D1732179

Governance and Public Management

Series Editors

Robert Fouchet
Universite Aix Marseille
France

Taco Brandsen
Nijmegen School of Management
Radboud University Nijmegen
The Netherlands

The Governance and Public Management series, published in conjunction with the International Institute of Administrative Sciences (IIAS), brings the best research in public administration and management to a global audience. Encouraging a diversity of approach and perspective, the series reflects the Institute's conviction for a neutral and objective voice, grounded in the exigency of fact. How is governance conducted now? How could it be done better? What defines the law of administration and the management of public affairs, and can their implementation be enhanced? Such questions lie behind the Institute's core value of accountability: those who exercise authority must account for its use to those on whose behalf they act.

More information about this series at
http://www.springer.com/series/15021

Sabine Kuhlmann • Geert Bouckaert
Editors

Local Public Sector Reforms in Times of Crisis

National Trajectories and International Comparisons

palgrave
macmillan

Editors
Sabine Kuhlmann
Full Professor
Political Science, Administration and
Organization
University of Potsdam, Germany

Geert Bouckaert
Professor
Faculty of Social Sciences
KU Leuven Public Governance
Institute, Belgium

Governance and Public Management
ISBN 978-1-137-52547-5   ISBN 978-1-137-52548-2   (eBook)
DOI 10.1057/978-1-137-52548-2

Library of Congress Control Number: 2016949426

© The Editor(s) (if applicable) and The Author(s) 2016
The author(s) has/have asserted their right(s) to be identified as the author(s) of this work
in accordance with the Copyright, Designs and Patents Act 1988.
This work is subject to copyright. All rights are solely and exclusively licensed by the
Publisher, whether the whole or part of the material is concerned, specifically the rights of
translation, reprinting, reuse of illustrations, recitation, broadcasting, reproduction on
microfilms or in any other physical way, and transmission or information storage and retrieval,
electronic adaptation, computer software, or by similar or dissimilar methodology now
known or hereafter developed.
The use of general descriptive names, registered names, trademarks, service marks, etc. in this
publication does not imply, even in the absence of a specific statement, that such names are
exempt from the relevant protective laws and regulations and therefore free for general use.
The publisher, the authors and the editors are safe to assume that the advice and information
in this book are believed to be true and accurate at the date of publication. Neither the publisher nor the authors or the editors give a warranty, express or implied, with respect to the
material contained herein or for any errors or omissions that may have been made.

Printed on acid-free paper

This Palgrave Macmillan imprint is published by Springer Nature
The registered company is Macmillan Publishers Ltd. London

PREFACE

In many European countries, the provision of public services, enacting the laws for their implementation, and the execution of administrative functions is largely, if not predominantly, carried out by local governments. The approximately 91,200 municipalities and 1100 second-tier local governments in the EU-27, covering some 50 percent of overall public employment and local government activities, represent a significant share (about 16 percent) of the entire gross domestic product of all EU member states as well as of the total of public expenditure (about 34 percent). From a political and democratic perspective, local self-government fulfills an important stabilizing and legitimizing function within the overall national government systems and in the supranational setting as well. It offers the opportunity for citizens to be directly involved in political decision making and to ensure spatial proximity for political problem solving. Eurobarometer surveys show that citizens' trust in local and regional public institutions is significantly higher than in national parliaments and governments. In the effective functioning and the acceptance of a constitutional democratic government in European countries, therefore, local self-government plays a crucial role. However, in the current comparative research about public sector modernization the local level has hitherto remained largely understudied. This is all the more a cause for concern as local governments are the most seriously hit by fiscal and economic crises, austerity policies, and pressures for reform in many countries. Reform intensity and activity can thus be assessed as particularly high at the local level, and local authorities in Europe are in a continuous process of institutional change and modernization.

This book provides comparative analyses and accounts of local public sector reforms in a wide range of countries (including Eastern and Western as well as Northern and Southern European systems) and reform measures (including territorial, functional and NPM/post-NPM reforms as well as democratic renewal and participatory innovations). Based on the research of the COST-Action "Local Public Sector Reforms: An International Comparison—LocRef" (IS1207), the volume is intended to address the abovementioned deficits by means of a strictly comparative approach using multinational teams of co-authors for each chapter. It exploits the expertise of about 60 internationally renowned scholars coming from 30 European countries, an outstanding source of knowledge that has not hitherto been integrated and synthesized in any book published on this topic.

This comprehensive comparative project would not have been feasible without the support of many colleagues and friends. The main resource for bringing scholars together, sharing knowledge, and bundling nationally scattered research has been LocRef, which we have the honor to serve as Chair and Vice-Chair. LocRef is funded by COST (European Cooperation in Science and Technology) and supported by the EU Framework program Horizon 2020. We are most fortunate to benefit from this unique opportunity for comparative research and collaboration with about 200 senior and early-stage researchers in our field coming from 31 countries and more than 50 renowned institutions in Europe. We owe many thanks to this excellent group of colleagues, who—in their various (mostly overlapping) roles as working group chairs/members, authors, commenters, discussants, conference organizers, coordinators, and so on—have joined forces for a common research and publication strategy. Among this group, we must mention in particular Christian Schwab who does an extraordinary job as Academic Coordinator of LocRef. Our thanks also go to the European Group for Public Administration (EGPA) for providing the opportunity of generating synergies between LocRef and the Permanent Study Groups of EGPA. We are also grateful for the stimulating comments received from the reviewers of the chapter typescripts and for the interest of the International Institute of Administrative Sciences (IIAS) and more specifically of two editors, Taco Brandsen and Robert Fouchet, of this IIAS-sponsored Palgrave series in our publication project. Finally, we would like to express our gratitude to the research staff in Potsdam, in particular Ina Radtke and Constanze Arnold, for their enormous support in coordinating the project, editing the text and preparing the final manuscript for publication. Any remaining weaknesses of the text remain, of course, the responsibility of the editors.

Geert Bouckaert
KU Leuven Public Governance Institute, Belgium

Sabine Kuhlmann
Political Science, Administration and Organization
University of Potsdam, Germany

Contents

1 Introduction: Comparing Local Public Sector
   Reforms: Institutional Policies in Context   1
   Geert Bouckaert, Sabine Kuhlmann

Part I Re-Scaling Local Governance: Amalgamation,
        Cooperation, Territorial Consolidation   21

2 A Comparative Analysis of Amalgamation Reforms
   in Selected European Countries   23
   Reto Steiner, Claire Kaiser, Grétar Thór Eythórsson

3 Explaining Trajectories of Municipal Amalgamations:
   A Case Comparison of the Netherlands and Flanders   43
   Wout Broekema, Trui Steen, Ellen Wayenberg

4 What Causes Municipal Amalgamation Reform?
   Rational Explanations Meet Western European
   Experiences, 2004–13   59
   Jostein Askim, Jan Erling Klausen, Signy Irene Vabo,
   Karl Bjurstrøm

5   Does Inter-Municipal Cooperation Lead to Territorial
    Consolidation? A Comparative Analysis of Selected
    European Cases in Times of Crisis   81
    Jochen Franzke, Daniel Klimovský, Uroš Pinterič

Part II   Managerial Reforms: From Weberian Bureaucracy
          to Performance Management?   99

6   Design, Trajectories of Reform, and Implementation
    of Performance Budgeting in Local Governments:
    A Comparative Study of Germany, Italy, Lithuania,
    and Norway   101
    Riccardo Mussari, Alfredo Ettore Tranfaglia, Christoph
    Reichard, Hilde Bjørnå, Vitalis Nakrošis, Sabina
    Bankauskaitė-Grigaliūnienė

7   Impacts of NPM-Driven Performance Management
    Reforms and Ideologies in Napoleonic Local
    Governments: A Comparative Analysis of France,
    Portugal, and Turkey   121
    Emil Turc, Marcel Guenoun, Miguel Ângelo V. Rodrigues,
    Yüksel Demirkaya, Jérôme Dupuis

8   Do They All Fail?: A Comparative Analysis of
    Performance-Related Pay Systems in Local
    Governments   139
    Isabella Proeller, Anne-Kathrin Wenzel, Dominik Vogel,
    Riccardo Mussari, Donatella Casale, Emil Turc,
    Marcel Guenoun

9   Human Resource Management Reforms and Change
    Management in European City Administrations from a
    Comparative Perspective   153
    Marco Salm, Christian Schwab

Part III   Re-Organizing Local Service Delivery:
           From Government to Governance?   185

10 Provision of Public and Social Services in European
   Countries: From Public Sector to Marketization
   and Reverse—or, What Next?   187
   Hellmut Wollmann

11 Municipal Waste Management in Norway and
   the Netherlands: From In-House Provision to
   Inter-Municipal Cooperation   205
   Harald Torsteinsen, Marieke van Genugten

12 On the Road Towards Marketization? A Comparative
   Analysis of Nonprofit Sector Involvement in Social
   Service Delivery at the Local Level   221
   Lars Skov Henriksen, Steven Rathgeb Smith,
   Malene Thøgersen, Annette Zimmer

13 The Governance of Childcare in Transition:
   A Comparative Analysis   237
   Nikos Hlepas, Pekka Kettunen, Dagmar Kutsar,
   Muiris MacCarthaigh, Carmen Navarro,
   Philipp Richter, Filipe Teles

14 Rescaling of Planning Power: Comparing Functional
   Planning Reforms in Six European Countries   253
   Panagiotis Getimis

Part IV   Local Participatory Reforms, Political
          Leaders, and Citizens   271

15 Giving Citizens More Say in Local Government:
Comparative Analyses of Change Across Europe
in Times of Crisis   273
Angelika Vetter, Daniel Klimovský, Bas Denters,
Norbert Kersting

16 Reforming Local Councils and the Role
of Councillors: A Comparative Analysis of
Fifteen European Countries   287
Anders Lidström, Harald Baldersheim, Colin Copus,
Eva Marín Hlynsdóttir, Pekka Kettunen, Daniel Klimovský

17 Have Mayors Will Travel: Trends and Developments
in the Direct Election of the Mayor: A Five-Nation
Study   301
Colin Copus, Angel Iglesias, Miro Hacek, Michal Illner,
Anders Lidström

18 Local Democratic Renewal by Deliberative Participatory
Instruments: Participatory Budgeting in
Comparative Study   317
Norbert Kersting, Jana Gasparikova, Angel Iglesias,
Jelizaveta Krenjova

19 Reforming Local Governments in Times of Crisis:
Values and Expectations of Good Local Governance in
Comparative Perspective   333
Bas Denters, Andreas Ladner, Poul Erik Mouritzen,
Lawrence E. Rose

20 Conclusion: Tensions, Challenges, and Future "Flags"
of Local Public Sector Reforms and Comparative Research   347
Geert Bouckaert, Sabine Kuhlmann

Index   355

Notes on Contributors

Jostein Askim is Associate Professor at the Department of Political Science at the University of Oslo. His research and teaching cover relations between central and local government, politics and administration in the executive, and ministries and agencies.

Harald Baldersheim has been Professor Emeritus at the University of Oslo, Department of Political Science since 2014. He was Professor of Political Science at the University of Oslo from 1995, and before that from 1977 until 1995 Professor of Public Administration at the University of Bergen. He was Head of the Norwegian Institute of Urban and Regional Research from 1982 to 1987. He will continue some of his duties as Academic Director of University of Oslo's Democracy Program. His research interests include European regionalism, municipal leadership, and e-governance.

Sabina Bankauskaitė-Grigaliūnienė is a PhD student at Vilnius University, Lithuania. Her main academic interests involve public management, change management, and Europeanization studies. Her PhD thesis investigates the relation between Europeanization processes and public management reforms. It focuses on the impact of institutional innovation networks on the adoption of managerial practices at central and local government level.

Hilde Bjørnå is Professor in the Department of Sociology, Political Science, and Community Planning, Faculty of Humanities, Social Sciences and Education, University of Tromsø—the Arctic University of Norway. Research interests include local leadership, local policies, and management in a comparative perspective, democracy, agencies, reputation management, and rural development.

Karl Bjurstrøm is a PhD Student and Research Fellow at the Department of Political Science at University of Oslo. His fields of research are public administration and local government studies.

Wout Broekema is Researcher and Lecturer at the Institute of Public Administration, Faculty of Governance and Global Affairs, at Leiden University. His research interests include organizational learning, incident and crisis management, and local governance. He holds a Master's degree with honors in Public Administration from Leiden University.

Geert Bouckaert is professor at the KU Leuven Public Governance Institute in Leuven, Belgium. He is President of the International Institute of Administrative Sciences (IIAS). His research focuses on performance, reform and financial management in the public sector.

Donatella Casale is a PhD candidate and Research and Teaching Assistant in Public Management at the Department of Business and Law of the University of Siena (Italy). She holds an MSc in Management and Business Administration from the University of Florence, where she worked mainly on business ethics. She previously worked as a research and management analyst and is currently research correspondent for Transparency International's Anti-Corruption Research Network (ACRN). Her research interests include local public sector reforms and public sector management, anti-corruption policies, public policy analysis, and evaluation research. In her PhD thesis she is focusing on the implementation of anti-corruption policies at a local level of government.

Colin Copus is the Director of the Local Governance Research Unit in the Department of Politics and Public Policy, De Montfort University, where he is Professor of Local Politics. His academic interests are central–local relationships and the constitutional status of local government, localism, local party politics, local political leadership, and the changing role of the councilor. Colin has worked closely with policy-makers and practitioners in central and local government; he was an advisor to the Political and Constitutional Reform Committee and is working with the Communities and Local Government Committee on the role of the councilor.

Yüksel Demirkaya is Associate Professor at Marmara University, Istanbul. His academic research and interest areas cover the fields of New Public Management reforms, local and regional government systems, strategic management in the public sector, alternative local public service models, corporate management, accountability and local participation in Turkish local governments, and the European local government systems. His study is supported by TÜBITAK (113 K427).

Bas Denters is full Professor of Public Administration and Head of the Department of Public Administration in the School for Management and Governance at the

University of Twente (Enschede, the Netherlands). He is also the Scientific Director of the Netherlands Institute for Government (NIG): the KNAW-accredited Dutch-Flemish graduate school for Political Science and Public Administration.

Jérôme Dupuis has a PhD in Management Sciences; at the IAE Lille he is director of "manager territorial" master;, and teaches strategic management, organization and management of local governments, monitoring and evaluation of public policies, and European local public services management. He is a member of the UMR CNRS 9221 LEM (Lille Economy Management); his research focuses on the analysis of local performance systems and more particularly on the changes and new dynamics of organization and management systems in local authorities in France and Europe. More recently, he studied innovation practices in local and territorial public policies.

Grétar Thór Eythórsson is Professor in Government and Methology at the University of Akureyri, Iceland (2008). He was Director of the University of Akureyri Research Institute and the Icelandic Institute for Regional Policy Research (2001–2005), Director of Bifröst University Research Centre (2005–2008) and Professor at Bifröst University (2005–2008).

Jochen Franzke has been Professor for Public Administration at the University of Potsdam since 2008. Furthermore, he has been since 2005 Director of Study Group IV "Local Governance and Democracy" of the European Group for Public Administration (EGPA) and since 2012 a member of the board of the Institute of Local Government Studies, University of Potsdam (KWI). He is a member of the Network of Institutes and Schools of Public Administration in Central and Eastern Europe (NISPAcee). The focus of his research includes the reform of public administration in Germany, particularly at the local and federal states level, the development of local democracy, and the transformation process in Central and Eastern Europe (especially in Poland and the Russian Federation).

Jana Gašparíková is Senior Researcher at the private School of Economic Management and Public Administration in Bratislava. She has served as chair of several international projects and grants on interdisciplinary issues, and also of domestic grants. Her recent interest is concentrated on issues of public administration and local democracy.

Marieke van Genugten is Assistant Professor of Public Administration at the Institute for Management Research at Radboud University in the Netherlands. She received her PhD in Public Administration at the University of Twente. In her current research she is examining the internal and external governance of municipally owned companies. She is also interested in the organization and governance of public service provision at the local level.

Panagiotis Getimis is Professor of Urban and Regional Planning and Policy, Department of Economic and Regional Development, Panteion University of Political and Social Sciences, Athens. Currently he is teaching and researching at the Universities of Dortmund and Darmstadt, Germany. His research interests are local government, urban and regional policies, spatial planning,and metropolitan governance. He is scientific coordinator in various European research programs (FP5, FP6, FP7, Interreg, DG Enlargement, DG Regio, and DG Social Affairs inter alia). He was Vice Rector of the Panteion University (1993–1998). He is a member of the executive board of the European Urban Research Association (EURA) and of the editorial board of the journal *Urban Research and Practice*.

Marcel Guenoun holds a PhD in management from ESSEC Business School and Aix-Marseille University School of Management. He is Associate Professor at the Institute of Public Management and Local Governance at Aix-Marseille University where he is in charge of executive programs. His research focuses on performance management in local government and citizen satisfaction measurement and participation. He is involved in several executive programs of civil service schools and is a member of the experts committee of the French National Center for Local Civil Service.

Miro Hacek is Professor at the Department of Political Science at the Faculty of Social Sciences, University of Ljubljana. From 2005 to 2007 he was the Head of the Political Science Department; he is currently again heading the same department (2013–2017); from 2007 to 2011 he was also Head of the Policy Analysis and Public Administration Department at the Faculty of Social Sciences at the University of Ljubljana. From 1999 to 2009 he was General Secretary of the Slovenian Political Science Association, while in May 2009 he was elected President of the Association and in June 2011 the Vice-President of the Association. In October 2012 he was elected the Vice-President of the Central European Political Science Association (CEPSA) and was reelected in September 2015. He also conducts a class on "Decentralized and Local Administration in Europe Compared (III)" in the international Master's program at the University of Trento. He was a Visiting Lecturer at the Hong Kong Baptist University (January 2005, January 2007), South Dakota State University (September 2009, April 2010) and at Hughes Hall in Cambridge (July 2001).

Lars Skov Henriksen is Professor at the Department of Sociology and Social Work at Aalborg University.

Nikos Hlepas is Associate Professor of Regional and Local Government, Department of Political Science and Public Administration at the National and Capodistrian University of Athens.

Eva Marín Hlynsdóttir is an Assistant Professor in Public Administration at the Department of Political Science at the University of Iceland. She has a PhD in

Political Science and an MPA in Public Administration. Her PhD thesis (2015) was about local government leadership roles in Iceland.

Angel Iglesias is a Professor of Political and Administrative Sciences at the University Rey Juan Carlos in Madrid. Previously he has taught at the Complutense University also in Madrid. His research focuses on issues of local government with regard to Spain and in a European comparative perspective, with particular focus on local democratic innovations and local public management. His second main area of research involves the study of Spain's political corruption, specifically addressing its role in local policy processes.

Michal Illner is Senior Research Associate in the Institute of Sociology–Academy of Sciences of the Czech Republic in Prague and was its Director in the 1990s. There he founded and was Head of the Department of Local and Regional Studies of which he has been member until the present. His research interests and publications have dealt with sociological, political, and legal aspects of local and regional government, regional and local development, and local and regional policy—particularly with their reconstruction after the fall of the communist regime. He directed several research projects on the post-communist transformation of local government in the Czech Republic, participated in several multinational research projects, and co-authored book chapters based on these studies. He has also commented on Czech legislation concerning the local and regional.

Claire Kaiser studied economics, business administration, communications, and media studies at the University of Bern, and—during an exchange semester—at the Università degli Studi di Roma "La Sapienza." She successfully completed her PhD in Public Administration at the University of Bern. Since 2009, she has been a Research Assistant at the Center of Competence for Public Management. She is involved in diverse research and consulting projects. In 2013, she was a Visiting PhD Researcher at Queen Mary University of London.

Norbert Kersting holds the Chair of Comparative Local and Regional Politics at the Department of Political Science at the University of Münster (Germany). He is Chair of the International Political Science Association's (IPSA) Research Committee 10 on "Electronic democracy" and a member of Board Research Committee 5 on "Comparative Studies on Local Government and Politics."

Pekka Kettunen PhD has a long experience in public administration, public policy, and evaluation research. He has also worked with a number of evaluation projects financed by the European Commission, ministries, and NGOs.

Jan Erling Klausen is an Associate Professor at the Department of Political Science at the University of Oslo, and a Senior Researcher at the Norwegian Institute for Urban and Regional Research in Oslo. His research focus is on local government studies, local politics, and state–local relations.

Daniel Klimovský completed his Master studies in the field of Public Administration in 2003. In 2009 he completed his PhD study in the field of Political Theory, and in 2015 he was academically habilitated in the same field. Since 2014 he has worked for the Institute of Public Policy, Faculty of Social and Economic Sciences of Comenius University in Bratislava, Slovakia. His contribution to chapters in this book is one of the outputs of his post-doc project, which was managed by Palacky University in Olomouc, Czech Republic.

Jelizaveta Krenjova is a PhD student at Ragnar Nurkse School of Innovation and Governance, Tallinn University of Technology, and a Project Manager in the e-Governance Academy. Her research interests comprise participatory instruments at the local level. More specifically, she focusing on participatory budgeting (PB)—a process of citizens' participation in the allocation of financial resources.

Sabine Kuhlmann has been Full Professor of Political Sciences, Administration and Organization at the University of Potsdam, Germany, since 2013. From 2009 to 2013, she was Full Professor of Comparative Public Administration at the German University of Administrative Sciences in Speyer. She chairs the COST Action "Local Public Sector Reforms: an International Comparison" and is a member of the National Regulatory Control Council that advices the German Federal Government on Better Regulation.

Her work and research focus on comparative public administration; administration modernization/international public sector reforms; comparative local and regional government; evaluation, better regulation, regulatory impact assessment; multi-level governance and decentralization.

Dagmar Kutsar is Associate Professor of Social Policy at the University of Tartu, Estonia. Her research interests are related to family, childhood, and welfare research and policies. She has been a partner in several international research projects, e.g. EU 6FP PROFIT, IPROSEC, NoE EQUALSOC, and EU FP7 FLOWS. She has been a member of the Standing Committee on Social Sciences of the European Science Foundation, a member of the Executive Committee and Chair of the National Associations Council of the European Sociological Association, and Expert of the EU FP7 Youth Social Inclusion Cluster at the European Commission.

Andreas Ladner is Professor for Political Institutions and Public Administration at the Institut de Hautes Études en Administration Publique (IDHEAP) at the University of Lausanne. His areas of research include the quality of democracy, local government, institutional change, political parties, and voting advice applications.

Anders Lidström is Professor and Head of the Department of Political Science, Umeå University, Sweden. His research focus is on urban, local, and regional politics and government, particularly in a comparative perspective. He is the convenor for the ECPR standing group on local government and politics.

Muiris MacCarthaigh is Lecturer in Politics and Public Administration at Queen's University Belfast. Among his current research interests are administrative reforms in the context of state retrenchment, issues with which he is involved in a number of international research networks, and with a particular focus on the Irish case. He is a member of the Political Studies Association of Ireland (PSAI), the UK Political Studies Association (PSA) and the International Political Science Association (IPSA).

Poul Erik Mouritzen is Professor of Political Science at the Department of Political and Public Management, University of Southern Denmark. His areas of research include local government, the welfare state, and recently university governance.

Riccardo Mussari is Professor of Public Financial Management at the School of Economics and Management of the University of Siena, Italy. During his academic carrier he has been a Visiting Scholar at several European, US, Australian, and Japanese Universities. His Doctoral thesis was focused on public management theory. He has been part of major national and international research projects comparing public sector reforms in Italy with those in various other countries. His research interests include public sector management and accounting, public value, performance measurement, and management. Dr Mussari is a member of the scientific boards of national and international academic journals.

Vitalis Nakrošis is a Professor in Public Administration in the Institute of International Relations and Political Science of Vilnius University. His main research interests include public management reforms, public sector organizations, and policy implementation and evaluation.

Carmen Navarro is Associate Professor at the Department of Political Science, University Autónoma of Madrid, where she has recently served as the Head of the Department (2010–2014). She focuses her research and teaching activities on local government and public policy. In recent years she has participated in a dozen financed research projects, mostly dedicated to local politics and policies such as "The European Mayor," "International Metropolitan Observatory," "Municipal Assemblies in European Local government," and "Local Public Sector Reforms."

Uroš Pinterič obtained PhD in political science at University of Ljubljana. He works as Associate Professor at the Faculty of Social Sciences, St Cyril and Methodius University in Trnava. He is post-doc researcher in the field of regional development at Charles University in Prague. He is president of the supervisory board of the Faculty of Organization Studies in Novo Mesto and a member of the scientific board at the Faculty of Social Sciences, St Cyril and Methodius University in Trnava. His past and current research activities have been connected to the local administration and local development.

Isabella Proeller is Professor for Public and Nonprofit Management at the University of Potsdam, Germany. Her main research interests are strategic and performance management.

Christoph Reichard is Emeritus Professor of Public Management and a member of the Potsdam Centre of Policy and Management and of the Institute of Local Government Studies, all at Potsdam University. His main fields of research include public management reforms, variants of public service delivery, performance management, public financial management and public personnel. His recent research projects deal with the evaluation of national and international trends of public management reforms, with corporate governance problems of public enterprises, with the use of financial data for managerial decisions, and with education and training in the German public sector. More information: www.pots-puma.de

Philipp Richter studied Political Sciences at the University of Potsdam and received his Diploma degree in 2009. From 2009 to 2014, he worked as a Research Assistant at the Chair for Comparative Public Administration, German University of Administrative Sciences Speyer, where he received his PhD in 2014. The Doctoral thesis was about performance effects of different macro organizations within German federalism. His main teaching and research topics are public administration, decentralization reforms, local government, federalism, and open government.

Miguel Ângelo V. Rodrigues is currently Assistant Professor at the Polytechnic Institute of Bragança in Portugal and a member of the Research Centre in Political Science, Department of International Relations and Public Administration, University of Minho, Portugal. His main research interests comprise topics in the fields of local government and public management, and he has published his work in *Local Government Studies* and the *International Review of Administrative Sciences*. He is a current member of the scientific board of the *Journal of Urban Affairs*.

Lawrence E. Rose is Professor Emeritus at the Department of Political Science, University of Oslo, Norway.

Marco Salm holds an MA in Economics, and is currently working at the German University for Public Administration in the field of public finance. The research was made possible by a PhD fellowship from the German Research Institute for Public Administration.

Christian Schwab studied Business Management and Political Science at the University of Mannheim and Public Administration at the German University of Public Administration Speyer, Germany. He is currently working as a research assistant at the Chair of Political Science, Administration, and Organization at the University of Potsdam and Project Coordinator of the COST-Action "Local Public Sector Reforms: An International Comparison—LocRef" (IS1207). Please visit his website for further information: http://www.uni-potsdam.de/ls-kuhlmann/lehrstuhl/schwab.html

Steven Rathgeb Smith is the Executive Director of the American Political Science Association. He previously held the Louis A. Bantle Chair in Public Administration at the Maxwell School at Syracuse University and was Nancy Bell Evans Professor at the Evans School of Public Affairs at the University of Washington. He has also been the editor of *Nonprofit and Voluntary Sector Quarterly* and President of the Association for Research on Nonprofit Organizations and Voluntary Action. He is President-Elect of the International Society for Third Sector Research. He received his doctorate in political science from MIT in 1988.

Trui Steen is Associate Professor at the Institute of Public Administration, Faculty of Governance and Global Affairs at Leiden University and is Associate Professor at the KU Leuven Public Governance Institute. Her research includes diverse such topics as professionalism, public service motivation, professional–citizen co-production of public services, and central–local government relations.

Reto Steiner is a Professor for Public Management at the University of Bern. He is a member of the Managing Board of the Center of Competence for Public Management at the University of Bern. In 2013, he was a Visiting Research Fellow at the Lee Kuan Yew School of Public Policy at the National University of Singapore (NUS) and at the Department of Politics and Public Administration at the University of Hong Kong. His research focuses on decentralization and local governance, the management of agencies, and state-owned enterprises.

Filipe Teles is Assistant Professor and Pro-Rector at the University of Aveiro, and holds a PhD in Political Science. His work deals primarily with issues of local governance, innovation and public policy, and his research interests include local public sector reform, regional governance, and community engagement. He is currently a member of the management committee of the COST-Action "Local Public Sector Reforms: An International Comparison—LocRef" (IS1207). He is also coordinator of the Aveiro's Regional Smart Specialization Strategy. He is a member of the Portuguese Political Science Association (APCP), the Political Studies Association (UK), the International Political Science Association, of the Governing Board of the European Urban Research Association.

Malene Thøgersen has a PhD in Political Science from the University of Southern Denmark. Today she is a Researcher at the Danish Institute for Non-Formal Education. Her main research interests are focused on voluntary associations and relations between the voluntary and the public sector, primarily at the local level.

Harald Torsteinsen is Associate Professor of Political Science and Management at the Institute for Economics and Social Sciences at Harstad University College, Norway, recently merged with UIT—the Arctic University of Norway, Tromsø. Torsteinsen received his Master's degree in political science from the University of Oslo and his PhD from UIT. His doctoral thesis focused on disaggregation and autonomization of local government service provision. In his current research he studies the internal and external governance of municipallyowned companies. He is also interested in the organization and governance of public service provision at the local level.

Alfredo Ettore Tranfaglia is a Doctoral Fellow in Public Management and Governance at the University of Siena, where he is Teaching Assistant in Public Management and Public Financial Management and he collaborates as Financial and Accounting Consultant with the National Association of Italian Municipalities. His main foci of research are on public financial accounting systems, publicly owned enterprises, innovative models of public service delivery, and coordination and performance management in times of crisis. His research project deals with coordination mechanisms and performance in interorganizational settings, with specific regard to public service delivery at lower levels of government.

Emil Turc is Associate Professor of Strategic Management and Organizational Behavior at the Institut de Management Public et de Gouvernance Territoriale, CERGAM, Aix-Marseille University. His research investigates strategic changes in public and private organizations, with a focus on the implementation of budgeting tools in central and deconcentrated administrations, and on the diffusion of performance management models and tools in local government organizations and intercommunal organizations. He is a current member of the steering committee of the European Group of Public Administrations (EGPA), and of the management committee of the EU-funded COST-Action "Local Public Sector Reforms: An International Comparison—LocRef" (IS1207).

Signy Irene Vabo is Professor in Political Science at the Department of Political Science at University of Oslo. Her research and teaching covers relations between central and local government, governance, local democracy, and welfare studies (care).

Angelika Vetter is Professor at the Department of Social Sciences at the University of Stuttgart (Germany). Her main research interests are in the fields of local government, political culture, and political behavior in a comparative perspective.

Dominik Vogel is a post-doc at the Chair of Public and Nonprofit Management at the University of Potsdam (Germany). His research interests are leadership in the public sector and motivation of public employees (especially public service motivation).

Ellen Wayenberg has been Associate Professor at the Department of Political Science, Faculty of Political and Social Sciences, Ghent University (Belgium) since October 2013. Ellen specializes in public policy and public administration with a specific interest for multi-level governance (MLG), intergovernmental relations (IGR), and local government. She is one of the Co-Chairs of the EGPA Study Group on Regional and Local Government and is actively involved in COST-Action "Local Public Sector Reforms: An International Comparison—LocRef" (IS1207).

Anne-Kathrin Wenzel is a PhD candidate and Research Assistant at the Chair of Public and Nonprofit Management at the University of Potsdam (Germany). She holds a Master's degree in Public Policy and Management from the University of Potsdam. Her research interests are performance pay and performance appraisals in the public sector as well as motivation of public employees.

Hellmut Wollmann is Professor (Emeritus) of Public Administration at the Humboldt University Berlin, Germany. His main fields of research and publications are comparative local government, comparative public administration and public policy, and evaluation research.

Annette Zimmer is Full Professor of Social Policy and Comparative Politics at the Institute of Political Science at the University of Münster, Germany. She holds a Doctoral degree in Political Science from the University of Heidelberg, and a Lecturer degree in Political Science from the University of Kassel, Germany. She was affiliated with the Program on Nonprofit-Organizations at Yale University, USA, and served as the DAAD Visting Professor of German and European Studies at the Centre for International Studies of the University of Toronto, Canada and as a Visiting Researcher at the American Centre for Contemporary Germany Studies in Washington, D.C. Her teaching experience covers BA, Master and PhD programs at universities in Germany (Kassel, Münster, Frankfurt), Canada (Toronto), the Netherlands (Twente), and France (Lille). Her research focuses on the topic of civil society–government relationships as well as on the role and function of nonprofit organizations in selected policy fields.

List of Figures

Fig. 1.1   Types of local public sector reform   7
Fig. 2.1   Analytical framework   25
Fig. 4.1   Theoretical model   60
Fig. 4.2   Predicted and actual amalgamation reforms 2004–13.
            AD partial-model predictions—after driving factors,
            AF full-model predictions—after filtering factors   67
Fig. 5.1   Possible institutional settings to reduce local fragmentation   84
Fig. 5.2   The most significant shifts in institutional settings in terms
            of reducing local fragmentation in the selected countries   95
Fig. 6.1   Framework of analysis   105
Fig. 9.1   Analytical design—change management and HRM linkages   158
Fig. 9.2   Change process and actors/groups involved   163
Fig. 9.3   Change process: before-and-after comparison   167
Fig. 9.4   Perceived changes in HRM-related measures—instrumental   168
Fig. 9.5   Perceived changes in HRM-related measures—personnel   169
Fig. 9.6   Perceived changes in HRM-related measures—organizational   170
Fig. 9.7   HRM-related organizational effects   171
Fig. 15.1   Presence of three institutional arrangements available for
            citizen involvement in local government in 28 European
            countries. Total number in 1990s and 2014   281
Fig. 19.1   Mean satisfaction with different aspects of municipal government
            performance by country   336
Fig. 19.2   Mean scores for four value orientations by country   338
Fig. 19.3   Mean scores for good local governance value orientations and
            satisfaction measures by country   340

LIST OF TABLES

Table 1.1	Context conditions and core-features of local government systems	11
Table 2.1	Development of the number of municipalities during the past 40 years	29
Table 2.2	Typology of amalgamation strategies	30
Table 2.3	Objectives	32
Table 2.4	Patterns of conflict	33
Table 2.5	Problems during the amalgamation process	35
Table 2.6	Outcome of amalgamations	37
Table 2.7	Significant correlations between different phases of the reform process	38
Table 3.1	Number of municipalities in the Netherlands over the period 1996–2005	45
Table 4.1	Amalgamation reforms in Western European countries, 2004–13	65
Table 4.A.1	Predicted amalgamation reforms 2004–13, partial model with pressure factors only. Reform predicted if pressure from any three of the four pressure factors, or if strong fiscal stress	72
Table 4.A.2	Predicted amalgamation reforms 2004–13 among countries experiencing reform pressure, full model including filtering factors. Reform predicted if negative scores on three of the four filtering factors	74
Table 5.1	Municipal territorial structures	87
Table 5.2	Legal frameworks	88
Table 5.3	Forms of IMC	89
Table 5.4	IMC and impacts	94

Table 6.1   A comparative view of PB systems and their implementation   106
Table 7.1   Weighting the national importance of local governments
             in France, Portugal, and Turkey   125
Table 7.2   Characterizing the performance measurement and
             management systems in the three LGOs of the sample   128
Table 8.1   Characteristics of the civil service in the three countries   141
Table 8.2   Reward structure in Italian public administration   147
Table 9.1   Public employment across levels of government   158
Table 9.2   Reform drivers, design, and duration   161
Table 9.3   Reform process objectives   162
Table 9.4   Change process measures   163
Table 9.5   Change process and the role of HRM/personnel unit   164
Table 9.6   Change process difficulties and tensions   165
Table 9.A.1 HRM-related instruments on leadership: implementation
             and importance   178
Table 9.A.2 HRM-related instruments on communication and
             cooperation: implementation and importance   179
Table 9.A.3 HRM-related instruments on performance/economic
             incentives: implementation and importance   181
Table 11.1   Types of agencies at the local level in Norway and the
             Netherlands   208
Table 11.2   Institutional forms of waste management in Norway and the
             Netherlands 2013–14   213
Table 12.1   Welfare regimes and nonprofit social service provision   223
Table 13.1   Coverage of child daycare in 2000 and 2014 and
             responsible public authority in 2014   247
Table 14.A.1 Local government and planning system typologies   266
Table 15.1   Presence of three institutional arrangements available for
             citizen involvement in local government in 28 European
             countries, 1990s and 2014   280
Table 16.1   Types of local government legitimacy in selected
             European countries   291

Introduction: Comparing Local Public Sector Reforms: Institutional Policies in Context

Geert Bouckaert and Sabine Kuhlmann

BACKGROUND AND OBJECTIVES

Local governments all over Europe are in a period of increased reform activity and intensity, especially since this level of government has been the most seriously affected by the continuously expanding global financial crisis and the austerity policies in some countries. The reforms involve a variety of trajectories ranging from New Public Management (NPM) modernization to reorganization of service delivery between the local public, private and non-profit sectors, functional re-scaling, territorial consolidation,

We would like to thank the members of the COST Action LocRef, specifically Yüksel Demirkaya, Nikos Hlepas, Andreas Ladner, Anders Lidstrøm, Pawel Swianiewicz and Ellen Wayenberg, for providing additional country data and for their constructive comments on previous versions of this contribution.

G. Bouckaert (✉)
Public Management Institute, Kath Universiteit Leuven, Leuven, Belgium

S. Kuhlmann
Chair for Political Science, Public Administration and Organization, University of Potsdam, Campus Griebnitzsee, Potsdam, Brandenburg, Germany

© The Author(s) 2016
S. Kuhlmann, G. Bouckaert (eds.), *Local Public Sector Reforms in Times of Crisis*, DOI 10.1057/978-1-137-52548-2_1

and inter-local cooperation. Many local governments have significantly shifted away from NPM-type reforms and moved to "something different" in order to correct the shortcomings of earlier NPM measures, which some commentators have labeled "post-NPM" (see Halligan 2010). The significance of NPM/post-NPM notwithstanding, European local governments have never concentrated solely on reforms of these kinds but have pursued a variety of (partly conflicting) reform trajectories. NPM reforms have undoubtedly prompted far-reaching institutional changes in some countries, yet in other countries they have been criticized or even ignored. Hence, "other-than-NPM measures" such as territorial reforms, functional re-allocations in the multi-level system, and democratic innovations have played an important role in many European local government systems. These diverse reform activities have contributed to transforming local government systems and patterns of local governance in Europe.

Against this background, it is cause for concern and criticism that analysis of the local level is conspicuously neglected in the current comparative research concerning public sector modernization. Even recent comparative studies on public management reform (see Bouckaert et al. 2010; Lægreid and Verhoest 2010; Pollitt and Bouckaert 2011) as well as investigations reported by the OECD (2010) and World Bank (2007) deal almost exclusively with central government and national administrative levels. A pressing need remains to assess how far those reforms have changed local governments, how they differ between various countries, to what extent they represent a new "wave" of reforms (is the pendulum really swinging back?), and whether all this makes a difference to the performance and functioning of local governments.

Based on the results of the COST Action "Local Public Sector Reforms: an International Comparison (LocRef)," this volume contributes to filling the respective gaps in comparative research by taking into account the huge spectrum of the abovementioned reforms from a European-scale comparative perspective. Capturing not only NPM/post-NPM, but also alternative approaches and reform trajectories, the overarching question of the volume is:

Which approaches and effects of local public sector reform can be identified from a cross-countries comparative perspective and how can these be explained?

The COST Action LocRef embraces 31 countries, 28 of which are referred to in at least one contribution of this book. These 28 countries represent six clusters of administrative traditions and local government systems in Europe characterized by specific combinations of institutional/cultural core features (see further below). In this chapter, we will elaborate a conceptual framework for understanding local public sector reforms from a cross-countries comparative perspective, on which, at the same time, the COST Action LocRef has drawn.

CONCEPTUALIZING LOCAL PUBLIC SECTOR REFORMS

We conceptualize local public sector reforms as a specific type of policy, namely *institutional policies*, which are directed at political and administrative institutional structures. The following areas of institutional analysis will be distinguished, and these also cover the main guiding questions of the LocRef conceptual framework:

- The first area of analysis pertains to the emergence of reform discourses, the *causes* of specific (national/local) reform agendas, and the formulation of institutional reform packages/policies by relevant stakeholders.
- The focus of the second area of analysis is on the actual adoption of reform measures, *institutional changes*, and degrees of reform implementation from a comparative perspective.
- The third analytical area deals with the *effects* of reform and the question of how specific measures influence the actual performance of local governments, citizens' satisfaction, and perceptions of how local government works, and whether there are also unintended (side) effects of various modernization efforts.

Our approach is not meant, however, to presume a deterministic relationship between the type of institutional policy and its implementation and performance. There are a number of factors to be taken into account when it comes to explaining modes, measures, and outcomes of institutional policies from a comparative perspective. One of these factors is the nature of the local tasks and functions subject to reforms. We might, for instance, assume more straightforward positive impacts of NPM-guided customer-oriented modernization efforts in the field of local service delivery functions that immediately affect the citizens than in the field of technical or environmental functions. Another important explanatory factor to be explored in more detail further below is "context" (see Pollitt 2013), that is, the institutional and cultural "starting conditions" (Pollitt and

Bouckaert 2011) of reforms in a given country (cluster) which we assume to exert major influence on the trajectories, adoption, and effects of local public sector reforms.

When local public sector reforms are viewed as institutional policy and conceptualized along the ideal type input–output model of the politico-administrative system, then a distinction can be made between more input-oriented *democratic reforms* and more output-oriented *administrative reforms* (see Scharpf 2002). Of course, empirically, there will most often be a mixture of both types. However, for analytical purposes, we differentiate between reforms directed at strengthening the input legitimacy by way of introducing new participatory instruments and elements of democratic innovation (*democratic reforms*) and reforms targeted at enhancing output legitimacy (*administrative reforms*; see also Kersting and Vetter 2003). The latter are aimed at improving the efficiency, effectiveness, and productivity of public service delivery through organizational, procedural, and instrumental changes within the public administration. Depending on which elements of institutional order are on the reform agenda, administrative reforms can be classified as *external* and *internal* variants. The external variant is intended to change the shape of the institutional order overall and to redefine institutional boundaries, functional and/or territorial jurisdictions, membership rules, and relations between organizations at different levels or sectors. Internal administrative reforms, by contrast, are concerned with changes in the distribution of responsibilities and resources within administrative organizations as well as the internal reorganization of decision-making rules.

External Administrative Reforms

(1) *Territorial re-scaling:* European local governments have been—to varying degrees—subject to both territorial upscaling (amalgamation) and/or trans-scaling (inter-local cooperation) of subnational jurisdictions fueled, in part, by recent austerity measures and the hopes of national policy makers that such reforms will facilitate economies of scale. On the one hand, a group of countries can be identified in which national governments acted to reinforce the administrative efficiency of local government by way of territorial and demographic extension (also termed "up-scaling"; cf. Baldersheim and Rose 2010, p. 20). Owing to the fact that this reform trajectory originated in Northern Europe (UK, Sweden,

Denmark; some northern parts of Germany), the international comparative literature therefore speaks of a "Northern European" reform model (Kuhlmann and Wollmann 2014, p. 150). In contrast with this country group stand a cluster of countries in which the small-scale, fragmented territorial structure of local government, whose origin often dates back to the eighteenth century, has remained largely unchanged. Since France, Italy, and Spain are prominent examples of this country group, the comparative literature refers to this as the "Southern European" reform model. In these countries, strategies (termed "trans-scaling" by Baldersheim and Rose) have been pursued that aim at ensuring the operative viability, even of very small-scale municipalities, by establishing inter-municipal bodies.

(2) *Re-organizing local service delivery:* Many European local governments have pursued NPM-driven externalization of local services to private or non-profit providers (contracting out, functional/asset privatization, corporatization, competitive tendering) and some of them have more recently undertaken post-NPM re-municipalizations of previously externalized local functions (Wollmann and Marcou 2010). In addition to this horizontal reorganization of local service delivery, a vertical dimension can be identified which addresses the reallocation of tasks between the local and upper levels of government (see Kuhlmann and Wayenberg 2015). Here, a crucial distinction needs to be made between political decentralization through which "real" decision-making powers are attributed to the local councils regarding the newly transferred tasks and administrative decentralization understood as a transfer of administrative functions from the state to the local government level without granting political powers to the latter (Kuhlmann et al. 2014, p. 206 et seq.).

Internal Administrative Reforms

(3) *Managerial reforms:* Guided by the NPM idea of transforming the bureaucratic Weberian administration into a customer-friendly *all uses* "service enterprise" to be managed in a performance oriented manner (Schedler and Proeller 2000), many local governments have embarked on reform projects of internal reorganization, process re-engineering, new budgeting and accounting systems, performance

management tools and human-resource-related modernization. Although a broadly convergent reform discourse is apparent in this respect, a radical managerialization of the public sector, as was characteristic of the United Kingdom (and New Zealand), has not taken place in the majority of European administrations (Pollitt and Bouckaert 2011). By contrast, the implementation of NPM concepts in Continental Europe has been significant, but by no means revolutionary (Bouckaert 2006; Kuhlmann and Wollmann 2014, p. 172). Nonetheless, this does not mean that reform activities at the local level have been minimal, but rather that different local government systems have adapted them to their respective cultural contexts (Peters 2013).

Democratic Reforms

(4) *Participatory reforms, direct democracy, and citizen involvement:* Major attempts in modernization have been directed at the revival of "old" participatory instruments as well as the introduction of "new" ones at the local level of government and the inclusion of civil society into local policy making. This reform area focuses on the strengthening of direct democracy (local referenda, direct election/ recall of local executives), on the one hand, and new forms of participatory and cooperative democracy on the other (citizens' forums, consultations, youth/neighborhood councils, e-democracy). Besides the introduction of direct elections of local political leaders/ mayors (Bäck et al. 2006; Reynaert et al. 2009), democratic reforms can be aimed at reinforcing the direct influence of residents through referenda, initiatives, and petitions. Finally, they can also be directed at allowing residents to participate in public debates, by introducing consultations and interactive and deliberative policy making.

The subsequent chapters of this book will use this typology of institutional reforms for mapping and clustering various reform activities and studying each of them from a cross-countries comparative perspective, referring to NPM and/or to post-NPM measures where applicable. Figure 1.1 summarizes the main reform components to be scrutinized.

COMPARATIVE APPROACH: INSTITUTIONAL POLICIES IN CONTEXT

As mentioned above, we consider the institutional "starting conditions" and "contexts" within which local public sector reforms take place as major explanatory factors for the adoption and outcomes of these reforms (see Peters 2013; Pollitt and Bouckaert 2011; Pollitt 2013). This assumption is conceptually inspired by historical institutionalism (cf. Pierson 2004), according to which answers to newly emerging problems are pre-structured by existing institutional arrangements and historically ingrained patterns of problem solving. Hence, the scope of reform options is limited by "path dependencies" (Hall and Taylor 1996, p. 941; cf. also Baldersheim and Rose 2010, p. 10 et seq.). Depending on its historically shaped institutional contexts and administrative cultures, each European country has thus viewed the concurring reform discourses (such as NPM) very differently. Likewise, similar administrative interventions can bring about very diverse effects in the contexts of the individual countries because they each encounter unique, pre-existing institutional arrangements, and institutional "legacies." These in turn can have either a promoting or blocking effect on specific types of reforms and the resulting outcomes.

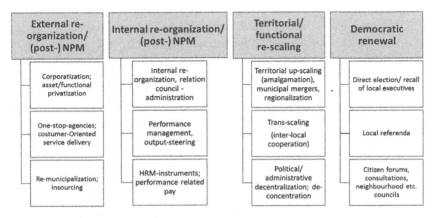

Fig. 1.1 Types of local public sector reform (Authors' own representation)

Context Conditions of Reforms

When taking the context of reforms into account, it appears to be useful to focus specifically on those institutional key features that—from theoretical and empirical viewpoints—are most likely to influence the nature of local public sector reforms. This applies to the following five aspects (see also Kuhlmann and Wollmann 2014; Pollitt and Bouckaert 2011):

(1) *State structure and type of government:* In unitary states with a centralized administration central governments can easily intervene in the affairs of subnational tiers of government. Thus they have, at least constitutionally, the possibility to impose local-level reforms and to monitor, control, and steer them from the center. In federal and highly decentralized states—characterized by strong subnational units, constitutionally protected local self-government, and vertical power sharing—local public sector reforms can theoretically be assumed to be more self-managed, voluntary, or organized in a collaborative manner. Furthermore, majoritarian systems are more likely to push far-reaching comprehensive reforms (but also to witness frequent policy reversals) than are consensus-oriented governments where negotiations, bargaining and an overall orientation towards compromise are predominant. Hence, reforms can be expected to be more incremental and cautious, but possibly also benefit from more comprehensive "ownership" and acceptance which might increase their sustainability over time.

(2) *Administrative culture and tradition:* As many of the reform measures treated in this book were originally borrowed from private sector enterprises, we would expect them to be implemented more hesitatingly in Continental European countries with legalist administrative cultures characterized by a separation between the public and private (legal) sphere and a predominance of rule orientation. This stands in contrast to countries with a public interest/common law tradition marked by a less clear-cut separation of public and private spheres, an instrumental notion of the "state" conceived of as "government" (Painter and Peters 2010, p. 20) and thus less hesitation in importing concepts and tools from the private sector. A further distinction must be made with regard to the inherited administrative traditions of post-communist countries whose institutional development was historically shaped by the centralist state model with municipalities acting as local offices for the state admin-

istration and an at-best rudimentary relevance of legal norms in day-to-day administrative work (Kuhlmann and Wollmann 2014, p. 19; Painter and Peters 2010, p. 27 et seq.). Yet, after 1990, the institutional development in post-communist Europe has taken place against the background of country-specific political conditions and pre-communist administrative traditions at different speeds and with different emphases (Swianiewicz 2014, pp. 292, 297).

(3) *Functional responsibilities and autonomy of local governments:* The scope and content of functional responsibilities and the extent of autonomy (local discretion) which the local authorities have in carrying out their tasks (see Page and Goldsmith 1987) can be expected to influence the emergence, steering mode, and impacts of reforms at the local level. We assume that local authorities with a broad range of functions are more inclined to reform their administrations than functionally weak local governments, because they face more intense pressures and a higher demand by citizens, politicians, superior levels of government, and so on for improvements in service delivery and efficiency. On a legal level, the strength and position of local authorities within an entire intergovernmental system can be seen from the existence or absence of a "general competence clause," which applies to Continental Europe and Scandinavia and stipulates that local councils are responsible (at least formally) for all matters relating to the local community. This stands in contrast to the British ultra vires principle by which local governments carry out only those responsibilities that have explicitly been assigned to them by parliamentary legislation and which can be revoked at any time (meanwhile attenuated by the local government legislation of 2000).

(4) *Territorial structures:* Size is an important condition for the operational viability, democratic quality (Denters et al. 2014), and—we assume—also of local governments' capacity for reform and/or pressures to reform they are faced with. Large-scale systems can be expected to be more capable of coping with the reform-related transaction and opportunity costs than are small municipalities, whose resources are used up by day-to-day business alone. Larger local authorities usually also have a more extensive human resource pool from which to draw and enough organizational leeway available to use for public sector modernization. Likewise, political and democratic reforms might be considered less relevant in smaller systems because direct participation is easier to achieve, whereas in

larger units the need to grant more participatory rights and direct involvement in local politics to the residents is likely to be regarded as more urgent.

(5) *Local democracy:* Finally, the nature and impacts of local public sector reforms can be expected to depend on the type of local democracy, specifically the distribution of decision-making powers within local authorities. In "strong mayor-systems" (cf. Heinelt and Hlepas 2006, p. 33; Mouritzen and Svara 2002) the individual local leadership is highly valued and the responsibilities are divided between the executive leader/mayor and the legislative/council with the—partly even directly elected—local leader/mayor being equipped with his or her own decision-making powers. Under these conditions, we might expect a greater locally based willingness to modernize the public sector than in so-called "committee systems" where strong mayors are generally unknown and the executive control of local administration lies with the elected local council or, more specifically, with council committees responsible for different domains (Wollmann 2008). In strong mayor systems with powerful local leaders it might thus be easier to steer and manage public sector reforms more effectively than in collective systems.

Country Clusters of Public Administration and Local Government Systems

The 28 countries represented in this volume can be grouped roughly into six country clusters of administrative traditions and local government systems each marked by distinct combinations of institutional and cultural characteristics (see Kuhlmann and Wollmann 2014):

(1) *Continental European Napoleonic type:* This type is marked first by the common Roman legal tradition and the importance of statutory law, and a powerful centralized bureaucracy. Traditionally, local governments are functionally weak (recent decentralization reforms notwithstanding) and a high number of (deconcentrated) locally operating field offices of the central state are characteristic.[1] Within the Continental European Napoleonic type, a Southern European subgroup can be identified (cf. Kickert 2011, p. 107 et seq.), whose administrative practice is shaped by exceptionally strong politicization, clientelistic relations and political party patronage with regard

to recruitment to the civil service (Kickert 2011, p. 107 et seq.; Sotiropoulos 2004, p. 408 et seq.).[2]

(2) *Continental European Federal type:* This type displays an essential commonality with the Napoleonic systems because of the strong legalistic orientation of administration and the rule-of-law culture following the Roman law tradition. A crucial difference from the Napoleonic group is, however, the important role of the subnational decentralized level and the principle of subsidiarity. As in federal countries many subnational tasks fall with the intermediate (*Länder/ Canton*) level, the percentage of local expenditures in these countries is party lower than in some unitary countries (see Table 1.1).

Table 1.1 Context conditions and core-features of local government systems

Country	Decentralization		Territorial structures[c]	Executive leader/mayor
	Functional responsibilities[a]	Discretion/Financial self-reliance[b]		
	>25% = strong (bold)	3 = strong (bold)	>10,000 = strong (bold)	1 = strong
Continental European federal type				
Austria	15.5	2	3,510	1
Germany	16.8	2	6,690	1
Switzerland	24.3	**3**	2,950	1
Continental European Napoleonic type				
Belgium	13.5	**3**	**17,910**	0
France	20.9	**3**	1,720	1
Greece	5.6	2	**33,600**	1
Italy	**31.3**	**3**	7,270	1
Portugal	14	2	**34,380**	1
Spain	13.3	**3**	5,430	1
Turkey	12.0	2	**52,200**	1
Nordic type				
Denmark	**64.3**	2	**55,480**	0
Finland	**40.6**	**3**	**12,660**	0
Iceland	24.2	**3**	4,150	0
Netherlands	**33.6**	1	**36,890**	0
Norway	**33.3**	**3**	**11,020**	0
Sweden	**48.2**	**3**	**31,310**	0
Anglo-Saxon type				
Ireland	10.3	**3**	**37,310**	
UK	**27.8**	1	**139,480**	0

(continued)

Table 1.1 (continued)

Country	Decentralization		Territorial structures[c]	Executive leader/mayor
	Functional responsibilities[a]	Discretion/Financial self-reliance[b]		
	>25%=strong (bold)	3=strong (bold)	>10,000=strong (bold)	1=strong
Central Eastern European type				
Czech Rep.	27	1	1,640	0
Estonia	24.7	1	5,930	0
Hungary	14.9	1	3,170	1
Latvia	**30.8**	0	**16,760**	0
Lithuania	**25.6**	1	**56,570**	1
Poland	**33**	2	**15,390**	1
Slovakia	18.2	2	1,870	1
South-Eastern European type				
Bulgaria	18.1	2	**29,090**	1
Croatia	16.6	3	8,014	1
Romania	23.9	1	6,800	1
Slovenia	20.4	0	9,560	1

Data sources:[6] DEXIA (2011), OECD (2013), United Cities and Local Governments (2010)

[a]% of local expenditure out of total public expenditure

[b]The extent to which local government revenues are derived from own/local sources (taxes, fees, charges); based on the LAI 2014 (Ladner et al. 2015 with further explanations): sources yield less than 10% of total revenues: 0; 10–25%: 1; 25–50%: 2; more than 50%: 3

[c]Ø PT of municipalities

(3) *Nordic type:* The Scandinavian/Nordic countries display significant overlap with Continental European countries in their administrative profiles since these countries are also rooted in the Roman law tradition (cf. Pierre 2010; Wollmann 2013). However, there is a peculiarity concerning the openness of the recruiting and career system in the public service and (specifically in Sweden) the explicit accessibility of the administrative system by the citizens (freedom of information, external transparency, citizen participation, and user democracy). Further commonalities with the Continental European federal nations are the subsidiarity principle in which responsibilities are allocated to the central and local administrative levels. These countries traditionally possess a highly decentralized administrative

structure with politically and functionally strong local governments, and (apart from the Netherlands[3]) a high degree of local autonomy.

(4) *Anglo-Saxon type:* The countries with an Anglo-Saxon (and Anglo-American) administrative model belong to the public interest or civic culture tradition. The cognitive and normative differences between the state and the social/economic sphere are not very pronounced and the crucial separation of the public and private legal sphere in Continental European administration is largely unknown in these countries. Local governments used to enjoy high levels of discretion and many functional responsibilities while staying comparatively weak in terms of local leadership. However, owing to reforms they have lost this traditionally strong position in many respects.

(5) The *Central Eastern European (CEE) type*[4] is characterized by a quite comprehensive break with the former legacy of the socialist administrative system. Public administration is highly decentralized and local governments enjoy a fairly wide scope of functions provided by local authorities, yet with different degrees of fiscal discretion. In the wake of the system change in 1989, these countries have made much progress in the (re)establishment of the Continental European constitutional and administrative model. Another qualification must be made regarding the Baltic States (Estonia, Latvia, and Lithuania), which resemble, in a number of features, the Nordic type (Vangas and Vilka 2003), specifically Lithuania as the CEE country with the highest average population of municipalities (57,000), whereas others are much more fragmented.

(6) *South Eastern European (SEE) Type:* Geographically, all countries of this cluster (Bulgaria, Croatia, Romania, and Slovenia) are located in the Balkans (Swianiewicz 2014, p. 305; Koprić 2009). In institutional terms, too, the local government systems of this group show many similarities with the South European type (see above); for instance, the narrower scope of functional responsibilities and the strong position of the mayors. Compared with the cluster of CEE countries, the SEE type is characterized by lower fiscal discretion and a weaker institutional position of local governments. Public administration is generally marked by a still quite centralized unitary structure (Kuhlmann and Wollmann 2014, p. 21). In some countries (e.g. Bulgaria and Romania), the administrative history was marked by highly centralist rules and the transformation process after 1990 was determined initially by the post-communist elite.

Table 1.1 gives an overview on some key features of local government systems and relevant context conditions of local public sector reforms in the (groups of) countries represented in the chapters of this volume.[5]

OVERVIEW OF THIS VOLUME

Drawing on the abovementioned reform typology, Part I of the book deals with the territorial rescaling of local governance, amalgamation, cooperation, and territorial consolidation. Proceeding from the empirical observation of significantly diverse territorial reform policies in Europe ranging from drastic mergers, through partial upscaling, to no amalgamation at all, Steiner, Kaiser, and Eythórsson (Chapter 2) focus on strategies, patterns of conflict, and outcomes regarding municipal merger reforms in 14 European countries. The broad variety of amalgamation strategies notwithstanding, the authors reveal that these reforms often result in a strengthened viability and improved service quality of the enlarged municipal units. Taking a predominantly explanatory approach, the comparison of the divergent reform patterns within a small-n design (the Netherlands and Flanders) presented by Broekema, Steen, and Wayenberg (Chapter 3) suggests that the degree of centralization/decentralization within a given country/region, the path of amalgamation in the past, and the role of the mayor, explain differences in reform outcomes. In a similar vein, Askim, Klausen, Vabo, and Bjurstrøm (Chapter 4) analyze potential driving forces (fiscal stress, urbanization and others) and filtering factors (for example municipal size) of amalgamation, using a large-n approach (17 European countries). They show that, inter alia, the degree of urbanization, the history of recent reforms, path dependencies, and municipal size are among those factors with the most predictive power for amalgamation reforms. Franzke, Klimovský, and Pinterič (Chapter 5) concentrate on the development and impacts of intermunicipal cooperation (IMC) as a potential alternative to mergers. Comparing the examples of Brandenburg, Slovakia, and Slovenia, they demonstrate that the various forms of IMC found in the country cases differ widely in their outcomes depending on (more favorable or more unfavorable) context conditions.

Part II of the volume addresses internal administrative reforms inspired by the NPM guided principles of performance management, performance budgeting, performance-related pay and other new forms of human resource management (HRM). The contribution by Mussari, Tranfaglia, Reichard, Bjørnå, Nakrošis, and Bankauskaitė-Grigaliūnienė (Chapter 6) deals with the design and implementation of local performance budgeting (PB) from the comparative perspective of four countries (Germany, Italy, Lithuania, and Norway). Highlighting the different concepts and trajectories of PB reform, the authors identify the major causes and drivers influencing processes of reform and show to what extent NPM-based principles, external pressures, and the 2007 financial crisis impacted the pace and contents of budgeting reforms in these four countries. Performance management is also the core concept analyzed by Turc, Guenon, Rodrigues, Demirkaya, and Dupuis (Chapter 7), who examine reform ideologies and diffusion in countries with a Napoleonic administrative tradition (France, Turkey, and Portugal). Their study suggests a visible resistance of Napoleonic local governments to NPM approaches of performance management. However, the comparative analysis also accounts for an enormous diversity of contexts and reforms in the sample of three countries. A critical view on performance related local government modernization is also taken by Proeller, Wenzel, Vogel, Mussari, Casale, Turc, and Guenoun (Chapter 8). Focusing on performance related pay (PRP) regimes in Germany, France, and Italy, the authors shed light on the causes by which PRP systems have lost their core position in the reform agendas of European local governments. Drawing on a survey in three "cities of excellence" nominated for the European Public Sector Award, Salm and Schwab (Chapter 9) explain to what extent and why HRM reforms can actually influence local government performance.

In discussing the external (post-)NPM-related reorganization of the local public sector, Part III of the volume concentrates on institutional changes in local service delivery, focusing on various local policies and services. Taking the examples of public utilities and elderly care, Wollmann (Chapter 10) provides a developmental (over time) and cross-countries/cross-policies analysis of institutional changes in local service delivery in both Western European countries and Central Eastern European ones. He suggests that after significant NPM -inspired and crisis-driven privatizations and outsourcing strategies, there are new signs of a "comeback" of the municipal sector and of an emerging engagement of the societal sphere. Torsteinsen and Van Genugten (Chapter 11) challenge this hypothesis of developmental stages and converging institutional trends in local service organization. Taking Norway and the Netherlands as the most similar cases, they find that the trajectories of reform do not match the general picture of similar reform trends and developmental patterns across Europe. By contrast, they reveal that NPM reforms have occurred in different decades in the two countries, that there are no signs of re-municipalization, but that there is instead a strong tendency towards inter-municipalization as a common feature. The search for convergence and divergence in local service organization is also at the center of the contribution by Henriksen, Smith, Thøgersen, and Zimmer (Chapter 12). They take a fresh look at the relation of municipal and non-profit actors by examining institutional changes in the welfare mix of local social service provision. Their analysis shows that, despite a general divergence in welfare regimes and non-profit–government relations, the country sample (Germany, Denmark, and the UK) exhibits major common institutional trends in local service provision. This observation of significant convergent developments in local service delivery despite persisting country (cluster) differences gains further support from Hlepas, Kettunen, Kutsar, MacCarthaigh, Navarro, Richter, and Teles (Chapter 13). Comparing seven countries (Estonia, Finland, Germany, Greece, Ireland, Portugal, and Spain) with regard to their reorganization of childcare governance, they identify the rescaling of care-related functions between levels of government as a common institutional trend. However, following a decade of investments in local childcare, the autonomy of municipalities in this sector has in the meantime been significantly reduced owing to the public debt crisis. The institutional consequences of the fiscal crisis are also the topic of the contribution by Getimis (Chapter 14) picking the example of local planning powers. A general trend towards decentralization of planning powers notwithstanding, he finds very different national responses, e.g. revealing the UK and Greece as "radical marketizers."

Part IV of the volume addresses local participatory reforms, innovations in local democracy and leadership, the impacts of reform on the local citizens, and their perceptions about "good local governance." Starting from the diagnosis of contested representative democracy, Vetter, Klimovský, Denters, and Kersting (Chapter 15) provide a comprehensive overview of local democratic reforms for all member states of the EU with a population of more than one million, plus Switzerland, Norway, and Iceland, over the period from 1990 to 2014. The authors conclude that most changes have occurred in minor fields of democratic reforms (such as free access to information) whereas with regard to more far-reaching attempts, e.g., the introduction of binding referenda, there is more reluctance. Lidström, Baldersheim, Copus, Hlynsdóttir, Kettunen, and Klimovský (Chapter 16) analyze attempts to restore and improve existing institutions of representative democracy—the councils and the councilors—in 15 European countries. They reveal that the observed variations between countries can largely be explained by the type of legitimacy that each local government system enjoys and that is based on different degrees of citizen trust and national government confidence in local government. Contested representative democracy at the local level is also the starting point of the contribution by Copus, Iglesias, Hacek, Illner, and Lidström (Chapter 17). Their concern is to examine the extent to which the debate about the direct election of the mayor has influenced change in local government and how, if at all, this model of local leadership has been adopted in their country sample (the Czech Republic, England, Slovenia, Spain, and Sweden). The question of discursive and instrumental convergence is also put forward by Kersting, Gasparikova, Iglesias, and Krenova (Chapter 18) with regard to new deliberative participatory instruments. Examining participatory budgeting (PB) as one of the most important reform instruments, they argue that the local administration and the directly elected mayors are key actors in the reform process, while councils are more hesitant to implement PB tools. Despite significant country differences, PB in Europe focuses more on public brainstorming and less on planning or actual conflict resolution. Finally, but importantly, Denters, Ladner, Mouritzen, and Rose (Chapter 19) shed light on citizens' perceptions in public sector reforms, governance, service provision, and democracy at the local level in Switzerland, Norway, Denmark and the Netherlands. Taking into account that reforming local government is not a value in itself but is meant to generate improvements for the population, the authors give the word directly to citizens and thus take a pronouncedly evaluative perspective. They scrutinize the importance of democratic values as compared with efficient provision of services and whether there is a trade-off n. between efficiency and democracy. Their analysis reveals that local governments, on the one hand, achieve satisfactory results in the eyes of their citizens in many respects. On the other hand, there are noteworthy differences, inter alia, concerning satisfaction with municipal output performance, responsiveness of local elected officials, citizens' expectations regarding good local governance (collective vs. individualist service provision), and democratic values (representative vs. more participatory).

Notes

1. Regarding Belgium, which has meanwhile been quasi-federalized, a differentiation between the Flemish region (with a more Nordic tradition) and the Walloon region (with a more Latin/Napoleonic tradition) must be made. However, for purposes of simplification we group Belgium with the Continental European Napoleonic cluster.

2. Although not belonging to Continental Europe geographically, Turkey displays many features of the Continental European Napoleonic administrative profile (Southern European sub-group) and is therefore classified with this group (country data taken from Turc et al. in this volume).

3. For some countries we have taken updated numbers (as far as available) in order to take major recent reforms into account: (1) *Greece*: average population significantly increased after the Kallikratis Reform of 2010 (from 10,750 in 2010 to 33,600 in 2015); (2) *Hungary* has witnessed a significant decline in functional responsibilities due to re-centralization processes (from 25.6 in 2011 to 14.9 in 2013); (3) *Latvia*: average population significantly increased after the reforms of 2010 (from 4,340 in 2010 to 16,760 in 2015).

4. Although the Netherlands are characterized by a historic legacy of the Napoleonic tradition it also shows many similarities with the Nordic countries (see John 2001), which have been further strengthened by way of recent (decentralization) reforms (Torsteinsen and Van Genugten in this volume).

5. We distinguish two types of Eastern European systems by combining parts of the more differentiated typology proposed by Swianiewicz (2014) that consist of five Eastern European sub-groups.

6. As Cyprus, Bosnia Herzegowina, and Israel, although being LocRef members, are not represented in this volume we have not included them in the table.

References

Bäck, H., H. Heinelt, and A. Magnier (eds.). 2006. *The European mayor. Political leaders in the changing context of local democracy*. Wiesbaden: VS Verlag für Sozialwissenschaften.

Baldersheim, H., and L.E. Rose. 2010. Territorial choice: Rescaling governance in European states. In *Territorial choice: The politics of boundaries and borders*, ed. H. Baldersheim and L.E. Rose, 1–20. New York: Palgrave Macmillan.

Bouckaert, G. 2006. Auf dem Weg zu einer Neo-Weberianischen Verwaltung. New Public Management im internationalen Vergleich. In *Politik und Verwaltung*, PVS-Sonderheft 37/2006, ed. J. Bogumil, W. Jann, and F. Nullmeier, 354–372. Wiesbaden: VS.

Bouckaert, G., G.B. Peters, and K. Verhoest (eds.). 2010. *The coordination of public sector organizations. Shifting patterns of public management*. Basingstoke: Palgrave Macmillan.

Denters, B., M. Goldsmith, A. Ladner, P.E. Mouritzen, and L.E. Rose. 2014. *Size and local democracy*. Cheltenham: Edward Elgar.

DEXIA. 2011. *EU subnational governments: 2010 key figures*. Paris: DEXIA Editions.

Hall, P. A., and Taylor, R. C. R. 1996. Political Science and the Three New Institutionalisms. In Political Studies 44 (5), S. 936–957.

Halligan, J. 2010. Post-NPM responses to disaggregation through coordinating horizontally and integrating governance. In *Governance of public sector organizations: Proliferation, autonomy and performance*, ed. P. Lægreid and K. Verhoest, 235–254. Basingstoke: Palgrave Macmillan.

Heinelt, H., and N. Hlepas. 2006. Typologies of local government systems. In *The European mayor: Political leaders in the changing context of local democracy*, ed. H. Bäck, H. Heinelt, and A. Magnier, 21–42. Wiesbaden: VS Verlag für Sozialwissenschaften.

John, P. 2001. *Local governance in Western Europe*. London/Thousand Oaks: Sage.

Kersting, N., and A. Vetter (eds.). 2003. *Reforming local government in Europe*. Wiesbaden: VS Verlag für Sozialwissenschaften.

Kickert, W.J.M. 2011. Public management reform in continental Europe: National distinctiveness. In *The Ashgate research companion to new public management*, ed. T. Christensen and P. Laegreid, 97–112. Surrey: Ashgate.

Koprić, I. 2009. Roles and styles of local political leaders on the territory of the former Yugoslavia: Between authoritarian local political top bosses and citizen-oriented local managers. *Hrvatska javna uprava* 9(1): 79–105.

Kuhlmann, S., and E. Wayenberg. 2015. Institutional impact assessment in multi-level systems: Conceptualizing decentralization effects from a comparative perspective. *International Review of Administrative Sciences* (forthcoming in 2016).

Kuhlmann, S., and H. Wollmann. 2014. *Introduction to comparative public administration. Administrative systems and reforms in Europe*. Cheltenham: Edward Elgar.

Kuhlmann, S., S. Grohs, and J. Bogumil. 2014. Reforming public administration in multi-level systems: An evaluation of performance changes in European local governments. In *Public administration and the modern state: Assessing trends and impact*, ed. E. Bohne, J.D. Graham, J.C.N. Raadschelders, and J.P. Lehrke, 205–222. Basingstoke: Palgrave Macmillan.

Ladner, A., Keuffer, N. and Baldersheim, H. 2015. Local Autonomy Index for European Countries (1990–2014). Release 1.0. Brussels: European Commission.

Lægreid, P., and K. Verhoest (eds.). 2010. *Governance of public sector organizations: Proliferation, autonomy and performance*, International Institute of Administrative Sciences. Basingstoke: Palgrave Macmillan.

Mouritzen, P.E., and J.H. Svara. 2002. *Leadership at the apex: Politicians and administrators in Western local governments*. Pittsburgh: University of Pittsburgh Press.

OECD. 2010. Public administration after "New Public Management". Paris: OECD Publishing.

OECD. 2013. *Government at a glance 2013*. Paris: OECD Publishing.

Page, E.C., and M.J. Goldsmith (eds.). 1987. *Central and local government relations: A comparative analysis of West European unitary states.* London: Sage.

Painter, M., and B.G. Peters. 2010. Administrative traditions in comparative perspective: Families, groups and hybrids. In *Tradition and public administration*, ed. B.G. Peters and M. Painter, 19–30. Basingstoke: Palgrave Macmillan.

Peters, B.G. 2013. Institutions in context, and as context. In *Context in public policy and management: The missing link?* ed. C. Pollitt, 101–114. Cheltenham: Edward Elgar.

Pierre, J. 2010. Administrative Reforms in Sweden. The Resilience of Administrative Tradition. In Tradition and public administration, ed. B. G. Peters und M. Painter, 191–202. Basingstoke: Palgrave Macmillan.

Pierson, P. 2004. *Politics in time: History, institutions, and social analysis.* Princeton: Princeton University Press.

Pollitt, C. (ed.). 2013. *Context in public policy and management: The missing link?* Cheltenham: Edward Elgar.

Pollitt, C., and G. Bouckaert. 2011. *Public management reform: A comparative analysis—New public management, governance, and the Neo-Weberian state,* 3rd ed. Oxford: Oxford University Press.

Reynaert, H., K. Steyvers, P. Delwit, and J.-B. Pilet (eds.). 2009. *Local political leadership in Europe: Town chief, city boss or loco president?* Bruges: Vanden Broele/Nomos.

Scharpf, F.W. 2002. *Governing in Europe: Effective and democratic?* Oxford: Oxford University Press.

Schedler, K., and I. Proeller. 2000. *New public management.* Bern: Haupt.

Sotiropoulos, D.A. 2004. Southern European public bureaucracies in comparative perspective. *West European Politics* 27: 405–422.

Swianiewicz, P. 2014. An empirical typology of local government systems in Eastern Europe. *Local Government Studies* 40: 292–311.

United Cities and Local Governments. 2010. *Local government finance: The challenges of the 21st century. Second global report on decentralization and local democracy (GOLD II).* Cheltenham: Edward Elgar.

Vangas, E., and I. Vilka. 2003. Local democracy in the Baltic countries: A new beginning? In *Local democracy in post-Communist Europe*, ed. H. Baldersheim, M. Illner, and H. Wollmann, 123–156. Opladen: Leske + Budrich.

Wollmann, H. 2008. *Reformen in Kommunalpolitik und -verwaltung: England, Schweden, Frankreich und Deutschland im Vergleich.* Wiesbaden: VS.

Wollmann, H. 2013. Zur (Nicht-)Verwendung von Evaluationsergebnissen in Politik und Verwaltung. Eine vernachlässigte Fragestellung der Evaluationsforschung. In der moderne staat - Zeitschrift für Public Policy, Recht und Management. 87–102.

Wollmann, H., and G. Marcou (eds.). 2010. *The provision of public services in Europe: Between state, local government and market.* Cheltenham: Edward Elgar.

World Bank. 2007. Administrative Capacity in the New EU Member States: The Limits of Innovation. Washington D.C.

Re-Scaling Local Governance: Amalgamation, Cooperation, Territorial Consolidation

A Comparative Analysis of Amalgamation Reforms in Selected European Countries

Reto Steiner, Claire Kaiser, and Grétar Thór Eythórsson

INTRODUCTION

Various European countries have implemented amalgamation reforms since World War II, and such reforms are still or again on the agenda of national and subnational governments. Politicians consider them a remedy to improve public service delivery and the financial situation of local and superordinate tiers of government, particularly in times of financial stress: Greece serves as a good example for this strategy, as it tremendously reduced its number of municipalities in 2010.

Although the advantages and disadvantages of amalgamations have been widely discussed, studies on the spread and outcome of this type of reform are mostly country-specific, fragmented, and only partially comparable (for example, Keating 1995; Council of Europe 2001; Fox and Gurley 2006).

Based on an expert survey, this chapter provides a comparative overview of the amalgamation strategies in local government in continental

R. Steiner (✉) • C. Kaiser
University of Bern, Bern, Switzerland

G.T. Eythórsson
University of Akureyri, Akureyri, Iceland

© The Author(s) 2016
S. Kuhlmann, G. Bouckaert (eds.), *Local Public Sector Reforms in Times of Crisis*, DOI 10.1057/978-1-137-52548-2_2

23

European countries, the implementation of these projects, patterns of conflict, and the outcome of these reforms. The main research question concerns whether the amalgamation reforms have achieved their goals thus far and whether the selection of a specific reform strategy leads to a certain reform path and outcome.

The chapter starts with the development of a framework, which structures the analysis of amalgamation reforms, and then provides an overview of the development of the local territorial structure in Europe and a classification of amalgamation strategies. We subsequently discuss the objectives of amalgamations, the patterns of conflict, and the outcome of the reform.

For this comparative cross-national study, we collected data from an expert survey that was sent to academic experts specialized in local government research in 20 countries participating in the working group on territorial restructuring of the LocRef COST Action research network, which include the majority of the continental European countries and Iceland. The questionnaire on territorial reforms focused, in the first part, on statistical data regarding municipal structure and size. In the second part, territorial reforms, particularly amalgamations, were addressed. The data were collected in 2014, and the response rate was 75% (15 countries participated in this survey: Belgium, Denmark, Finland, Germany, Greece, Iceland, Italy, the Netherlands, Norway, Poland, Portugal, Slovenia, Spain, Sweden, and Switzerland).

FRAMEWORK FOR THE ANALYSIS OF AMALGAMATION REFORMS

The analysis of amalgamations in European countries is structured based on an analytical framework, as presented in Fig. 2.1: amalgamations are first classified by the *characteristics* of the not-yet-amalgamated municipalities and the *context* that influences the *objectives* that actors want to reach with the reform. These objectives are expected to be achieved through the selection of *a reform strategy* and its *implementation*. The implementation will cause *patterns of conflicts*, which, among other factors, will influence the *outcome* of the reform. The reform process is nonlinear. The outcome will be the starting point of future reforms, and each aspect of the process may influence other aspects, e.g., patterns of conflict can trigger a change in the strategy or implementation process.

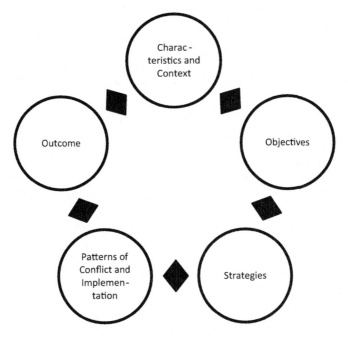

Fig. 2.1 Analytical framework

This chapter focuses on the "objectives," "strategies," "patterns of conflict," and "outcome" of amalgamation reforms. The contribution by Askim et al., Chap. 4 in this volume discusses the drivers, i.e., characteristics and context, of such reforms.

Objectives

The objectives that politicians want to achieve with amalgamations focus on not only the resources of a municipality (human resources and local finances) and the output of amalgamation (quality and quantity of public services, correctness of legal decisions) but also the room for maneuvering that is granted to an amalgamated municipality (from outside the political-administrative system of the municipality, local autonomy; from inside the political-administrative system, local democracy and identity with a municipality).

These effects are frequently discussed in the literature and are crucial characteristics of local government performance (see Poister 2003; Padovani and Scorsone 2009).

Proponents usually argue that task fulfillment could be improved (Reingewertz 2012; Steiner 2002) and that costs can be reduced through economies of scale (Fox and Gurley 2006; Council of Europe 2001). Professionalization of the administration is expected in larger municipalities because personnel are better educated and able to work in more specialized areas (Dafflon 1998). The position of the local tier of government vis-à-vis higher tiers is expected to become stronger because more tasks can be transferred to the local tier and because the local tier can gain more negotiation power; moreover, the local government should gain more municipal autonomy (Steiner 2002). However, opponents of mergers often argue that democracy will be hindered by a reduction in political participation and direct contact between local councilors and citizens and by a loss in local identity (Linder 1999; Copus 2006; De Ceuninck et al. 2010).

In addition, if promoters of amalgamations formulate objectives, they are not necessarily consistent and clear. Indeed, for political reasons, a lack of knowledge, or conflicting interests, governments may follow an inconsistent agenda with contradictory objectives.

Strategies

Countries can choose between different reform strategies. In a first dimension these strategies can range from bottom-up to top-down strategies, and in a second dimension they can range from comprehensive to incremental approaches. A bottom-up amalgamation strategy can be defined as a proposal for boundary change that is generated at the local tier of government. These reforms are usually voluntary—that is, the municipalities and its citizens decide on their own whether they want to merge with one or more neighbor municipalities. There are no threats of intervention or law enforcement at the superior state level in case the merger project fails. In some cases, superordinate tiers of government may set financial incentives to promote mergers Kaiser (2014). In contrast, a top-down amalgamation strategy involves an intervention by central government (or by the superior state level), and changes are imposed on local governments (Baldersheim and Rose 2010, p. 13). Top-down mergers are usually coercive—that is, the higher-ranking state level can force a municipality to merge with one or more neighbor municipalities against the will of the municipality concerned or the majority of its citizens.

With respect to the second dimension, comprehensive and incremental approaches can be distinguished (Baldersheim and Rose 2010, p. 13). When a comprehensive strategy is chosen, the entire local government structure in the country is analyzed at one point in time. Such an approach can be considered conceptual and normative. In the incremental approach, however, only parts of a territorial structure in a country are considered for reform; the procedure may be stepwise (Kaiser 2015; see also the Chap. 3 by Broekema et al., in this volume for a qualitative perspective on comprehensive and incremental amalgamation strategies).

Patterns of Conflict and Implementation

The chosen strategy will likely cause different patterns of conflict during the implementation process. A top-down-initiated reform is likely to meet resistance at the local level (Brantgärde 1974) and to cause conflicts between central and local government, large and small municipalities and rich and poor municipalities. A top-down initiative by the government can easily be considered power-gathering by the central government. Smaller and poorer municipalities may indeed consider themselves victims of such reforms.

The same may be true with comprehensive reforms. Such reforms will likely cause a greater number of conflicts because they have an impact on all the smaller and poorer municipalities. Thus, resistance to amalgamations may be reduced if the reforms are introduced bottom-up and incrementally.

Not only the chosen strategy but also the objectives may influence whether resistance will arise. Certain reform objectives, such as increasing efficiency, may cause greater skepticism by the citizens. The impact can take time to actualize, and the expected effects are sometimes difficult to calculate ex ante. Additionally, such objectives may be questioned because other aspects related to a municipality, such as responsiveness and local democracy, are considered more important and endangered. However, objectives such as resolving the financial problems of a municipality would be easier to justify beforehand and therefore likely face less resistance. Providing concrete knowledge of the tasks that are being transferred from the superordinate tier to the local tier of government could also engender a more positive attitude toward a reform.

Reforms are usually associated with the initiative of political parties in power. Hence, conflicts may be visible between left-wing and right-wing parties.

During the implementation process, different problems can arise. There may be opposition from not only politicians but also employees, and the potentially different views and approaches of a rather technocratic administration or of a government and a parliament in a political argument could cause resistance to change. Both groups could be winners or losers of the reform, and the outcome may be affected.

Additionally, the reform process may lack thorough preparation, or resources may be wanting for a timely proceeding. Should other reform projects occur at the same time, these issues could create conflicts between the different reforms.

Outcome

The outcome of an amalgamation reform is the consequence of the chosen reform strategy, patterns of conflict, and the way conflicts are handled, as well as factors that cannot be influenced by the involved actors, such as a decrease in tax revenues in times of recession. From the viewpoint of the promoters of the reform, the one-to-one achievement of all reform objectives is the expected result. From a more objective, outsider's view, outcomes different from the expected ones may still lead to a municipality with greater legitimacy regarding input and output. Without rating the outcome, we want to examine the realized results of amalgamations.

Development of the Municipal Structure and Amalgamation Strategies

The majority of the 15 continental European countries observed have reduced their number of municipalities during the past 40 years. The most drastic upscaling between 1973 and 2013 occurred in Greece and Belgium, at –94.6% and –75.0%, respectively. In addition, Iceland, Denmark, and the Netherlands lost more than half their municipalities during this period. By contrast, in Slovenia, the number of municipalities increased between 1993 and 2013, from 147 to 212 units. Additionally, Poland, Portugal, Spain, and Italy saw a slight increase in the number of municipalities from the 1970s onwards.

Table 2.1 presents the mean population size of the municipalities in the 15 European countries observed. The largest municipalities can be found in Northern Europe, where amalgamations took place in most countries.

Denmark and the Netherlands have the largest municipalities, and Portugal, Greece, and Sweden follow, with a mean population size of more than 30,000 inhabitants each. Switzerland, Iceland, Spain, Germany, and Italy have the smallest municipalities, where municipalities have less than 10,000 inhabitants on average.

Table 2.1 Development of the number of municipalities during the past 40 years[a]

Country	1973	1993	2013	Change 1973–2013 in%	Mean population
Northern Europe					
Norway	443	439	428	−3.4	11,802
Finland	483	455	320	−33.7	16,151
Sweden	464	286	290	−37.5	33,240
Denmark	275	275	98	−64.4	56,943
Iceland	224	196	74	−67.0	4,447
Western Europe					
Switzerland[b]	3,095	3,015	2,396	−22.6	3,163
Germany	15,009	16,043	11,197	−25.4	6,742
The Netherlands[c]	913	636	408	−55.3	41,000
Belgium	2,359	589	589	−75.0	18,593
Southern Europe					
Slovenia[d]	–	147	212	+44.2	10,000
Portugal	304	305	308	+1.3	34,293
Spain		8,088	8,117	+0.8	5,815
Italy[e]	8,056	8,100	8,092	+0.4	7,550
Greece	6,061	5,921	325	−94.6	33,653
Eastern Europe					
Poland	2,366	2,462	2,480	+4.8	15,600
Total (mean)	*3,081*	*3,130*	*2,336*	*−29.3*	*19,933*

[a]Composition of geographical regions according to the United Nations Statistics Division

[b]In 1960, 1980, 1993, 2003 and 2013

[c]In 1970, 1980, 1995, 2003 and 2013

[d]In 1995, 2003 and 2013

[e]In 1971, 1981, 1991, 2001 and 2011—that is, the years when the Central Statistics Office conduct a census

Iceland and Switzerland with their small municipalities demonstrate that the historical context and the density of the population in the municipality play a crucial role: although amalgamations took place, the municipalities have remained quite small. However, Portugal with its rather large municipalities has not seen mergers thus far.

If we classify the amalgamation strategies of the countries, we can distinguish, as already discussed, between those countries that have conducted amalgamations and those that have not thus far. The countries with an amalgamation strategy can be subdivided into countries with top-down and bottom-up approaches. A top-down approach can be comprehensive or incremental. Furthermore, mixed strategies as they exist in federal countries have to be considered. Countries without amalgamations may be subdivided into those with no amalgamation strategy (favoring intermunicipal cooperation), and those with a fragmentation strategy. Table 2.2 illustrates how the countries can be grouped into these different categories.

Looking at the time period since the 1970s, countries with a *comprehensive top-down* amalgamation strategy include Denmark, Finland, Greece, Iceland, and the Netherlands, although the Danish reform had some voluntary aspects in the choice of partners and the reform in Iceland was voluntary in the sense that no amalgamation could be implemented without the acceptance of the citizens in a referendum. Additional countries with a top-down strategy, though incremental, are Norway and Spain. With these top-down reforms, the number of municipalities was often reduced drastically, such as the territorial consolidation in Greece (Hlepas 2010) or the structural reforms in Denmark (Vrangboek 2010).

Table 2.2 Typology of amalgamation strategies

Amalgamation strategy	Countries
Top-down strategy (comprehensive)	Denmark, Finland, Greece, Iceland, the Netherlands
Top-down strategy (incremental)	Spain, Norway
Mixed strategy	Belgium, Germany (some Länder), Switzerland (some cantons)
Bottom-up strategy	Switzerland (some cantons)
No amalgamation strategy	Germany (some Länder), Italy, Portugal, Sweden, Switzerland (some cantons)
Fragmentation strategy	Poland, Slovenia

Mixed strategies are found, for example, in Belgium and some German *Länder*, where this strategy has also been called the "carrot-and-stick" strategy. In the first voluntary phase, municipalities could decide themselves how to implement the reform scheme. Amalgamation intentions were also supported by financial incentives (the "carrots"). In the second phase, however, for the local governments that failed to implement the reform scheme before a date fixed by legislation, binding legislation came into force (the "stick"). Very few Swiss cantons have chosen a similar strategy (e.g., Thurgau). Additionally, the East German *Länder*, with the exception of Sachsen, after 1990 (i.e., after German unification), followed the same reform path (Wollmann 2010).

Some Swiss cantons apply an *incremental bottom-up* strategy for mergers. The cantonal governments support mergers with certain incentives, but they wait for the initiative of the local government.

No amalgamation strategies as such can be found in some German *Länder*, Italy, Portugal, Sweden, and some Swiss cantons. Intermunicipal cooperation is usually widely spread in these countries to overcome the problem of minimum size. Sweden had two waves of enforced mergers in the 1950s and between 1964 and 1974; since then, the number of municipalities has remained constant. Therefore, stability may also be an indication that amalgamation waves occurred during earlier times.

Territorial *fragmentation* has been a reform trend in several, mainly Eastern European countries, such as Slovenia and Poland (Swianiewicz 2010). Fragmentation is often a reaction to earlier consolidation reforms by communist regimes. The Czech Republic—although not part of the country sample in this chapter—serves as a good example. After a territorial consolidation of local government in the 1960s and 1970s decreed by the central government, the country underwent a fragmentation of municipalities after the fall of the communist regime in the 1990s (Illner 2010). The number of municipalities was reduced from more than 10,000 in 1950 to 4,120 in 1989. After the fragmentation process, the Czech Republic had more than 6,200 local governments in 2007.

For the further analysis of amalgamations in European countries, we include only the 10 countries with amalgamations during the last 40 years, and Sweden, which had finished its amalgamations in 1974. Not all questions have been answered by all countries.

OBJECTIVES

Increasing efficiency has been the most important objective of amalgamation reforms in all the observed countries. The professionalization of staff as another way to improve the efficiency of the use of a municipality's resources has been much less relevant (see Table 2.3). The hope of achieving efficiency gains is bundled in almost all countries with an expected improvement in service quality.

Table 2.3 Objectives

Objectives	Countries		
	No importance[a]	Medium importance	High importance
Improving input			
Efficiency (economies of scale, economies of scope)			Belgium, Denmark, Finland, Germany, Greece, Iceland, Italy, the Netherlands, Norway, Sweden, Switzerland
More specialized staff	Denmark, Italy	Belgium, Finland, Iceland, Greece, Switzerland	
Improving output			
Improving service quality		Denmark	Belgium, Finland, Germany, Greece, Iceland, Italy, the Netherlands, Norway, Sweden, Switzerland
Improving room for maneuvering			
Evolution/ Delegation of powers	Denmark	Iceland, Italy, Switzerland	Belgium, Finland, Germany, Greece, the Netherlands, Norway, Sweden
Democratization/ Participation/ Accountability	Denmark, Germany, Iceland, the Netherlands, Sweden, Switzerland	Belgium, Italy	Greece, Norway

[a]The experts assessed the various items on a scale from 1 (not important) to 5 (important). We have clustered the answers 1 and 2 as "No Importance," 3 as "Medium Importance," and 4 and 5 as "High Importance."

Interestingly, the objective of increasing a municipality's room for maneuvering is important for most countries from the viewpoint that more tasks would be delegated to the municipality. With regard to strengthening democracy and increasing the room for maneuvering for citizens, only a few countries consider this objective important. The reason might be that amalgamation reforms are not considered to be the right strategy to achieve this objective.

PATTERNS OF CONFLICT AND IMPLEMENTATION

Territorial reforms are drastic changes for the concerned municipalities because they touch jurisdictional boundaries that have often existed for long periods of time. Amalgamation processes, therefore, often accompany opposition and resistance. In different countries, different patterns of conflict prevail, depending on the nature of the reform and the historical traditions in the particular country (Baldersheim and Rose 2010, p. 14).

According to the expert survey (see Table 2.4), the main pattern of conflict in territorial reforms occurs along the central–local division. Municipalities often try to prevent such reforms and oppose the central government's projects. The rift between large and small municipalities,

Table 2.4 Patterns of conflict

Conflicts	Countries		
	No importance	Medium importance	High importance
Central-Local		Italy, Switzerland	Belgium, Denmark, Finland, Germany, Greece, Iceland, the Netherlands, Norway, Sweden
Rich-Poor	Belgium, Denmark, Greece, Iceland, Italy, Norway, Sweden	Finland, Germany	The Netherlands, Switzerland
Large-Small	Denmark, Italy, Sweden	Finland	Belgium, Germany, Greece, Iceland, the Netherlands, Norway, Switzerland
Left-Right	Denmark, Finland, Iceland, Switzerland	Germany, Italy, the Netherlands, Norway	Belgium, Greece, Sweden
Technocracy-Politics	Belgium, Denmark, Sweden	Germany, Switzerland	Finland, Greece, Iceland, Italy, Norway

which likely results from the conflicting interests between large urban municipalities and their agglomerations, on the one hand, and smaller peripheral, rural municipalities, on the other hand, is also rather important. The results from studies on both Swedish and Icelandic municipalities demonstrate in both cases that the strongest explanatory variable for resistance against amalgamation is each municipality's expected status in the new/potential municipality. The potential loss of status and power is something that does not seem to be acceptable for either voters or local leaders. Further, the lack of status could mean that the small municipalities are overruled or swallowed by the larger municipalities. The risk of not being the center for services and administration in the newly created municipality is, not surprisingly, strongly connected with the population size of the municipality. The largest municipality in each context is of course most likely to take on that role. Therefore, the status dimension and the size dimension are interrelated (Eythórsson 1998, 2009; Brantgärde 1974).

Regarding the conflict between large and small municipalities, there is, for example, great variation in Northern Europe, as Finland and Iceland have much higher grades than Sweden and Denmark. The different countries' different variation in the size of municipalities might explain this result, as it is much greater in Finland and Iceland than in Sweden and Denmark, where the reforms have managed to reduce these differences in size.

The different political viewpoints between left-wing and right-wing parties appear to play a fairly important role in some countries. However, there is no clear pattern according to country type. The same is true for the technocracy–politics conflict that can be observed in half of the countries. Such a result is understandable for countries such as Greece, where the reform has been requested by outside institutions owing to its financial problems.

Table 2.5 shows the greatest problems encountered during the reform process. The most important overall factor is strong opposition from politicians. Such strong opposition can be explained by public choice theory. This theory assumes that individuals try to maximize their personal egoistic interests. Facing changes such as municipal amalgamations, elected local politicians can clearly have a personal interest in keeping their jobs and status—by being reelected (Mouritzen 2006). Amalgamations reduce both the number of municipalities and, therefore, the number of elected politicians. Another reason may be that politicians are usually elected in

Table 2.5 Problems during the amalgamation process

Implementation problems	Countries		
	No importance	Medium importance	High importance
Strong opposition of politicians	Sweden	Italy, Switzerland	Belgium, Finland, Germany, Greece, Iceland, the Netherlands, Norway
Strong opposition of employees	Belgium, Finland, Germany, Iceland, Sweden		Greece, Italy, the Netherlands, Norway, Switzerland
Insufficient resources for reform implementation	Belgium, Norway, Sweden	Finland, Germany, Iceland, Switzerland	Greece, Italy, the Netherlands
No time to prepare the implementation	Belgium, Italy, Sweden, Switzerland	Finland, Germany, Greece	Iceland, the Netherlands
Other reform projects at the same time	Belgium, Greece, Iceland, Norway, Sweden, Switzerland	Germany, Italy	Finland, the Netherlands
Unclear/Inconsistent reform objectives	Belgium, Greece, Iceland, the Netherlands, Norway, Sweden, Switzerland	Germany, Italy	Finland

electoral districts. By opposing amalgamations, the politicians of rural and poorer areas receive the support of their voters. Moderately important factors are the opposition of employees (who may fear the loss of their jobs), insufficient resources for the implementation of the reform, and the lack of time to prepare for the implementation well in advance.

OUTCOMES

The most important effect of amalgamations thus far has been improved service quality, which has been reported by all countries. Cost savings have been observed as well, but more countries report that cost savings have occurred only to some extent. Interestingly, improved service quality does not go together with improved citizen orientation. Indeed, increased professionalization may lead to more standardization, which may not necessarily touch the heart of the citizens. Legal correctness is also not a major outcome of amalgamation reform, which is understandable because the rule of law and its application play a crucial role in continental Europe even in small municipalities, and because it is superordinate tiers of government that oversee it.

The strengthening of local autonomy appears to be another outcome that can be observed in most countries with amalgamations. At first sight, this result may seem to reflect a contradiction; however, by losing autonomy (through amalgamation with a neighbor municipality), a municipality gains autonomy in the long run because of the increase in financial power, the transfer of additional tasks to the municipality, and the decrease in the necessity for intermunicipal cooperation. Although autonomy increases, some countries state that the influence of the superordinate tier of government has increased as well. With respect to the municipality itself, local mayors and executives appear to profit more in their status after an amalgamation than the citizens themselves (Table 2.6).

CORRELATIONS BETWEEN DIFFERENT PHASES OF THE REFORM PROCESS

As a next step, we want to examine more closely the correlations between the different phases of the reform process. We assume that the set objectives that actors want to achieve with amalgamation reforms lead to the choice of a specific reform strategy. The chosen strategy will lead to typical patterns of conflict and shape the outcome of the reform, as we have discussed in the conceptual paragraph of this chapter. These potential correlations are tested with Spearman's Rho as a measure of association. All significant correlations are shown in Table 2.7.

Surprisingly, there are no significant correlations between the various objectives of the reform and the chosen strategy. The countries appear to select a strategy independently of the goals they want to achieve.

However, strong correlations can be observed between the chosen strategies and the patterns of conflict, on the one hand, and the outcome of the reform, on the other hand. Bottom-up reforms touch the heart of the citizens, as they are far more acceptable to citizens and are associated with higher citizen orientation. Moreover, mandatory reforms strengthen mayors and executives.

Table 2.6 Outcome of amalgamations

Outcome	Countries		
	No importance	*Medium importance*	*High importance*
Improving input			
Cost savings		Finland, Italy, Sweden, Switzerland	Belgium, Germany, Greece, Iceland
Improved output			
Improved professional quality	Italy		Belgium, Finland, Germany, Greece, Iceland, Sweden, Switzerland
Improved legal correctness	Finland, Germany, Italy, Switzerland	Iceland, Sweden	Belgium, Greece
Improved citizen orientation	Finland, Germany, Sweden	Belgium, Greece, Iceland, Italy, Switzerland	
More equal treatment of citizens	Sweden	Finland, Germany, Greece, Italy, Switzerland	Belgium, Iceland
Room for maneuvering			
Strengthened local autonomy		Belgium, Finland, Germany, Iceland	Greece, Italy, the Netherlands, Sweden, Switzerland
Increased influence of the superordinate tier of government	Iceland, Italy, Sweden, Switzerland	Belgium, Finland, Germany, Greece, the Netherlands	
Strengthened local mayors/executives		Finland, Iceland, Italy, Switzerland	Belgium, Germany, Greece, the Netherlands, Sweden
Strengthened local citizenship	Finland, Germany, Iceland, the Netherlands, Sweden	Greece, Italy, Switzerland	Belgium

In contrast, the scope of the reform does not influence patterns of conflicts. The only significant difference between incremental and comprehensive reforms with respect to the outcome lies in the improved legal correctness of the municipality. Perhaps, comprehensive reforms better focus on this aspect rather the technocratic aspect owing to the involvement of national legal experts.

Table 2.7 Significant correlations between different phases of the reform process

Correlation		Measure of association (Spearman's Rho)
Objectives	Strategies	
No significant correlation		
Strategies	Patterns of conflict	
Reform initiative (1 = bottom-up; 5 = top-down)	Reform accepted by the public (1 = not at all; 5 = widely accepted)	−0.635*
Scope of reforms (1 = incremental; 5 = comprehensive)	Rich-Poor (1 = not important at all; 5 = very important)	−0.779**
Convincing/Gaining support (1 = incentives/inclusion; 5 = threats/exclusion)	Left-Right (1 = not important at all; 5 = very important)	0.776**
Strategies	Outcome	
Reform initiative (1 = bottom-up; 5 = top-down)	Improved citizen orientation (1 = not at all; 5 = very important)	−0.760*
Scope of reforms (1 = incremental; 5 = comprehensive)	Improved legal correctness (1 = not at all; 5 = very important)	0.883**
Voluntariness of reform (1 = yes; 5 = no)	Strengthened local mayors/ executives (1 = not at all; 5 = very important)	0.778*
Patterns of conflict	Outcome	
Technocracy-Politics (1 = not important at all; 5 = very important)	Explicit reform goals achieved (1 = not at all; 5 = very important)	−0.709*
Small-Large (1 = not important at all; 5 = very important)	Cost savings (1 = not at all; 5 = very important)	0.808*
Central-Local (1 = not important at all; 5 = very important)	Strengthened local mayors/ executives (1 = not at all; 5 = very important)	0.742*

Note: Spearman's Rho; $N = 11$; *$p < 0.05$. ** $p < 0.01$

If the promoters of a reform use threats instead of incentives, the conflict between left-wing and right-wing parties becomes more visible.

Conflicts between politicians and technocrats have a negative impact on the achievement of reform goals. Collaboration between bureaucrats and politicians appears to be a necessity for successful reforms. Interestingly, conflicts per se do not hinder goal achievement; some conflicts even have a positive impact on the outcome. For instance, conflicts between small and large municipalities lead to cost savings—likely because smaller municipalities often produce more expensive public services and if their resistance toward reforms is diminished, cost savings could be achieved. A similar effect of conflicts between the central government and local governments can be observed, where mayors and executives are the winners as they can likely exchange the approval for amalgamation for more influence.

CONCLUSIONS

The choice of a territorial structure is a complex phenomenon. Often, "territorial choices are fuzzy affairs with numerous battlefronts and bewildering claims of benefits and pitfalls..." (Baldersheim and Rose 2010, p. 234). The present comparative chapter has aimed to provide an overview of the municipal structures, reform objectives, strategies, and patterns of conflicts and outcomes associated with amalgamation reforms in selected European countries on the basis of the perception of country experts.

The results indicate that the objectives of amalgamation reforms primarily concern efficiency and service delivery criteria. Differences in items such as improving local democracy are substantial, suggesting that there is considerable variation in the objectives of mergers. The amalgamation strategies chosen by the countries are also very heterogeneous. Whereas some countries chose top-down strategies with intervention from the central government, others prefer bottom-up ones, where a decision to merge is left to the municipalities. In some cases there is however a mix of the two.

Patterns of conflict during amalgamation processes are related primarily to the divide between central and local government as well as between small and large municipalities. This result is not surprising because territorial reforms touch jurisdictional boundaries, which have often been shaped through historical processes. Opposition occurs when the central government attempts to intervene or when smaller municipalities fear being "swallowed" and overruled by larger municipalities. The greatest problems during the amalgamation processes appear to be connected with the strong resistance of politicians. We argue that owing to the reduction of municipalities through amalgamation, the number of local council seats would also be reduced. Therefore, politicians tend to defend their own situations, status, and jobs by trying to prevent these reforms.

The analysis of the amalgamation reforms in the observed European countries indicates that the most important outcomes are improved service quality and, to some extent, cost savings. In addition, autonomy appears to increase after mergers. However, it should be kept in mind that often these effects do not occur "automatically"; rather, they result from the decisions and actions of local authorities after the merger.

Policy makers should not only carefully plan and implement amalgamation reforms but also devote attention to the stabilization process of the newly created municipalities. Actions taken or not taken could influence the course of the reform: to touch the hearts of citizens and include the financial goals and the professionalization of the municipality in the political agenda, it would be wise to select a reform strategy that involves the municipalities and citizens affected by the planned reforms. In times of crisis, such a goal may not be feasible. In such cases, it is at least beneficial to know that service quality can usually be improved through amalgamation; however, financial improvement may not necessarily be evident: amalgamations require a careful implementation process, and other reforms may have similar effects as well.

REFERENCES

Baldersheim, Harald, and Lawrence E. Rose (eds.). 2010. *Territorial choice: The politics of boundaries and borders.* Basingstoke: Palgrave Macmillan.

Brantgärde, Lennart. 1974. *Kommunerna och kommunblocksbildningen.* Göteborg Studies in Politics 4. Göteborg. (e. The municipalities and the amalgamation reform).

Copus, Colin. 2006. British local government: A case for a new constitutional settlement. *Public Policy and Administration* 21(2): 4–21.

Council of Europe (ed.). 2001. *Relationship between the size of local and regional authorities and their effectiveness and economy of their action.* Strasbourg: CDLR.

Dafflon, Bernard. 1998. *Suisse: Les Fusions de Communes dans le Canton de Fribourg. Analyse Socioéconomique.* In Annuaire des Collectivités Locales, edited by Crédit Local de France et Direction Générale des Collectivités Locales. Paris: Grale.

De Ceuninck, Koenraad, Herwig Reynaert, Kristof Steyvers, and Tony Valcke. 2010. Municipal amalgamations in the low countries: Same problems, different solutions. *Local Government Studies* 36(6): 803–822.

Eythórsson, Grétar Thór. 1998. *Kommunindelningspolitik i Island. Staten kommunerna och folket om kommunsammanslagningar.* Göteborg: CEFOS.

Eythórsson, Grétar Thór. 2009. Municipal amalgamations in Iceland: Past, present and future. In *Remote control: Governance lessons for and from small, insular, and remote regions*, ed. Godfrey Baldacchino, Larry Felt, and Robert Greenwood. St. John's: Iser Books.

Fox, William F., and Tami Gurley. 2006. *Will consolidation improve sub-national governments?* World Bank working paper 3913, 1–45. Washington, DC: The World Bank.

Hlepas, Nikolaos-K. 2010. Incomplete Greek territorial consolidation: From the first (1998) to the second (2008–09) wave of reforms. *Local Government Studies* 36(2): 223–249.

Illner, Michal. 2010. Top-down or bottom-up? Coping with territorial fragmentation in the Czech Republic. In *Territorial choice: The politics of boundaries and borders*, ed. Harald Baldersheim and Lawrence E. Rose, 214–233. Basingstoke: Palgrave Macmillan.

Kaiser, Claire. 2014. Functioning and impact of incentives for amalgamations in a Federal State: The Swiss case. *International Journal of Public Administration* 37(10): 625–637. doi:10.1080/01900692.2014.903265.

Kaiser, Claire. 2015. Top-down versus bottom-up: Comparing strategies of municipal mergers in Western European Countries. *dms—der moderne staat* 1: 113–127.

Keating, Michael. 1995. Size, efficiency and democracy: Consolidation, fragmentation and public choice. In *Theories of urban politics*, ed. David Judge, Gerry Stoker, and Harold Wolman. London/Thousand Oaks/New Delhi: Sage.

Linder, Wolf. 1999. *Schweizerische Demokratie: Institutionen, Prozesse, Perspektiven.* Bern/Stuttgart/Wien: Haupt.

Mouritzen, Paul Erik. 2006. Et år i fusionslaboratoriet: Dannelsen av det nye kommunekort i Danmark. In *Stort er Godt. Otte fortællinger om tilblivelsen av de nye kommuner*, ed. Paul Erik Mouritzen. Odense: Syddansk Universitetsforlag.

Padovani, Emanuele, and Eric Scorsone. 2009. Comparing local government's performance internationally: A mission impossible? *International Review of Administrative Sciences* 75(2): 219–237.

Poister, Theordore H. 2003. *Measuring performance in public and nonprofit organizations.* San Francisco: Jossey-Bass.

Reingewertz, Yaniv. 2012. Do municipal amalgamations work? Evidence from municipalities in Israel. *Journal of Urban Economics* 72: 240–251.

Steiner, Reto. 2002. *Interkommunale Zusammenarbeit und Gemeindezusammenschlüsse in der Schweiz.* Bern/Stuttgart/Wien: Haupt.

Swianiewicz, Pawel. 2010. Territorial fragmentation as a problem, consolidation as a solution? In *Territorial consolidation reforms in Europe*, ed. Pawel Swianiewicz, 1–24. Budapest: Open Society Institute.

Vrangboek, Karsten. 2010. Structural reform in Denmark, 2007–09: Central reform process in a decentralised environment. *Local Government Studies* 36(2): 223–249.

Wollmann, Hellmut. 2010. Territorial local level reforms in the East German regional states (Länder): Phases, patterns, and dynamics. *Local Government Studies* 36(2): 251–270.

CHAPTER 3

Explaining Trajectories of Municipal Amalgamations: A Case Comparison of the Netherlands and Flanders

Wout Broekema, Trui Steen, and Ellen Wayenberg

INTRODUCTION

Based on the rationale of increasing administrative power and obtaining efficiency through economies of scale, municipal upscaling in Western European states has intensified in recent years. Despite this general tendency, the specific trajectories of municipal amalgamations vary strongly between countries. Sometimes local government re-scaling evolves incrementally; sometimes it occurs in a more drastic way, or not at all. So far, these differences in trajectories have not been satisfactorily explained. There have been a number of studies describing the amalgamation process or analyzing its effects (mostly financial) in specific countries (for example, Dollery and Crase 2004; Kushner and Siegel 2005; Kjaer et al.

W. Broekema • T. Steen (✉)
Institute of Public Administration, Leiden University, Leiden, The Netherlands

E. Wayenberg
Faculty of Economics and Business Administration, Ghent University, Ghent, Belgium

© The Author(s) 2016
S. Kuhlmann, G. Bouckaert (eds.), *Local Public Sector Reforms in Times of Crisis*, DOI 10.1057/978-1-137-52548-2_3

43

2010; Reingewertz 2012). Comparative explanatory studies between countries on the subject, however, remain scarce and fragmented (some exceptions are Steiner 2003; Brundgaard and Vrangbæk 2007). This is remarkable in view of the important and growing role of local governments in delivering goods, services, and democratic values to citizens.

This chapter explores *what factors help to explain the differences in municipal amalgamation trajectories between Western European countries*, on the basis of a comparative case study of the Netherlands and Flanders. The chapter fits in with the LocRef research, which aims at understanding national trajectories of reform through international comparison. Despite a number of policy evaluations, academic studies on municipal mergers in the Low Countries have been scarce (exceptions are Toonen et al. 1998; De Ceuninck et al. 2010; De Peuter et al. 2011; Smulders 2012; Abma 2013). After a discussion of the analytical framework and research design, we provide a brief overview of municipal amalgamations in the two cases, followed by an in-depth analysis of the factors explaining amalgamation trajectories in the Netherlands and Flanders. We conclude by discussing the factors we found to be crucial for explaining amalgamation trajectories.

ANALYTICAL FRAMEWORK AND RESEARCH DESIGN

We took a predominantly inductive approach, using a wide analytical framework as the starting point. The model proposed by Pollitt and Bouckaert (2004) provides a general insight into factors influencing public management reform. It includes (1) socio-economic forces, such as economic forces, socio-economic policies, and socio-demographic change; (2) the political system, including deep-structural features of the system, as well as dynamic elements such as new management ideas, pressures from citizens, and party political ideas; (3) elite decision-making on what is desirable and feasible; (4) change events, such as scandals or disasters; and (5) the administrative system, covering content of reforms, implementation, and results.

Municipal amalgamations are highly complex and case-embedded processes in which multiple factors interact. We argue that to do justice to this complexity, in-depth case analysis is required first, to function as a basis for more (quantitative) research in the future. Therefore, we opted for a comparative in-depth case study design, selecting the Dutch and Flemish cases. In the Netherlands in the past decades, municipal amalgamations have been occurring in an incremental way, while in Flanders in the same period no municipal amalgamations have occurred at all. Although we see contrasting trajectories of municipal amalgamations (dependent variable), both cases have relatively similar government systems and cultures due to their shared history as one country (until 1830).

The analytic model provides wide categories that help to structure our comparison. The two cases are systematically compared on the factors outlined above for trajectories in the period 1996–2015. We use this time frame to limit the number of intervening variables that play a role, especially because the government system in Belgium has changed substantially. We present the findings in the form of a thick description, which does justice to the complex contextual situation: factors are complex; they have divergent explanatory powers, abstraction levels, and levels of analysis; and they are often deeply interwoven with each other. We integrate data from secondary sources: academic articles, evaluation reports, policy documents, statistical monitors, and newspaper articles.

Divergent Trajectories of Municipal Amalgamations

Incremental Change vs. Large Waves

In the Netherlands, the number of municipalities has been gradually decreasing for a long time, starting as early as the 19th century. The gradualness of the amalgamation process in the Netherlands, a pattern that also characterizes the past two decades as such (see Table 3.1), is noteworthy. Although the outcome fits with the general trend of municipal mergers in most of Western Europe, owing to the incrementality of the process for a few decades until the beginning of the 1990s, the Netherlands lagged behind many other countries as regards increasing the local government scale (Toonen et al. 1998).

Table 3.1 Number of municipalities in the Netherlands over the period 1996–2005

Year	1996	1997	1998	1999	2000	2001	2002	2003	2004	2005
Number of municipalities	625	572	548	538	537	504	496	489	483	467
Year	2006	2007	2008	2009	2010	2011	2012	2013	2014	2015
Number of municipalities	458	443	443	441	431	418	415	408	403	393

Source: CBS (2015)

Although in Flanders the number of municipalities also dropped drastically in the 20th century, the reform process unfolded along a completely different path. The number of municipalities stayed relatively stable until 1961, after which re-scaling took place in large waves of reforms. In 1961, the Unity Law gave the Executive the authority to abolish municipalities. As a result, over the period 1961–71 the number of municipalities in Belgium decreased from 2663 to 2359 (Wayenberg and De Rynck 2008). In 1976, through a large-scale reform of municipal amalgamations, the number of municipalities in Belgium dropped from 2359 to 596 (De Ceuninck 2009). Since the 1976 reforms, no significant municipal re-scaling has taken place. In 1983, the city of Antwerp merged with seven surrounding municipalities. Since then the number of municipalities has remained the same, with 308 of the 589 Belgian municipalities situated in Flanders (De Ceuninck et al. 2010; De Peuter et al. 2011). Recently, the Flemish government has attempted to initiate municipal amalgamations (Coalition Agreement 2009; ABB 2014a). So far, however, its strong efforts remained unsuccessful.

In sum, we see two very different reform paths resulting in municipalities that count twice as many inhabitants in the Netherlands as in Flanders (in 2014: on average, 41,760 in the Netherlands versus 20,720 in Flanders; CBS 2015; ABB 2014b).

Socio-Economic Forces

Austerity Governments and Policy in Times of Crisis

When we consider socio-economic forces as a possible explanation for municipal amalgamations in the Netherlands and Flanders, we find that especially economic factors play a role. As in other European countries, the recent economic recession puts financial pressure on the public sector as a whole. With the appointment of austerity governments, budget cuts have been implemented and efficiency programs are run. The Dutch national government aims at cutting 180 million euros from spending on municipalities in 2017, along with the general austerities amounting to an estimated 307 million euros a year (Boon 2013), creating an estimated financial deficit for the local government of 6.1 billion euros in 2017 (Allers et al. 2013). To enhance efficiency, the national government has decided to radically reform the local and regional government structure in the coming years. Similarly and simultaneously, budget cuts have been put through in Flanders. The Flemish government runs a policy of local and regional scale reforms, including, for example, a radical cutback of competencies at the provincial level, and a forced policy of merging local administration and social policy administration (separate until now) at the level of cities and municipalities. In both cases, municipalities need to reduce their expenses drastically. One possible way to keep performing their tasks is to make use of scale benefits by merging with neighboring municipalities.

POLITICAL SYSTEM

Deep-Structural Features of the Government System: Consensus vs. Consensus in the Making

In the Netherlands, the relationship between national and local government is based on a mix of autonomy, co-governance, and supervision. Although in certain areas local governments can take their own initiatives (autonomy), and mostly carry out policies made at a higher level (co-governance), national government has the power to overrule local decisions (supervision) (Breeman et al. 2012). For the execution of its policies, national government is highly dependent on the quality and cooperation of local governments. As a result, the intergovernmental relations in the Netherlands are not so much based on formal hierarchy as on consensus (the so-called "polder model"). This typically leads to incremental pragmatic changes, or, if there is no consensus, to things remaining as they were (Steen and Toonen 2010a, b). When it comes to municipal amalgamations, this works in two directions. On the one hand, it seems to facilitate local government reform, because municipalities cooperate with the national government in reaching goals, in this case larger municipalities. On the other hand, the system makes it more difficult to hierarchically impose reforms on municipalities. The culture of intergovernmental bargaining requires the national government to follow an intensive path of consultation and persuasion of the local level in order to get reforms accepted. The consensus system results in an incremental reform process of municipal re-scaling in which resistance is also spread over the years.

Historically, Belgium is more centralized, with municipalities disposing over limited formal competences and autonomy (Wayenberg and De Rynck 2008). However, over the past decades, the system has been subject to a process of federalization. As a result, regional government currently plays a central role in supervising and regulating local governments within its territory. In 2005, the Flemish region adopted a Municipal Decree that created more autonomy for local governments in Flanders. The Flemish government stresses the issue of local autonomy and has pledged to transform the system of intergovernmental management, from "control" to "support" and "partnership." However, in reality the traditionally highly centralized system and culture in which municipalities were told what to do still has its impact. This helps to explain reform conservatism especially amongst the small(er) municipalities as the primary target group of amalgamation reform, of which there are a relatively high number in Flanders: in 2013 27% of the municipalities had less than 10,000 inhabitants (ABB 2014b).

Decentralization of Tasks

A closely related factor characterizing the intergovernmental system is the division of competencies between levels of government. In the Netherlands, owing to a series of decentralizations the number of municipal tasks has steadily grown over the past decades. Current policy is directly related to the economic context and the austerity policies described above. In 2014, the national government decided to decentralize three major social welfare tasks to the local level (CPB 2013). However, municipalities often do not have sufficient scale and scope to carry out these tasks, nor do they receive the corresponding share of financial resources to perform them. As a result, decentralizations push municipalities to upscale and closely cooperate or merge with surrounding ones. In this way, the decentralization to some degree again leads to centralization (Allers 2013), a process known as the "decentralization paradox."

In Flanders, the decentralization of tasks has been less pronounced. Yet here, too, the trend is towards increasing numbers of tasks and competencies at the local level. While the Flemish government promised that every decentralization would take place in consultation with local government and would be accompanied with the transfer of necessary means, personnel, and financial resources (Coalition Agreement 2014, p. 33), the question arises as to what extent this will put additional stress on municipalities to cooperate and/or merge in the (near) future.

Local Politics and Identity

Additionally, characteristics of the local political system play a role. Especially in Flanders, local government officials and citizens alike both fear the loss of local identity and being swallowed up by larger neighboring municipalities, or simply fear reform. The imposed reforms of 1976 led to the disappearance of many municipalities, as these became part of configurations mostly identified with the largest community. For the new municipality, often the name of the largest municipality was taken. According to Van Ostaaijen (2007), in Belgium citizens feel more connected with their local identity, whereas in the Netherlands citizens experience a stronger connection to the state. The former creates a form of conservatism. Although of less importance in the Netherlands, the issue of local identity also plays a role. Every now and then, when plans for specific municipal mergers are initiated, the issue of municipal rescaling becomes politicized and meets with resistance, especially when small municipalities merge with an adjacent larger urban community (Vriesema 2014).

A strong local leader with the political will to implement reform can mitigate local resistance by means of communication and persuasion (ABB 2014a, p. 10). Although in many respects the position of mayor in the Netherlands resembles that of Flanders, there are some important differences. Compared with the Netherlands, the Flemish mayor has a more political function and is more connected with his or her own municipal area and politics, representing the local identity. This is reflected in the fact that mayors have a vote in the local council and are appointed from the local council (Van Ostaaijen 2007). The appointment of a mayor is strongly based on the results of the local elections, whereas in the Netherlands a new mayor is often appointed from outside the municipality. In the Netherlands, the office of mayor is seen much more as a step towards other government positions. Owing to these institutional differences, we expect Flemish local officials to be more troubled than their Dutch counterparts by the possibility of losing their position if a municipality is to merge with surrounding municipalities, and therefore more likely to try to stall the process. As an interesting fact of local politics, almost half of the mayors in the Netherlands support the idea of larger municipalities (Logtenberg and Vriesema 2014).

ELITE DECISION MAKING

Why Are Amalgamations Desirable?

In the Netherlands and Flanders, the main arguments used by central government in favor of municipal amalgamations are similar and clear-cut: increased administrative power and economies of scale. Mergers enable carrying out complex tasks in an efficient way. At the same time, it is thought that municipal amalgamations bring the administration closer to the citizen, because it makes it easier to provide services (for example, online) (BZK 2013a; Flemish Government 2010). Especially given the scope of current decentralizations in the Netherlands, mergers are viewed as a solution (CPB 2013). Another argument used is preventing 'administrative crowdedness', especially current in Flanders, a subject the discussion of which accompanies the debate in both the Netherlands and Flanders about a reform of the provincial level of government. In Flanders, the current government drastically cut the competencies of the provinces, whereas the Dutch government so far has not achieved sufficient support for its plan to merge provinces into larger "country-regions."

External Pressure by the Central Government

As a result of the considerations outlined above, in both our cases, central government[1] directly and indirectly pressures for municipal amalgamations. In its 2012 coalition agreement, the Dutch government stated that it would aim at creating larger municipalities. In 2009, and again in 2014, the coalition agreements of the Flemish government strongly encouraged voluntary municipal amalgamations. Both governments influence the process in a similar way: by setting the outline for municipal reorganizations, by creating political pressure, and by initiating a broad public debate. The Dutch Ministry of the Interior created a formal policy framework (BZK 2013a), issued a handbook (BZK 2014), and assesses proposals for municipal amalgamations. In its turn, the Flemish government drew up a framework to support voluntary municipal amalgamations (Flemish government 2010), and a white book on internal state reform (Flemish government 2011). A blueprint model was created to guide municipalities through the amalgamation process (KPMG and Eubelius 2011). The Flemish administration published a memorandum on how to create a stronger local government in the near future (ABB 2014a). Currently, the government is funding research aimed at providing a practical handbook for local reform, including municipal amalgamations.

In the Netherlands, political pressure from central government is expressed by the strong words of Minister Plasterk in the mass media, expressing clear goals concerning municipal amalgamations. The central government announced that it aims to increase the number of municipal amalgamations by doubling them from 10 to 20 per year (Boon 2013). To a certain extent, municipalities are pressured into merging, as illustrated by the municipalities that merged with the municipality Alphen aan den Rijn in 2014 despite strong resistance on their part (Vriesema 2014). The Dutch central government has also created a financial incentive for amalgamations, providing financial support in the amount of €400,000 per municipality. This sum, which can be up to 10% of what municipalities receive from the Municipal Fund, can cover part of the friction costs of mergers (BZK 2013b; Bekkers and Koster 2013).

Similarly, the Flemish government exercises political pressure, creates incentives to encourage municipal amalgamations and fuels the public debate on the topic. The former government promised both substantive and financial assistance to municipalities if they would decide to merge on 1 January 2013. The 2014–2019 coalition agreement stated the plan to provide a financial bonus to encourage voluntary mergers. Interestingly, the current government formulated the intention to differentiate between municipalities in terms of their population, and to increase autonomy and grant additional tasks to medium-size and large cities and municipalities (Coalition Agreement 2014, pp. 32–33). In contrast to the Netherlands, however, the active role of the Flemish government in promoting municipal amalgamations and initiating an intensive public debate on the topic has not yet resulted in actual mergers. Smulders (2012, p. 73) suggests that the higher degree of financial autonomy held by Flemish municipalities diminishes the central government's potential to direct the local level. Nonetheless, the Flemish government is hoping the incentives will have a catalyzing effect on municipal amalgamations in the near future.

Change Events

The municipal amalgamation wave of 1976 still helps to explain why there have been no municipal amalgamations in Flanders in the past decades. The mergers were imposed by the Belgian central government in a highly top-down process, in which local preferences were taken into account only to a limited extent. Strong political resistance from many municipalities could not prevent the decisions from being implemented (De Ceuninck 2013).

Although the reforms were implemented almost thirty years ago, they have stuck in minds: government officials are still referring to the problems encountered then which continue to create resistance to change at this moment.

ADMINISTRATIVE SYSTEM

A Bottom-Up Process?

First, we discuss the extent to which decisions on and implementations of amalgamations are embedded in a bottom-up process. In the Netherlands, the local level of government is entitled to initiate and decide upon amalgamations according to the law general rules reorganization' of 1984 and the policy framework on municipal reorganization (BZK 2013a). In its policy documents, the national government continuously stresses that municipal re-scaling is a bottom-up process (BZK 2013b). The idea is that municipal reforms can be successful only if initiated at the local level, if consultations are done at the local level, and if the reform has the voluntary support of local authorities (BZK 2013a, 2014). In some cases, the provincial level is involved in this process. In Flanders, likewise, municipal amalgamations are formally a bottom-up process. The voluntary initiation of amalgamations by municipalities is included in the Municipal Decree. Formally, municipalities are free to initiate municipal amalgamations. The Flemish government stresses that amalgamations should be initiated by the local level as a bottom-up process, and as set out in a framework for supporting voluntary municipal amalgamations (Flemish Government 2010; ABB 2014a).

Seen from a formal rules perspective, municipal amalgamations are predominantly a bottom-up process. The voluntary initiation of municipal mergers may explain the incremental trajectory of municipal amalgamations in the Netherlands. Although the formal rules in Flanders are rather similar, efforts by the Flemish government to initiate municipal amalgamations have not been successful. An explanation might be that in Flanders current rules on municipal amalgamations have only been in place for a few years. Municipalities need some time to get used to the new reform ideas. Moreover, the wide experience with best practices of implementing amalgamations that is available in the Netherlands provides support for municipalities that start a reform process, something that cannot be said of the situation in Flanders (Smulders 2012). This makes past reform experience a distinguishing factor.

Intermunicipal Cooperation: An Alternative and/or a First Step?

Second, we discuss the issue of intermunicipal cooperation (IMC) as an alternative for or step towards amalgamations. IMC has taken place in the Netherlands ever since municipalities were established. Recent decentralizations have drawn extra attention to IMC because municipalities are often unable to perform new tasks on their own, and IMCs are viewed as an alternative to amalgamations when it comes to dealing with these new challenges (Fraanje and Herweijer 2013). Motivations to initiate IMCs resemble the motivations for amalgamations: to create efficiency profits through scale benefits, and to gain the expertise necessary to handle new complex tasks. Moreover, IMCs especially enable smaller municipalities to retain their local identity. At the same time, in the Netherlands, IMCs are seen as a first step towards amalgamations (e.g. Fraanje and Herweijer 2013), because intensified cooperation on multiple topics makes a subsequent merger less drastic.

Within the context of the debate on municipal amalgamations in Flanders, the impact of structural reforms on democratic legitimization is clearly an issue. This is discussed in the context of local government being a democratically legitimized actor, unlike forms of IMC, which have not been democratically legitimized through direct elections. The Flemish government coalition agreement 2014–2019, for example, states that "Flanders will install new forms of cooperation only if an extensive note of motivation demonstrates that the policy aims intended cannot be realized within an existing cooperation" (2014, p. 35). In Flanders, IMCs are seen as inhibiting rather than facilitating amalgamations. The attention given to IMCs rather than to amalgamations during the period 1976–2009 has resulted in a distinct path-dependence effect, making it difficult to re-initiate municipal amalgamations (Smulders 2012).

CONCLUSION AND DISCUSSION

Although there has been a general trend towards local government mergers in Western European countries, with an upsurge in recent years, the trajectories of municipal amalgamations vary widely by country. Comparative research has been limited and fragmented, despite the importance of local government for providing goods, services, and legitimacy. Through a comparative in-depth analysis of the Netherlands and Flanders, we explored what factors help to explain the differences between trajectories of municipal amalgamations, as a starting point for understanding why municipal amalgamations do or do not occur.

We found a vast number of factors that were influential, and these were often overlapping and interdependent. In both cases, the external economic context can be viewed as an underlying driving force for municipal amalgamations. Central governments are confronted with a global financial recession, making them implement budget cuts on the local level. This creates an incentive for generating scale efficiency through larger municipalities. The rational arguments used in both cases are to a large extent similar: increased administrative power and benefits from economies of scale. Also, despite the fact that in both cases amalgamations are formally bottom-up processes, central governments exert great external pressure to adopt amalgamations by setting the outline for the process, providing incentives, and initiating societal debate.

These factors seem influential, but they apply to both cases and so apparently do not serve to explain the differences between the respective trajectories of amalgamations in the Netherlands and Flanders. What then are the main factors that explain these different trajectories? First, the incremental trajectory of municipal amalgamations in the Netherlands can be explained by the consensus system of intergovernmental bargaining. Municipalities and national government cooperate when realizing goals, yet the system also requires intensive consultation and persuasion. Second, whereas in Flanders there have been some decentralizations, in the Netherlands much more drastic decentralizations have been put through. Decentralization of tasks puts immediate pressure on municipalities to increase scale in order to be able to carry out the new tasks, which makes it a major explanatory factor for trajectories of municipal amalgamations. Third, the incremental reform trajectory in the Netherlands can be explained by path dependence. Wide experience with best practices, for example, supports the initiation of new reform projects. The higher resistance to municipal amalgamations in Flanders can also be explained historically, because the large national top-down municipal amalgamations imposed in 1976 stopped as central government saw it for municipal amalgamations for a while, and is still a cause of resistance. The traditionally strongly centralized system also helps to explain local reform conservatism. Additionally, the fact that thus far Flemish government has not succeeded in initiating municipal amalgamations seems partly explained by differences in the local political system and identity between the Netherlands and Flanders. In Flanders, local identity plays a more important role, among other reasons because the role of the mayor is much more connected with his or her own municipality, which creates a form of conservatism. Finally, IMCs provide no clear explanation for trajectories of municipal amalgamations, because an IMC can be an alternative to or a first step towards municipal amalgamation, that is, a facilitator or an inhibitor.

Can our findings provide a first explanation for the trajectories of municipal amalgamations even beyond our two cases? It is clear that amalgamation trajectories are highly complex and very much embedded in the case-specific contexts. Our findings suggest that major factors influencing municipal amalgamations trajectories relate to an explanation of path dependence (e.g., Baumgartner and Jones 1993). Path dependence provides an explanation for incremental reform, reform shocks, and deadlock. It also explains differences in alternatives—for example, installing IMCs rather than mergers. We saw that the financial crisis and economic situation functioned as a rationale for reform, which can also be seen as a "change event." The same goes for related large decentralizations in the Netherlands that provided a "shock" for local government. In contrast, in Flanders, the 1976 reform was a major change event, still explaining the current deadlock. Similarly, there is an institutional path-dependent explanation for the influence of the intergovernmental system and for local government characteristics—for example, local identity and leadership.

Because our findings are based on an in-depth study of two cases, their generalizability may be limited. We found that the factors affecting the trajectories of municipal amalgamations are closely interwoven, and we realize that categorizations can be made in many other ways. In addition, we are aware that the effects of current dynamics in both cases are as yet unknown. We propose further research on the topic, also including more countries in the analysis, and looking into differences between municipalities in one country. The overview of factors involved, and our conclusion that path dependence is a highly relevant framework for studying trajectories of municipal amalgamations, may form a point of departure for future research. However, the complexity of amalgamation processes carries the threat of easy oversimplification. Our conclusion, therefore, is that the deeper processes must be understood as a basis for studies that use more simplified, quantified data.

NOTE

1. Because we are comparing the Netherlands (country) and Flanders (region), we use the term "central government" here to denote the Dutch national and Flemish regional governments, respectively.

REFERENCES

ABB (Agency for Internal Administration). 2014a. *Beleid van de Vlaamse regering tot stimulering van vrijwillige fusies van gemeenten.* Brussels: ABB.

ABB. 2014b. *Vlaamse profielschets: Vlaamse gemeenten in kaart gebracht.* Brussels: ABB.

Abma, K. 2013. Kiezen tussen kwaden. Gemeentelijke herindeling in Nederland. *Vlaams Tijdschrift voor Overheidsmanagement* 18: 8–26.

Allers, M.A. 2013. Decentralization with national standards. The case of the Netherlands. In *Balance between decentralization and merit,* ed. J. Kim, J. Lotz, and N. Jørgen Mau, 119–130. The Korea Institute of Public Finance and the Danish Ministry for Economic Affairs and the Interior.

Allers, M.A., B. Steiner, C. Hoeben, and J.B. Geertsema. 2013. *Gemeenten in perspectief.* Groningen: COELO.

Baumgartner, F.R., and B.D. Jones. 1993. *Agendas and instability in American politics.* Chicago: University of Chicago Press.

Bekkers, H., and Y. Koster. 2013. Plasterk maakt herindelingen financieel aantrekkelijker. *Binnenlands Bestuur,* 17 Jan 2013.

Boon, L. 2013. Plasterk probeert onrust gemeenten over herindeling te sussen. *NRC Handelsblad,* 14 Mar 2013.

Breeman, G.E., W.J. Van Noort, and M.R. Rutgers. 2012. *De Bestuurlijke kaart van Nederland.* Bussum: Coutinho.

Brundgaard, U., and K. Vrangbæk. 2007. Reform by coincidence? Explaining the policy process of structural reform in Denmark. *Scandinavian Political Studies* 30(4): 491–520.

BZK (Ministry of Internal Affairs and Kingdom Relations). 2013a. *Beleidskader gemeentelijke herindeling.* The Hague: BZK.

BZK. 2013b. *Nadere toelichting met betrekking tot gemeentelijke herindeling.* 13 maart 2013.

BZK. 2014. *Handboek gemeentelijke herindeling.* The Hague: BZK.

CBS (Statistics Netherlands). 2015. *Statline.* http://statline.cbs.nl. Accessed 27 Apr 2015.

Coalition Agreement. 2009. *De Vlaamse Regering 2009–2014. Een daadkrachtig Vlaanderen in beslissende tijden.* Brussels.

Coalition Agreement. 2012. *Bruggen slaan. Regeerakkoord VVD—PvdA.* The Hague.

Coalition Agreement. 2014. *De Vlaamse regering 2014–2019. Vertrouwen, Verbinden,* Vooruitgaan. Brussels.

CPB (Netherlands Bureau for Economic Policy Analysis). 2013. *Decentralisaties in het sociaal domein.* The Hague: CPB.

De Ceuninck, K. 2009. *De gemeentelijke fusies van 1976.* Een mijlpaal voor de lokale besturen in België. Brugge: Vanden Broele.

De Ceuninck, K. 2013. Fusies van gemeenten, spielerei of noodzaak? Een korte blik over de grenzen. *Vlaams Tijdschrift voor Overheidsmanagement* 18(1): 31–44.

De Ceuninck, K., H. Reynaert, K. Steyvers, and T. Valcke. 2010. Municipal amalgamations in the low countries: Same problems, different solutions. *Local Government Studies* 36(6): 803–822.

De Peuter, B., V. Pattyn, and E. Wayenberg. 2011. Territorial reform of local government: Evaluation criteria underpinning decisions and debate in Flanders. *Local Government Studies* 37(5): 533–552.

Dollery, B., and L. Crase. 2004. Is bigger local government better? An evaluation of the case for Australian municipal amalgamation programs. *Urban Policy and Research* 22(3): 265–275.

Flemish Government. 2010. *Nota aan de Vlaamse regering. Betreft: Uitvoering Vlaams regeerakkoord—Vaststelling van een kader ter ondersteuning van vrijwillige fusies van gemeenten—Financiële en organisatorische ondersteuning.*

Flemish Government. 2011. *Witboek interne staatshervorming.* Brussels: Vlaamse overheid.

Fraanje, R., and M. Herweijer. 2013. Innoveren in samenwerking: een alternatief voor herindeling? *Bestuurswetenschappen*, 3.

Kjaer, U., U. Hjelmar, and A.L. Olsen. 2010. Municipal amalgamations and the democratic functioning of local councils: The case of the Danish 2007 structural reform. *Local Government Studies* 36(4): 569–585.

KPMG and Eubelius. 2011. *Dossier vrijwillige fusieoperatie gemeenten. Rapport TO BE.* Brussels: Agentschap voor Binnenlands Bestuur.

Kushner, J., and D. Siegel. 2005. Are services delivered more efficiently after municipal amalgamations? *Canadian Public Administration-Administration* 48(2): 251–267.

Logtenberg, H., and I. Vriesema. 2014. NRC-enquête: bijna helft burgemeesters wil grotere gemeenten. *NRC Handelsblad*, 1 Mar 2014.

Pollitt, C., and G. Bouckaert. 2004. *Public management reform: A comparative analysis.* Oxford: Oxford University Press.

Reingewertz, Y. 2012. Do municipal amalgamations work? Evidence from municipalities in Israel. *Journal of Urban Economics* 72(2–3): 240–251.

Smulders, J. 2012. *De vrijwillige fusie van gemeenten. Een vergelijkende studie tussen Vlaanderen en Nederland.* Leuven: KU Leuven.

Steen, T., and T. Toonen. 2010a. The institutional analysis of central-local relations applied to the case of the Netherlands and Germany. In *Policy, performance and management in governance and intergovernmental relations*, ed. E. Ongaro, A. Massey, M. Holzer, and E. Wayenberg, 77–88. Cheltenham: Edward Elgar.

Steen, T., and T. Toonen. 2010b. The Netherlands. In *Changing government relations in Europe: From localism to intergovernmentalism*, ed. M.J. Goldsmith and E.C. Page, 145–162. Milton Park: Routledge.

Steiner, R. 2003. The causes, spread and effects of intermunicipal cooperation and municipal mergers in Switzerland. *Public Management Review* 5(4): 551–561.

Toonen, T., M. Van Dam, M. Glim, and G. Wallagh. 1998. *Gemeenten in ontwikkeling. Herindeling en kwaliteit.* Assen: Van Gorcum.

Van Ostaaijen, J. 2007. *Nog steeds vreemde buren? De rol van de burgemeester in Vlaanderen en Nederland.* Tilburg: Tilburgse School voor Politiek en Bestuur.

Vriesema, I. 2014. Fuseren is strijd—alleen al om de nieuwe naam. *NRC Handelsblad,* 5 May 2014.

Wayenberg, E., and F. De Rynck. 2008. Kingdom of Belgium. *Decentralization and local governments in the world: country profiles.* Global Observatory on Local Democracy and Decentralisation; United Cities and Local Governments (UCLG).

CHAPTER 4

What Causes Municipal Amalgamation Reform? Rational Explanations Meet Western European Experiences, 2004–13

Jostein Askim, Jan Erling Klausen, Signy Irene Vabo,
and Karl Bjurstrøm

INTRODUCTION

Amalgamation has been on the political agenda in most European countries during the last few decades, in some places resulting in national reform initiatives that substantially reduce the number of local governments, in others not (Baldersheim and Rose 2010). The question addressed in this chapter is why amalgamation reforms occur. Building on existing research, we develop a theoretical model consisting of factors that exert pressure to undertake amalgamation reforms (for example, fiscal stress), and factors that mediate the causal relationship between pressure to reform and decisions to implement amalgamation reform (for example, political system characteristics). We then test the model's viability by exploring whether it can predict the amalgamation reforms undertaken by 17 Western European countries in the period 2004–13.

J. Askim (✉) • J.E. Klausen • S.I. Vabo • K. Bjurstrøm
Department of Political Science, University of Oslo, Oslo, Norway

© The Author(s) 2016
S. Kuhlmann, G. Bouckaert (eds.), *Local Public Sector Reforms in Times of Crisis*, DOI 10.1057/978-1-137-52548-2_4

When to Expect Amalgamation Reform

The existing literature offers several analytical frameworks to explain the occurrence of public administration reforms. Some frameworks have been developed to explain a broad selection of reforms (see, for example, Pollitt and Bouckaert 2011); others target particular types or clusters of reforms, such as privatization and new public management (see, for example, Hood 1994). Our model, illustrated in Fig. 4.1, seeks to explain national amalgamation reforms as a distinct class of public administration reforms.

Driving Factors

Our theoretical model has a two-step logic. In the first step (horizontal arrow in Fig. 4.1), we consider amalgamation reform to be a functional response to pressure. We expect to see amalgamation reform in countries that have experienced pressure from any three among the following four factors: fiscal stress, urbanization, decentralization of policy functions from national to local government level, and recent amalgamation reform. In addition, we expect strong fiscal stress to be able to drive amalgamation reform by itself.

Fiscal Stress Fiscal stress pressures governments to cut public spending wherever possible. Lowering service standards angers citizens, however, and so administrative reforms are often the preferred option. Fiscal stress

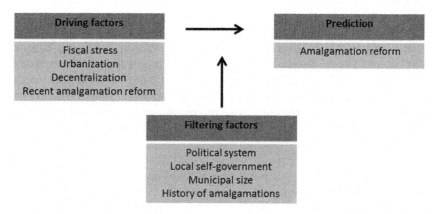

Fig. 4.1   Theoretical model

has therefore frequently been seen as a driver for cost-cutting public sector reforms. No theoretical or empirical agreement exists regarding whether larger public entities are more cost effective than smaller ones, to what extent municipal tasks yield significant economies of scale (Dollery and Fleming 2006), and whether cost reductions outweigh transaction costs incurred by amalgamation reforms (Blom-Hansen et al. 2014). Nevertheless, amalgamation of local governments has repeatedly emerged on national reform agendas in periods of recent, current or anticipated fiscal stress at the national level (Hansen et al. 2014). Amalgamation is often portrayed as a means to reduce administrative costs and improve managerial and political capacities to prevent costs from exceeding budgets.

We define fiscal stress as a situation where the country's GDP, in total or per inhabitant, increases less than the OECD average. We define growth 20% or more below the average—in the decade prior to the period studied—as strong fiscal stress and growth 10–19% below the average as medium fiscal stress.

Urbanization Socio-demographic change (for example, immigration, increased life expectancy, improved health status, and increased income levels) is an important driver for public sector reform (Pollitt and Bouckaert 2011). Most central to the question of amalgamation reform, however, is the global movement of people to urban areas (urbanization), due to broader changes in the economy (e.g., reduced employment in traditional occupations like farming, mining and fishing). When residence patterns change, what Hood (1994) calls the "habitat" of an existing policy changes too, thereby introducing or increasing pressure to reform the scale and structure of local governments. Centralization causes population decline in peripheral areas. A diminishing client base for public services can in turn lead to efficiency losses due to reverse economies of scale. Moreover, the corresponding population growth in urban areas can exacerbate challenges commonly associated with metropolitan governance, notably coordination of spatial planning, public transportation and infrastructural development across administrative boundaries (Klausen and Swianiewicz 2007).

Urban habitation denotes the share of the population that resides in an urban area at a given time, and the term "urbanization" denotes increase in urban habitation over time. We consider growth in urbanization above the OECD average—in the decade prior to the period studied—to exert pressure for amalgamation reform.

Decentralization The policy responsibilities of local governments vary considerably between countries, as reflected in differences in, for example, local government percentages of public sector employment, expenditure, and tax revenues (Loughlin et al. 2011). Decentralization can result, for example, from national welfare policies expanding beyond what central governments can deliver themselves (Kersting et al. 2009, p. 6). Regarding production costs, optimal jurisdiction size varies between sectors and services, so that at any given time considerations about a municipality's optimal size must balance the size imperatives of the various tasks in its portfolio, each with its own u-shaped cost curve. Overall, however, substantial decentralization of policy responsibilities can be expected to strengthen arguments in favor of larger local entities (Christofilopoulou-Kaler 1991).We assume that a growing local portfolio changes the existing map's habitat and exerts pressure for reform.

To measure change in local governments' policy functions, we track each country's changes in local government expenditure as a percentage of total public sector expenditure, and in local government employment as a percentage of total public sector employment. An increase above the OECD average in either—in the decade prior to our period of study—is considered to exert pressure for amalgamation reform.

Recent Amalgamation Reform Reform histories vary across the countries. Among the 17 countries studied here five underwent amalgamations during the ten years prior the period studied (Germany, Greece, Iceland, the Netherlands, United Kingdom), some between 1945 and 1990, and some never in recent history (see appended Tables 4.A.1 and 4.**A.2**). We assume that reform is self-reinforcing in the short term. In some countries amalgamation appears to be—as Weick and Quinn (1999) describe it—a continuous rather than an episodic change phenomenon. A preference for amalgamation is in a sense embedded into such countries' DNA. Also, students of episodic organizational change argue that organizations need time to recover from radical change. "Refreeze" does not follow immediately after "unfreeze" (Weick and Quinn 1999). Often, new borders do not enclose a historically recognized area. It may take decades before they become institutionalized and therefore are defended against change. A "new" municipal structure is therefore vulnerable to new reform. Based on these assumptions, we expect to see reforms during 2004–13 in Germany, Greece, Iceland, the Netherlands, and the United Kingdom.

FILTERING FACTORS

Elite decision-makers at the center of public sector reforms face not only internal and external forces that push reforms forward but also internal and external obstacles that can make reforms undesirable and infeasible (Christensen and Lægreid 2010, p. 410). In a second step, illustrated by the vertical arrow in Fig. 4.1, we therefore introduce factors that mediate the assumed causal relationship between pressure for reform and amalgamation reform. We expect that a combination of any three among the following four factors filters away the chance that national political elites will respond to pressure by implementing amalgamation reforms.

(1) *Consensual political systems:* Comprehensive municipal amalgamation is a radical public administration reform affecting many policy sectors and stakeholders. National political elites in consensual democracies are less able than those in majoritarian democracies to assemble the political support necessary to implement such radical reforms (Pollitt and Bouckaert 2011, pp. 37–8), and so amalgamation reforms are least likely in these countries. In consensual democracies, political parties with ties to opponents of any given radical public sector reform will often be able to dilute or stop radical reform initiatives.

We base the distinction between majoritarian and consensual democracies on Lijphart's executive-parties index, where countries are given index scores based on how they score on five variables: effective number of parliamentary parties, minimal winning one-party cabinets, executive dominance, electoral disproportionality, and pluralism of interest groups (Lijphart 2012, p. 241, pp. 305–6). We define as most consensual those countries scoring above the mean index value for the 17 countries analyzed.

(2) *Strong protection of local self-government:* Most European countries have ratified the European Charter of Local Self-Government, guaranteeing local governments some level of political, administrative and financial independence. The emphasis on self-government varies, however (Sellers and Lidström 2007). The level of protection of local self-government, by constitution or by political tradition and custom, is normally a deeply rooted aspect of a country's political system, similar to the majoritarian–consensual distinction. Major restructuring of subnational jurisdictions is difficult in countries with a high degree of protection for local self-governance (John 2001; Sellers and Lidström

2007). We therefore expect that amalgamation reform is least likely in these countries.

The degree of protection of local self-government is measured by the use of Sellers and Lidström's (2007) index on fiscal and politico-administrative supervision (national supervision). A high value on the index, which varies from zero to two, denotes strong supervision of local government—effectively weak protection of local self-government. We define countries as having relatively strong protection of local self-government if they score below the 17-country mean.

(3) *Large local governments at starting point*: The size of local governments (measured by population) is a key variable for theories of economies of scale. Size varies considerably among European countries. Some countries have a tradition of relatively large local governments. For countries with such "starting conditions," we do not expect further local government amalgamation to be seriously considered as a reform strategy to meet challenges arising from fiscal stress, urbanization, or functional decentralization. We expect such countries to view the amalgamation option as exhausted, and to instead seek other strategies.

We measure size as the average population size of a country's municipalities. We do not expect amalgamation in countries with average municipality size above the 17-country median, and especially not in countries with average municipality size more than 5,000 above the median (that is, about half the magnitude of the median). We define countries whose average municipality size is more than 5,000 below the 17-country median as having extraordinarily small municipalities.

(4) *Historical absence of amalgamation reform*: As mentioned, some Western European countries have not undergone amalgamation reforms for decades. We assumed that reform is self-reinforcing in the short term and can work as a driver for new reforms. We also assume that non-reform is self-reinforcing and can work as a filter against reforms. In countries where local governments' territorial structure has remained virtually unchanged for many decades, municipal borders become infused with value among local political elites and among local populations; municipalities become carriers of identity, not just vehicles for service production and other tangible functions (Hesse and Sharpe 1991; Brunazzo 2010). Such institutionalization increases

resistance to amalgamation. Based on this assumption, and given pressure to reform from factors mentioned above, we do *not* expect France, Italy, Portugal, Spain, and Switzerland to undertake amalgamation reforms in 2004–13 (for details and references, see appended Table 4.**A.2**).

FINDINGS

Amalgamation Reforms

Table 4.1 presents an overview of amalgamation reforms in 17 Western European countries during 2004–13. We register a country as having undergone an amalgamation reform if the number of municipalities is reduced by 5% or more.

Table 4.1 Amalgamation reforms in Western European countries, 2004–13

Country	Number of local governments 2004	Change in number 2004–13 (%)	Reform initiated (year)
Austria[a]	2,359	–0.2	
Belgium	589	0.0	
Denmark	271	–64.0	2007
Finland	446	–28.0	2005
France[a]	36,565	0.3	
Germany	12,260	–8.0	1990
Greece[a]	1,033	–69.0	2011
Iceland	105	–30.0	2004
Ireland	80	0.0	
Italy[a]	8,101	–0.1	
Netherlands	489	–17.0	2004
Norway	434	–1.4	
Portugal	308	0.0	
Spain	8,108	0.1	
Sweden	290	0.0	
Switzerland	2,842	–8.7	2004
United Kingdom[a]	467	0.2	

Sources: See notes to Tables 4.A.1 and 4.A.2 and: For Denmark: Blom-Hansen and Heeager (2011, p. 224); Finland: Sandberg (2010, p. 43); Italy: Istat (2015); Switzerland: Ladner (2011, p. 196): United Kingdom: Wilson (2005, p. 161); The Council of European Municipalities and Regions (2015)

[a]Time of measurement (number of units) differs slightly from 1993 or 2004, due to availability of data

In *Denmark* 238 municipalities were merged into 65 in 2007, while 33 remained unchanged. While the reform involved a certain element of local discretion in that municipalities were allowed to propose amalgamations, the reform was predominantly mandatory and comprehensive because proposals had to satisfy size criteria set by central government (Blom-Hansen and Heeager 2011). In *Finland*, the 2005 amalgamation reform was implemented as a nationally initiated reform process based on voluntary local initiatives (Sandberg 2010, p. 42). In *Germany*, the substantial number of amalgamations relates to the fundamental reform of the local government system in the five *Länder* that constituted the DDR prior to reunification (Walter-Rogg 2010, p. 153). This reform was implemented by the *Länder* governments themselves, and the scope and pace of amalgamations varied (Kuhlmann and Wollmann 2014, pp. 163–7). *Greece* underwent a territorial reform in 2011, reducing the number of municipalities from 1033 to 325 (Tavares and Feiock 2014, p. 31). In *Iceland* (Eythórsson 2009) and *the Netherlands* (Boedeltje and Denters 2010, pp. 120–1), amalgamation reform has been on national policy agendas for decades. However, because amalgamations in both countries are initiated primarily by regional or local governments, reforms have resulted in a markedly incremental and uneven reduction of the number of municipalities. In *Switzerland*, all mergers result from local, bottom-up initiatives (Ladner 2010, p. 212). Yet an increasing focus on the need for reform in later years has resulted in a small surge of voluntary amalgamations in 2004–13.

Predictions Versus Findings

Figure 4.2 summarizes a comparison of actual amalgamation reforms and predictions based on our theoretical model, with driving and filtering factors. Country-wise and detailed information on each variable is documented in the appended Tables 4.A.1 and 4.**A.**2.

The partial model, based on driving factors alone, predicts amalgamation reforms in 2004–13 in seven countries. Four predictions are correct (Germany, Iceland, the Netherlands, and Switzerland) and three wrong (Italy, Portugal, and United Kingdom). The full model, which includes filtering factors, predicts amalgamation reforms in four countries. Three predictions are correct (Germany, Iceland, and the Netherlands) and one wrong (United Kingdom). Moreover, the full model fails to predict four amalgamation reforms that did occur—those in Denmark, Finland,

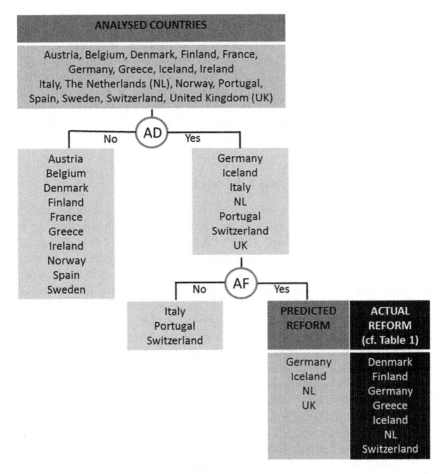

Fig. 4.2 Predicted and actual amalgamation reforms 2004–13. *AD* partial-model predictions—after driving factors, *AF* full-model predictions—after filtering factors

Greece and Switzerland. Our inability to predict those reforms stems from a fault in the driving factor stage of analysis, while our inability to predict the reform in Switzerland stems from a fault in the filtering factor stage. Overall, the filtering stage nonetheless improved the model's fit with the data.

Concluding Discussion

Maintaining that amalgamation reforms are rational responses to driving factors, mediated by filtering factors, possible reasons for our model's weaknesses should be discussed. Below we consider, first, potential problems with the measurements, second, the model's construction, and whether relevant variables are included, and third, potential weaknesses with our definition of the dependent variable. Finally, we offer suggestions for future research into the causes of amalgamation reforms.

Correct Model, Wrong Measurements?

Starting with the drivers, *fiscal stress* is the common denominator of the four correct predictions, and the sole basis for predicting reform in Switzerland. According to our definition however, only five of the 17 countries did *not* experience fiscal stress in the reference period, among which two (Finland and Greece) reformed anyway. The absence of amalgamation reform in most fiscally stressed countries suggests that no causal relationship exists between austerity and this kind of reform. Alternatively, measures other than GDP might be better, and the causal effect may be further delayed, suggesting that a longer reference period is needed. Moreover, economic outlook might better predict reform than economic experience does.

Three of five rapidly urbanizing countries implemented a reform (Finland, Netherlands, and Switzerland), indicating that *urbanization* could be a significant reform driver. The remaining four reforming countries did not experience urbanization in the reference period, but the low number of rapidly urbanizing countries precludes definite conclusions.

We assumed that *decentralization* of policy functions would be a driver for reform, but the predictive power of this variable was insignificant. Of the six countries that underwent amalgamation reform, only Iceland and to some extent the Netherlands had decentralized during the reference period. Taken alone, the variable incorrectly predicted reform in six countries. While these findings weaken the assumption of a direct relationship between functional and territorial reform, measurement problems could exist. Perhaps a longer reference period is needed owing to time lag. Also, the effect of decentralization on the likelihood of amalgamation reform may depend on local governments' initial level of functional responsibility, suggesting a non-linear relationship between the two variables, and that an interplay variable should be used to measure decentralization.

Four out of seven countries that undertook amalgamation reform in 2004–13—Germany, Greece, Iceland, and the Netherlands—share a history of *recent amalgamation reform*. This finding supports the theoretical assumption that reform ("unfreeze") carries with it a time lag before new structures settle ("refreeze") and therefore temporarily weakens institutional insulation against new reforms (Weick and Quinn 1999).

The filtering variables overall served the model well. The correct predictions of reform in Germany, Iceland, and the Netherlands survived the filtering process. Furthermore, the drivers incorrectly predicted reforms in Italy and Portugal, but the filter removed these from the equation. The *weak protection of local self-government* in these two countries, in combination with a prolonged absence of reform, seems to have negated the pressure for amalgamations indicated by the drivers.

Overall, the assumption of a *historical path dependency* of reform is strongly supported by the analysis. When all the temporal reform variables included in the model—historical (filter), recent (driver) and current (dependent)—are seen in conjunction, it is noteworthy that Italy, Portugal, Germany and the Netherlands are all coded with the same value (positive or negative) on all three variables. The United Kingdom and Iceland score the same value on two out of three. Switzerland is the only deviant case, as its current reform has neither recent nor historical precedent. It is however difficult to assess the relative effect of the "historical" as compared with the "recent" variable, since the historical absence of reform in Iceland and Switzerland did *not* preclude amalgamations in the period studied. Our inability to explain why the relative strengths of the drivers and the filters were different in these countries as compared with the others suggests that the model is incomplete, a matter discussed next.

The theoretical assumption concerning a filtering effect of *consensual political systems* is not supported by the analysis. Including this variable in the full model remedies the partial model's false prediction of reform in Italy, but it also indicates a reduced probability of reform in Germany, Iceland, the Netherlands and Switzerland—the four countries correctly predicted by the drivers. It also predicts wrongly the occurrence of reform in the United Kingdom—by far the most majoritarian country studied.

Municipal size emerges as one of the most successful variables in the model, regarding predictive power. It correctly negates the prediction of amalgamations of the very large municipalities in Portugal and the United Kingdom, and it supports the correct predictions of reforms of the very small municipalities in Iceland and Switzerland.

Model Specification The limited overall predictive power of the model suggests that the probability of amalgamations could be influenced by factors not included in the model. Some suggestions for additional variables are offered here.

Territory While municipalities that were already populous appeared less prone to further amalgamations, size could alternatively be defined in territorial terms. The literature notes several examples of reforms being initiated because the small size of many municipalities precluded their fulfillment of planning and development functions. For instance, the quite drastic amalgamation reform in Belgium in 1976 has been attributed to the difficulty of planning industrial zones in narrowly circumscribed municipal territories (Delmartino 1991, p. 340). Average size of municipalities in square kilometers could be included in the model as a driver for reform, with the expectation of a negative correlation.

Intermunicipal Cooperation Arguments favoring amalgamations are commonly related to the need for stronger and more competent local administrations, for instance in Greece (Getimis and Hlepas 2010) and Denmark (Mouritzen 2010). Intermunicipal cooperation has, however, often been regarded as an optional strategy for achieving similar aims. For instance, Goldsmith et al. (2010, p. 257) cite this as a "means of overcoming some of the problems concerned with service delivery and infrastructure provision posed by having large numbers of small municipalities." Intermunicipal cooperation could be included as a filtering variable, with a high frequency expected to decrease the likelihood of amalgamation reform.

Functional Status As noted, variations in the functional status of local governments in different countries are substantial (Loughlin et al. 2011). Yet the model included only *increasing* decentralization as a driver for change, regardless of *initial* differences in functional status. Possibly, the likelihood of reform is most affected by the general strength and importance of the local government system. A measure of functional status could, given this, be included as a filtering variable rather than as a driver. We would expect a positive correlation, based on the assumption that the net benefits of a reform would outweigh the costs only if local governments were to play an important role in service provision or exerting authority.

The Dependent Variable: Amalgamation Reforms

Scrutinizing results of the analysis reveals an interesting pattern. According to previous studies, amalgamations in Germany, Iceland, the Netherlands, and Switzerland—the four reforms correctly predicted by the driving factors in our model—are all based on local or regional initiatives. These reforms are markedly incremental, to the extent that the appropriateness of the label "reform" is debatable. The drivers failed however to predict the reforms in Denmark, Greece, and Finland. Whereas amalgamations in Finland were based on municipal initiatives and resulted in an incremental reform pattern (Sandberg 2010), amalgamations in Denmark and Greece were mandatory and comprehensive, redrawing much of the municipal map within a very short time frame. Although the prediction of Switzerland's incremental reform was incorrectly negated by the filtering variables, the model appears better at predicting incremental reforms based on local or regional initiatives than it does mandatory, comprehensive reforms.

An extended time frame for the analysis could provide better evidence for testing this assumption. The post-war ("historical") period includes several reforms of a comprehensive and somewhat mandatory nature, for instance, in Belgium, Denmark, Norway and Sweden.

A possible implication is that incremental reforms based on local or regional initiatives belong to a different class of phenomena than do mandatory, comprehensive reforms, and so follow a different logic of causality. An interesting approach for further research would, in this regard, be to compare diverging patterns of stability and change over a prolonged period. Why have countries such as Denmark and Greece experienced isolated instances of radical, comprehensive reform, whereas others, such as the Netherlands and Iceland, have experienced an incremental reform pattern over a long period? Why have countries such as Spain, Italy, or France managed to remain stable, avoiding change altogether?

Appendix

Table 4.A.1   Predicted amalgamation reforms 2004–13, partial model with pressure factors only. Reform predicted if pressure from any three of the four pressure factors, or if strong fiscal stress

Country	Fiscal stress $\Delta 1993$– 2003^1	Urbanization $\Delta 1990$–2000^2	Decentralization in expenditure (in employment) $\Delta 1995$–2003^3		Recent amalgamation reform ($\Delta 1993$– $2003)^{10}$		Predicted reform after driving factors?
Austria	51.9[a]	0.0	−3.0	(−0.3)	No	(0%)	No
Belgium	53.0[a]	0.8	1.2	(1.4)	No	(0%)	No
Denmark	56.2[a]	0.3	6.1[a]	(2.3)[a]	No	(−2%)	No
Finland	72.0	2.8[a]	7.2[a]	(1.6)	No	(−2%)	No
France	54.5[a]	1.8	1.3	(3.0)[a]	No	(0%)	No
Germany	39.3[b]	−0.1	0.5	(−1.5)	Yes[a]	(−23%)	Yes
Greece	73.0	1.2	1.4[4]	(NA)	Yes[a]	(−82%)	No
Iceland	56.1[a]	1.7	6.6[a5]	(10)[a6]	Yes[a]	(−46%)	Yes
Ireland	160.1	2.2[a]	10.0[a]	(11.5)[a]	No	(0%)	No
Italy	43.1[b]	0.5	6.4[a]	(−0.1)	No	(0%)	Yes
Netherlands	70.9[a]	8.1[a]	−4.5	(2.4)[a]	Yes[a]	(−24%)	Yes
Norway	93.4	4.1[a]	−4.5[7]	(−13.7)	No	(−1%)	No
Portugal	65.8[a]	6.5[a]	2.5[a]	(0.9)	No	(−1%)	Yes
Spain	81.1	0.9	1.9	(1.3)	No	(0%)	No
Sweden	61.3[a]	0.9	6.3[a]	(−0.7)	No	(1%)	No
Switzerland	38.9[b]	0.1	−2.1	(−0.9)	No	(0%)	Yes
United Kingdom	65.2[a]	0.5	2.4[a]	(1.8)	Yes[a]	(−13%)	Yes
Mean 17 countries	*66.8*	*1.9*	*2.30*	*(0.60)*			
Mean OECD^7	*71.5*	*1.8*	*2.27^8*	*(2.02)^9*			

[a]Expected positive association with amalgamation reform

[b]Expected strong positive association

Notes:

[1]Percentage change in GDP (GDP per capita was also calculated, returning identical patterns). *Source*: OECD (2015a)

[2]Change in percentage of people living in urban areas. *Source*: UNDP (2014). Percentage of Population at Mid-Year Residing in Urban Areas by Major Area, Region and Country, 1950–2050. For methodological details, see http://esa.un.org/unpd/wup/Methodology/WUP2014-Methodology.pdf

[3]Expenditure: Change (in percentage points) in local government expenditure as percentage of total government expenditure. *Source*: OECD (2015b). Employment: Change (in percentage points) in employee

compensation at local government level as percentage of total government employee compensation. *Source*: OECD (2015c). Note that local governments are defined by OECD as institutional units whose fiscal, legislative and executive authority extends over the smallest geographical areas distinguished for administrative and political purposes (OECD 2001)

[4]Data for Greece is from 2000–6 and collected from Leibfritz (2009)

[5]Data for Iceland covers the period 1995–2004 and is collected from Statistics Iceland (2010) and Althingi (2015a)

[6]Data for Iceland covers the period 1995–2004 and is collected from Althingi (2015b) and Althingi (2015c). This number refers to the change (in percentage points) of public employees at local levels as percentage of total public employees. It is therefore not directly comparable with data for the other countries

[7]Data refers to 1996–2003

[8]Because of several missing values, the OECD mean more or less equals the mean of included countries (missing values for Australia, Chile, Estonia, Japan, Korea, Mexico, New Zealand, Poland, Turkey, and the United States)

[9]Data for Estonia refers to 2000–3

[10]Amalgamation reform is decided on the basis of changes in the number of municipalities (5 % reduction or more is counted as reform). Data on the number of municipalities stem from the COST Survey (2014), supplemented with the following sources: For Austria: Statistics Austria (2015). France: Borraz and Le Galés (2005, p. 13), Pinson (2010, p. 70), Cole (2011, p. 307). Greece: Hlepas and Getimis (2011, p. 426). Italy: Denters (1991, p. 525), Piattoni and Brunazzo (2011, p. 332). Netherlands: Centraal Bureau voor de Statistiek (2015). United Kingdom: Wilson (2005, p. 151, 161)

Table 4.A.2 Predicted amalgamation reforms 2004–13 among countries experiencing reform pressure, full model including filtering factors. Reform predicted if negative scores on three of the four filtering factors

Country	Maj./cons. political system[1]	Local self-government (weak)[2]	Average municipal size (year)[3]	Historical reform 1945–92[4]	Filtering effect	Predicted reform after filtering factors?	Actual reform (see Table 4.A.1)
Germany	0.63[a]	1.26	5,069 (1993)	1968–80	Inactive	Yes	Yes (−8.0 %)
Iceland	0.55[a]	NA	1,339 (1993)	None[a]	Inactive	Yes	Yes (−30.0 %)
Italy	1.13[a]	0.93[a]	7,041 (1991)	None[a]	Active	No	No (−0.1 %)
Netherlands	1.17[a]	1.26	23,669 (1993)	1969–92	Inactive	Yes	Yes (−17.0 %)
Portugal	0.04	1.15[a]	32,639[a] (1993)	None[a]	Active	No	No (0.0 %)
Switzerland	1.67[a]	0.52[a]	2,431 (1993)	None[a]	Active	No	Yes (−8.5 %)
United Kingdom	−1.48	1.23	106,043[a] (1990)	1972–74	Inactive	Yes	No (0.2 %)
Mean 17 countries	0.50	1.19	18,927				
Median 17 countries			9,703				

[a]Expected negative association with amalgamation reform

Notes:

[1]Values below the mean for the included countries denote a majoritarian-oriented party system, above denotes a consensus-oriented party system. *Source:* Lijphart (2012, pp. 305–6). Data for 1981–2010

[2]Data is collected from various sources in the period 1986–2002. Sellers and Lidström's (2007) index on Fiscal and Politico-Administrative supervision (national supervision) comprises seven indicators: (1) local supervision officials (prefect or equivalent), (2) supra-local appointment of local executive, (3) supra-local control of governmental form, (4) trans-local civil service, (5) grants as percentage of local revenue, (6) local tax autonomy and (7) supervision of local borrowing. The index ranges from 0 (= minimum supervision) to 2 (= maximum supervision). Values above the mean for the included countries denote weak protection of local self-government. *Source:* Sellers and Lidström (2007)

[3]Data on population is in general collected from Eurostat (2015). In addition, population statistics are also collected from OECD (2015d). The number of municipalities is also collected from the COST-Survey (2014), and from the following sources: Italy: Denters (1991, p. 525); Netherlands: Centraal Bureau voor de Statistiek (2015); United Kingdom: Wilson (2005, p. 154)

[4]*Sources:* Germany: Gunlicks (1986); Walter-Rogg (2010). Iceland: Eythórsson (2009). Italy: Brunazzo (2010). Netherlands: Denters et al. (1990). Portugal: Magone (2010). Switzerland: Ladner (2010). The United Kingdom: John (2010)

References

Althingi. 2015a. Parliamentary Q&A. http://www.althingi.is/altext/127/s/0544.html. Accessed 16 Apr 2015.

Althingi. 2015b. Parliamentary Q&A. http://www.althingi.is/altext/138/s/0261.html. Accessed 16 Apr 2015.

Althingi. 2015c. Parliamentary Q&A. http://www.althingi.is/altext/132/s/0910.html. Accessed 16 Apr 2015.

Baldersheim, H., and L. Rose. 2010. Territorial choice: Rescaling governance in European states. In *Territorial choice: The politics of boundaries and borders*, ed. H. Baldersheim and L.E. Rose. Basingstoke: Palgrave Macmillan.

Blom-Hansen, J., and A. Heeager. 2011. Denmark: Between local democracy and implementing agency of the state. In *The Oxford handbook of local and regional democracy in Europe*, ed. J. Loughlin, F. Hendriks, and A. Lidström. Oxford: Oxford University Press.

Blom-Hansen, J., K. Houlberg, and S. Serritzlew. 2014. Size, democracy, and the economic costs of running the political system. *American Journal of Political Science* 58: 790–803.

Boedeltje, M., and B. Denters. 2010. Step-by-step: Territorial choice in the Netherlands. In *Territorial choice: The politics of boundaries and borders*, ed. H. Baldersheim and L.E. Rose. Basingstoke: Palgrave Macmillan.

Borraz, O., and P. Le Galés. 2005. France: The intermunicipal revolution. In *Comparing local governance: Trends and developments*, ed. B. Denters and L.E. Rose. Basingstoke: Palgrave Macmillan.

Brunazzo, M. 2010. Italian regionalism: A semi-federation is taking shape—Or is it? In *Territorial choice: The politics of boundaries and borders*, ed. H. Baldersheim and L.E. Rose. Basingstoke: Palgrave Macmillan.

Centraal Bureau voor de Statistiek. 2015. Gemeentelijke indeling. http://www.cbs.nl/nl-NL/menu/methoden/classificaties/overzicht/gemeentelijke-indeling/2003/default.htm. Accessed 7 June 2015.

Christensen, T., and P. Lægreid. 2010. Complexity and hybrid public administration—Theoretical and empirical challenges. *Public Organization Review* 11: 407–432.

Christofilopoulou-Kaler, P. 1991. Local government reform in Greece. In *Local government and urban affairs in international perspective: Analyses of twenty Western industrialised countries*, ed. J.J. Hesse. Baden-Baden: Nomos.

Cole, A. 2011. France: Between centralization and fragmentation. In *The Oxford handbook of local and regional democracy in Europe*, ed. J. Loughlin, F. Hendriks, and A. Lidström. Oxford: Oxford University Press.

COST-Survey. 2014. *Local public sector reforms: An international comparison ('LocRef'). Expert survey.* European Cooperation in Science and Technology.

Delmartino, F. 1991. Local government in Belgium: Decentralizing the state. In *Local government and urban affairs in international perspective: Analyses of twenty industrialised countries*, ed. J.J. Hesse. Baden-Baden: Nomos.

Denters, B. 1991. The fragmented reality of Italian local government. In *Local government and urban affairs in international perspective: Analyses of twenty Western industrialised countries*, ed. J.J. Hesse. Baden-Baden: Nomos.

Denters, B., H.M. Jong, and J.A. Thomassen. 1990. *Kwaliteit van gemeenten: een onderzoek naar de relatie tussen de omvang van gemeenten en de kwaliteit van het lokaal bestuur.* 's-Gravenhage: VUGA.

Dollery, B., and E. Fleming. 2006. A conceptual note on scale economies, size economies and scope economies in Australian local government. *Urban Policy and Research* 24: 271–282.

Eurostat. 2015. Population change—Demographic balance and crude rates at national level. http://ec.europa.eu/eurostat/web/population-demography-migration-projections/population-data/database. Accessed 16 Mar 2015.

Eythórsson, G.T. 2009. Municipal amalgamations in Iceland: Past, present and future. In *Remote control: Governance lessons for and from small, insular and remote regions*, ed. G. Baldacchino, R. Greenwood, and L. Felt. St. John's: ISER Books.

Getimis, P., and N. Hlepas. 2010. Reinventing local government in Greece. In *Territorial choice: The politics of boundaries and borders*, ed. H. Baldersheim and L.E. Rose. Basingstoke: Palgrave Macmillan.

Goldsmith, Michael J., and Edward C. Page. 2010. *Changing government relations in Europe: from localism to intergovernmentalism.* London: Routledge.

Gunlicks, A.B. 1986. *Local government in the German federal system.* Durham: Duke University Press.

Hansen, S.W., K. Houlberg, and L.H. Pedersen. 2014. Do municipal mergers improve fiscal outcomes? *Scandinavian Political Studies* 37(2): 196–214.

Hesse, J.J., and L.J. Sharpe. 1991. Local government in international perspective: Some comparative observations. In *Local government and urban affairs in international perspective: Analyses of twenty Western industrialised countries*, ed. J.J. Hesse. Baden-Baden: Nomos.

Hlepas, N., and P. Getimis. 2011. Greece: A case of fragmented centralism and "behind the scenes" localism. In *The Oxford handbook of local and regional democracy in Europe*, ed. J. Loughlin, F. Hendriks, and A. Lidström. Oxford: Oxford University Press.

Hood, C. 1994. *Explaining economic policy reversals.* Buckingham: Open University Press.

Istat. 2015. PublicAdministration Stat. *Statistical indicators on central and local government, number of institutional unities (Municipalities).* Italian National Institute of Statistics, http://dati.statistiche-pa.it/?lang=en. Accessed 7 June 2015.

John, P. 2001. *Local governance in Western Europe*. London/Thousand Oaks/New Delhi: Sage.

John, P. 2010. The endless search for efficiency in the UK. In *Territorial choice: The politics of boundaries and borders*, ed. H. Baldersheim and L.E. Rose. London: Palgrave Macmillan.

Kersting, N., J. Caulfield, R.A. Nickson, D. Olowu, and H. Wollmann. 2009. *Local governance reform in global perspective*. Wiesbaden: VS Verlag für Sosialwissenschaften.

Klausen, J.E., and P. Swianiewicz (eds.). 2007. *Cities in city regions: Governing the diversities*. Warsaw: University of Warsaw.

Kuhlmann, S., and H. Wollmann. 2014. *Introduction to comparative public administration: Administrative systems and reforms in Europe*. Cheltenham: Edward Elgar.

Ladner, A. 2010. Switzerland. In *Changing government relations in Europe: From localism to intergovernmentalism*, ed. M.J. Goldsmith and E.C. Page. London: Routledge.

Ladner, A. 2011. Switzerland: Subsidiarity, power-sharing, and direct democracy. In *Oxford handbook of local and regional democracy in Europe*, ed. J. Loughlin, F. Hendriks, and A. Lidström. Oxford: Oxford University Press.

Leibfritz, W. 2009. *Fiscal federalism in Belgium: Main challenges and considerations for reform*, Economics Department working paper No. 743. Paris: OECD.

Lijphart, A. 2012. *Patterns of democracy: Government forms and performance in thirty-six countries*, 2nd ed. New Haven/London: Yale University Press.

Loughlin, J., F. Hendriks, and A. Lidström (eds.). 2011. *The Oxford handbook of local and regional democracy in Europe*. Oxford: Oxford University Press.

Magone, J.M. 2010. Portugal: Local democracy in a small centralized republic. In *Oxford handbook of local and regional democracy in Europe*, ed. J. Loughlin, F. Hendriks, and A. Lidström. Oxford: Oxford University Press.

Mouritzen, P.E. 2010. The Danish revolution in local government: How and why? In *Territorial choice: The politics of boundaries and borders*, ed. H. Baldersheim and L.E. Rose. Basingstoke: Palgrave Macmillan.

OECD. 2001. Glossary of statistical terms. Local government. https://stats.oecd.org/glossary/detail.asp?ID=1550. Accessed 16 Apr 2015.

OECD. 2015a. National accounts at a glance. Gross domestic product (GDP). http://stats.oecd.org/Index.aspx?DataSetCode=NAAG#. Accessed 30 Mar 2015.

OECD. 2015b. OECD fiscal decentralisation database. Consolidated expenditure as percentage of total general government expenditure (consolidated). http://www.oecd.org/tax/federalism/oecdfiscaldecentralisationdatabase.htm. Accessed 30 Mar 2015.

OECD. 2015c. National Accounts at a Glance. Government deficit/surplus, revenue, expenditure and main aggregates. https://stats.oecd.org/Index. aspx?DataSetCode=SNA_TABLE12. Accessed 22 Feb 2015.

OECD. 2015d. Population. http://stats.oecd.org/Index.aspx?DatasetCode= POP_FIVE_HIST. Accessed 12 Mar 2015.

Piattoni, S., and M. Brunazzo. 2011. Italy: The subnational dimension to strengthening democracy since the 1990s. In *The Oxford handbook of local and regional democracy in Europe*, ed. J. Loughlin, F. Hendriks, and A. Lidström. Oxford: Oxford University Press.

Pinson, G. 2010. France. In *Changing government relations in Europe: From localism to intergovernmentalism*, ed. M.J. Goldsmith and E.C. Page. London: Routledge.

Pollitt, C., and G. Bouckaert. 2011. *Public management reform. A comparative analysis: New public management, governance and the Neo-Weberian state.* Oxford: Oxford University Press.

Sandberg, S. 2010. Finnish power-shift: The defeat of the periphery? In *Territorial choice: The politics of boundaries and borders*, ed. H. Baldersheim and L.E. Rose. Basingstoke: Palgrave Macmillan.

Sellers, J.M., and A. Lidström. 2007. Decentralization, local government, and the welfare state. *Governance: An International Journal of Policy, Administration, and Institutions* 20: 609–632.

Statistics Austria. 2015. *Number of municipalities at 1973, 1983, 1993, 2003 and 2013.* Data received by request.

Statistics Iceland. 2010. *General government outlays by functions 1998–2008*, Statistical series. National Accounts 2010:1.

Tavares, A. F., and R. C. Feiock. 2014. Intermunicipal cooperation and regional governance in Europe: An institutional collective action framework. In *Presented at the European Consortium for Political Research*, Glasgow.

The Council of European Municipalities and Regions. 2015. Local and regional Europe (map). http://www.ccre.org. Accessed 7 June 2015.

UNDP. 2014. United Nations, Department of Economic and Social Affairs, Population Division (2014). *World urbanization prospects: The 2014 Revision.* CD-ROM Edition. http://esa.un.org/unpd/wup/CD-ROM/Default.aspx. Accessed 30 Nov 2014.

Walter-Rogg, M. 2010. Multiple choice: The persistence of territorial pluralism in the German federation. In *Territorial choice: The politics of boundaries and borders*, ed. H. Baldersheim and L.E. Rose. Basingstoke: Palgrave Macmillan.

Weick, K.E., and R.E. Quinn. 1999. Organizational change and development. *Annual Review of Psychology* 50: 361–386.

Wilson, D. 2005. The United Kingdom: An increasingly differentiated polity? In *Comparing local governance: Trends and developments*, ed. B. Denters and L.E. Rose. London: Palgrave Macmillan.

CHAPTER 5

Does Inter-Municipal Cooperation Lead to Territorial Consolidation? A Comparative Analysis of Selected European Cases in Times of Crisis

Jochen Franzke, Daniel Klimovský, and Uroš Pinterič

In recent times of financial crisis, the territorial municipal structures and the distribution of responsibilities across various governmental levels have come under pressure in many European countries (see Steiner et al., Chap. 2 in this volume). Some central governments have used this situation to increase the pressure to bring about more effective and efficient administrative structures; local governments have faced a challenge of developing inter-municipal cooperation (IMC) more than at any previous time.

J. Franzke (✉)
University of Potsdam, Potsdam, Germany

D. Klimovský
Comenius University, Bratislava, Slovakia

U. Pinterič
St. Cyril and Methodius University, Trnava, Slovakia

© The Author(s) 2016   81
S. Kuhlmann, G. Bouckaert (eds.), *Local Public Sector Reforms in Times of Crisis*, DOI 10.1057/978-1-137-52548-2_5

One central research issue of this chapter is to analyze IMC development and its impact on territorial fragmentation, dealing in particular with
the challenges posed by the recent crisis. Three cases form the basis for
our international comparison, namely Brandenburg (as one of the German
federal states), Slovakia, and Slovenia. The difference in constitutional status between the two independent countries, Slovakia and Slovenia, and
the East German federal state of Brandenburg is obvious. From the perspective of our research, however, it is of only minor relevance, as in all
three cases the legal competencies to (re)define municipal/local affairs
and territorial boundaries lies with the upper-level government, that is the
national government in Slovakia and Slovenia and the *Land*-government
in Brandenburg.

The rationale behind this selection is based on five arguments: All cases
have undergone similar transformations leading to the introduction of
democratic local government systems. In the 1990s in particular, post-
communist legacies influenced how local government systems developed.
External pressure has played a crucial role in their transformations. Each
has been confronted with a challenge of inappropriate territorial structure
at the beginning of the transformation. Each has implemented structural
reforms that have influenced the position of local governments within the
state structure.

LOCAL GOVERNMENTS, SIZE, AND IMC

Recently, the "old" debate about the size and performance of local governments (for example, Keating 1995) has heated up again (Baldersheim
and Rose 2010). Considering the relationship between population size,
politico-administrative structure and system capacity has led some scholars to skeptical conclusions about the "beauty of bigness" (Denters et al.
2014, p. 333). However, IMC usually plays only a limited or secondary
role in this debate. In some countries, on the other hand, IMC may form a
possible alternative to mergers of municipalities (for example, Teles 2014).

There are still significant differences among European countries in
terms of the size of their local authorities (for example, Denters et al.
2014). Generally, a small average population size is linked to a fragmented structure of local governments (see Broekema et al., Chap. 3
in this volume). Obviously, other characteristics can also indicate a high
level of fragmentation—for instance, area size, transport accessibility, or
tax capacity.

Although public choice theory may favor a fragmented structure of local governments in order to support the quality of local democracy by way of inter-local competition, the practices in different countries lead us to serious doubts. On this matter, Tiebout's famous theory (1956) can be used only in a limited way, since it avoids, inter alia, spatial obstacles of mobility (Swianiewicz 2002), the existence of externalities, and shifts in electoral preferences. A discussion of municipal fragmentation implies that the size of local governments is not optimal from the perspectives of governance, economy, service delivery, administrative ease, and the responsiveness of local governments to global changes (Skaburskis 2004, p. 41), including reactions in times of crisis. As Skaburskis (2004) further points out, while fragmented local governments may lose control over economic entities, larger local governments may retain some control. On the other hand, any amalgamation increases not only local administrative capacities but potentially also the quality and outputs of public decision-making (for example, Spicer 2012).

The issue of the "optimal size" of local governments based on their ability to meet local public service requirements is circular when the selection of services is determined by their size (Skaburskis 2004, p. 45). This is especially evident in countries with highly fragmented structures of local governments, where an IMC on a voluntary basis is usually used and compulsory mergers garner strong resistance from the local governments' representatives.

Despite the widespread use of IMC, it has not yet been subjected to systematic comparative research (Hulst and van Montfort 2012, p. 121). However, a few studies of IMC as a public service delivery reform or an alternative to territorial consolidation have been published (for example, Carr and Feiock 2004; Hulst et al. 2009; Tavares and Camões 2007).

Widening the scope of publicly provided services by IMC and increasing democratic control lead to new institutional settings, finally to amalgamation (see Fig. 5.1). From this perspective, it may act as a driver for reducing local fragmentation (for example, Soguel 2006). Experience from other countries, however, shows that impacts of IMC may lead to the conclusion that mergers are superfluous. Amalgamation reform is only one of the alternatives in the context of widespread IMC (see Askim et al. Chap. 4 in this volume). In some countries, this argument is instead of an economic nature. Its supporters stress improving the cost effectiveness as well as the administrative capacity for providing local services (for example, Mäeltsemees et al. 2013). In other countries,

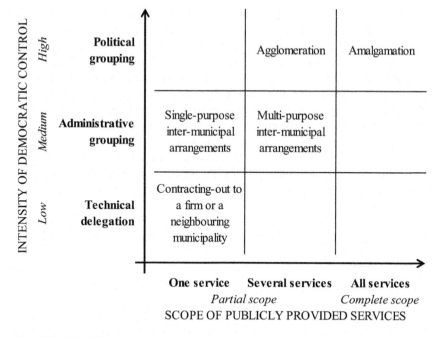

Fig. 5.1 Possible institutional settings to reduce local fragmentation (*Source*: Soguel (2006, p. 175))

the arguments of local autonomy and the undemocratic nature of any non-voluntary mergers prevail. Taking into account the facts mentioned above, IMC might potentially be the first institutional step towards amalgamation, though there is no automatic link. In addition, it remains theoretically controversial whether to prefer a fragmented structure or a consolidated one.

Pros and Cons of the IMC and Its Types

Incentives supporting IMC vary greatly. First, IMC arises from the desire to provide local services more efficiently or more broadly (Sancton et al. 2000, p. 1). Another popular argument is to improve the quality and/or availability of local public services (for example, Mäeltsemees et al. 2013). Generally, many authors consider IMC a suitable instrument to overcome a fragmented structure of local governments (for example, Hertzog 2010) as well as to increase the planning and performance capacities of individual local governments. However, it seems that IMC is not urgently needed in territorially consolidated countries (for example, Kelly 2007; Klimovský et al. 2014). Another motivation is potentially a better allocation of additional (especially financial) resources. Last but not least, IMC may help open a policy window to a broad amalgamation reform or at least to individual mergers.

Regardless of IMC's indisputable advantages and strengths, one can also identify significant disadvantages and weaknesses. It may fail because of negative side effects, unintended outcomes (especially in terms of local democracy), and the like (for example, Swianiewicz 2010). Improvements in the quality of local democracy and/or the availability of local public services are not automatically achieved just because of implementing IMC (for example, Dollery and Akimov 2008; Ermini and Santolini 2010). To better understand why such failures may occur, scholars tend to use either network or organization theories. In addition, despite the fact that some recent empirical works (for example, Bel et al. 2014; Zafra-Gómez et al. 2013) have demonstrated that IMC saves costs, others (for example, Sørensen 2007) have concluded the opposite. Within this context, it seems that small local governments may benefit more than larger ones from cooperation, as the former are more likely to achieve a reduction in the average cost of service delivery. Last but not least, IMC can serve as a functional substitute for a territorial consolidation (Koprić 2012).

One can observe various types of IMC (for example, Wollmann 2010). While higher politico-administrative authorities often favor compulsory IMC, local governments prefer voluntary ones. Savitch and Vogel (2000) consider the latter a good pattern to overcome metropolitan illnesses; however, they stress at the same time that it can be difficult to sustain such cooperation. From this point of view, the voluntary IMC is no panacea (Lackowska 2009), and may even lead to unsystematic or chaotic "solutions" far from the expected or desired state (Klimovský 2010).

Following Hulst and van Montfort (2012), we compare, in this study, four different types of IMC: (1) quasi-regional governments, (2) planning forums, (3) service delivery organizations, and (4) service delivery agreements. We have based our research on this typology and have added one more type, namely (5) ad hoc project cooperation.

COMPARATIVE ANALYSIS OF THE IMC IN BRANDENBURG, SLOVAKIA, AND SLOVENIA

Although relevant research literature targeting various local government issues is available, studies focusing on the forms, trends, and impacts of IMC are either rare or quite unsystematic. On the other hand, because of crises, the topic of IMC and efficiency in local public service delivery has become interesting of late (for example, Kuhlmann and Wollmann 2014; Bogumil and Kuhlmann 2010; Büchner and Franzke 2001 for Germany/ Brandenburg; Klimovský 2010, 2014; Klimovský et al. 2014; Tichý 2005 for Slovakia; Žohar 2014 for Slovenia).

Within this context, this chapter contributes to filling the research gap mentioned. Our three cases will illustrate the variability associated with IMC. Starting with the municipal territorial structures, legal provisions and reasons behind IMC development, we examine the forms that IMC may take and their related impacts in our three cases.

MUNICIPAL TERRITORIAL STRUCTURES

Slovenian municipal structure has faced systematic fragmentation since the end of the 1980s. The number of municipalities has increased threefold compared with 1989. Although Slovakia never experienced such an intense fragmentation wave, its territory is highly fragmented. The lowest number of municipalities was reached in 1989, but this increased to 2,891 a few years later. Despite the fact that the total number of municipalities has increased since 1989, it has not been a straightforward and gradual increase. Brandenburg had a fragmented municipal territorial structure in the late 1980s, consisting of almost 1,800 municipalities. Through a series of reform steps, including a general territorial reform in 2003, it has dramatically reduced the number of its municipalities.

The aforementioned trends led to different municipal population sizes in our three cases: while, on average, Slovak municipalities are among the smallest in Europe (almost 1,900 inhabitants), the municipalities in Brandenburg are larger (almost 5,900 inhabitants). Paradoxically, despite real fragmentation, the average population size of Slovenian municipalities (about 9,700 inhabitants) is the largest in our comparison (Table 5.1).

Table 5.1 Municipal territorial structures

Indicators	Brandenburg	Slovakia	Slovenia
Number of municipalities (1989)	1,793	2,669	63
Number of municipalities (2014)	418	2,890	212
Relative change (%) in number of municipalities (1989–2014)	–76.7	+8.3	+236.5
Average population size of municipality (2014)	5,900	1,900	9,700
Present share (%) of municipalities with fewer than 500 inhabitants (2014)	5	41	1

Sources: Statistical Office of the Slovak Republic: Register of Spatial Units (REGPJ), Databasis STATdata, Statistical office of the Republic of Slovenia: Regional overview, Statistisches Jahrbuch Brandenburg 2014

Reasons for Development

The reasons for developing forms of IMC vary significantly in Brandenburg, but economic reasons prevail. Two reasons in particular are crucial—namely, help in solving problems that go beyond the limits of a single municipality, and achieving higher efficiency by lowering costs. Slovenian local governments have recognized, especially in the last decade, the importance of IMC, not only because of increased opportunities for allocating additional resources (for example, EU funds) but also owing to the necessity of increasing their administrative efficiency.

In the 1990s, IMC was used to a limited extent in Slovakia. A significant shift occurred after a huge devolution, but IMC development has been rather non-strategic and unsystematic. The local governments' representatives, especially local politicians who wanted to retain their offices, have refused any mergers. The central government adopted this attitude after 2006, considering IMC an appropriate tool to overcome shortcomings caused by existing fragmentation. A second important reason has been the possibility of obtaining additional financial resources (especially from EU funds), since most of the local governments individually have insufficient capacity to apply for and manage projects of this type.

Legal Frameworks

In Brandenburg and Slovakia, the constitution guarantees the usage of IMC by the local governments. In general, German local governments can decide autonomously on cooperation with other local authorities and on the form in which they fulfill their public tasks (for example, the local authority itself, municipal-owned enterprises, contracting out, or IMC). In Slovakia, the constitution similarly contains explicit provisions regarding IMC (Table 5.2).

In all three cases compared, general acts on local government contain provisions focused on IMC. In Slovakia, each local government is authorized to cooperate with other territorial or administrative units. Any specific IMC entity must be of a private nature, and five forms of cooperation (agreements) are possible: on performance of tasks; on establishment of joint municipal offices; on establishment of municipal associations; on establishment of legal entities; and on establishment of associations of legal entities. Other laws (for example, the Act on Budgetary Rules of Territorial Self-Government) amend these provisions. Finally, the Ministry of Interior published the "Methodological Instruction on Establishing the Joint Municipal Offices" in 2002.

The original version of the Slovenian Local Government Act defined IMC as a joint municipal administration. The law has been changed several times, and the 2005 amendment of the Act on Municipal Finances significantly influenced the management of a joint municipal administration. The cooperating local governments receive an additional donation from the national budget of up to 50%.

As for the case of Brandenburg, a special local government law (the "Communal Constitution") defines the associations of municipalities and relevant regulation of their activities. The Brandenburg Act on Activities of a Joint Local Authority regulates IMC, and specifies that the local governments and their associations may together exercise all public tasks to which they are entitled or obliged. The law enables public sector

Table 5.2 Legal frameworks

Indicators	Brandenburg	Slovakia	Slovenia
Constitutional provisions	Yes	Yes	No
General legal provisions	Yes	Yes	Yes
Special law/act	Yes	No	No
Specific legal provisions contained in other laws/acts	Yes	Yes	Yes
Official governmental or ministerial recommendations	Yes	Yes	No

Source: Authors' own compilation

legal forms of IMC (for example, municipal working groups, public law agreements, special-purpose associations) as well as private legal forms of IMC (for example, limited-liability companies and joint-stock companies). Any informal IMC is also possible in addition to these forms.

IMC Forms

Compulsory forms of IMC cannot be found in Slovakia or Slovenia (Table 5.3), but only in Brandenburg, which has three different ones. The most important one of these is the association of municipalities (*Ämter*). Established by law in 1992, they form special legal entities each with the nature of a public corporation. Almost 65% of all local governments (270 of 418) are part of 52 municipal associations at this time. The asso-

Table 5.3 Forms of IMC

Indicators	Brandenburg	Slovakia	Slovenia
Numbers of general forms (associations of municipalities)	2	2	3
Compulsory specific forms	Yes	No	No
Voluntary specific forms	Yes	Yes	Yes
Dominant form (number of units): type	Association of municipalities / *Amt* (52): quasi-regional government	Joint municipal office / *spoločný obecný úrad* (233): quasi-regional government	Joint municipal administration / *skupna občinska uprava* (48): service delivery organization
Main reasons for development	Higher efficiency in local public service delivery xxx Increasing capability to deliver additional local public services	Ensuring minimal capability to perform one's own and delegated competences xxx Possibility to obtain additional resources	Higher efficiency in local public service delivery xxx Possibility to obtain additional resources
Direct financial support from the state	Yes (compulsory specific IMC forms) No (other cases)	Yes (joint municipal offices) No (other cases)	No

Source: Authors' own compilation

ciations perform administration for member municipalities in order to increase their efficiency; on the other hand, they maintain political self-governmental rights. The associations have mandatory tasks assigned by law or other legal regulations (for example, registry offices), and contractual tasks transferred from the member municipalities (for example, primary school administration). The local governments receive federal state subsidies to fulfill the mandatory tasks. For the rest, the member local governments pay for the management of these tasks.

Another compulsory form is the regional planning association (*Regional Planungsgemeinschaft*), established in 2008. Nowadays, there are five associations in Brandenburg with both counties and county-free municipalities as members. As in the previous case, each is a separate legal entity having the nature of a public corporation, supervised by the Federal State Planning Authority. Regional planning associations are responsible for carrying out the mandatory task of elaborating, updating, amending, and supplementing regional plans. The Federal State Planning Authority pays a basic fee, and the federal state and the associated members share the costs for additional tasks.

Special-purpose associations (*Zweckverbände*) traditionally comprise one of the most important forms of IMC in Brandenburg. Approximately 80 of them are officially registered. They are separate legal entities, each with the nature of a public corporation, and are mostly voluntary but in some cases compulsory. These associations work especially in the sectors of tourism, water management, culture, energy, transport, and so on. Various fees plus sums allocated by their members constitute the financial basis for their activities. Additionally, they may apply for financial support from the federal state authority in case of emergency.

Voluntary IMC forms used in the countries compared are very diverse. In the 1990s, contracts or agreements on IMC for particular tasks (*zmluvy o medziobecnej spolupráci pri výkone konkrétnej úlohy*) were quite common in Slovakia. After a huge devolution (2002–04), voluntary single- or multi-purpose joint municipal offices (*spoločné obecné úrady*) replaced them. Nowadays, 233 offices perform exclusively delegated state administration. The state provides grants for them based on their population. In many cases, these grants are sufficient, and the municipalities do not need to contribute. Each municipality may belong to several different offices. Voluntary institutionalized sub-regional associations called micro-regions (*mikroregióny*) have not yet been legally defined. Nevertheless, they are usually territorially small units involving several municipalities with a common historical development, economic interconnection, and so on. Although their borders often correspond to existing borders of the joint municipal offices (Klimovský 2010, pp. 248–9), some of them do not respect official administrative borders. Hence, many municipalities are involved in more than one micro-region. There are currently 220 officially registered micro-regions, but the number of active micro-regions is unknown because a significant proportion of them exist only officially and do not perform any activity at all (especially in the pre-accession period, there was a kind of "fashionable trend" to be involved in a micro-region). Similarly, joint municipal companies (*spoločné obecné podniky*) are quite common, though their exact number is unclear. They perform tasks in the fields of waste management, sewage disposal, and so on. Ad hoc project IMC (*projektová medziobecná spolupráca*) is very common at present. Additionally, an implementation of the LEADER (*Liaison entre actions de développement de l'économie rurale*) initiative has significantly affected development of IMC in Slovakia. As a result, 29 local action groups (*miestne akčné skupiny*) have been established. Each of them consists of both public and private entities, but the local governments and their representatives play the leading role.

Concerning Slovenia, the main motivations for establishing joint municipal administration (*skupna občinska uprava*) are increasing professionalism in task management, increasing productivity of public servants, additional financial allocations, and/or reducing local administration costs. At present, 48 such cooperation units involve 195 local governments. According to Žohar (2015), they focus their activities on inspection, security service, urban planning, and so on. In Slovenia, other voluntary specific IMC forms are not so well developed. Regional development agencies and local action groups are particularly worth mentioning. The agencies are not necessarily public entities. Even if they play some role in local development promotion, they are subject to private law and have no governing competences. About 33 local action groups cover more than 90% of the Slovenian rural population. They are popular in Slovenia, but more in facilitating support for local NGOs and/or SMEs. Finally, there is an uncoordinated package of various ad hoc contracts between local governments in fields such as construction, provision of social services, and so on.

In Brandenburg, there are a large number of voluntary agreements between local authorities. However, a conclusive overview of these agreements is not possible owing to the lack of any central record of them. The local governments and their associations may agree that any of them will carry out selected tasks on behalf of the others, and the parties will cover the costs. The most informal and soft form of IMC is that of voluntary joint municipal working groups (*Kommunale Arbeitsgemeinschaften*). These are widespread in Brandenburg under different names (for example, round tables or expert panels), and have no right to be involved in official decision-making, usually providing "only" some opinions or statements.

IMPACTS

Only in recent years has IMC become more effective in Slovenia. Currently, almost all local governments use some form of it; however, the associations of municipalities/local governments play no significant role in public policy-making. Much more important are joint municipal administrations, which have been widely used recently, replacing the need for any systematic change in territorial structure. One can even argue that in Slovenia these administrations have played a part linked to territorial stability by establishing some functionally limited regionalization, their network having in this regard taken over the role of the regions themselves.

Slovakia is among the countries (including for example, France and Spain) where IMC is substituted for any consolidation reform. The local governments are strong in terms of their competences and have proper fiscal tools at their disposal, but most of them have insufficient capacity and remain dependent on state transfers. IMC is understood not only as a crucial element for the local governments' survival (that is, a tool to save their independence), but also as a project management tool for those who apply for various external funds. At the same time, it is a main argument used by those who deny the necessity of amalgamation. Thus, IMC contributes to maintaining the status quo of territorial fragmentation in Slovakia.

The Ministry of the Interior evaluated the impact of IMC in the planning process of municipal territorial reform in Brandenburg in 2003. Afterwards, more than 65% of municipal territories voluntarily decided to change their status, based largely on many years of positive experience with IMC. Despite this fact, the federal state government, which took office in 2014, plans some additional reforms. According to the first plan, municipal mergers of a voluntary nature should be encouraged, and an average population of more than 10,000 inhabitants is desirable. Although the IMC is considered a positive measure in general and all major political actors in Brandenburg support further development of IMC, in some official strategic documents there are clear statements that IMC does not necessarily lead to stable and sustainable structures. In addition, opinion-building in the decision-making bodies is associated with problems linked, inter alia, to democratic legitimacy (Landtag Brandenburg 2014).

Concerning the crisis, in none of the cases we have analyzed has it had a direct impact on the development of IMC. The absence of such an impact in Slovakia is apparent through the lack of any significant changes in IMC forms and the intensity of their use. This confirms the claim that the main drivers of IMC development in Slovakia were devolution in the early 2000s and the local governments' intentions to avoid any merger and "survive." The Slovenian case is slightly different, because there has recently been a gradual increase in IMC units. This increase had already started before the beginning of the crisis, however, and IMC was intensified more for reasons related to legal amendments connected with local finances. From this point of view, if there is any impact of the crisis on IMC and its development, then it has either a secondary or an indirect nature. The same applies to Brandenburg. However, the crisis has indirectly deepened the rift between well-financed and ill-equipped local governments. Thus, obstacles to further IMC development between local governments belonging to these two groups have increased.

Conclusions

Various IMC forms are used in different ways in the countries compared. In Brandenburg, all IMC types (based on Hulst and van Montfort 2012) are utilized intensively. Different types of IMC exist in Slovakia as well, but quasi-regional governments and service delivery organizations are the most dominant. In Slovenia, one dominant IMC form is a service delivery organization, though ad hoc project cooperation is also widespread.

In general, IMC is an important measure to address challenges of a sub-optimal municipal size and to overcome related shortcomings associated with a high level of territorial fragmentation. The analysis presented shows significant diversity in terms of outcomes and impacts (Table 5.4, Fig. 5.2). Under favorable conditions (for example, an active reform policy of the central government), as in Brandenburg, IMC has led to territorial consolidation. Under unfavorable conditions, as in Slovakia and Slovenia, it may even be inefficient, opportunistic and sustain territorial fragmentation as well as preventing any amalgamation reform. However, the two cases clearly differ. On one hand, the arguments based on the cost

Table 5.4 IMC and impacts

Impact	Brandenburg	Slovakia	Slovenia
Sustaining the status quo in regard to territorial fragmentation	No	Yes	Yes
Direct impact on reducing territorial fragmentation	No	No	No
Indirect impact on reducing territorial fragmentation	Yes	No	No
Creation of mezzo-/quasi regional governmental level—institutional perspective	No	No	No
Creation of mezzo-/quasi regional governmental level—functional perspective	To some extent yes (in the field of regional planning)	Very limited (in the field of delegated state administration)	To some extent yes
Ensuring capacity of the local governments to deliver minimal number of local public services	Yes	Yes	Yes
Increasing capacity of the municipalities to deliver additional local public services	Yes	To some extent yes	No
Increasing efficiency of delivery of local public services	Yes	To some extent yes	Yes
Increasing allocation of additional (especially financial) resources	No	Yes	Yes
Direct significant quantitative impact of the crisis on IMC development and intensity of its use	No	No	No
Direct significant qualitative impact of the crisis on IMC development	No	No	No

Source: Authors' own compilation

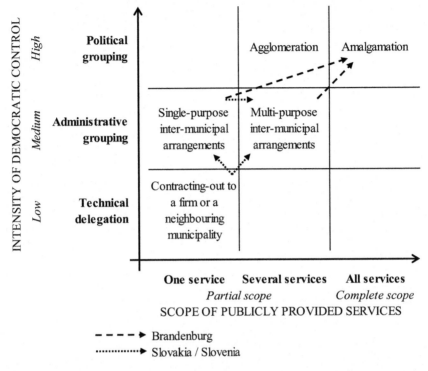

Fig. 5.2 The most significant shifts in institutional settings in terms of reducing local fragmentation in the selected countries (*Source*: Soguel (2006, p. 175) [modified by the authors])

effectiveness, higher efficiency, and improvements in the local administrative capacity have dominated in Slovenia. On the other, in Slovakia, the need for local autonomy maintenance has been stressed. Any attempt at non-voluntary mergers is regarded there as an undemocratic tool. Relevant stakeholders in both countries appreciate an allocation of additional financial resources, but the crisis has no direct impact on IMC and its development. Concerning the quality of local democracy, the form IMC takes does not contribute directly to its improvement in any of the countries compared. One main argument is that there is no directly elected body of any IMC form, and therefore, the decisions taken by the main bodies of IMC forms tend to be of a more technocratic, "top-down" nature than a democratic "bottom-up" one.

Whether IMC may help overcome territorial fragmentation and lead to territorial consolidation apparently depends less on the tool itself, but rather on the ability of the central government to provide and promote effective local administrative structures.

REFERENCES

Baldersheim, H., and L.E. Rose. 2010. *Territorial choice: The politics of boundaries and borders.* Basingstoke: Palgrave Macmillan.

Bel, G., X. Fageda, and M. Mur. 2014. Does cooperation reduce service delivery costs? Evidence from residential solid waste services. *Journal of Public Administration Research and Theory* 24(1): 85–107.

Bogumil, J., and S. Kuhlmann (eds.). 2010. *Kommunale Aufgabenwahrnehmung im Wandel—Kommunalisierung, Regionalisierung und Territorialreform in Deutschland und Europa.* Wiesbaden: VS Verlag für Sozialwissenschaften.

Büchner, Ch., and J. Franzke. 2001. Kreisgebietsreform in Brandenburg: Leitbild, Implementation und eine Zwischenbilanz nach sechs Jahren. In *Reorganisationsstrategien in Wirtschaft und Verwaltung,* ed. T. Edeling, W. Jann, and D. Wagner, 229–244. Berlin: VS Verlag für Sozialwissenschaften.

Carr, J.B., and R. Feiock (eds.). 2004. *City-county consolidation and its alternatives: Reshaping the local government landscape.* New York: Sharpe.

Denters, B., M. Goldsmith, A. Ladner, P.E. Mouritzen, and L.E. Rose. 2014. *Size and local democracy.* Northampton: Edward Elgar.

Dollery, B., and A. Akimov. 2008. Are shared services a panacea for Australian local government? A critical note on Australian and international empirical evidence. *International Review of Public Administration* 12(2): 89–102.

Ermini, B., and R. Santolini. 2010. Local expenditure in Italian municipalities. Do local council partnerships make a difference? *Local Government Studies* 36(5): 655–677.

Hertzog, R. 2010. Inter-municipal co-operation: A viable alternative to territorial amalgamation? In *Territorial consolidation reforms in Europe,* ed. P. Swianiewicz, 289–312. Budapest: OSI/LGI.

Hulst, J.R., and A.J.G.M. van Montfort. 2012. Institutional features of inter-municipal co-operation: Cooperative arrangements and their national contexts. *Public Policy and Administration* 27(2): 121–144.

Hulst, J.R., A.J.G.M. van Montfort, A. Haveri, J. Airaksinen, and J. Kelly. 2009. Institutional shifts in inter-municipal service delivery: An analysis of development in eight Western European countries. *Public Organization Review* 9(3): 263–285.

Keating, M. 1995. Size, efficiency and democracy: Consolidation, fragmentation and public choice. In *Theories of urban politics,* ed. D. Judge et al., 117–134. London: Sage.

Kelly, J. 2007. The curious absence of inter-municipal cooperation in England. *Public Policy and Administration* 22(3): 319–334.

Klimovský, D. 2010. Territorial consolidation and inter-communal co-operation at the local level in the Slovak Republic. In *Territorial consolidation reforms in Europe*, ed. P. Swianiewicz, 237–253. Budapest: OSI/LGI.

Klimovský, D. 2014. *Inter-municipal cooperation in Slovakia: The case of regions with highly fragmented municipal structure.* Novo mesto: Faculty of Organization Studies.

Klimovský, D., O. Mejerė, J. Mikolaityte, U. Pinterič, and D. Šaparniene. 2014. Inter-municipal cooperation in Lithuania and Slovakia: Does size structure matter? *Lex Localis—Journal of Local Self-Government* 12(3): 643–658.

Koprić, I. 2012. Consolidation, fragmentation, and special statuses of local authorities in Europe. *Croatian and Comparative Public Administration* 12(4): 1175–1196.

Kuhlmann, S., and H. Wollmann. 2014. *Introduction to comparative public administration: Administrative systems and reforms in Europe.* Cheltenham/Northampton: Edward Elgar.

Lackowska, M. 2009. Why is voluntary co-operation condemned to failure? Reflections on the polish and German background. *Lex Localis—Journal of Local Self-Government* 7(4): 347–369.

Landtag Brandenburg. 2014. *Abschlussbericht der Enquete-Kommission 5/2 „Kommunal- und Landesverwaltung—bürgernah, effektiv und zukunftsfest— Brandenburg 2020".* On-line at: http://www.landtag.brandenburg.de/media_fast/5701/Drs_5_8000.pdf.

Mäeltsemees, S., M. Lõhmus, and J. Ratas. 2013. Inter-municipal cooperation: Possibility for advancing local democracy and subsidiarity in Estonia. *Halduskultuur—Administrative Culture* 14(1): 73–97.

Sancton, A., R. James, and R. Ramsay. 2000. *Amalgamation vs. inter-municipal cooperation: Financing local and infrastructure services.* Toronto: ICURR Press.

Savitch, H.V., and R. Vogel. 2000. Paths to new regionalism. *State and Local Government Review* 32(3): 158–168.

Skaburskis, A. 2004. Goals for municipal restructuring plans. In *Redrawing local government boundaries: An international study of politics, procedures, and decisions*, ed. J. Meligrana, 38–55. Toronto: University of British Columbia Press.

Soguel, N.C. 2006. The inter-municipal cooperation in Switzerland and the trend towards amalgamation. *Urban Public Economics Review* 6: 169–188.

Sørensen, R.J. 2007. Does dispersed public ownership impair efficiency? The case of re-fuse collection in Norway. *Public Administration* 85(4): 1045–1058.

Spicer, Z. 2012. Post-amalgamation politics: How does consolidation impact community decision-making? *Canadian Journal of Urban Research* 21(2): 90–111.

Statistical Office of Republic of Slovenia, Ljubljana *Regional overview*. Online at: http://www.stat.si/StatWeb/en/field-overview?id=20&headerbar=16.

Swianiewicz, P. (ed.). 2002. *Consolidation or fragmentation? The size of local governments in Central and Eastern Europe.* Budapest: OSI/LGI.

Swianiewicz, P. 2010. If territorial fragmentation is a problem, is amalgamation a solution? An East European perspective. *Local Government Studies* 36(2): 183–203.

Tavares, A.F., and P.J. Camões. 2007. Local service delivery choices in Portugal: A political transaction costs framework. *Local Government Studies* 33(4): 535–553.

Teles, F. 2014. Local government and the bailout: Reform singularities in Portugal. *European Urban and Regional Studies* (pub online 27. January 2014) 1–13.

Tichý, D. 2005. Združovanie obcí ako predpoklad rýchlejšieho rozvoja samospráv a regiónov. *Ekonomický časopis* 53(4): 364–382.

Tiebout, Ch M. 1956. A pure theory of local expenditures. *The Journal of Political Economy* 64(5): 416–424.

Wollmann, H. 2010. Comparing two logics of interlocal cooperation: The cases of France and Germany. *Urban Affairs Review* 46(2): 263–292.

Zafra-Gómez, J.L., D. Prior, A.M. Plata-Díaz, and A.M. López-Hernández. 2013. Reducing costs in times of crisis: Delivery forms in small and medium sized local governments' waste management services'. *Public Administration* 91(1): 51–68.

Žohar, F. 2014. *Delovanje skupnih občinskih uprav v Sloveniji.* Ljubljana: Skupnost občin Slovenija, Združenje občin Slovenje & Ministrstvo za notranje zadeve in javno upravo.

Žohar, F. 2015. *Avtonomnost občin in medobčinsko povezovanje z namenom spodbujanja regionalnega razvoja.* PhD thesis, School of Advanced Social Studies, Nova Gorica.

PART II

Managerial Reforms: From Weberian Bureaucracy to Performance Management?

Design, Trajectories of Reform, and Implementation of Performance Budgeting in Local Governments: A Comparative Study of Germany, Italy, Lithuania, and Norway

Riccardo Mussari, Alfredo Ettore Tranfaglia, Christoph Reichard, Hilde Bjørnå, Vitalis Nakrošis, and Sabina Bankauskaitė-Grigaliūnienė

R. Mussari (✉) • A.E. Tranfaglia
University of Siena, Siena, Italy

C. Reichard
Potsdam University, Potsdam, Germany

H. Bjørnå
University of Tromsø, Tromso, Norway

V. Nakrošis • S. Bankauskaitė-Grigaliūnienė
Vilnius University, Vilnius, Lithuania

© The Author(s) 2016
S. Kuhlmann, G. Bouckaert (eds.), *Local Public Sector Reforms in Times of Crisis*, DOI 10.1057/978-1-137-52548-2_6

INTRODUCTION

Since the 1980s, many European countries have approved reforms inspired by so-called "new public management" (NPM) (Hood 1991, 1995). The rhetoric of reform has been supported largely by principles imported from business practices that, by privileging the quantification and measurement of economic performance (economy, efficiency, and effectiveness), and shifting the focus of public administration from procedures to results, have given budgeting and accounting a central role to play, promoting what Hood defined as "a different style of accountingization" (Hood 1995, p. 94).

Although known and practiced previously, performance management and measurement has become more relevant for public sector organizations with the NPM movement. Consequently, the use of financial and non-financial performance information has also become a key element of budget reforms, and several countries have substituted traditional "line-item" budgets with forms of budget aimed at establishing a link between forecast expenses/expenditures and results to be achieved, in terms of outputs and/or outcomes, in order to provide public officials "not only with more spending discretion but also, and simultaneously, with more responsibility for reaching agreed performance targets" (Zapico-Goñi 1996, p. 71).

This chapter deals with the design and implementation of performance budgeting (PB) at the local level of government. The analysis focuses on municipal budgeting systems in four European countries in order to appraise whether, to what extent and why they have moved (or are moving) towards PB. The selected countries represent four sets of geographical regions in Europe: (1) Nordic countries (Norway); (2) countries of Continental Europe (Germany); (3) countries of Southern Europe (Italy); and (4) countries of Eastern Europe (Lithuania). The objectives of this chapter are: (i) to provide a description of the evolution of budgeting systems towards PB models at the local level of government by highlighting different concepts and trajectories of reform in the countries investigated; (ii) to identify the main causes influencing processes of reform in the different countries, focusing specifically on whether and to what extent NPM-based principles, external pressures, or the 2007 financial crisis impacted the pace and contents of budgeting reforms.

The chapter proceeds as follows: the section "Theoretical Approaches and Research Design" presents and discusses the theoretical framework and briefly explains the research design; the section "Comparison Among PB Systems" presents a comparative view of the different PB systems; the section "Comparative Analysis and Discussion" discusses the design of the PB systems and the *status quo* of their implementation from a comparative viewpoint. The "Conclusion" presents some final considerations.

THEORETICAL APPROACHES AND RESEARCH DESIGN

Performance budgeting emerged as a concept in the second half of the twentieth century. Starting from the first Hoover Commission Report in 1949, via the Planning Programming Budgeting System (PPBS) in the 1960s, Management by Objectives (MBO) in the early 1970s, and Zero-Based Budgeting (ZBB) in the late 1970s, interest in the concept of PB progressively increased among various governments around the world (Schick 2014). After an initial boom phase in the 1970s and its subsequent decline, PB became relevant and fashionable again with the advent of the NPM doctrine.

Generally, a performance budget is a form of budgeting that relates funds allocated to measurable results (Van Dooren et al. 2010). Depending on the degree of linkage between appropriations and performance information, three variants of PB can be distinguished (OECD 2007): *presentational, performance-informed,* and *formula-based.* In practice, however, over the last few decades the general idea of PB has been implemented in very different ways, depending on the type and level of detail of the data, its role in different stages of the budget cycle, and its integration into general performance management (for more details and a critical assessment of the PB concept, see Schick (2014)). Here, we consider PB as the whole process aimed at linking resources employed (inputs) to measurable results (outputs/outcomes) in order to improve the efficiency, effectiveness, and transparency of goals and results. Thus, the purpose of PB is to satisfy both managerial and political needs. The former should be met by increasing internal accountability (making each organizational unit responsible for the resources allocated, activities defined, and results planned), while the latter focus more on external accountability (providing information to the public regarding performance objectives and results).

To achieve our research objectives we use the *transformative approach* as the overarching theoretical framework (Christensen and Lægreid 2001). It argues that external pressures (Olsen 1992) and international trends/fashions are transformed into country-specific factors that influence the design and implementation of reforms via the filtering of various contextual features of the respective country (Verhoest et al. 2010, pp. 41–2). Furthermore, we refer to institutional isomorphism (DiMaggio and Powell 1991) to understand how NPM can shape the spread of PB. If mimetic adaptation to "international fashion" is characterized as the voluntary adoption of "best practices," coercive adaptation occurs when an external authority imposes certain concepts/practices on particular countries. While EU institutions have applied hard governance instruments (like the conditionality of EU membership) prior to accession, softer mechanisms, such as "naming and shaming" or the "sharing of good practices", have prevailed after enlargement (Schimmelfennig and Sedelmeier 2005). The former instruments correspond to the logic of coercive adaptation, whereas the latter are based on the logic of mimetic adaptation.

Domestic responses to external pressures or international trends depend on various political and administrative factors (for example, legal systems or types of government) at both central and local levels of government. First, public management reforms can take a more legalistic and "top-down" course in "Rule of Law" systems (Reichard 2003), compared with the more managerial and "bottom-up" nature of reform initiatives in legal systems where the principles of common law prevail (Verhoest et al. 2010). Second, institutional arrangements and central–local government relations impact the design and implementation of PB reforms. For instance, higher autonomy and flexibility of local governments in budgeting can be associated with stronger incentives to engage in PB reforms. Furthermore, processes of reform implementation also depend on the capacity (knowledge and expertise) of local governments to manage budgeting processes and tools effectively.

In order to support the interpretation of the research results, the following analytical framework has been adopted (see Fig. 6.1). In line with the life-cycle approach to performance management (Bouckaert and Halligan 2008), the process of budget reform is considered as a three-stage path, spanning from the design of a new PB system to its implementation and finally to its operation and use by decision-makers and top managers. From a broader analytical viewpoint, the intended and unintended effects of a PB system (for example, on efficiency or accountability) are also relevant. However, since Italy is only starting its PB implementation from 2015 onwards and Lithuania is in the process of revising its PB system

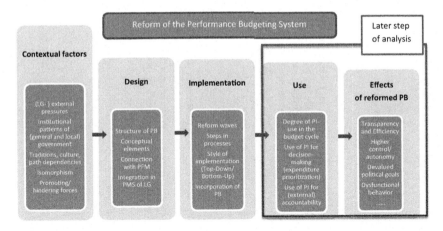

Fig. 6.1 Framework of analysis

at the local level, we will focus on the first two stages alone (design and implementation).

Figure 6.1 presents a picture of several factors external and internal to local government (LG) that influence the design, and also the implementation, of a PB system. Furthermore, the design of a PB is characterized by different features, such as the general structure of the PB, the characteristics of the underlying PB concept, the connection of PB with other parts of the financial management system, and the degree of integration of the PB into the LG's general performance management system. The implementation of a PB by a LG can be characterized by aspects such as certain reform "waves" (namely NPM), by reform steps, the style of PB implementation, and the degree of PB incorporation into LG.

COMPARISON AMONG PB SYSTEMS

Table 6.1 below shows a comparative picture of the PB systems designed and implemented in the four countries under review. The table highlights patterns of convergence, divergence, or persistence (Kuhlmann 2010; Kuhlmann and Wollmann 2014) among the different PB systems. The information it contains is based on country reports and summarizes the "starting conditions" of LG in the four countries, the essence of reforms, the reform trajectories, and the antecedents and drivers of reforms.

Table 6.1 A comparative view of PB systems and their implementation

Criterion	Aspect	Germany	Italy	Lithuania	Norway
A. General information and context	Financial autonomy of LG (% of own revenues)	Moderate	Moderate	Low and diminishing further	Moderate
	Prevailing public accounting and budgeting system in general	Mostly traditional: 'cameralist' cash accounting; accrual accounting and budgeting introduced at local level since 2003	Mostly traditional: cash accounting; highly itemized cash and commitment-based budgeting; accrual accounting will be compulsory from 2015	Accrual accounting (but national budget still accounted on a modified cash basis), semi-program budgeting (mixing traditional budgeting with some elements of performance budgeting)	Central government: cash accounting and budgeting; local government: modified accrual accounting and budgeting
	Traditional budgeting concept at LG level (before actual reform)	Traditional line-item budget, no focus on results, cash-based (as in whole country)	Loosely results-focused, cash and commitment based	Input-oriented, line-item budget without performance information	Traditional budgets were detailed, reporting on centrally established sectors (departments)
B. Major elements of budgeting reforms	Type of financial data	Accrual data (expenses and revenues)	Cash and commitment-based data (expected expenditures and revenues)	Accrual data (expenses and revenues)	Accrual data (expenses and revenues)
	Time-period (annual vs. midterm)	Annual with three-year perspective	Midterm with a three (five)-year perspective	Annual budget with a three-year perspective	Annual, with four-year perspective

Level of detail	Quite detailed (more than 100 products on average)	A bit less detailed than the previous format	Quite detailed (containing performance aims, measures, targets, and so on for each program)	Much less detailed than prior to 2001
Main structural units	Products	Programs	Programs	Frame budgets with ceilings for *de facto* organizational units
Focus on results	Targets and performance information per product	Targets and performance information per program[a]	Targets and performance information per performance aim	Although not mandatory, performance information is most often included in budget documents
Process of budget formulation	Starting top-down (key figures)	Starting top-down	Top-down (estimating revenues, then gathering needs)	Starting top-down. Then left to sector units
Process of budget execution	Flexibility to shift and to carryover within a partial budget	Increased flexibility to shift items within certain expenditure ceilings	Flexibility to reallocate funds within individual LG (but not individual budgetary institutions)	Flexibility to shift and to carryover within a sector unit budget
Budget statement (report)	The income statement (= component of financial report); plus interim reports	The income statement and the balance sheet (= component of financial report)	Annual budget execution reports	Annual and interim reports with expenses and revenues from the entire municipality (also covering municipally owned companies)

(continued)

Table 6.1 (continued)

Criterion	Aspect	Germany	Italy	Lithuania	Norway
	Interrelation with accounting system (type of data and so on)	Closely interrelated (same financial data [accrual], same accounting system)	Loosely interrelated (cash and commitment based budgeting but compulsory accrual accounting)	Weak interrelation (budget accounted on a modified cash basis, not mandatory accrual accounting)	Close link (accrual data in annual budget and accrual accounting system)
	Link of budget to strategic documents	Not mandatory, some municipalities have a link	Directly linked to all strategic documents; the link is established via programs	Directly linked to all strategic documents; the link is established via programs	Strong link. Four year economic plan is the main strategy for all activities (revised annually). Development plan, other plans and annual budget are to be adjusted to the economic plan
	Links between budget and other tools of performance management	Indirectly, for example with departmental performance reports, benchmarking	Directly linked to the performance plan and the performance report (until 2014) and to the MEP—Management Executive Plan)	Weak links between the budgeting process and performance management; better links are expected from 2014 thanks to annual performance plans	Linked to MBO, sector (department) performance, strategies, benchmarking

C. Trajectories and implementation				
Major reform waves	1. 1993–2003: experimental stage with flexible budget execution 2. Since 2003: mandatory performance budget on accrual base	1. Until 2009: traditional budget but performance information included in the MEP 2. 2009–2014: *performance cycle* (aimed at integrating the process of collecting, measuring and using PI) 3. from 2015 onwards: Program Budget	1. 1998–2000: program based budgeting was adopted 2. 2010–2011: strategic planning reforms were implemented; the finalization stage of the accrual accounting reform	1. Before 1992: detailed budgets, no long-term strategy focus 2. 1992: introduction of MBO and four-year economic plan 3. 2001: Flexibility in budgetary chapters and less detailed budgets. Mandatory reports to government on performance indicators (KOSTRA system)
Status of change achieved (new budget formally in place)	70% of municipalities have (formally) established the new budget	The PFM reform will come into force only in 2015 (so far, 5% of municipalities have successfully experimented with the new system)	All municipalities have adopted semi-program-based budgeting and switched from cash to accrual-based accounting	All municipalities have four-year economic plans and frame budgets for internal sectors (departments). Most municipalities (70–90%) use PI in annual reports and strategic plans
Role and quality of PI in the new budget	Dominance of physical input data, not much outcome information provided	Output-oriented performance information is included in the DUP and in the MEP	Performance information is provided in the description of budget programs: a mix of financial and performance information	Output-oriented performance information is used in annual reports and in strategic documents for control and planning and to further MBO (but not mandatory)

(continued)

Table 6.1 (continued)

D. Causes/ antecedents and promoters/ drivers				
Role of NPM	Very influential, main driver	Very influential, perhaps main driver	Moderate	Very influential, main driver
Role of external pressure (for example EU)	No clear indications	Moderate/high (for example Domestic Stability Pact issued in 1999; consistency with budget formats issued by the European System of Accounts, ESA 2010, and so on)	Very influential, especially during accession to the EU, accessibility of EU structural assistance to performance management after accession	No indications
Role of fiscal crisis	Moderate	Very influential: Domestic Stability Pact set constraints on the LGs' spending and hiring freedom, cutback management policies in 2012, and so on	Very influential (during the previous crisis of 1998–1999 and the current crisis)	Very low/none
Major promoters/ drivers	KGST (municipal think tank), consultants, state government	General Accounting Office; LGs experimenting with the new PFM system; ANCI (National Association of Italian Municipalities), intergovernmental bodies	Prime Minister's/ Government Office, also the Ministry of Finance, the National Audit Office; to some extent consultants and IT companies	Municipal association (KS), Municipal Revision Association (NKKF), municipalities, central government

ᵃComplex and integrated budgeting process: objectives, targets and resources are allocated per program in the Single Planning Document (DUP), then referred to programs in the Budget, and further detailed in the Management Executive Plan (MEP)

COMPARATIVE ANALYSIS AND DISCUSSION

Design of the Various PB Systems

In general, many features of the "pre-reform" local budgeting systems were quite similar across the four countries: budgets were highly itemized, did not provide information about results (input-oriented), and were inflexible (no shifting, no carrying over). With regard to the accounting basis, however, the countries show some divergence: in Germany and Lithuania local budgets prior to the recent reforms relied on pure cash accounting and applied cameralist (single-entry) bookkeeping; in Norway the annual budget followed a modified accrual approach for a long time; while Italian municipal budgets relied on cash and commitment accounting. Nowadays, all the countries analyzed have some kind of PB at LG level (or are just starting with its introduction, as in the case of Italy). The introduction of PB is always part of a larger financial management reform, usually in line with a change of the LG accounting system from cash to accrual. Only the Italian budget system remains cash- and commitment-based. The level of aggregation of performance information (PI) in the budget differs between the various countries: while German budgets are quite detailed (focusing on single products or services), the budgets in the other countries are relatively aggregated (concentrating on missions and programs).

In the four countries PB usually provides data and facts regarding different kinds of PI (inputs, processes, outputs, efficiency, effectiveness, quality, impacts, and outcomes). In Germany, input figures (for example, data on existing capacities) and physical output figures (for example, number of trained students) are most popular. Quality information is less frequently displayed, while information about impacts and outcomes, which usually comes from policy evaluations, can be found only very rarely. Norwegian municipalities have an interesting extra source of PI in their budgets: they can refer to performance measurements that are required by the government in annual reports, based on a common software system (KOSTRA) (Statskonsult 2001). This system aggregates more than 1,000 specific performance indicators from each municipality and is publicly available. In Italy, the performance budget is a program budget (Robinson 2013). Expenditures are aggregated in missions and programs, both associated with performance information (outcome, effectiveness, or output). In Lithuania, municipal budgets are organized according to budgetary institutions and programs that contain performance aims, objectives, and measures at the level of products and outcomes.

The style of budget formulation is similar in the four countries: it always starts top-down with indications of the revenues available and the distribution of expenditures/expenses to policy sectors by the LG's top management. On that basis the departments/responsibility centers start estimating appropriations for the coming year with regard to the various programs or services. This procedure helps to prevent unrealistic appropriations being made by line departments and reduces the length and intensity of budget negotiations between line departments and the treasurer. Interestingly, LGs in all four countries enjoy considerable flexibility during the budget execution stage. The shifting of appropriations between budget items is possible everywhere, within certain limits. Furthermore, non-spent funds can be carried over to the next budget year to increase spending efficiency. However, in Lithuania carrying-over is limited to appropriations for special programs and projects, as well as to unused EU financial support and cofunding. Thus, LGs in all four countries have departed from some of the traditional budget standards such as the principles of annuality or item-specificity.

The PB concepts in the four countries differ with regard to the kind of financial data used for budgeting. In Germany and Norway the LG budgets consist primarily of accrual data: they display the revenues and expenses expected to occur in the respective budget year (also covering, for example, depreciation and provisions). More specifically, in Germany the budget provides information about accrual data and about expected cash flows in the budget year. In contrast, the Lithuanian LG budget displays financial data on a modified cash basis. Similarly, the new Italian LG budget will provide information about expected cash flows and commitments.

In essence, the performance budgets of all the countries reviewed can be characterized as "presentational budgets" (OECD 2007): their performance figures are not, or are only very loosely, coupled with the appropriations in the budget. The PI disclosed regards targeted or expected performance levels, so appropriations are not based on a formula or contract with specific performance or activity indicators (OECD 2007). Furthermore, PI disclosed in the budgets seems to be used primarily for allocation decisions in the budget formulation stage. This is particularly true for the German PB. However, municipalities in Lithuania and Norway prepare regular performance reports (interim as well as annual) and thus compare the target performance data of the PB with "real" performance figures resulting from policy evaluations.

The discrepancies between the budgeting and reporting concepts in the four countries are striking: while all of them have moved to accrual accounting at some stage, only Germany and Norway have expanded the use of accrual data to their LG budgets. Reformers in Italy and Lithuania seem to be very cautious about using accrual data for budgeting—most probably because they are worried that accrual data makes financial planning less transparent and may be subject to manipulation (Grandis and Mattei 2012). Another reason is that small municipalities do not possess sufficient financial resources and skills to engage in a full accrual system. Consequently, reformers in these latter two countries only want to disclose in the budget financial figures that are directly related to cash inflows or outflows in the respective year. However, in doing so they neglect to make future financial burdens (for example, provisions) transparent, to provide information about global resource consumption, or to follow the principle of intergenerational equity (Marini and Scaramozzino 1999; Doran 2008). Furthermore, their budgeting systems are not fully compatible with their reporting systems.

Implementation of the PB Systems

The timing of introduction, experimentation and implementation of PB is quite different across the four countries. Norway was an early mover, including performance targets in LGs' long-term budgets since 1992. Performance indicators are usually included in annual reports (up to 90 percent) and some LGs include them in the annual budget on a voluntary basis. Lithuania also adopted PB quite early (after 1998) throughout its government sector (Nakrosis 2008). This country was not hindered in its reforms by legacies and budgeting traditions, as its government undertook a fundamental change after the transformation. Germany—after a decade of NPM-driven PB experimentation—started quite late, partly because of its weighty "cameralist" legacies, but also owing to the complexity and lengthiness of the process of change in a large federal state. Italy is still in an experimental phase of its introduction of the PB. However, a different but similar concept has been in use since 1995—the MEP, which includes PI but is not subject to decision-making by the city council. The late start of Italian LGs can also be explained by the notoriously time-consuming legal process. Altogether, the timing of PB reforms in the four countries cannot be said to follow a common pattern—there are no "parallel waves."

The degree of PB implementation is also quite different among the four countries: in Germany, 10 years after the formal decision regarding budgeting reforms, 71 percent of municipalities had formally established PB (Reichard 2012). However, the "performance side" of the new budget was largely neglected in the early stages of the reform process in Germany: in 2011, only 25 percent of municipalities included PI in their budgets (Reichard 2014). Even if PI is formally disclosed, it primarily regards input data (for example, capacity utilization) and processes, and only partially concerns outputs (for example, number of products). Outcome information is quite rare so far.

In Italy attempts to incorporate performance information into the budget process have drastically increased over the last 20 years (Mussari 2005; Grossi et al. 2016; Mussari, under review for publication). Appropriations are increasingly linked to expected results in the MEP, but performance data is not included in the "official budget" to be approved by the city council. This will change with the current reform and hopefully the increasing number of pilot municipalities (from 49 in 2012 to 373 in 2014) implementing the new budgeting system should foster the success of the reform in the near future. In Lithuania, all municipalities have drawn up strategic development or performance plans, although so far there is no clear hierarchy between the planning documents, while the integration of the plans with municipal finances is insufficient and their implementation lacks effective monitoring and accountability procedures (Government of Lithuania 2013). Budgeting and implementation processes are focused on appropriations and their spending, rather than on the achievement of strategic objectives. Performance indicators are commonly included in the Norwegian LG budgets and reports. The inclusion of PI in the budget process has increased over the years (Cap-Gemini, Ernst & Young 2002; Statskonsult 2001) and the latest research indicates that up to 90 percent of LGs include performance information (based on KOSTRA; see above) in their budget documents (Johansen and Juul 2011; Nyland and Pettersen 2012).

Even though the overall impact of PB-related reforms in the four countries considered remains to be evaluated, this comparison of experiences makes it possible to highlight the similarities and differences to date. The common feature is the inclusion of performance information in the budgeting process. In all four countries it is no longer sufficient for LGs to estimate how much money should be spent for the various different purposes (missions, programs, functions, and services). It is now essential for them to identify the expected level of "results" that should derive from the use of public resources, even though the impact of performance information on budgetary decision-making remains limited, perhaps with the exception of Norway. The existing capacities of municipal staff is a feature that quite commonly limits LG's ability to implement the PB, except in Norway (where LG's capacity was quite appropriate, owing to previous long-term experiments and the openness of staff towards public finance management (PFM) reforms). In contrast, the capacity of LGs in Italy, Germany, and Lithuania is more restricted because of the traditional patterns of prevailing PFM practices and the legalistic culture of their staff. The technical procedures chosen for preparation of the budget and to connect planned spending to expected performance are different. The LGs do not follow a common "best practice" and the budgeting formats are quite diverse, consistently with the differences in the implementation of NPM concepts observed in the literature (Pollitt and Bouckaert 2011).

CONCLUSION

The implementation of PB-related reforms can be interpreted as a response to an external and global trend. This trend is twofold: on the one hand, some countries have adopted internationally widespread reform concepts such as NPM because this has become the prevailing doctrine (DiMaggio and Powell 1991). These countries expect advantages from being perceived as modern and innovative when implementing such ideas. On the other hand, some countries have faced external pressures for reform from third parties (particularly the EU). In our country set, Norway and Germany followed the pattern of the voluntary adoption of NPM practices, whereas Italy and Lithuania (albeit for different reasons) were influenced by external authorities, in line with the logic of coercive adaptation. Furthermore, the analyzed countries differed substantially in terms of the impact of the 2007 financial crisis on performance budgeting. Whereas the crisis had a large impact on the implementation of reform initiatives in Italy and Lithuania, its effect was only moderate in Germany and not relevant in Norway.

Thus, such reforms are affected by situational factors. They are initiated locally by an active administrative policy, which is constrained by environmental factors, polity features and administrative culture and traditions. They then undergo a process of transformation within which trajectories of reform are modified and interpreted according to the political-administrative culture, the style of government and polity factors (Christensen and Lægreid 2001). These countries are responding to PB trends and challenges differently, depending on their specific historical and institutional contexts. The institutional environment determines how reforms are designed and implemented. Accordingly, there are differences between the reform strategies pursued by the four countries selected. Reform initiatives in Italy and Lithuania have followed a top-down course, while Germany and Norway have implemented their reforms according to a more bottom-up pattern. This can be explained partly by the established traditions of the respective countries. Italian LGs, for instance, have long been kept on a short leash by central government, and Lithuania—which was exposed to the powerful external triggers of EU membership and the recent financial crisis—has adopted the most centralized approach to PFM reforms. On the other hand, German and Norwegian LGs traditionally enjoy considerable autonomy.

From the perspective of fiscal control, the integration of the local level financial management system into the broader budgeting and reporting context of the respective countries' central governments is of great importance. In Lithuania the financial management systems of central and local government are intertwined. Similarly, the new accounting and budgeting model of Italian LGs is based on a harmonized concept, involving the country's whole government machinery (Mussari and Giordano 2013). Consequently, the conditions for more coordinated fiscal steering are better in these two countries. In Germany and Norway, the financial management systems practiced at the different levels of government are not comparable with each other, which makes external fiscal steering and control of LGs less effective. The adoption of NPM reforms like PB may have profound effects if they are followed up by the political and administrative leadership and are compatible with historical and institutional traditions. They may, however, produce few changes if they are consciously blocked or avoided by local leaders or lack compatibility with traditional norms (Brunsson and Olsen 1993; Christensen and Lægreid 2001).

REFERENCES

Bouckaert, G., and J. Halligan. 2008. *Managing performance: International comparison.* New York: Routledge.

Brunsson, N. and J.P. Olsen. 1993. *The Reforming Organization.* London: Routledge.

Christensen, T., and P. Lægreid. 2001. *New public management. The transformation of ideas and practice.* Aldershot: Ashgate.

DiMaggio, P.J., and W.W. Powell. 1991. *The new institutionalism in organization analysis.* Chicago: University of Chicago Press.

Doran, M. 2008. Intergenerational equity in fiscal policy reform. *Tax Law Review* 61: 241–293.

Ernst & Young. 2002. *Evaluering av KOSTRA.* Oslo: Kommunal og regionaldepartementet.

Government of Lithuania. 2013. *Survey of local government bodies on strategic planning practices.* Office of the Government of the Republic of Lithuania Vilnius (unpublished document).

Grandis, F.G., and G. Mattei. 2012. Is there a specific accrual basis standard for the public sector? Theoretical analysis and harmonization of Italian government accounting. *Open Journal of Accounting* 2: 27–37.

Grossi, G., C. Reichard, and P. Ruggiero. 2016. Appropriateness and use of performance information in the budgeting process: Some experiences from German and Italian municipalities. *Public Performance and Management Review* 39(3): 581–606.

Hood, C. 1991. A public management for all seasons? *Public Administration* 69(1): 3–19.

Hood, C. 1995. The "new public management" in the 1980s: Variations on a theme. *Accounting, Organizations and Society* 20(2/3): 93–109.

Johansen, M.L., and M. Juul. 2011. *Norske kommuners bruk av KOSTRA til intern styring.* Bergen: Masteroppgave, Norges Handelshøyskole.

Kuhlmann, S. 2010. New public management for the "Classical Continental European Administration": Modernization at the local level in Germany, France, and Italy. *Public Administration* 88(4): 1116–1130.

Kuhlmann, S., and H. Wollmann. 2014. *Introduction to comparative public administration. Administrative systems and reforms in Europe.* Cheltenham: Edward Elgar.

Lüder, K. 2008. Accrual accounting in German governments. In *Het Beroep Accountant Centraal,* ed. R.C.W. Eken and P.M. Zanden. Tilburg: Universiteit.

Marini, G., and P. Scaramozzino. 1999. Social security and intergenerational equity. *Journal of Economics* 70(1): 17–35.

Mussari, R. 2005. Public sector financial management reform in Italy. In *International public financial management reform: Progress, contradictions, and challenges*, ed. J. Guthrie, C. Humphrey, O. Olson, and L.R. Jones. Charlotte: Information Age Press.

Mussari, R. Accounting harmonization as a whole-of-government response to the Italian financial crisis. Article under review for publication.

Mussari, R., and F. Giordano. 2013. Emerging issues in Italian fiscal federalism: The case of municipalities. In *Making multilevel public management work: Stories of success and failure from Europe and North America*, ed. D. Cepiku, D.K. Jesuit, and I. Roberge. Boca Raton: CRC Press.

Nakrošis, V. 2008. Reforming performance management in Lithuania: Towards result-based government. In *Mixes, matches and mistakes: New public management in Russia and the former Soviet Republics*, ed. B.G. Peters. Budapest: Open Society Institute.

Nyland K. and I. J. Pettersen, 2012, *Reforms and clinical managers' responses: a study in Norwegian hospitals.* Journal of Health Organization and Management, Vol. 26 (1), pp.15–731.

OECD. 2007. *Performance budgeting in OECD countries*. Paris: OECD.

Olsen, J.P. 1992, *Analyzing Institutional Dynamics*, Staatswissenschaften unStaatspraxis, 2, 247–71.

Ongaro, E. 2011. The role of politics and institutions in the Italian administrative reform trajectory. *Public Administration* 89(3): 738–755.

Pollitt, C., and G. Bouckaert. 2011. *Public management reform: A comparative analysis—new public management, governance, and the Neo-Weberian state*, 3rd ed. Oxford: Oxford University Press.

Reichard, C. 2003. Local public management reforms in Germany. *Public Administration* 81(2): 345–363.

Reichard, C. 2012. Umsetzung und Praxis des neuen kommunalen Haushalts- und Rechnungswesens. *Verwaltung and Management* 18(3): 118–121.

Reichard, C. 2014. Leistungsinformationen im neuen Kommunalhaushalt— welche Rolle spielen diese Daten in der Praxis? *Verwaltung and Management* 20(3): 125–129.

Reichard, C., and H. Bals. 2002. Resource-based accounting and output-budgeting as common patterns of public sector financial management Reforms. In *Evaluation and accounting standards in public management*, ed. D. Bräunig and P. Eichhorn. Baden-Baden: Nomos.

Robinson, M. 2013. Performance budgeting. In *International handbook of public financial management*, ed. R. Allen, R. Hemming, and B.H. Potter. Basingstoke: Palgrave Macmillan.

Schick, A. 2014. The metamorphoses of performance budgeting. *OECD Journal on Budgeting* 13(2): 1–31.

Schimmelfennig, F., and U. Sedelmeier (eds.). 2005. *The Europeanization of Central and Eastern Europe*. Ithaca: Cornell University Press.

Statskonsult. 2001. *Kartlegging av kommunenes bruk av KOSTRA*. Oslo: Kommunal og regionaldepartementet (KRD).

Van Dooren, W., G. Bouckaert, and J. Halligan. 2010. *Performance management in the public sector*. New York: Routledge.

Verhoest, K., P.G. Roness, B. Verschuere, K. Rubecksen, and M. MacCarthaigh. 2010. *Autonomy and control of state agencies: Comparing states and agencies*. Basingstoke: Palgrave Macmillan.

Zapico-Goñi, E. 1996. Performance monitoring for budget management: A new role of the budget center. In *Monitoring performance in the public sector*, ed. J. Mayne and E. Zapico-Goñi. New Brunswick: Transaction Publishers.

CHAPTER 7

Impacts of NPM-Driven Performance Management Reforms and Ideologies in Napoleonic Local Governments: A Comparative Analysis of France, Portugal, and Turkey

Emil Turc, Marcel Guenoun, Miguel Ângelo V. Rodrigues, Yüksel Demirkaya, and Jérôme Dupuis

The contribution of Pr. Yüksel Demirkaya has received the financial support of the 'Scientific and Technological Research Council of Turkey', (TÜBİTAK, project no 113K427).

E. Turc (✉) • M. Guenoun
Aix-Marseille Univ, CERGAM-IMPGT, Aix-en-Provence, France

M.Â. V. Rodrigues
CICP, University of Minho, Braga, Portugal

Y. Demirkaya
Marmara University, Istanbul, Turkey

J. Dupuis
IAE Lille, Lille, France

© The Author(s) 2016
S. Kuhlmann, G. Bouckaert (eds.), *Local Public Sector Reforms in Times of Crisis*, DOI 10.1057/978-1-137-52548-2_7

121

This chapter addresses the question of the resistance of the Napoleonic administrative model to the diffusion of the NPM model and reforms at the local government level. Performance management and measurement systems (PMMS) are regarded as the main pillar of management reform in recent years, as well as an indicator of managerialization and an outpost of NPM in local governments. This leads to two subjacent questions: (1) Can NPM coexist with non-Anglo-Saxon administrative cultures? (2) To what extent do Napoleonic local governments (LGs) integrate the NPM's focus on public sector performance measurement and management?

These questions contribute to fill a gap in the literature by looking at the effects of performance management reforms (PMR) from the South (Napoleonic countries) and from below (with a focus on municipalities). With few exceptions, reforms of continental Napoleonic countries have received more attention at the central government level, whereas the local government level remains largely unexplored (Kuhlmann 2010; Ongaro and Valotti 2008). Moreover, comparative research often holds a monolithic view of the Napoleonic tradition, despite the extent and diversity of the devolution processes across Europe (Heinelt and Hlepas 2006). These are reputed to have increased the diversity of managerial practice and processes in LGOs, and to boost their modernizing and innovative capacities (Kuhlmann 2006; Ongaro 2009). Yet the effects of performance management reforms are not guaranteed. Conservative forces are fostered by the challenging sophistication of PMMS, the inertial bureaucratic controls of the *RechtsStaat* model of public administration, and the cultural distance between NPM-inspired reforms and the Napoleonic context of their implementation (Peters 2008; Spanou 2008).

To address these issues, we use a *paradigmatic* case selection strategy (Flyvbjerg 2006) to identify three LGOs in France, Portugal, and Turkey which provide a sense of the average municipality in each Napoleonic country. Their PMMS are analyzed using Bouckaert and Halligan's (2008) typology for managing performance in public organizations. The context-sensitive and in-depth qualitative approach provides an opportunity to understand how these municipalities react to the country-specific variations of the Napoleonic model and reform strategies, and to attempt analytic generalizations at the European level. The French case belongs to the original Napoleonic model, although it now represents the highest degree of decentralization and self-administration in the sample, with state regulation mostly focused on financial and accounting processes. Turkey is the most conservative and centralized Napoleonic country, intent on transforming local government with top-down PMM reforms. Portugal provides an intermediate case, with end-of-century decentralization reforms, and tight state regulation of LGOs in finance and human resources due to the recent economic crisis. This diversity offers a contrasting view of the benefits, feasibility, and conditions of implementation of PMR in a Napoleonic context, and sparks ex post investigations into their trajectories, successes, and failures.

LOCAL GOVERNMENTS IN NAPOLEONIC COUNTRIES: MODEL STABILITY AND PERFORMANCE MANAGEMENT ISSUES

While most of the research on PMR in Napoleonic countries has focused on the central government level (Ongaro 2009), we intend here to look at NPM reforms "from below," focusing on local governments and particularly their first layer: municipalities. This requires a preliminary inquiry into the stability of the Napoleonian concept at the local government level.

From the beginning, the traditional strength of the central state in Southern European countries imposed common and specific features on local governments. Mainly they appeared as weak organizations under the tutelage of a centralized state. In contrast to Anglo-Saxon countries, however, centralization did not lead to a principal–agent relation. In Napoleonic countries, local governments have strong institutional protection but are administratively weak. Later on, the model started to evolve as all Napoleonic countries engaged in a devolution process: French decentralization in 1981; the Portuguese Constitution in 1976; Turkish decentralization in 1983–89. This brought up the question of whether a de-napoleonization process took place in European public administrations.

Therein, problems of classification of local administration models were explored in the literature. These contributions appear to confirm the continuing coherence of the Napoleonic model at the local level but also a refinement of its features. Three classifications stand out.

First, Page and Goldsmith (1987); Page (1991); and John (2001) explored the different roles local government plays in liberal representative systems across Europe using three criteria: the array of *functions* under local authority; the *discretion* in administering services and allocating resources; and the *access* of local decision-makers to central authorities and resources. The authors identified important differences between Southern and Northern European systems, where Southern municipalities have few functions and competencies, low legal discretion, and good access by local politicians to the central (and regional) level of government. This southern cluster overlaps the Napoleonic countries, including the three southern countries studied here (France, Portugal, and Turkey). In a second phase, Hesse and Sharpe (1991) contested the simplicity of the previous typology. Taking into account three criteria [(1) distribution of competencies in service provision, (2) political influence of the local level in relation to upper-level government, and (3) importance of local democracy)] they identify three groups of local government systems: the Anglo group, the North and Middle European group, and the Franco (or Napoleonic) group. Again, the coherence of the southern group is maintained and reveals even more clearly the coherence of the Napoleonic classification: strong constitutional status, low autonomy and high control by the central government (tutelage, ex ante legal control, and prefect). In a third phase, Heinelt and Hlepas (2006) took into account the substantial changes in central–local relations since the 1990s, as well as the power relations between mayors, councils, and the municipal administration. The coherence of the Franco (or Napoleonic) group remains, as France, Greece, Italy, Portugal, Turkey, and Spain are concentrated in the "strong mayor" form.

Complementary to this analysis, the literature opens some perspectives and hypotheses on the link between the Napoleonic features of local governments and the adoption and diffusion of performance management systems. On one hand, their political autonomy makes it difficult for central governments to steer internal management procedures. Following Kuhlmann's (2010) comparative framework, it is predictable that in Napoleonic countries PMMS will be not centrally initiated and imposed, but initiated by local actors on a voluntary base. On the other hand, political autonomy is balanced with low administrative autonomy. Thence, some performance indicators and efficiency and effectiveness ratios may be imposed by central ministries to certain local services and public policies. The absence of comprehensive PMMS imposed by central governments does not prevent the implementation of compulsory indicators in several policy sectors (in a silo-based, fragmented, top-down approach). Yet, these findings may lead to over-generalization, and a closer look into country specificities may suggest different mechanisms and outcomes of reforms.

VARIATIONS OF THE MODEL AND OF LOCAL PMM REFORMS: THE CASES OF FRANCE, TURKEY, AND PORTUGAL

Our selection of three countries of the Napoleonic cluster procures the advantage of presenting a set of different economic and political contexts which maximize the variety of the "starting conditions" for PMM reforms

Table 7.1 Weighting the national importance of local governments in France, Portugal, and Turkey

	Average population size of municipalities	Local public employment as % of total public	Local public spending as % of total public spending	Investment as % of total public investment	Public debt as % of GDP
France	1,720	34.6%	21%	73%	8.3%
Portugal	34,049	26.64%	10%	58%	2.05%
Turkey	52,200	11%	12%	35%	5.5%

(Table 7.1). French LGOs have by far the strongest employment, expenditure, and investment figures of the cluster. Turkish LGOs are lighter although they cover more population on average, while the Portuguese model appears at mid-interval in all indicators. According to Kuhlmann (2010), disparities in size, and differences between urban and rural areas, can explain the various degrees of performance implementation in LGs. But another differentiating factor in our comparison resides in the design of the PMM reforms.

In France, the decentralization process of 1981–83 produced a legal and accounting framework which promoted the adoption of performance management. Constraining rules were imposed during this period: (a) adoption of double-bookkeeping accounting, (b) "golden rule" of balanced and sincere budgets, (c) compulsory budget orientation debates, and (d) evaluation of management control by the regional audit chambers. Managerial improvements were also the result of endogenous factors, based on innovation and mimetism (Kuhlmann 2006; Ongaro 2009). PMM practices quickly diversified into a vast array of tools which were progressively but unevenly diffused across LGOs during the 1990s. Management research shows that since that period 50 percent of local governments have used analytical accounting, 30 percent have implemented some form of scoreboard, 10 percent used management by objectives, and 10 percent a system of zero-based budgeting (Pariente 1998). A new label of "performance processes" covers the haphazard choices of performance management tools by LGOs (Carassus et al. 2012).

In Turkey, LGOs remain an integral part of a unitary public administration system, operating under the overall responsibility of the Council of Ministers, despite recent reforms which expanded their area of intervention (public services, promotion of social and economic development). Starting with 2003, a succession of performance management reforms were voted into law (for example, the Law on Public Financial Management and Control 2005) and tools imposed such as strategic planning, multi-annual budgeting based on programs, the introduction of standards and performance indicators for public services, the establishment of internal control systems (mostly based on ex post audits), and citizens' information and participation in decision-making processes. These encountered important problems of implementation due to the managerial capacities of local civil servants. Programs supported by development agencies and international donors were set up to provide technical assistance and training to enhance reform capacities in local administrations (Local Administration Reform programmes I & II, initiated in 2005 and, respectively, 2009) through a limited number of pilot projects. The lack of comprehensive studies makes it difficult to assess the impacts of these reforms, but it is generally considered that the difficulty of setting effective targets and indicators and of measuring and managing the performance of local authorities is the main obstacle in the Turkish LG reform process.

In Portugal, the 1976 Constitution opened a trend of decentralization and, as part of this, the Local Finances Act established financial autonomy and the budgetary principles of local governments. More functions were transferred to local governments and more autonomy and the ability to make pluri-annual investment plans (1998). These powers were increased in the 2000s. Accrual accounting was adopted to foster better use of public resources and to improve transparency. In the meantime performance management initiatives were implemented through HRM in 2006 with a compulsory program for objective measurement of achievement. The recent financial crisis reoriented this trend towards more financially oriented reforms. New laws forced the creation of supramunicipal non-elected entities to share or merge local public services, to right-size municipal structures, and to reduce the number of local entities. A financial law (2011) was passed to regulate endowments from the central government. If financial stress is proven, a central council can enforce LG plans to rationalize spending, maximize own revenues, and implement instruments of internal control. The expression of municipal autonomy is bound to financial stability.

In summary, only one of the three countries (Turkey) has a performance management orientation driven by top-down legal measures. In France and Portugal (at least until the financial crisis), central strategies to foster local performance management were based on input and output regulation (black-box strategy: reduction of grants, obligation to balance budgets...), since local freedom of administration prevented central government from controlling the internal production process. Nevertheless, the differences tend to dissipate if we consider that, owing to economic pressure, central government in France and Portugal started during the 2000s to demonstrate to LGs their interest in performance efforts through indirect initiatives (HRM in Portugal, addition of reports in France claiming the necessity to adopt standard costs for grant calculation...). This diversity of situations and reform styles suggests that the Napoleonic model, despite its supposed uniformity, may reveal a wide array of PMR mechanisms and outcomes.

RESEARCH METHODOLOGY

This research uses a case study methodology (Evers and Wu 2006) to understand to what extent performance management reforms and ideologies have overridden (or not) the inertia and cultural conservatism of Napoleonic LGOs by promoting sophisticated systems of performance management. More specifically, it categorizes the PMMS of representative LGOs in three different countries, and questions the impact of the various features of the local Napoleonic models and national reforms on the adoption of performance management systems.

The Turkish, Portuguese, and French municipalities are identified using a paradigmatic strategy of case selection (Flyvbjerg 2006; Rialp et al. 2005) which stresses the general shared characteristics in each population. They capture a sense of the "average municipalities" and general approach of PMMS in each country. In each country, case selection was based on two interviews with experts in the field: a member of a professional association and a specialized researcher. These discussions explored both the meaning of an average PMMS in national LGOs, and the relevance of potential cases.

The PMMS of the three municipalities were characterized using a structured analytical tool (Yin 1994) based on Bouckaert and Halligan's (2008) typology for managing performance. Their systematic framework gives rise to four ideal types of PMMS: (a) performance administration, (b) management of performances, (c) performance management, and (d) performance governance. We mention them here in the authors' "expected" succession as, according to the authors, public organizations tend to progress from one model to the other through the enforcement of their *performance measurement* (types of indicators, span, depth); the increasing *incorporation of performance* in documents, procedures, and discourse (level and degree of incorporation); and the better *use of performance information* (intensity, reporting focus, time orientation, and automatization). Data collection was based on a common case study protocol, identifying interviewees and key questions in the form of the categories proposed by Bouckaert and Halligan (2008). Interview data was completed with internal documents analysis and secondary data issued from public reports (Table 7.2).

Table 7.2 Characterizing the performance measurement and management systems in the three LGOs of the sample

		Case A (France)	*Case B (Portugal)*	*Case C (Turkey)*
		Imminent departure from performance administration	*Financial performance administration under a strong mayor*	*Proximity with performance administration*
1. Measurement	**Type of measurement**	Mechanistic and closed	Mechanistic and closed	Mechanistic and closed
	Design of measurement system	Ad hoc schemes by department managers. Multiple and contradictory definitions of performance	Ad hoc: based on the mayor's best judgment	Few ad hoc schemes by department managers
	Span of measurement	Limited: economy and efficiency	Input and efficiency	Limited and selective: economy, input and activity
	Depth of measurement	Micro and meso (only for inputs)	Micro and meso	Micro, and limited at meso level
	Specific dimension of measurement	Quality requires separate focus (measured in few departments)	Quality not measured	Quality not measured

(*continued*)

Table 7.2 (continued)

		Case A (France)	Case B (Portugal)	Case C (Turkey)
		Imminent departure from performance administration	Financial performance administration under a strong mayor	Proximity with performance administration
2. Incorpo-ration	Level of incorporation	Static	Static	Static, mainly for legal reporting and financial control
	Degree of incorporation	Disconnected, isolated, but development of a top management scoreboard	Isolated and disconnected of any other scheme	Disconnected, isolated
3. Usage	General use	Limited and technical; incipient integration with policy cycles	Limited but important financial indicators	Limited and technical
	Main reporting focus	Internal hierarchy	Internal hierarchy and external responsiveness	Internal hierarchy; national reporting
	Learning by using (standards)	Single-loop learning	Single-loop, limited to finance	None
	Accountability for performance	Administrative	Administrative and political	Administrative and political
	Potential value added of performance	Limited	Limited	Limited

CASE PRESENTATIONS AND FINDINGS

Case A (France): An Imminent Departure from Performance Administration

Municipality A has 230,000 inhabitants, with a staff of 4684 municipal employees. It enjoys a lasting political stability, the same party governing the city since 1955. The city showcases the stability of the performance administration model in spite of multiple initiatives (policy segmentation, cost accounting) launched since the 1980s. Yet current projects and the accumulation of management and quality tools suggest a potential upgrade to the next PMMS model.

Performance Measurement

Performance measurement is dominated by logics of management and budget control. In line with institutional discourse, the most important modernization initiative was the *partial adoption of the national program-budgeting (LOLF) framework.* Budgetary envelopes were ventilated per functions and missions, but personnel costs continued to be centralized within the HR account. Accountability was not enforced: the departments "watch the expenditures flow" as interviewees put it, more than they manage envelopes. Minimalistic aggregation tools for management control are developed (a master scorecard), although no precise definition is given to indicators or objectives. Elected officials use a table of updated budget expenditures structured along public policies and limited to financial data.

The case does not confirm the existence of a systematic approach to defining indicators and objectives, although the departments analyzed in depth (sports, cleaning, and sanitation) produce data about activities and output used in the departments' management processes. A new project of executive information system promises more data quality and standardization.

Performance Incorporation

The integration of measures is pursued separately by each department. In effect, management information is communicated essentially to the departments' directors, and seldom to general management.

As a global performance approach and tools are lacking, the tools developed by the finance department (budget execution monitoring, multi-annual investment plans, and scoreboard) are the only transversal supports for performance analysis. A static, rather than dynamic, incorporation shows financial indicators used for monitoring rather than projection purposes. Available data in operational departments is not systematically channeled to the manager controllers. There are gaps between data that are produced, usable, and used. The *limits of the management culture* are thus made apparent.

Performance Use
Data use may be characterized broadly as limited, internal-bound, and administrative. The departments' indicators serve mainly for inter-period comparisons. They are meant to engage fine adjustments of objectives, and not policy turnarounds. Analyses are retrospective in the main, and inquire into productive efficiency and operational efficacy.

While the model of performance administration is well established for the French case, some features signal a potential departure from it. (1) The elected officials have clear delegations for budgetary missions; they are accountable for budget envelopes and mark a progressive coupling between political and management cycles. (2) The decision-makers adopt a sensible rather than mechanistic approach to management measures. (3) Devices with a higher degree of integration are developed in operational units. (4) Service quality receives increasing attention. These elements suggest a potential orientation towards a "managements of performances" model.

Case B (Portugal): Financial Performance Administration

This case concerns a city of 120,000 inhabitants which experienced a major political change in the 2009 municipal election, bringing in a new vision of its mission and managerial procedures. Over the subsequent five years, case B was highlighted as being one of the municipalities with the most efficient use of taxpayer money. The level of indebtedness dropped and financial autonomy increased at the same time as the budget started to record successive surpluses. Beyond some specificities, the case presents a management of performance based mainly on cost savings and due-process logics.

Performance Measurement
Municipality B does not have a formal or well-established PMM. Performance measurement is subjected to a logic of budget efficiency and control. Mainly, it is based on an ex ante control of public expenditures, keeping track of all financial operations. There is no formal plan to control performance, no set of indicators to measure output, nor any indicators defined cross-functionally. Collaterally, a more informal, ad hoc process is run, controlled, and evaluated by the central figure of the mayor. Within a close chain of command, managers control the inputs and assess the

outputs and the feasibility of efficiency levels. Under the constraints of the central government system, several departments produce activity reports as compulsory exercises in red tape. External entities, such as parishes and municipal enterprises, have more formal performance management. Their compulsory quarterly reports begin to incorporate a closer link to outputs and value for money.

Performance Incorporation

Management information follows a path from elected officials to each department of the local government structures. The integration of measures is an informal process that flows from the mayor to the deputies and, subsequently, to the rest of the structure. All public servants have clear knowledge of what they should do and what is expected of them: that they will control expenditures. There is no global incorporation tool for performance information. Incorporation proceeds through budget control but financial objectives are not connected with non-financial programs and objectives. This modus operandi is enforced by the *control exerted by central government.*

Performance Use

The municipality resorts to two main indicators of performance: budget execution and the level of indebtedness. The first is seen as an efficiency indicator. The mayor uses this information to readjust the set of objectives and goals of the rest of the structure. The second functions mostly as a financial alert. Municipalities have a legal limit on borrowing, and exceeding it entails severe financial punishments. Whenever the limit grows near, management opts for a contingency plan based on financial cuts. This threat explains the mayor's focus on financial accountability organization-wide. A single-loop process underlines the system: the mayor sets what he considers to be the best level of performance, and evaluates behaviors accordingly.

In summary, case B appears as an instance of robust performance administration, in a context of severe financial constraints. It is reputed to be a case of "best practice" of LG management. In complement to the strict financial control built into the tools and processes of the municipality, the mayor assumes a political control bound on overall performances, whereas the reporting required by the state is seen as a source of red tape rather than strategic steering. Some trends however announce a possible enrichment of the model with features of the management of performance model. First, the quarterly reports of parishes and municipal firms bring into focus the importance of goal achievement, financial performance, and budgetary responsibility. Second, the municipality goes beyond bureaucratic self-centeredness through the mayor's insistence on systematic reports of main achievements and budgetary information for the citizens.

Case C (Turkey): Performance Administration

The municipality has 494,000 inhabitants and may be considered representative of provincial Turkish cities in socioeconomic terms. Case C has been led by center-right political parties and sensibly the same political team for the last 20 years. It has implemented some of the national tools of performance management under the supervision of the directorates of finance and strategic development. However, a shared belief holds that a better PMMS should be in place in order to compete with the surrounding rival cities.

Performance Measurement

Elected officials and top managers see performance data as a means of accountability towards the state and the public, although they share the dominant view that Turkish LGOs should behave as state-driven bureaucracies. Thus, despite nominal political autonomy and local elections, municipalities still struggle against cognitive barriers to acting independently, and expect central directions and guidance for internal improvements. The 2006 legal obligation to implement strategic planning (Strategic Plan, Annual Performance Plan and Annual Facility Plan) *produced an isomorphic process*, in which targets result from bureaucratic aggregation, and *the statistical nature of the data overshadows its administrative purpose*. Accordingly, their instrumentation at intermediate levels is scarce, and there are questions about the integrity of data collection for annual reports.

Mostly, performance measurement is limited to financial and budget data which are collected regularly as the basic material for legal reporting, internal audit, and inspections. On an uneven basis, department heads enrich the data sets with basic input and activity data for the use of inspectors and of the directorates of planning and financial control. Collected at department level and with a technical focus, this data is enriched in municipality C by a local initiative to measure the capacities and efficiency of the personnel. So far, doubts have been expressed about the latter's effectiveness and impact on staff.

Performance Incorporation

The municipality lacks a corporate integration of measures, which are pursued separately by some departments. Managers are only and directly responsible by providing their own data without comparison and integration with other departments. This explains concerns for the reliability of the data produced internally.

A much-tiered hierarchy and bureaucratic structure also preclude transversal learning and the use of other departments' data, a difficulty which extends even to the strategic management department. Only the mayor and deputy mayors have the capacity to access data from all departments. However, the Annual Performance Plan and Annual Facility Plan cover the main indicators of all the departments' activities, and are communicated both internally and externally.

Performance Use

Systematic and reliable internal data are collected from the departments for compulsory legal reporting requirements. However, data usage is limited to the allocation of resources, financial control, and some reporting aspects of the municipality. In general, internal data use may be characterized as limited, internal-bound, and administrative. There is a clear unawareness of the importance of internally consolidated data usage.

Overall, *neither the culture, nor the finalities of performance management* seem to be integrated by the members of the municipality. Despite external legal obligations of performance reporting, the model corresponds to an unintegrated type of performance administration.

DISCUSSION AND CONCLUSIONS

This study of performance management and measurement systems in France, Turkey, and Portugal suggests the resistance of the Napoleonic local governments to NPM approaches of performance management. The three paradigmatic cases appear as slight variations of the performance administration model which, according to Bouckaert and Halligan's (2008) framework, is one of the least sophisticated approaches to public performance, focused on resource allocation and conformity with standards, and best adapted to the formal regulations of Weberian bureaucracy. This dominant PMMS can be considered the most congruent with the Napoleonic features of uniformity and strict input control. Yet such conservatism accounts poorly for the diversity of contexts and reforms in our sample.

Indeed, the mechanisms which explain the shared innocuousness of NPM performance reforms and ideologies in the three countries appear to vary. They occur as an interplay between the country-specific degrees of decentralization and reform approaches. Thus, Turkey provides the most recent and limited decentralization. The state maintains its tutelage over local governments, and promotes top-down legal reforms which implement and monitor performance measurement systems. Despite central authority and legitimacy, strategic steering reforms are superficially adopted and act as institutional façades (Brunsson 1989). The weakness of Turkish LGs (lower functions, employment, and investment) correlate with lower administrative capacities and prevent the diffusion of performance management tools. As strategizing remains a matter of politics and hierarchy, the bureaucratic and centralistic features of the Napoleonic model are enforced. Meanwhile, in Portugal and France the principle of "freedom of administration" is firmly established. The state encourages diffusion of PMMS through indirect strategies of grant reductions and the increasing regulation of local public services. With wider functions and budgets under pressure, French LGs slowly internalize the need for performance management tools and tend to enrich those they employ under the overarching label of "performance processes" (Carassus et al. 2012). Yet, over-intense state pressures may have the opposite effect. In Portugal the crisis-driven pressure from central government comes to be perceived as a threat to local autonomy. A "threat-rigidity" effect (Barker and Mone 1998) accentuates the "strong-mayor" feature of the Napoleonic model. Centralized power and tightened bureaucratic controls tie in closely the performance processes to the mayor's priorities, and ultimately limit further expansion of PMMS. Thus, direct and indirect reforms in Turkey and Portugal suggest that the Napoleonic model and "performance administration" systems can both be enforced along different paths.

Of course, the external validity of this case-based comparison may be limited. However, analytic generalization from three different countries is a reliable source for new theorizing and ideas for further research. As a trend, the chapter confirms the infertile ground of Napoleonic LGs for NPM performance reforms. Their rationale and technique can conflict with existing values and, paradoxically, enforce the existing models and systems. But the variety of mechanisms is inspiring and further research is needed to account for the diversity of LGs in each country. Wider samples may reveal prospectors and innovators ready to take advantage of both

NPM and post-NPM approaches to public performance management and could signal new evolutions of the Napoleonic model.

REFERENCES

Barker, V.L., and M.A. Mone. 1998. The mechanistic structure shift and strategic reorientation in declining firms attempting turnarounds. *Human Relations* 51: 1227–1258.

Bouckaert, G., and J. Halligan. 2008. *Managing performance: International comparisons*. London: Routledge.

Brunsson, N. 1989. *The organization of hypocrisy: Talk, decisions and actions in organizations*. Chichester: John Wiley & Sons.

Carassus, D., C. Favoreu, D. Gardey, and P. Marin. 2012. La caractérisation et le management des déviances organisationnelles liées à la mise en œuvre d'une démarche de performance publique: application au contexte local français. *Management International* 16(3): 102–117.

Evers, C.-W., and E.-H. Wu. 2006. On generalising from single case studies: Epistemological reflections. *Journal of Philosophy of Education* 40: 511–526.

Flyvbjerg, B. 2006. Five misunderstandings about case-study research. *Qualitative Inquiry* 12: 219–245.

Heinelt, H., and N.-K. Hlepas. 2006. Typologies of local government systems. In *The European mayor: Political leaders in the changing context of local democracy*, ed. H. Bäck, H. Heinelt, and A. Magnier, 21–42. Wiesbaden: VS Verlag für Sozialwissenschaften.

Hesse, J.J., and L.J. Sharpe. 1991. Local government in international perspective: Some comparative observations. In *Local government and urban affairs in international perspective: Analyses of 20 Western industrialised countries*, ed. J. Hesse. Baden-Baden: Nomos Verlagsgesellschaft.

John, P. 2001. *Local governance in Western Europe*. London: Sage.

Kuhlmann, S. 2006. Local government reform between "Exogenous" and "Endogenous" driving forces. Institution building in the city of Paris. *Public Management Review* 8: 67–86.

Kuhlmann, S. 2010. New public management for the "Classical Continental European Administration": Modernization at the local level in Germany, France and Italy. *Public Administration* 88: 1116–1130.

Ongaro, E. 2009. *Public management reform and modernization: Trajectories of administrative change in Italy France, Greece, Portugal and Spain*. Cheltenham: Edward Elgar.

Ongaro, E., and G. Valotti. 2008. Public management reform in Italy: Explaining the implementation gap. *International Journal of Public Sector Management* 21(2): 174–204.

Page, E. 1991. *Localism and centralism in Europe*. Oxford: Oxford University Press.

Page, E., and M. Goldsmith. 1987. *Central and local government relations*. Beverly Hills: Sage.

Pariente, P. 1998. Intérêt des approches contingentes en contrôle de gestion: le cas des collectivités locales. *Politique et Management Publics* 16(4): 1–17.

Peters, G.-B. 2008. The Napoleonic tradition. *International Journal of Public Sector Management* 21(2): 118–132.

Rialp, A., J. Rialp, D. Urbano, and Y. Vaillant. 2005. The born-global phenomenon: A comparative case study research. *Journal of International Entrepreneurship* 3(2): 133–171.

Spanou, C. 2008. State reform in Greece responding to old and new challenges. *International Journal of Public Sector Management* 21(2): 150–173.

Yin, R.K. 1994. *Case study research: Design and methods*. Second Edition. Applied Social Research Method Series, Vol. 5. Beverly Hills, CA: Sage Publications.

CHAPTER 8

Do They All Fail?: A Comparative Analysis of Performance-Related Pay Systems in Local Governments

Isabella Proeller, Anne-Kathrin Wenzel, Dominik Vogel, Riccardo Mussari, Donatella Casale, Emil Turc, and Marcel Guenoun

INTRODUCTION

Performance-related pay (PRP) regimes have been promoted as instruments to boost efficiency, motivation, and performance orientation of the public sector and its employees. However, experiences of implementation have revealed that PRP is not a quick-and-easy-win instrument, and that the results expected from it could not often be realized.

I. Proeller (✉) • A.-K. Wenzel • D. Vogel
University of Potsdam, Potsdam, Germany

R. Mussari • D. Casale
University of Siena, Siena, Italy

E. Turc • M. Guenoun
Aix-Marseille Université, Marseille, France

© The Author(s) 2016
S. Kuhlmann, G. Bouckaert (eds.), *Local Public Sector Reforms in Times of Crisis*, DOI 10.1057/978-1-137-52548-2_8

Previous evaluations have identified severe weaknesses in PRP schemes in the public sector (Perry et al. 2009). Not only were expected effects like motivation crowding-in regularly not realized; looking at the reform discourse and development in some European countries it seems that PRP regimes have been loosened or even taken off the reform agenda, often with the notion that PRP systems were not operated as planned, failed to deliver, and ultimately were stalled as being a control instrument that was incompatible with the existing administrative culture. Local government level in Germany, France, and Italy are among the areas where such developments occurred, and where accounts of the successful implementation of PRP systems were given only somewhat reluctantly. These three national local government levels will serve as comparative cases to explore just why PRP systems have failed to manifest a core position in performance-oriented reform agendas. In terms of research the interest of this chapter lies in finding out what can explain why a once clearly positioned and regulated reform policy like PRP should be taken off the reform agenda rather quickly. From a rational perspective, the abandonment or repositioning of a reform could be explained as functionalist, e.g. the reform did not deliver what it was designed for and was therefore dismissed for lack of problem-solving capacity. From a sociological, neo-institutionalist perspective, it could be argued also that the abandonment of a certain reform trajectory can follow a logic of appropriateness (March and Olsen 1989). As a process of mimetic isomorphism, to *not* push further for this particular reform policy would then become the newly emerged social norm. By comparative analysis of the three case studies against those theoretical perspectives, we aim to better identify potential influencing factors and mechanisms. In the instance of France, we observe a case that has degraded its PRP reform, while in Italy and Germany, though some sobering results have also been experienced with PRP, it still remains a part of the reform package. Methodologically, we therefore have two similar cases and a dissimilar one with respect to our object of analysis: the continuity of PRP as reform trajectory. In the following, we will outline the origins, designs, and contemporary accounts of the experiences of implementation in the three countries, before we synthesize the comparison with regard both to our own research interest and to the further research to come (Table 8.1).

Table 8.1   Characteristics of the civil service in the three countries

Characteristics of the civil service	Germany	Italy	France
Number of public employees	4.6 Mio (2011)	3.4 Mio (2010)	5.4 Mio (2011)
Number of local employees	3.18 Mio (incl. Länder)	0.57 Mio	1.81 Mio (2011)
Proportion of personnel at the local level (as % of tot. public employees)	79%	16.7%	19.4%
Distribution per layer	Länder 60% Municipalities 27%	Municipalities 76%, Provinces: 11% Regions: 7%	Municipalities 63% Intercommunal organizations: 13% Provinces: 20% Regions: 4%

Source: Authors' compilation

PRP in Germany

Origin

In 2003, a commission on the reform of the public sector recommended the introduction of an effective reform of the system of remuneration including PRP (Regierungskommission 2003). The suggestions finally led to the reform of the "Collective Agreement for the Public Service" (TVöD and TV-L). This imposed on public administrations at all levels the duty to introduce PRP starting in 2007. In the following, we will concentrate on the description of PRP for public employees and disregard the completely different regulations for civil servants who only amount to 13.3% of people employed at local level.

It was intended that with the introduction of PRP, the motivation, self-responsibility, and leadership skills of employees working in public services should increase. Initially, PRP was launched with a budget of 1% of the basic pay of all employees of the respective organization in the previous year and has now risen to 2%. It has been planned to increase the amount up to 8%. PRP is paid on top of the regular salary and the latter cannot be reduced as a result of lower performance. All employees of an organization are eligible to get PRP and no official quota is applied.

Design

German public administrations enjoy a lot of discretion in designing the concept of PRP. The collective agreement for the public sector (§ 18 TVöD) merely regulates the basic framework of the performance payment; more specific regulations have to be decided in mutual agreements (*Dienstvereinbarung*) by the bargaining parties—the employer and the staff council—within the respective organization. In mutual agreements, the employer and especially the staff council have to concur on the type of performance appraisal, the distribution of PRP, and the performance appraisal methods.

There are three types of PRP. The most commonly used is the performance bonus, which is usually paid once a year. In addition, organizations can pay bonuses based on the fulfillment of economic goals by single employees as well as making team and incentive bonus payments, both of which however are rarely used.

Regarding the allocation of the budget, an organization can decide whether to divide its PRP budget into sub-budgets or use one budget for all employees. In the case of division by departments, there is an individual budget for each department and only the performance ratings of employees within it are compared and transformed into the individual amounts of PRP. It is often argued that this is fairer as it reduces the chance of different performance appraisers using different criteria.

Two methods of performance appraisal can be applied: agreement on goals, and systematic performance appraisals. Agreement on goals amounts to a voluntary contract between a single employee or a team and the supervisor on three to five targets. In employing systematic performance appraisals, supervisors have to use objective and measurable criteria for the performance assessment. It depends on the mutual agreement whether only one method of performance appraisal is used or both.

Different studies provide evidence that employees perceive agreements on goals as notably fairer, more transparent, and participative compared with systematic performance appraisals (Meier 2013; Erez et al. 1985). It remained unclear for a long time whether it made a difference if the goals were agreed between the employer and a single employee or a team; the results of a survey by Meier (2013) confirmed however that team agreements on goals led to less envy between employees than other appraisal methods. Nevertheless, individual agreements on goals are shown to have a stronger influence than do team agreements on the transparency and fairness of the performance appraisal as well as on participation within the goal-setting process (ibid.).

Implementation and Criticalities

Despite several years of the application of PRP in German public administrations including LGOs, there are few evaluation studies that demonstrate what effect performance pay actually has and how the employees perceive the different appraisal methods (Meier 2013; Schmidt and Müller 2013; Schmidt et al. 2011).

In 2013, Meier surveyed 21 German county councils and cities with county status in order to analyze whether the introduction of PRP into the public service resulted in crowding effects of intrinsic motivation and public service motivation (PSM). The design of the performance appraisal schemes turned out to be by far the most significant factor in the perception of PRP, with the schemes' apparent fairness and transparency being particularly influential.

In the international context critics have frequently stated that there is a tendency to "reward" a very high proportion of employees with the best possible rating within the performance appraisal process (Perry et al. 1989; Landy and Farr 1983); the limited data suggest that more than 90% of employees receive at least some performance pay (Meier 2013), while the percentage of those who get the best performance appraisal is very high and varies from 56% (Meier 2013) to 59% (Schmidt and Müller 2013). The study by Meier (2013) has also shown that the choice of performance appraisal method influences the chance of getting the highest rating: agreements on goals offer significantly greater chances, while the chances seem to be very low for employees rated with systematic performance appraisals. This finding is especially relevant for those organizations which implemented both appraisal methods.

The low amount of PRP is often seen as a reason for employees being dissatisfied with it. This could explain the leniency of the appraisers, who could see (too) good performance appraisals as having a potential for employee motivation while more realistic performance appraisals might demotivate. In the end, however, this attitude must totally defeat the principle of performance pay.

The differentiation between public employees and civil servants also leads to problems; although both groups work together in the same teams, they do so under completely different rules governing PRP. The regulations of § 18 TVöD apply only to public employees, while the different rules affecting civil servants vary between the federal states (Weber 2013).

In the end, PRP has caused a lot of discussions and problems in the German public sector. In 2009, it was abolished at the federal level. Since 2014, there has been no duty to distribute PRP at state level. The trade union argues essentially that PRP does not fulfill its purpose and leads to discord and envy between employees (ver.di 2011).

PRP in France

Origin

Performance bonuses in the French civil service are a relatively new development, gaining strength and visibility during the late 2000s (Carrez 2007). The PFR (bonus for functions and results—*prime de fonctions et de résultats)* was rapidly translated into law (2008). Along with Law 2010-751, this ended the decades-long ban on personalized variable pay in the French civil service.

From an organizational standpoint, the mission of PFR was to replace the existing approximately 1,800 bonuses across the national and local government administration, and secure a more equitable treatment for employees with comparable jobs in public administrations (Silicani 2008). Departing from the general culture of uniformity and bonuses based on "impersonal" criteria, the PFR was also seen as a means to expand managerial leeway, giving direct supervisors the possibility of incentivizing subordinates through individual goal-setting, evaluation, and bonuses. Eventually, and in a context of austerity, the PFR was to reconcile and improve the management of salary budgets, wage rises, and the recognition of professional value and work performances. Concurrently, the government introduced in 2010 the possibility of collective incentive schemes. However, the interest for this PRP tool was quickly stalled, with trade unions perceiving it as a disguised mechanism for personnel reduction and financial cutbacks (2011).

Design

According to the law, the PFR includes two parts: the functional bonus PF (*prime de fonctions*) and the performance-related bonus PR (*prime de résultats*). The assessment of each follows specific calculations, but they are jointly paid on top of the yearly base salary as determined by the career index and national grids. First, the functional part is meant to acknowledge the professional trajectory of the agent. While the PF bonus may have appeared as a recognition of professional worth, it is more closely aligned to the OECD's (2005) vision of allowances for certain posts and working conditions. Specifically, the PF depends on new "objective" categorizations of jobs produced by the ministries and LGOs and has no connection with the personal characteristics of the employee.

Second, the *prime de résultats* (PR) part is formally connected to the annual assessment interview of each civil servant. It integrates multiple criteria such as the commitment to serve, the achievement of annual objectives set by the supervisor, personal involvement, interpersonal skills, and the acquisition of other competencies and skills required on the job. This explains the de facto categorization of the PR part as a PRP tool, although the merit bonus (for professional worth and competence) and payment for results (which is goal-related) are not separated and follow a single procedure of assessment and attribution.

As for amounts, the PFR may make a significant difference. For instance, middle managers in the national civil service could reach in 2011 a PF bonus of €15,600 and a PR bonus of €10,200 per year. A concern for equity is apparent, as the superior margins of the PFR's parts are bound by national limits for each category of civil servants. As for volunteering LGOs, their councils must validate and enact all the limits and modalities of their PFR systems.

Implementation and Criticalities

While the PFR has been widely promoted as supporting civil servant motivation, its design appears as a barrier to this goal. The beginnings of PRP in the local civil service coincide with those of the national services (law 751/2010, decree 1705/2010). But the pace of reforms in LGOs was reduced by the constitutional principle of freedom of administration. The extension of PFR was seen as an optional process, depending on the decisions of LGO councils to either try it out or else continue with the previous system of bonuses and allowances.

To analyze the level of implementation of PRP tools and their effects, original qualitative interview data was gathered[1] and was completed by second-hand data and a literature review. So far, the application of PRP tools calls for the following comments:

1. Their implementation and diffusion is extremely limited, almost anecdotal. The ensuing budgetary inflation is widely acknowledged by the profession as an essential reason why PFR was not diffused more widely across the LGOs in the context of economic crisis.
2. Local adaptations of the design of PFR limit drastically the part connected with the employee's results, hence its kinship to PRP systems. The *PF* part, which depends on the position occupied by the employee, ended up dominating the *PR* part (60:40).
3. Within the context of LGO administrative culture the implementation of PFR came at the cost of budget inflation and significant distortions of its initial goals. The PFR was based on a uniform method, in which widespread communication on LGO-wide criteria and procedures was appreciated by both administrators and employees. Yet, as experiments went on, the decision-makers were unsettled. The inflationary effects of PFR on total payroll contributed to reduce the LGO's financial leeway.
4. Lastly, the local adaptations of PFR were swift to reach their limits, leading to demands for a renewal or abandonment of the system. Their resource-intensive implementation and the perceived budgetary inflationary were incompatible with the decreasing finances of French LGOs.

Eventually, the vote into law of a new bonus system (IFSE, 20/05/2014) made optional the results-based bonus for the whole civil service. This confirms the profession's preference for a simplification tool, rather than a performance-based HR instrument.

PRP in Italy

Origin

The PRP system has been recently reformed following a typical top-down approach through the introduction of decree 150/2009 that aimed at strengthening the already existing principles introduced by previous reforms during the past years. In fact, the intense public management reform in Italy in the 1990s mainly concerned institutional design, career

Table 8.2   Reward structure in Italian public administration

	Ministries	Regions	Provinces	Municipalities
Number of managers	21.3%	37.4%	9.5%	31.8%
Average gross annual pay	87.248	86.199	80.592	73.866
% pay for performance	5%	9.7%	8.5%	7.4%

Source: Authors' elaboration from Cristofoli et al. (2007)

progressions, and remuneration systems (Mele 2010; Ongaro 2009; Capano and Gualmin 2006) and special units devoted to performance management, *Nuclei di Valutazione,* were introduced in every local council (decree 142/1990). Subsequently, a comprehensive reform of the civil service introduced a first assemblage of performance instruments in LGOs (decree 29/1993). Notwithstanding these efforts, any organic performance-related pay system for public managers has not been introduced till 2009 (Mussari and Ruggiero 2010) (Table 8.2).

Design

The above-mentioned reform of 2009 (decree 150/2009) introduced a comprehensive and sophisticated system of PRP aimed at the evaluation and measurement of individual and organizational performance in the Italian public sector. The main principles and promoted values are the obligation to measure and evaluate performance, along with the enhancement of merit through the provision of bonuses linked to individual and organizational performance.

The decree introduced a process (a performance cycle) organized around a three-year planning document (a performance plan) indicating the strategic and operational objectives along with the indicators selected to measure organizational and individual performance. Besides the planning document, each administration must issue a performance report that functions as a feedback on achievement of both strategic and operational objectives by providing a breakdown of the strategic objectives included in the performance plan into annual objectives.

The performance of all employees of local administrations is evaluated. The evaluation of individual performance is made in accordance with the executive management plan (*piano esecutivo di gestione*) and the formal attribution of individual objectives in each LGO. In particular, every organization must adopt the executive management plan and formally allocate individual objectives.

The bonuses available are distributed according to the results of the formal evaluation of individual performances and are calculated implementing specific algorithms, which are defined in accordance with collective integrative decentralized bargaining (*contrattazione collettiva decentrata integrativa*). According to the legislation three types of bonuses are designed to promote performance orientation: (1) *Bonuses based on performance*, which are the annual excellence bonuses for managerial and non-managerial staff, and efficiency bonuses that consist of allocation of a quota of 30% of resources derived from contingent savings. (2) *Bonuses based on special success*, which are annual innovation bonuses for the best projects in terms of improvement, change regarding internal processes, organizational performance, and/or the quality of a public service. (3) *Incentive bonus payments*, which consist of economic and career progressions. In particular, the bonuses for individual and/or collective productivity are defined according to article 17 CCNL 1.4.1999 and article 37 CCNL 22.1.2004 plus article 26 and following articles of CCNL 23.12.1999 (*comparto dirigenti*). The resources devoted to the bonuses are defined in accordance with articles 31 CCNL 22.1.2004 and 26 CCNL 23.12.1999.

Implementation and Criticalities

A recent survey of 169 local administrations conducted in 2010–11 by Di Mascio and Natalini (2013) found that 54.8% of the LGOs observed do not effectively use performance-related pay. In addition, since the municipalities are required to publish PRP-related data on their websites, the above-mentioned survey showed that only 23% of the administrations proved to be compliant with this requirement.

In general, performance management suffers because of difficulty of application due to the complexity of the structures and the nature of activities of the public sector. The context of widespread emphasis on performance measurement despite the public sector's loss of competitiveness and productivity and fiscal stress (Italian Court of Auditors 2012, 50; law 94/2012; decree 07/05/2012) undermines the capability of LGOs to distribute resources in accordance to the above-mentioned bonuses outlined by the legislation. Moreover, the differences in the implementation within Italian LGOs (Ruffini et al. 2011; Spano and Asquer 2011; Borgonovi 2005) also show the problems in adapting to the newly introduced performance schemes in different organizations, which demonstrate resistance to change and collision with consolidated bureaucratic cultures.

CONCLUSION

Diffusion and implementation practice in the three countries shows significant differences and leads to relevant heterogeneity as well as variance of implementation of PRP. While PRP is implemented in most of Italian LGOs and the majority of German LGOs, diffusion of PRP is very limited in France. A main reason involves the different legal requirements associated with the implementation of PRP. Italian LGOs are expected by law to use PRP, and German LGOs at least have to spend the budget dedicated to PRP. In contrast, French LGOs are allowed to decide on their own to use PRP or not, and if they do what reorces they can and will allocate resources to it. But differences and heterogenity among LGOs is not limited to the decision level as referred to by variety in regime designs (Brunsson 1989), it also reaches into the action level (Brunsson 1989) of LGOs and creates further heterogenity there. So, for example, the survey by Meier (2013) shows that up to 58% of LGOs in each federal state ignore and pervert the PRP system on the action level by simply assigning everybody the same PRP bonus.

Our main research interest was on the continuity of PRP as reform trajectory. Italy, and to date also Germany on the local level, are continuing their current systems and at present show no lessening or loosening of their controls and regulations for PRP, while in France we observe a de facto withdrawal from the *prime de résultats*, e.g. the performance-oriented part of the bonus system. Evaluating developments through a theoretical lens it seems that the functionalist argument has only limited explanatory power. The sketchy and limited evaluative accounts that exist to date on the effects of the PRP reforms rather point to the conclusion that any gains in motivation and efficiency have lagged behind expectations in every national context. Even though there are—for instance in the German case—also examples and groupings where motivation has been systematically increased, overall the effects are sobering. Taking into account the findings of recent international research on the motivational effects of PRP, to boost motivation it would be important to stress the supportive character of the PRP procedures (Jacobsen and Andersen 2014; Meier 2013; Andersen and Pallesen 2008). However, in the case studies, neither adjustments to produce reforms nor efforts to foster intended effects were described as core features, which might be interpreted as a lack of interest in making the systems work beyond just having them in place. As to the logic of appropriateness, the different coping and dismissal strategies that were observed in France can be explained and interpreted in this light, as well as the continuing compliance approach that describes both Italian and German practices. While at the beginning of the reforms the logic of appropriateness seemed to have a distinctly international structure and influence, leading also to an international reform trajectory for PRP, in actual fact during the course of the reforms what is deemed appropriate has shown a decidedly national variance. As our case studies illustrated, there is variance between the national LGOs of what is considered as accepted, legitimate, appropriate, expected implementation and development of the reform. Hereto, the different degree of institutional and systematic linkage of the PRP system to other, comprehensive control systems might be a relevant explanatory factor. Hence, in Italy we observe a highly interlinked PRP system which is embedded and systematically linked to a more comprehensive, performance-oriented administrative control system. In France and in Germany, PRP systems were operated rather on their own, with many more discretionary links to other, not necessarily performance-oriented control systems. Obviously this first, general comparative analysis of PRP systems in Italian, French, and German LGOs is of limited validity and reliability. However, the theoretically driven analysis points us to an area worthy of further research beyond the analysis of direct and indirect effects of PRP systems on motivation. So, as this chapter sees a potential reason in different developments of PRP systems in their systematic links to other control systems, future research might take up this strand and further explore the effects of integrating PRP systems in administrative control systems, in order, ultimately, to clarify further whether systems where PRP is linked and integrated into a wider performance-oriented control system actually work better in terms of motivational and efficiency gains.

NOTE

1. In summer 2014 five interviews were conducted in French LGOs with HRM officers who were involved in professional associations and some of whom had implemented PRP.

REFERENCES

Andersen, Lotte, and Thomas Pallesen. 2008. Not just for the money? How financial incentives affect the number of publications at Danish Research Institutions. *International Public Management Journal* 11: 28–47.

Borgonovi, Elio. 2005. *Principi e sistemi aziendali per le amministrazioni pubbliche*. 5. ed. I manuali/[EGEA] 25. Milano: EGEA.

Brunsson, Nils. 1989. *The organization of hypocrisy: Talk, decisions and actions in organizations*. Chichester: Wiley.

Capano, Giliberto, and Elisabetta Gualmini. 2006. La pubblica amministrazione in Italia (Ed.).

Carrez, G. 2007. *Rapport fait au nom de la Commission des finances, de l'économie générale et du plan sur le Projet de loi de finances pour 2008* (n° 189).

Cristofoli, D., A. Turrini, and G. Vallotti. 2007. *Da burocrati a manager: Una riforma a metà. Primo Rapporto sulla Dirigenza Pubblica Italiana*. Milano: EGEA.

Di Mascio, F., and A. Natalini. 2013. Context and mechanisms in administrative reform processes: Performance management within Italian local government. *International Public Management Journal* 16(1): 141–166.

Erez, Miriam, P.C. Earley, and Charles L. Hulin. 1985. The impact of participation on goal acceptance and performance: A two-step model. *Academy of Management Journal* 28(1): 50–66.

Italian Court of Auditors. 2012. Corte dei Conti (2012) Relazione 2012 sul costo del lavoro pubblico.

Jacobsen, Christian, and Lotte Andersen. 2014. Performance management in the public sector: Does it decrease or increase innovation and performance? *International Journal of Public Administration* 37: 1011–1023.

Landy, Frank J., and James L. Farr. 1983. *The measurement of work performance: Methods, theory, and applications*. New York: Academic Press.

March, James G., and Johan P. Olsen. 1989. *Rediscovering institutions: The organizational basis of politics*. New York: The Free Press.

Meier, Anne-Kathrin. 2013. *Determining factors of the perception of performance-pay systems. An analysis of a survey in German local administrations*. Paper presented at the EGPA Annual Conference, Edinburgh, 11–13 Sept 2013.

Mele, Valentina. 2010. Innovation policy in Italy (1993–2002): Understanding the invention and persistence of a public management reform. *Governance* 23(2): 251–276.

Mussari, Riccardo, and Pasquale Ruggiero. 2010. Public managers' performance evaluation systems and public value creation: Behavioral and economic aspects. *International Journal of Public Administration* 33(11): 541–548.

OECD. 2005. *Performance-related pay policies for government employees*. Paris: OECD.

Ongaro, Edoardo. 2009. *Public management reform and modernization: Trajectories of administrative change in Italy, France, Greece, Portugal and Spain.* Cheltenham/Northampton: Edward Elgar.

Perry, J.L., B.A. Petrakis, and T.K. Miller. 1989. Federal merit pay, round II: An analysis of the performance management and recognition system. *Public Administration Review* 49(1): 29–37.

Perry, James L., Trent A. Engbers, and So Y. Jun. 2009. Back to the future? Performance-related pay, empirical research, and the perils of persistence. *Public Administration Review* 69(1): 39–51.

Regierungskommission, N.R. 2003. *Zukunft des öffentlichen Dienstes–Öffentlicher Dienst der Zukunft. Anlageband zum Bericht der Regierungskommission NRW.* Düsseldorf: Innenministerium des Landes NRW.

Ruffini, R., L. Bottone, and R. Giovannetti. 2011. *Il performance management negli Enti Locali. Logiche e metodologie in applicazione della Riforma Brunetta.* Rimini: Maggioli Editore.

Schmidt, Werner, and Andrea Müller. 2013. *Leistungsorientierte Bezahlung in den Kommunen: Befunde einer bundesweiten Untersuchung.* Berlin: Ed. Sigma.

Schmidt, Werner, Nele Trittel, and Andrea Müller. 2011. Performance-related pay in German public services: The example of local authorities in North Rhine-Westphalia. *Employee Relations* 33(2): 140–158.

Silicani, J.-L. 2008. *Livre blanc sur l'avenir de la fonction publique: faire des services publics et de la fonction publique des atouts pour la France.* Paris: La documentation Française.

Spano, Alessandro, and Alberto Asquer. 2011. Performance review and assessment of public managers: Some evidence from local governments in Italy. *International Journal of Public Administration* 34(7): 461–472.

ver.di. 2011. *Antrag E 150 (Abschaffung des § 18 TVöD) an den Bundeskongress 2011.* http://bundeskongress2011.verdi.de/antraege/antrag.html?cat=E&sort=150&aid=9367. Accessed 11 June 2013.

Weber, Klaus. 2013. Leistungsbezahlung im Beamtenbereich. Überblick über dienstrechtliche Gegebenheiten. *Der Personalrat* 3: 101–105.

CHAPTER 9

Human Resource Management Reforms and Change Management in European City Administrations from a Comparative Perspective

Marco Salm and Christian Schwab

INTRODUCTION

In its latest "Cities of Tomorrow" report, the European Commission emphasized that cities are facing important current and future challenges, such as economic crises, economic stagnation, demographic change, and/ or social polarization (European Commission 2011). In addition to these "external conditions" that must be addressed, there are also New Public Management (NPM)-driven "internal reform drivers." City administrations have to adapt themselves to their changing environment in terms of these internal and external reform drivers, leading to sub-national modernization policies. The administrative adaptations involve various institutional changes in order to achieve set reform objectives. Variations in adaptations, changes, and objectives may further imply different impacts

M. Salm
German University of Administrative Sciences Speyer, Speyer, Germany

C. Schwab (✉)
University of Potsdam, Potsdam, Germany

© The Author(s) 2016   153
S. Kuhlmann, G. Bouckaert (eds.), *Local Public Sector Reforms in Times of Crisis*, DOI 10.1057/978-1-137-52548-2_9

on local governments' results and performances in the delivery of services. In order to deal with these challenges, many cities have reacted with either holistic or specific reform programs, in which human resource management (HRM) is becoming increasingly important. The reform of HRM is only one reform component, but it is—probably more than ever before—a primary focus of city administrations.

Both scientists and practitioners have found that empirical evidence with regard to the reform of HRM has been neglected in the past decades and needs to be examined more closely. A review of the current literature shows that public management reforms downplay the role of HRM. Furthermore, the effects of HRM reforms are a neglected research issue and scarcely discussed in the reform context (OECD 2015). A recent article, which reviews HRM reforms and performance, finds a general lack of empirical evidence linking HRM reforms with (the expected) results (Jordan and Battaglio 2013). Moreover, there is little empirical evidence on the role of HRM in terms of change management (Sedlack 2010). Yet, the management of change in organizations is very much linked to HRM. Therefore, more scientific (empirical) attention needs to be directed toward HRM reforms and their corresponding results, effects, and outcomes at the local level of government.

This chapter examines three case studies of "reform excellence" by analyzing an online survey conducted among the key actors from three cities nominated for the European Public Sector Award in 2009 and 2011, namely Bilbao (Spain), Mannheim (Germany), and Tampere (Finland). The focus of the survey was the city reform approach as a whole and especially HRM reform approaches.

The chapter follows two analytical guiding questions in order to discover whether HRM reforms and change management make a difference, at least in city administrations classified as "best performers." These questions are:

(a) Which approaches to and effects of HRM reform can be identified in cities of (supposed) "excellence"? Are there major commonalities or differences? And is there a general reform trend in Finland, Germany, and Spain from a cross-country comparative perspective?

(b) Which *organizational, personnel, and instrumental* changes affect the organizational performance of the city administration?

In summary, this chapter provides some insights into the correlation between change management and HRM reforms and their (presumed) effects. First, it highlights some ambiguities, tensions, and problems inherent within change processes. Second, it scrutinizes the scope and extent of the implementation of new HRM-related *instruments* and *organizational structures* as well as the *results* of HRM reforms on the *organizational performance* of the city administrations. The findings seek to stimulate future research by advancing hypotheses drawn from the case study results. Whether the hypotheses hold true and lead to more nomothetic knowledge is a question to be answered by subsequent research.

In the following sections, the applied conceptual framework is laid out (section "Conceptual Framework, Method and Case Selection") before a more general comparative overview of HRM reforms in Finland, Germany, and Spain is given (section "HRM Reform Profiles: Comparing Finland, Germany, and Spain"). The next section examines the change management and HRM reform process in the three case cities (section "HRM Reforms and Change Management in Three City Administrations: The Cases of Mannheim, Bilbao, and Tampere"). Concluding, we highlight crucial findings and draw some hypotheses.

CONCEPTUAL FRAMEWORK, METHOD AND CASE SELECTION

The theoretical framework draws on the *neo-institutionalist* approach (Hall and Taylor 1996; Immerguth 1998; Peters 2007). For the conceptualization of the causes and effects of HRM reforms, the analysis relies on an institutional understanding in the sense of an *actor-centered institutionalism* (Mayntz and Scharpf 1995; Ostrom 2007). It considers reforms as the attempt of administrative and political actors to change the institutional order (polity) with a non-deterministic correlation between the institution's behavior and that of the actor. Instead, they lead to different action strategies inside a restricted corridor for non-institutional factors (Benz 2004; Jann 2006), which is also the explanatory statement for our survey target group (it can be seen below as the main reason why we related key actors, since they matter significantly). As shown elsewhere (Salm and Schwab 2015), *key reform actors* have a significant influence on the success or failure of a change process.

The starting point of the case selection is the evaluation of the administrative reform process of the city of Mannheim, which could be labeled as a "best practice" benchmark for local government reform in Germany (Färber et al. 2014) and to which the authors had extensive field access. Mannheim established guidelines for leadership, communication, and cooperation in order to promote a cultural change within the city administration (Salm and Schwab 2015). In order to address HRM reform activities in a broader, European context, the sample of cities was expanded to three best practice cities within Europe: *Bilbao (Spain), Mannheim (German), and Tampere (Finland)*. These cities were nominated for (and won) the European Public Sector Award (EPSA) of the European Institute of Public Administration (EIPA) in 2009 and 2011 (Bosse et al. 2013). Although best practice approaches and especially the "awarding" procedures can be criticized (Gannon et al. 2012, p. 516), best practice or at least good practice approaches are commonly accepted and used not only in business administration but also in public administration (Rackow 2011), since they can be used at least analytically for benchmarking.

From a methodological point of view, the comparative research design is based on "similar cities with different reform concepts." Drawing on a most-similar case design (MSCD) concept, the classification of a city as a city of excellence is the most important selection criterion in terms of "similarity." Furthermore, selected cases are non-capital cities that play important economic and cultural roles in their respective nations. Overall, the three cities under comparison are "similar" in size and socio-economic conditions, yet followed "different" reform concepts; thus, they provide a fruitful basis for comparison. By applying MSCD, it is possible to analyze institutional changes triggered by the reform process and the perceived effects of these changes. Although it is not possible to totally discount the influence of other city-specific contextual factors in the outcome, the "common context" of the city cases is sufficient to account for the major possible exogenous drivers and thus justify their selection by contemporaneously controlling for other variables such as reform willingness (mayor and council majority), socio-economic conditions, and so on.

Empirically, this chapter draws on data from an online survey conducted in the three selected cities in 2015. The standardized questionnaire was addressed to the *key reform actors*. In all three cities, one key actor from each of the five following target groups responded (n = 15): (1) mayor/head of directorate; (2) municipal council/faction leader; (3) staff council/employee committee; (4) organizational development unit/change manager; (5) personnel/human resource management unit.

Since municipal administrations cannot be considered as unitary actors, one needs to differentiate between the different actor groups, because any change always affects the groups involved to differing degrees. Therefore, a *multi-perspective approach* is used, concentrating on the key actors involved in the change processes. Moreover, the use of key actors as the unit of analysis is methodologically recommended (Holtkamp 2012, p. 112), first, for research-pragmatic reasons, and second, because the knowledge of the staff involved is often limited to their fields of responsibility. To guarantee anonymity, the answers have been consolidated into a single response for each sample city. Each "consolidated city answer" has been ex post validated and accepted by the cities. While the strengths of this explorative approach (i.e. analyzing only cities of excellence) were discussed above, it is obvious that focusing only on this sample is also a weakness in terms of generalization and results overinterpretation.

Content-wise, the development of the questionnaire was derived from several sources linked to the New Public Management (NPM) movement. We assume that the reform of HRM (especially the introduction of new instruments) is strongly linked to the doctrines of New Public Management (Christensen and Laegreid 2007). The introduction of new types of civil service organizations (on the national level) and the introduction of new budgeting and accounting standards (mainly on the local level) may be cited as examples. Therefore, the survey focused on NPM-oriented reforms on the national level (Bogumil et al. 2007) and on private-sector-oriented studies that draw on the same ideological roots as NPM (Sedlack 2010). Additionally, the questionnaire draws from the self-evaluation scheme of the Common Assessment Framework (CAF), especially with respect to the "enablers" and key performance results.

The concept for the analysis applied to assess the institutional changes to, and effects of, HRM reforms is adapted from the "three-step model to evaluate institutional policies" (Kuhlmann and Wollmann 2011, p. 481). As shown in Fig. 9.1, the original model was adapted and reduced into a "two-step model": first, the institutional change in the city administrations under scrutiny, due to the change process (and triggered by endogenous and exogenous reform drivers) is captured. Second, the institutional changes are assessed against the backdrop of success and/or failure and (performance) effects.

HRM Reform Profiles: Comparing Finland, Germany, and Spain

To cast the setting of cases in a broader light and enable some cross-country comparisons, as well as the identification of (possible) countrywide trends, one has to look into the "HRM profile" of the selected countries.

The public sector is highly decentralized within all three countries, with 75 percent to 80 percent of public employees located at the local level. According to OECD (2011) data, job cutbacks on the central government level have been quite significant in the last decade (2001–11), especially in Spain. However, the picture is different at the local level (2008–11). While the share of employment of the central level went from 17 percent down to 13 percent in Germany, the share of employment on the sub-central level was rather stable, 80 percent and 79 percent respectively (the remaining percentage corresponds to the social security system). The same situation is to be found in Finland and Spain (Table 9.1).

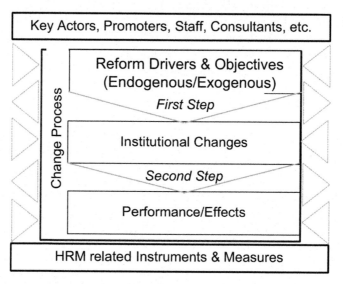

Fig. 9.1 Analytical design—change management and HRM linkages (*Source*: Authors; Kuhlmann and Wollmann (2011))

Table 9.1 Public employment across levels of government

		Germany		*Finland*	*Spain*
Employment at … central level	*2001*	17.1%	24.6%	39.9%
	2011	12.9%	22.9%	19.7%
Sub-central level	*2008*	79.8%	76.0%	79.8%
	2011	78.5%	75.4%	80.3%

Source: Authors; OECD (2011)

Various points of departure for the reform in our case countries can be identified. These can generally be classified as either external or internal factors. External factors, such as budgetary constraints, are one determinant of public administration modernization for national governments. Overall, budgetary constraints have placed additional performance pressure on most OECD countries. Spain was among the states with the "highest budgetary pressure and consolidation requirements" during the financial crisis of 2008–13 (OECD 2015). This is reflected in some of the measures implemented on the national level, such as no replacement of operating staff, recruitment freezes, salary cuts, and bonus payment cuts (OECD 2012). As Germany and Finland were among the OECD states experiencing "modest budgetary pressure and consolidation requirements," their cutbacks were less severe, focusing on staff reductions through productivity measures and rationalization of support services.

In Finland, one main driver of reform is the aging population. Finland has the fastest-aging population in the EU with the resulting well-known consequences for human resource management and public service provision. The "Finwin—Towards a New Leadership" program was established in 2006 in order to reach a common understanding and vision concerning the challenges ahead. Finwin constitutes a platform for all levels of government to disseminate and draw best practice from the changing environment.

Furthermore, international, national, and/or sectoral developments (also from the private sector) revealing outdated processes constitute another reform driver. This is mainly the case in Germany as a so-called "NPM laggard" (Eymeri-Douzans and Pierre 2010), where human resource reforms could be seen as a bottom-up movement with the national level's role more limited compared with the local level. The "translation" of the New Public Management concept into the German local government context, the so-called New Steering Model (NSM), has involved a broad NPM-driven reform process on the local level since the 1990s. Among the NSM elements are HRM-related innovations, such as recruiting management expertise, teamwork and participation, performance-related pay, and modern HRM systems (Kuhlmann et al. 2008). While the overall NSM reform process in Germany has been evaluated as a partial failure (Kuhlmann et al. 2008), this might not apply to adjunct HRM reforms. Färber et al. (2014) indicate that the NSM reforms were accompanied also by a general modernization of HRM.

Internal factors, such as political motives and legal gaps, led to modernization processes in Spain and Finland. In Spain, a major reform program for human resource management started in 2007, encompassing all levels of government. The "Basic Statute for Public Employees (EBEP)" aims at consistent practices with regard to human resource management in the public sector. Furthermore, improving the provision and quality of public services through the adoption of a performance-oriented culture constitutes a main objective (Huerta Melchor 2008).

This short overview shows that there are different primary drivers for HRM reforms in the public administrations of Finland, Germany, and Spain and that different levels of government are at the forefront of HRM reforms in each case. While comparing the effects and outcomes of HRM reforms is not possible (owing to a lack of empirical evidence), one can derive some lessons learned from these HRM reforms, especially with regard to change management. These insights can be very helpful, because successfully managing change requires supportive HRM measures and instruments (Huerta Melchor 2008; Färber et al. 2014; Kuhlmann et al. 2014).

In particular, communication (such as information and dialogue) among all types of stakeholders plays a vital role through the entire change process. A vision and derived strategies/objectives gives people a direction and a basis for communication and cooperation. Leadership is one main determinant of success: Even though top managers are not initiators of the process, they have a pivotal role within the process (that is implementing change, communication of change, motivating change, and generally setting an example to all employees). In a reform process in which all levels of government are addressed, an incremental approach towards a change increases receptiveness to it.

HRM Reforms and Change Management in Three City Administrations: The Cases of Mannheim, Bilbao, and Tampere

Institutional Setting

Change processes are generally challenging owing to the nature of the administrative policy field of reform (often referred as "polity policy" (Wollmann 2003) as well as, in part, specific regional and local contexts. These peculiarities are reflected in every single administrative change process.

Table 9.2 Reform drivers, design, and duration

	Bilbao	Mannheim	Tampere
Name of reform[a]	Political management based on economic stringency and strategic budgets	CHANGE[2]	Tampere flows
Reform driver	City strategy	City strategy, organizational changes, process optimization, citizen involvement	Process optimization, customer orientation
Reform design	Top-down	Top-down	Top-down[a]
Time frame[a]	2007–11	2008–3	2007–20

Source: Authors, online-survey, Bosse et al. (2013)[a]

While Bilbao's initial motivation for reform was to improve the city's strategic direction (that is, introduction of a vision, objectives, strategic planning, and budgeting), Tampere sought to optimize their processes and further emphasize customer orientation. Mannheim's reform drivers constituted a combination of the other two cities (Table 9.2). Personnel issues (that is training, recruitment, and so on) were not part of the reform drivers in any of the cities examined.

The various reform drivers resulted in different municipal-specific reform objectives (Table 9.3) designed to meet the municipal-specific needs: Bilbao was facing budgetary constraints and Mannheim and Tampere aimed to improve their administrative culture, while the latter also tried to focus more on customer needs. Similarities among the cities' objectives pertain to efficiency, effectiveness, and transparency. None of the cities had fiscal consolidation as a reform objective.

This is in accordance with Bosse et al. (2013, p. 11), as Bilbao and Mannheim were running a holistic reform process while Tampere was focusing on a more specific customer-oriented approach. The main objective of the cities of Bilbao and Mannheim was to implement management principles for the administration and political leadership in order to facilitate strategic planning, measure outputs and outcomes—thereby increasing transparency—and rationalize the overall decision-making process. Furthermore, they put substantial reform effort into the field of internal

Table 9.3   Reform process objectives

	Bilbao	Mannheim	Tampere
Increase organizational efficiency (processes)	✓	✓	✓
Increase political steering capacity and effectiveness	✓	✓	✓
Increase citizen orientation and transparency	✓	✓	✓
Increase market orientation and competitiveness	–	–	✓
Cost reduction	–	–	✓
Change of administrative culture (for example, improve communication, leadership behavior)	–	✓	✓
Improve service delivery/quality	–	–	✓
Fiscal consolidation	–	–	–
Budgetary consolidation	✓	–	–

Source: Authors, online survey

management and dialogue processes as well as external communication with citizens and social groups. In contrast to this holistic NPM-oriented reform process, Tampere took a customer-oriented approach focusing on strategic and organizational changes—that is, they focused on good management and on the broader customer's wellbeing, which was only indirectly part of the other cities" objectives.

Change Process Description (Questionnaire Results)

All three cities defined a timeframe for the change process (definition of start and end) (Table 9.4). Each city also formulated overall municipal strategies, visions, and/or objectives right at the beginning of reform. Two cities—Mannheim and Tampere—based their municipal strategy on a SWOT analysis. Tampere included a dialogue process already in the planning phase. In a further step, in Bilbao and Tampere the municipal strategies were broken down into operative objectives, management targets, and indicators. These two cities also set criteria to measure success. Consultants were included in the early stage of the reforms in Mannheim and Tampere.

The most important actor in the reform process was the mayor, who was classified as *"very important"* in all three cities' responses (Fig. 9.2). Thereafter, the *municipal council* was classified as *"very important,"* except in *Mannheim* were it was classified as *"fairly important."* Consultants received a *"neutral"* rating, while all *other actors* were classified as *"fairly important."*

Table 9.4 Change process measures (planning phase)

	Bilbao	Mannheim	Tampere
Development of project(s) timeframe(s)	✓	✓	✓
Formulation of overall municipal strategy, vision, or strategic objectives	✓	✓	✓
SWOT analysis	–	✓	✓
Formulation of operative objectives and/or management targets and indicators	✓	–	✓
Definition of criteria to measure success (Result/output and/or outcome measurement)	✓	–	✓
Inclusion of consultants	–	✓	✓
Determination of reform demand (for example, dialogue, participation, survey)	–	–	✓
Definition of responsibilities	–	–	✓

Source: Authors, online survey

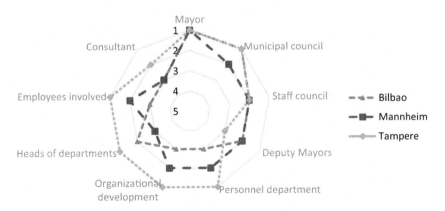

Fig. 9.2 Change process and actors/groups involved (according to importance) (*Source*: Authors, online survey. *Note*: *1* very important, *2* fairly important, *3* neutral, *4* not very important, *5* not at all important)

The *municipal council* and the *staff council* played an important role within the change process, but while HRM issues were addressed *regularly* in Mannheim and Tampere, they were only *occasionally* addressed in the municipal and staff council in Bilbao. According to the respondents, the *human resource* unit was not a crucial player in the reform process (Table 9.5).

Table 9.5   Change process and the role of HRM/personnel unit

	Bilbao	Mannheim	Tampere
Providing personnel expertise	–	✓	✓
Project manager	–	✓	–
Promoting function	–	–	✓
Provision of administrative expertise	–	–	–
Project initiator	–	–	–
Expert in change management	–	–	✓
Coaching of middle/top management	–	–	✓
Communicator/facilitator of HRM-related aspects	✓	–	✓
Personnel management was not involved	–	–	–

Source: Authors, online survey

For future reform efforts, it is of particular importance to consider the various difficulties that arose along with the change process. Noticeable within all three cities were conflicts of interest among the top management level and their insufficient involvement and commitment. Furthermore, there were interface problems among departments and agencies. However, it is remarkable that many well-known problems that usually arise in the context of change processes did not occur in the sample cities (Table 9.6). The reason may be that overall the reform processes were well run (labeled as "excellent"); another possible reason is their concrete implementation of essential reform instruments.

INSTITUTIONAL REFORM CHANGES TO HRM INSTRUMENTS

A vast number of HRM-related instruments support change processes. We split a preliminary selection of instruments that are widely considered to be the most important into three broader categories of instruments: *leadership*; *communication and cooperation*; and *performance/economic incentives*. Furthermore, we then classified the instruments with regard to their implementation time (before the change process or as part of it). This subdivision is important in order to identify if instruments were introduced because of the objectives pursued and in order to evaluate their effects (Annex Tables 9.A.1, 9.A.2, and 9.A.3).

All instruments listed under the category of *leadership* were implemented in all three cities, with the exception only of rules of conduct in Tampere (Annex Table 9.A.1). Noticeable is that the implemented reform

Table 9.6 Change process difficulties and tensions

	Bilbao	Mannheim	Tampere
Conflicts among the administrative top management	✓	✓	✓
Conflicts among the administrative top management and the municipal councilors	–	–	–
Interface problems across functional departments and/or agencies	✓	✓	✓
Lack of resources	–	–	✓
Lack of managerial skills	–	✓	–
Lack of support from top management	–	–	–
Lack of expertise within the project team(s)	–	–	–
Insufficient involvement/commitment of top and middle management	✓	✓	✓
Lack of communication	–	–	–
Inadequate conflict management	–	–	✓
Inadequate performance review	–	–	✓
Lack of motivation of involved operative staff	–	–	–
Lack of clear objective(s)	–	–	–
Increase of responsibility without salary adjustment	–	–	✓
Excessive workload/intensification of work	–	✓	–
Decreased career opportunities and gender equality (due to flattening of hierarchy/decentralization)	–	–	–
Fear of job cuts and job losses	–	–	–
Collected data/indicators are not used or applicable in day-to-day work	–	–	–
Opposition coalitions against change process (e.g., political, administrative)	–	–	✓

Source: Authors, online survey

instruments are closely linked with change objectives in the case of Bilbao and Mannheim. During the change process, Bilbao implemented relevant leadership instruments, such as a central steering unit and a change management system, in order to achieve their objectives, while Mannheim introduced the complete list of instruments. Tampere was already working with relevant leadership instruments in order to achieve their reform objectives. In addition, Mannheim introduced some additional newly invented leadership concepts, such as the mayor's dialogue—a dialogue session between randomly chosen employees and the mayor.

A more diverse picture can be identified with regard to *communication and cooperation* (Annex Table 9.A.2). Bilbao and Mannheim introduced a change management unit, (partly) taking over some original tasks of human resources (see Table 9.5). Basic instruments such as intranet, news-letter, and participation instruments (for example, staff, citizens' surveys) had been implemented before the change process. All cities introduced feedback instruments, such as summaries or improvement actions, which are necessary in order to run strategic-oriented approaches such as those taken by these cities. The concept of lifelong learning was introduced only in Tampere.

Turning to *performance and economic incentive related instruments*, we can see that Bilbao already introduced—with the exception of prizes/awards—all instruments listed before the change process (Annex Table 9.A.3). While all cities make use of performance appraisal and evalu-ation, HRM-related indicators, and contract management, only Bilbao and Tampere are "closing the management cycle" with performance-related pay. Mannheim has not implemented performance-related pay due to strong opposition by the staff council.

Finally, the instruments can be classified according to their importance (see rating Annex Tables 9.A.1, 9.A.2, and 9.A.3). Evident is a correlation between newly introduced instruments and a positive perception—especially in the case of Mannheim. Bilbao has a very positive perception of instru-ments implemented during the change process, such as central steering and a change management unit, change management system, and feedback instruments. Simultaneously, performance-related instruments, which were already implemented in Bilbao prior to the reform process, are perceived as neutral. In Tampere, all instruments are perceived as "fairly" helpful.

Impact Assessment: Change Process and HRM Instruments

The following section covers the results regarding change management and HRM instruments as perceived by the key actors. They expressed their views by choosing among the following categories: "strongly increased," "increased," "neutral," "decreased," and "strongly decreased." The answers were clustered according to perceived changes on the *instrumental, personnel,* and *organizational* level.

Assessment of Change Process

With regard to *instrumental changes*, the respondents indicated that access to and quality of training has (*strongly*) increased in relation to the stra-tegic objectives of the organization (*Bilbao*) (Fig. 9.3). Consultation and dialogue for the operative staff has also increased within all three cities.

Fig. 9.3 Change process: before-and-after comparison (*Source*: Authors, online survey. *Note*: 1 strongly increased, 2 increased, 3 about the same, 4 decreased, 5 strongly decreased)

Furthermore, the respondents said that careers and competencies are now more systematically developed.

Results on the *personnel level* are perceived as neutral with regard to the quantity of top and middle management staff in Bilbao and Mannheim. An increase in perception of the quantity of operative staff is seen in Mannheim. Tampere is the only city where both management and operative staff levels were perceived as having increased.

On the *organizational level*, the involvement of top and middle management in decision-making processes and their awareness of mission, vision, and values has increased in Mannheim and strongly increased in Bilbao and Tampere. Analogously, the ability to steer the organization (that is setting goals, allocating resources, evaluating the global performance of the organization, and HRM strategy) has (strongly) increased (Bilbao and Tampere). The respondents in Bilbao perceive a (strong) increase in the efficiency (input vs. output) of the organization in managing the available resources. Furthermore, the organizational culture has increased in

Bilbao and Mannheim, and the working atmosphere (for example, how to deal with conflicts, grievances or personnel problems, and bullying in the workplace) has increased in Bilbao and Tampere. Especially noteworthy is that transaction costs (such as costs of cooperation, coordination, and communication) have, according to the respondents, increased within all three city administrations. Overall costs of the administrative reform are classified as neutral in Bilbao and Mannheim, but have increased in Tampere.

Assessment of HRM Instruments

With regard to seven preconfigured selection possibilities for HRM-related *instruments* (Fig. 9.4), there are two instruments perceived as having a "positive" impact ("increased" or "strongly increased") that can be assigned to the category of leadership: Top management encourages/provides feedback from/to employees, and delegation of responsibilities and competencies. Less positively, the strategy to develop competencies, such as training plans based on current and future organizational and individual competency needs, was classified as neutral in Mannheim and Tampere. Clear criteria for recruitment, for remuneration, and for assigning mana-

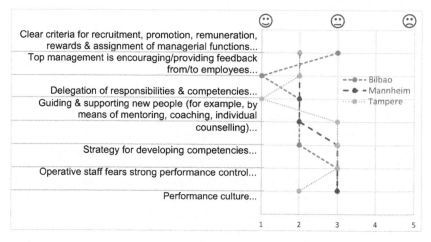

Fig. 9.4 Perceived changes in HRM-related measures—instrumental (*Source*: Authors, online survey. *Note*: *1* strongly increased, *2* increased, *3* about the same, *4* decreased, *5* strongly decreased)

gerial functions increased in Mannheim and Tampere but were neutral in Bilbao.

Staff motivation is crucial for the success of change processes, as a change process always involves *personnel* (Fig. 9.5). With regard to the motivation of top/middle management, all cities reported an increase— in Bilbao even a strong increase. On the operative level, staff motivation increased in Bilbao and Tampere, but not in Mannheim. Both the top/ middle management and the operative staff have also seen a strong increase with regard to their workload, while on the management level in Bilbao and Mannheim this has only increased. Job satisfaction on the operative level is perceived as neutral in Mannheim and Tampere and has slightly increased in Bilbao. Social considerations, such as flexible work time, paternity and maternity leave, sabbaticals, gender and cultural diversity, and employment of disabled people increased in Mannheim and Tampere.

The *organizations'* focus (Fig. 9.6) is on efficiency (relation between inputs and outputs) and effectiveness (relation between objectives and outputs) of HRM-related instruments. Generally, HRM-related costs have increased in Mannheim due to the change process, while Bilbao and Tampere kept their budget constant. The change process is seen as being neutral regarding cooperation and communication among departments in Tampere, but has increased in Mannheim and Bilbao. Effective internal and

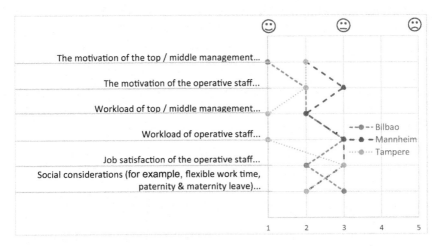

Fig. 9.5 Perceived changes in HRM-related measures—personnel (*Note: 1* strongly increased, *2* increased, *3* about the same, *4* decreased, *5* strongly decreased)

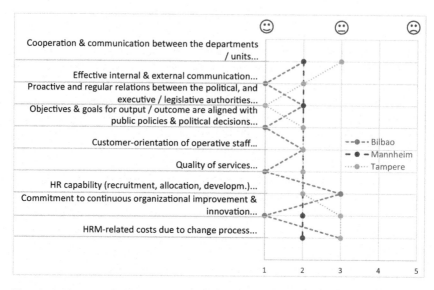

Fig. 9.6 Perceived changes in HRM-related measures—organizational (*Source*: Authors, online survey. *Note*: *1* strongly increased, *2* increased, *3* about the same, *4* decreased, *5* strongly decreased)

external communication has increased overall, and even strongly increased in Bilbao. These two preconfigured selection possibilities indicate that communication has improved in all cities, but that cooperation has not improved in Bilbao and Tampere. Relations between the different levels of hierarchy (political and executive and legislative) have strongly increased in Tampere and increased in Mannheim and Bilbao. Furthermore, HRM-related instruments and measures have had a positive impact on customer orientation and on quality of services.

Overall Assessment of HRM-Related Changes

As a final step in the analysis, we turn our attention to overall HRM related changes. This illustrates how HRM measures have had (un)supportive impacts on change management and the organization and in what way they influence success and/or failure (Fig. 9.7).

HRM related *instruments* have an impact on communication (within the administration), cooperation (with other departments and cross-

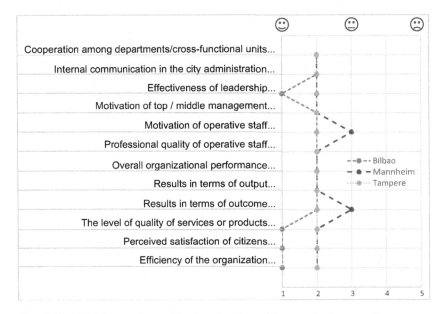

Fig. 9.7 HRM-related organizational effects (*Source*: Authors, online survey. *Note*: *1* strongly improved, *2* improved, *3* about the same, *4* worsened, *5* strongly worsened)

functional units), and leadership. The measures undertaken have had a positive impact on communication, cooperation, and leadership, with all three having improved across the three cities.

On the *personnel level* motivation is a pivotal element for success. According to the respondents, motivation has improved within the management and staff levels—with the exception of the operative staff in Mannheim. Within all three cities, the professional quality of the operative staff has increased.

The *organizational level* was positively influenced by HRM measures. Overall, the respondents testified to an increase in organizational performance. In terms of outputs (that is quantity and quality in the delivery of services and products) and outcomes (the effects of the delivered output of services and products in society as well as on the direct beneficiaries), HRM-related measures had an overall positive impact on the organization though are seen as neutral in Mannheim with regard to outcomes. The service quality (such as products delivered in relation to standards and regulations) and, accordingly, the perceived satisfaction (that is reduced processing and/or waiting times) of citizens has increased in Mannheim and Tampere and strongly increased in Bilbao. The same results are testified to regarding organizational efficiency in managing available resources (which includes HRM) in an optimal way.

CONCLUSIONS AND HYPOTHESIS

This study has thrown light on a neglected field of research: "today, the problem with HR reform is not that there are too few reforms or too little innovation. In fact, the real challenge is the lack of evidence on the effects of reforms, the neglected role of HRM as such and the ongoing importance of perceptions and clichés" (OECD 2015, p. 14). To fill this gap, the above sections examined HRM reform processes in Finland, Germany, and Spain. The, albeit limited amount of, relevant literature indicates that the main HRM reforms were initiated, broadly speaking, because of an aging population in Finland (Finwin), the introduction of NSM concepts in Germany, and the need to establish coherent HRM practices in the public service sector (EBEP) in the context also of budgetary constraints in Spain. The reform initiatives were addressed from the national level in Spain and Finland, while Germany clearly shows a bottom-up-approach, with the implementation of NPM instruments on the municipal level, while the state and central levels lagged behind.

Reviewing the cities of excellence, it is apparent that there is a link between HRM and local change processes. The change and HRM process in Bilbao and Mannheim focused on a holistic management cycle with NPM elements, while Tampere specifically addressed the improvement of customer services. More specifically, all three cities aimed to improve efficiency, effectiveness, and transparency, but each city had also further objectives: Bilbao sought budgetary consolidation, Mannheim the improvement of administrative culture, and Tampere the improvement of service delivery/quality and administrative culture.

Observing the conditional change factors, for example, macro-trends and reform drivers in the three countries, and contrasting them with the knowledge obtained from the sample cities, one can clearly state that there is a high cross-country variance, an outcome observable due to the most similar case design applied herein.

Institutional Changes

The key actors within the institutional settings are the respective mayors (mean value, 1.3), which is not surprising given that all three cities followed a (mostly) top-down driven change management approach (Fig. 9.2). The most important stakeholders that had to be addressed within this approach were the municipal council (1.3), followed by staff representatives and all employees regardless of their position (2.0). The only rather neutral position was assigned to consultants (2.6).

Financial and budgetary constraints seem to influence the degree of "centrality" (top-down) in the implementation of the change process, at least in the city sample selected. Bilbao, where the fiscal pressure was highest, had the most stringent top-down approach with a consolidation objective. It was also the city where mayoral influence was highest and employee and citizen involvement was lowest (Fig. 9.2). The middle position was taken by Mannheim; followed by Tampere (both had no explicit consolidation objective during the change process, although Mannheim has recently introduced one). Assuming that this observation is generalizable, one can state:

(H1a) the higher the external financial pressures on city administrations (fiscal and budgetary), the more likely a top-down approach will be followed (for example, avoiding deliberative and participatory elements and a citizens' orientation, less likely to involve employees and other departments, including HRM units, instead fostering mayoral influence and so on).

With regard to the institutional setting and respective competencies, it is striking that the organizational and HRM units were kept almost entirely out of the implementation process (Table 9.5). Instead, a strict top-down approach was followed. This leads to the proposal that:

(H1b) cities of "excellence" make heavy use of the available HRM measures "tool kit," but when it comes to the implementation of these measures, the administrative units in charge of the process (irrespective of phase, for example, planning or implementation) are NOT the HRM/organizational unit.

Assessment of Change Management

To run change successfully, it seems necessary that a clear timeframe and vision/objectives are set. The strengths and weaknesses (SWOT) have to be identified right at the beginning of the change process (a SWOT analysis was not conducted in Bilbao, perhaps because of the budgetary consolidation and was identified as the main "weakness" in that city's approach) (Table 9.5). Furthermore, in order to successfully manage change operative objectives and management targets (including indicators) have to be derived from the vision and criteria to measure success have to be set. Overall, this strategic approach might explain that:

(H2) conditional factors and "starting conditions" (rule of law tradition, budgetary framework conditions, administrative discourse and so on; Kuhlmann and Wollmann 2014) have a non-significant influence on the success of overall change processes—more relevant is the pursuit of a "strategic pathway to change."

Assessment of HRM Instruments

In addition to the reform path, HRM instruments (might) play an important role in successfully run change. With regard to instruments, Bilbao could be classified as the most modern public administration, as they were already working with almost the whole set of instruments prior to the reform (Annex Tables 9.A.1, 9.A.2, and 9.A.3). They thus had to implement only 10 out of 37 instruments. Finland had only to implement a customer-oriented approach, as they worked already with most of the leadership and communication instruments. Overall, they needed to implement 11 more of 37 instruments. Further, Mannheim had to newly implement 23 out of 37 proposed instruments. In this context, they could be classified as the reform laggard within the city sample.

Currently, all preconfigured instruments in the questionnaire have been implemented in all three cities, with only minor exceptions. These findings notwithstanding, all cities of excellence had a similar emphasis in their choice of reform instruments, this being an excessive use and assessment of leadership, communication and cooperation instruments, but a reluctant use and assessment of performance/economic incentive instruments. Based on this it could be proposed that:

(H3) conditional factors have an insignificant influence on the implementation of HRM instruments, indicating that there is a mix of "core" instruments that are used, leading to a "convergence of instruments."

Overall, less positively rated are all instruments with regard to performance measurement and all items pointing into a performance culture or regime (Annexes Tables 9.A.1, 9.A.2, and 9.A.3). The key actors rather "neutrally" assessed performance measurement. These findings are consistent with other studies, such as in the UK, showing that audit and performance regimes tend to be critical in the long run for several reasons (for example, data cemetery, over-steering, transaction costs and so on) (Lowndes and Pratchett 2012).

HRM measures' assessment on the organizational performance is rated overall positively (Figs. 9.4, 9.5, and 9.6). An increase in motivation at the top and middle management level is observable, whereas the operative staff reaction tends to be rather neutral or moderately positive. This is quite surprising because the workload resulting from the change process increased mainly for the top-level management and not for the operative staff. This puzzle, an increase in motivation despite an increase in the workload, can be solved if one takes the results from another study into account (Färber et al. 2014): in-depth interviews with key reform actors showed that a clear city strategy, leading to transparently defined and broadly communicated operative objectives, results in an enormous increase in intrinsic motivation, as everyday work gains "meaning" and the purpose of work becomes more comprehensible.

Further, a positive impact on the organization with regard to organizational efficiency and effectiveness can be observed. Remarkably, HRM-related costs arising from the change process are neutral—they increased only in Mannheim—while at the same time there are performance improvements for all organizational issues (efficiency, effectiveness, service quality, and customer orientation).

Summing up the findings of the assessment of HRM instruments, we can say that:

(H4) *some instruments (for example, feedback instruments) or catego-*
ries of instruments (leadership; communication and cooperation) are
better rated (with more positive effects) than others (performance and
economic incentives), regardless of when they were implemented (before
or after the change process). This indicates that time of implementation
is not crucial for successful HRM reforms. The implementation of the
"right" instruments (regardless of the point in time) not only helps to
achieve positive overall effects, but also avoids unintended negative effects
like reductions in motivation or quality due to work overload.

Overall Effects

To gain an insight into HRM-related effects, it is fruitful to contrast reform objectives (Table 9.3) and the overall impact assessment of HRM instruments (Fig. 9.7). All three cities addressed efficiency and effectiveness as reform objectives. According to the respondents, both of these aspects (even strongly) improved (in Bilbao) owing to HRM reforms. The objective of "budgetary consolidation" set in Bilbao was achieved and surpassed—Bilbao is the only large municipality in Spain that is debt-free. Moreover, Bilbao also shows the best results among the sample cities with regard to the efficiency of the organization and the effectiveness of leadership (since all other items are perceived alike in Mannheim and Tampere).

Beyond these findings, there is no correlation between additional objectives set and positive HRM-related effects on change. For example, Mannheim and Tampere aimed to enhance the administrative culture, but motivation has increased in the same way in Bilbao despite it not having specifically addressed the issue. Further, Tampere aimed to improve service delivery and quality, but Bilbao has achieved better results with regard to the quality of services even while not setting it as an objective. Of course, this discourse neglects the fact that all three cities faced different starting positions; therefore, one city might have achieved "more" in absolute or relative terms, while showing "less" improvement within this rating.

In addition to the problems accompanying change processes, such as the acceptance of innovations, long decision-making processes, inflexible hierarchies, and coordination problems between different management levels, there is one peculiarity worth mentioning: the clearly evidenced need to mainstream and establish a culture of "project management" alongside the hierarchical steering of the city administrations. Most of the new HRM and change process measures need to be carried out as a "project" throughout the whole organization. This means technical teams (whether in the ICT unit, the HRM or personnel unit, organizational and administrative reform units, or other cross-functional units) need to be empowered to carry out those tasks. A striking finding is, therefore, that all three cities of excellence established a central steering unit, which served more or less as an "internal counseling" unit with its staff acting as project managers to advance the respective projects on all levels of the organization. Therefore, one can state that:

(H5) successful change processes rely on the empowerment of technical teams as a necessary but not sufficient condition of ensuring a project management that secures the successful implementation of reform measures.

Lastly, this study has shown that it is possible to successfully transform city administrations with change concepts and supporting HRM measures even in times of crisis. However, some *critical success factors* must be taken into account: proper planning of strategy, clearly communicated and transparent (overall) objectives, formulation of mission statements appealing to staff and management, technical empowerment, fiscal responsibility, and—last but not least—a strong top-down approach with a very high level of commitment and involvement by the top management. Through combining these factors, a "continuous culture of improvement" may be achieved. This leads to the conclusion that:

(H6) ceteris paribus, even in a hostile economic climate, successful change processes and HRM reforms can be effectively conducted as long as critical success factors are taken into account.

Finally, with regard to further research, more attention has to be given to the *question of causality and the direction of effects.* In other words, causal links between proper planning, a "correct" mix of instruments, and/or the inclusion of all relevant actors as well as other conditional factors such as local law or municipal voting systems must be empirically tested in order to clearly identify what distinguishes "success" from "failure."

ANNEXES

Table 9.A.1   HRM-related instruments on leadership: implementation and importance

	Bilbao		Mannheim		Tampere		B	M	T
	Already impl.	Impl.	Already impl.	Impl.	Already impl.	Impl.			
Establishment of a central steering unit		✓	✓		✓		1	1	2
Establishment of a change management system (for example, project management, pilot projects, monitoring, reporting on the follow-up)		✓	✓		✓		1	1	2
Top-down feedback		✓	✓		✓		1	1	2
Structured personnel selection process	✓		✓		✓		2	1	2
Establishment of a personnel development, training, and education unit	✓		✓		✓		2	1	2
Introduction of competence profiles, job and function descriptions for recruiting and personnel development	✓		✓		✓		2	1	2
Norms of good leadership		✓	✓			✓	1	2	2
Upward feedback		✓	✓		✓		1	2	2
Coaching		✓	✓			✓	2	1	2
Agreed tasks/responsibilities between political and administrative level	✓		✓		✓		2	1	2
Decentralized responsibility within departments	✓		✓		✓		2	2	2
Guidelines of good behavior and/or rules of conduct	✓		✓		–		3	1	–

Source: Authors, online survey

1 very helpful, *2* fairly helpful, *3* neutral, about the same, *4* not very helpful, *5* not at all helpful

Table 9.A.2   HRM-related instruments on communication and cooperation: implementation and importance

	Bilbao		Mannheim		Tampere		B	M	T
	Already impl.	Impl.	Already impl.	Impl.	Already impl.	Impl.			
Culture of open communication and dialogue (for example, top management conferences, mayor–staff dialogue)	✓			✓	✓		1	1	2
Feedback on the quality of the management	✓			✓		✓	1	1	2
Change management unit (for example, internal consultation, staff communication)		✓		✓	–		1	1	2
Environment for gaining ideas and suggestions from employees (for example, suggestion schemes, work groups, brainstorming)	✓		✓		✓		1	2	2
Participation instruments (for example, staff/citizens' surveys)	✓		✓		✓		1	2	2
Feedback instruments (for example, summaries/interpretations/improvement actions on results)		✓		✓		✓	1	2	2
Involvement of employees and their representatives (for example, staff council) in the development of plans, strategies, goals, etc.	✓		–		✓		1	–	2
Cross-departmental workshops (for example, coordination of processes across the organization/development of cross organizational processes)		✓	✓		✓		2	–	2
Task forces across organizations/service providers to tackle problems	✓			✓		✓	2	1	2
Transparency concerning the decision-making processes (for example, by publishing annual reports)		✓	–		✓		1	–	2

(continued)

Table 9.A.2 (continued)

	Bilbao		Mannheim		Tampere		B	M	T
	Already impl.	Impl.	Already impl.	Impl.	Already impl.	Impl.			
Intranet	✓				✓		–	1	2
Newsletter, employee magazine	✓		✓		✓		–	2	2
Job rotation	✓			✓	✓		–	1	2
Team-oriented forms of organization	✓			✓	✓		–	1	2
Conflict management	✓		–		✓		–	–	2
Concepts of lifelong learning	–		–		✓		–	–	2

Source: Authors, online survey

1 very helpful, *2* fairly helpful, *3* neutral, *4* not very helpful, *5* not at all helpful

Table 9.A.3 HRM-related instruments on performance/economic incentives: implementation and importance

	Bilbao		Mannheim		Tampere		B	M	T
	Already impl.	Impl.	Already impl.	Impl.	Already impl.	Impl.			
Non-financial rewarding (for example, by supporting social, cultural and sport activities focused on people's health and wellbeing)	✓	✓	✓		✓		3	1	2
Contract management between council and mayor(s)/heads of departments	✓		✓			✓	3	1	2
Performance appraisal and evaluation	✓		✓		✓		3	1	2
HRM-related indicators and measures	✓		✓			✓	3	1	2
Contract management between top and middle management	✓		✓			✓	3	2	2
Performance-related pay for top and middle management	✓		–			✓	3	–	2
Performance-related pay for operational staff	✓		–			✓	3	–	2
Performance budgeting	✓		–			✓	3	–	2
Prizes and awards	–		–		✓	·	–	–	2

1 very helpful, *2* fairly helpful, *3* neutral, *4* not very helpful, *5* not at all helpful

REFERENCES

Benz, A. 2004. Institutionentheorie und Institutionenpolitik. In *Institutionenwandel in Regierung und Verwaltung*, ed. A. Benz, H. Siedentopf, and K.-P. Sommermann, 19–31. Berlin: Duncker & Humblot.

Bogumil, J., S. Grohs, S. Kuhlmann, and A. Ohm. 2007. *Zehn Jahre Neues Steuerungsmodell. Eine Bilanz kommunaler Verwaltungsmodernisierung*. Berlin: Edition Sigma.

Bosse, J., A. Heichlinger, E. Padovani, and J.O. Vanebo. 2013. *In search of local public management excellence: Seven journeys to success*. Maastricht: EIPA.

Christensen, T., and P. Laegreid. 2007. *Transcending new public management: The transformation of public sector reforms*. Aldershot: Ashgate.

European Commission. 2011. *Challenges, Visions, Way Forward. European Commission, Directorate General for regional Policy*. Brussels: doi:10.2776/41803.

Eymeri-Douzans, J.-M., and J. Pierre. 2010. *Administrative reforms and democratic governance*. London: Routledge.

Färber, G., M. Salm, and C. Schwab. 2014. Evaluation des Verwaltungs-modernisierungs-prozesses CHANGE[2] der Stadt Mannheim. Speyrer Forschungsbericht 276.

Gannon, J.M., L. Doherty, and A. Roper. 2012. The role of strategic groups in understanding strategic human resource management. *Personnel Review* 41(4): 513–546.

Hall, P.A., and R.C.R. Taylor. 1996. Political science and the three new institutionalisms. *Political Studies* 96(5): 936–957.

Holtkamp, L. 2012. *Verwaltungsreformen—Problemorientierte Einführung in die Verwaltungswissenschaft*. Wiesbaden: VS-Verlag.

Huerta Melchor, O. 2008. *Managing change in OECD governments: An introductory framework*, OECD working papers on public governance No. 12. Paris: OECD publishing.

Immerguth, E. 1998. The theoretical core of the new institutionalism. *Politics and Society* 26: 5–34.

Jann, W. 2006. Die skandinavische Schule der Verwaltungswissenschaft: Neo-Institutionalismus und die Renaissance der Bürokratie. In *Politik und Verwaltung*, ed. J. Bogumil, W. Jann and F. Nullmeier, 121–148. Wiesbaden: VS-Verlag.

Jordan, T., and R.P. Battaglio. 2013. Are we there yet? The state of public human resource management research. *Public Personnel Management 2014* 43(1): 25–57.

Kuhlmann, S., and H. Wollmann. 2011. The evaluation of institutional reforms at sub-national government levels: A still neglected research agenda. *Local Government Studies* 37(5): 479–494.

Kuhlmann, S., and H. Wollmann. 2014. *Introduction to comparative public administration—Administrative systems and reforms in Europe.* Cheltenham/ Northampton: Edward Elgar Publishing.

Kuhlmann, S., J. Bogumil, and S. Grohs. 2008. Evaluating administrative modernization in German local governments: Success or failure of the "new steering model"? *Public Administration Review* 68(5): 851–863.

Kuhlmann, S., S. Grohs, and J. Bogumil. 2014. Reforming public administration in multilevel systems: an evaluation of performance changes in European local governments. In *Public administration and the modern state: assessing trends and impact,* ed. E. Bohne, 205-222. Basingstoke: Palgrave Macmillan.

Lowndes, V., and L. Pratchett. 2012. Local governance under the coalition government: Austerity, localism and the 'big society'. *Local Government Studies* 38(1): 21–40.

Mayntz, R., and F.W. Scharpf. 1995. *Gesellschaftliche Selbstregelung und politische Steuerung.* Frankfurt/New York: Campus Verlag.

OECD. 2011. Government at a Glance 2011. Paris: OECD Publishing.

OECD. 2012. *Human resources management: Country profiles.* Paris: OECD Publishing.

OECD. 2015. *Impact of budgetary constraints on HR reforms* (forthcoming). Paris: OECD Publishing.

Ostrom, E. 2007. Institutional rational choice: An assessment of the institutional analysis and development framework. In *Theories of the policy process,* 2nd ed, ed. P.A. Sabatier, 21–64. Boulder: Westview Press.

Peters, G.B. 2007. *Institutional theory in political science: The new institutionalism.* London/New York: Continuum.

Rackow, M. 2011. *Personalmarketing in der öffentlichen Verwaltung: Analyse und Implikationen eines Best Practice-Ansatzes.* KWI Potsdam, Schriftenreihe für Public and Nonprofit Management, Band 5.

Salm, M., and C. Schwab. 2015, forthcoming. *Die Bedeutung von Führung, Kommunikation und Zusammenarbeit: Teilergebnisse der Evaluation des Verwaltungsmodernisierungsprozesses CHANGE² der Stadt Mannheim.* Schriftenreihe der Deutschen Sektion des Internationalen Instituts für Verwaltungswissenschaften, Band 39. Baden-Baden: Nomos.

Sedlack, B. 2010. *Change management—Veränderungsprozesse aus der Sicht des Personal managements.* Düsseldorf: Deutsche Gesellschaft für Personalführung.

Wollmann, H. 2003. Evaluation and public-sector reform in Germany: Leaps and lags. In *Evaluation in public-sector reform: Concepts and practice in international perspective,* ed. H. Wollmann, 118–139. Cheltenham: Edward Elgar.

PART III

Re-Organizing Local Service Delivery: From Government to Governance?

Provision of Public and Social Services in European Countries: From Public Sector to Marketization and Reverse—or, What Next?

Hellmut Wollmann

THE ISSUE: THE REORGANIZATION OF THE PUBLIC SECTOR IN EUROPEAN COUNTRIES—WHENCE TO WHERE?

In discussing the "external" reorganization of the public sector this chapter addresses the institutional changes which the provision of public utilities and of (personal) social services has undergone. It draws, inter alia, on the chapters in Wollmann et al. (2016, forthcoming) that were generated and authored within Working Group 1 of COST Action. For further sources relevant to the topic, see EPSU 2010; Wollmann and Marcou 2010a; Hall 2012; Bauby and Similie 2014; Wollmann 2014.

H. Wollmann (✉)
Humboldt University of Berlin, Berlin, Germany

© The Author(s) 2016
S. Kuhlmann, G. Bouckaert (eds.), *Local Public Sector Reforms in Times of Crisis*, DOI 10.1057/978-1-137-52548-2_10

Selection of Services Discussed in This Chapter

The provision of *public services* essentially encompasses water supply, sewage, waste management, public transport, and energy provision (for a detailed discussion of the concept of public services, see Marcou 2016b). In Anglo-Saxon terminology and context they are usually called "public utilities," in French *services publics industriels*, in Italian *servizi pubblici* or *servizi di pubblica utilità*, and in German *Daseinsvorsorge* ("provision of the necessaries for existence"). In European Union (EU) policy the term *services of general economic interest* (SGEI) has been introduced to signify this service sector (see European Commission 2011, p. 2 ff.; see also Bauby and Similie 2014, Marcou 2016a;).

By contrast, *personal social services* as well as *health services* relate to attending to individual social (or health) needs. In EU terminology they are labeled "social services of general interest" (SSGI) and include "health care, childcare, care for the elderly, assistance to disabled persons or social housing" (see European Commission 2011, p. 2).

While in the literature these two service sectors are mostly treated separately, the COST Working Group 1, from which this chapter originates, has made it a point to comprise both fields in order to achieve more comprehensive analyses.

The following discussion will dwell largely on the provision of energy and water (as public utilities) and on care for the elderly (as personal social service).

COUNTRY SELECTION

The sample of EU member states dealt with in this chapter comprises countries in the West–East divide between Western European (WE) countries and the (ex-communist) Central Eastern European countries (CEE countries) as well as countries in the North–South divide (between "Nordic" and "Mediterranean" countries) (see Wollmann 2016).

ANALYTICAL AND EXPLANATORY FRAMEWORK

To analyze and explain the institutional development, our discussion draws on variants of the "neo-institutionalist" debate (Peters 2011; Kuhlmann and Wollmann 2014, p. 44 ff. with references), particularly on *historical institutionalism* which highlights the impact of institutional, political, as well as cultural traditions (legacies, "path-dependencies"), on *actor-centered institutionalism* which emphasizes the influence of relevant political and economic actors, and on *discursive institutionalism* which accentuates the leverage of discourses (political, ideological, or others) and their supportive advocacy/discourse coalitions (see also Wollmann 2016).

DEVELOPMENTAL ("OVER TIME") APPROACH

In aiming at a developmental ("over time") analysis four phases are distinguished—to wit,

Development in the (late) nineteenth-century.
Advancing and advanced welfare state up to the 1970s.
The impact of NPM and EU market liberalization since the 1980s.
The most recent, "post-NPM" phase since the mid/late 1990s.

(On the concept of sequential phases see Millward 2005; Röber 2009; Wollmann and Marcou 2010b; Wollmann 2014, p. 49 ff).

GUIDING QUESTION: CONVERGENCE OR DIVERGENCE?

The guiding question is whether (and why) the institutions of public and social services delivery have shown cross-country and cross-policy convergence or divergence during the respective developmental phase.

NINETEENTH-CENTURY DEVELOPMENT

In the course of the nineteenth century, the provision of "infrastructural" public utilities (water, sewage, waste, public transport, energy) in their early basic forms was seen mainly as a responsibility of the local authorities, and was contemporarily labeled (by conservatives polemically) "municipal socialism" (see Kühl 2001). By contrast, the provision of elementary personal social services and social care was largely left to charities, philanthropic engagement, workers' organizations, self-help groups and so on.

WESTERN EUROPEAN (WE) COUNTRIES: ADVANCING AND ADVANCED WELFARE STATE

Public Utilities

In West European (WE) countries, following the rise of the advanced welfare state which climaxed in the 1970s, the public utilities were predominantly provided by the public (state as well as municipal) sector: directly ("in house," *en régie*) or through "corporatized" ("hived off") public/municipal companies ("municipally owned enterprises," MOEs; see Grossi and Reichard 2016) and organizations. The "quasi-monopoly" wielded by the public sector in service provision was meant to ensure service provision took place under the (direct or indirect) control of (elected) public authorities ("government") as the advocate of the "public interest" and "political rationality." The non-public, non-profit ("third") sector, let alone the private sector, was largely sidelined in such service provision (see Wollmann 2014).

For instance, the energy sector was "nationalized," that is, taken from ownership and operation by predominantly municipal (or private) interests and placed in the hands of the state. This took place in the UK in 1946 under the incoming (social democrat) Labour government and in "Gaullist" (conservative, nationalist, centralizing) France in 1948 by the creation of the state-owned energy giants Electricité de France (EdF) and Gaz de France (GdF).

The water sector was owned and operated by the municipalities and their companies in Germany, Italy, and Sweden, while in France the municipalities traditionally largely "outsourced" water provision (*gestion déléguée*) to private companies (see Citroni 2010; Lieberherr et al. 2016). By contrast in the UK the water sector was nationalized as well.

Personal Social Services

Under the premises of the advanced welfare state the personal social services (such as care for the elderly) were rendered primarily by the public/municipal sector personnel proper. Again the UK is exemplary: after 1945, the local authorities built up extended social-service-related structures—critically identified by some as "municipal empires" (Norton 1994). By contrast, in Germany, (path-dependently) rooted in the traditional so called "subsidiarity" principle, personal social services were provided primarily by non-public, not-for profit ("welfare") organizations (see Bönker et al. 2016).

Post-1945 Development in Central Eastern European (CEE) Countries

In CEE countries, after 1945, following the imposition of the communist rule and of its centralist "socialist" (late-Stalinist) state, public and social services were carried out by the central state or by centrally controlled local level units (for country reports on Poland, Czechoslovakia, and Hungary see Mikula 2016; Nemec and Soukopova 2016; Horvath 2016; respectively). A conspicuous exception was Yugoslavia, where a decentralized, "self-management" system with comprehensive local level public and social services was put in place (on Croatia, see Kopric et al. 2016).

WE Countries Since the 1980s: NPM-Inspired and EU-Driven (Neo-Liberal) Market Liberalization

Since the early 1980s in WE countries, the NPM-inspired and EU "neo-liberal" market-liberalization-driven reorganization of the public sector was set to dismantle the sector's dominance and its quasi-monolithic institutional fabric by (asset) privatization (that is, by transferring the public ownership and operation to private sector actors), by "corporatization" (that is, "hiving off" or "corporatizing" units that, while remaining publicly/municipally owned, are given operational, financial and other forms of quasi-autonomy) (see Grossi and Reichard 2016) and by "outsourcing" (that is, "commissioning" and "contracting out" service provision to outside, preferably private sector, providers). Hence, through institutional horizontal "decentralization" and pluralization of service providers a multitude of public/municipal, semi-public, private, "mixed" (public/private) and non-public, non-profit (NGO-type) providers and organizations emerged.

Public Utilities

In the public utilities sector in the UK, the Conservative government under Margaret Thatcher was the first and went furthest among European countries in the pursuit of the neo-liberal agenda by, inter alia, (asset) privatizing the ("nationalized") energy and water sectors (see Wollmann 2014 for further details).

Personal Social Services

In the UK during the 1980s the government under Thatcher passed legislation on competitive tendering that was directed at putting an end to the quasi-monopoly of local authorities in service provision and opening the service market for all (preferably) private sector providers (see Munday 2010; Bönker et al. 2010, p. 106 ff.; McEldowney 2016). Similarly in Germany. the federal legislation of 1994 was designed to abolish the traditional quasi monopoly of the non-public, non-profit (welfare) organizations and to open the service market to all, not least including private commercial providers (see Bönker et al. 2010, p. 111, 2016).

By and large, the UK again epitomized the neo-liberal restructuring of the public sector in public utilities as well in personal social services after it had been exemplary, after 1945, in the public sector dominance of the advanced welfare state.

CEE Countries After 1990: The Fundamental Post-Socialist Transformation of the Politico-Administrative Structures

After 1990, following the collapse of the communist regimes, the entire politico-administrative structure, including the institutions of public and social service provision, underwent a fundamental institutional transformation. It was driven not least by the adoption of the European "classical" politico-administrative model, including decentralized local government. Moreover the institutional remolding was strongly influenced by the "neo-liberal" and "NewPublicManagement"-guided modernization concepts that then ran rampant in WE countries. Finally, EU policies, not least in their market liberalization thrust, have increasingly impacted on the institutional transformation in CEE countries that from the mid 1990s onwards were preparing for accession to the EU (see Horvath 2016; Mikula 2016; Nemec and Soukopova 2016).

SINCE THE MID TO LATE 1990S: INSTITUTIONAL DEVELOPMENT IN WE AND CEE COUNTRIES

Since the mid–late 1990s the delivery of public and social services has, in WE as well as in CEE countries, experienced significant institutional changes on noticeably different trajectories the divergence of which has been contingent on various factors. Among the latter the conceptual-ideological and politico-cultural downturn of NPM dominance (in the "post-NPM" wake of the worldwide financial crisis triggered by the bankruptcy of Lehman Brothers in 2006) and the ensuing budgetary ("sovereign debt") crisis and fiscal austerity policies have loomed large.

Public Utilities

Further Pursuit and Variance of "Corporatization"
Since the mid–late 1990s the trend of "corporatizing," particularly in the form of "municipally owned enterprises" (MOEs), has gained further momentum driven by the search for more operational flexibility and efficiency typical of NPM. In a similar vein, "mixed" (public/municipal private) companies (with an increasing share of private sector, not least international, companies) and (organizational and contractual) PPPs have multiplied (see Grossi and Reichard 2016).

Since such "external" actors are, as a rule, guided by their own specific (functional, often first of all *economic*) logic and "rationality" horizontally "pluralized" and "fringed-out" ("governance" type) actor networks have taken shape and have revealed some "centrifugal" dynamics in operating largely outside the direct or indirect influence and control of the (elected) political authorities (governments) and their "political rationality" (for the government vs. governance debate, see the seminal Rhodes 1997; for the distinction and juxtaposition of "economic and political rationality," see Wollmann 2014, p. 50, 2016). However, within this general trend of "corporatization," significant variance due to country and service sector specific givens can be observed.

In Sweden where public services, "such as municipal housing, water and sewage services, energy distribution, public transport have to large extent been transformed into municipal companies ... with a new push for corporatization since 2007" (see Montin 2016), the MOEs have exhibited a "hybrid" orientation in that, on the one hand, in being exposed to the competition by private sector companies, they adopt an "entrepreneurial" and profit-seeking "economic rationality," while, on the other, in remaining embedded in the local political context of local government, they also follow a "political rationality" by also taking non-economic goals, such as social, ecological and other issues, into account (see Montin 2016; Wollmann 2014).

In Germany too the trend towards ("corporatized") municipal companies (MOEs) has seized almost all sectors (see Bönker et al. 2016; Grossi and Reichard 2016). The centrifugal dynamics and "self-interest" of their MOEs have posed a serious "steering" problem for the local authorities which they try to cope with by establishing specific administrative "steering" units.

In Italy during the 1990s the great number of the some 5,000 MOEs (*municipalizzate*) were targeted by NPM-inspired national legislation that was, for one, designed to create a countrywide net of so-called districts of "optimal territorial size" (*ambito territorio ottimale*, ATO), each comprising several municipalities. Second, water (as well as waste) was to be rendered, within each ATO, by a sole provider to be contracted by way of market competition. In its gist, the ATO legislation aimed at reducing the number of MOEs concerned and at opening the service market to private sector companies, including international ones. However, in 2011 the legislation on ATOs was repealed, leaving it to the regions to define their own systems, which resulted in a "situation now more chaotic and uncontrolled than ever" (Citroni et al. 2016).

A similar strategy to curb the process of "corporatization" of service provision has been embarked upon in Greece where, since the early 1980s, under social-democrat leadership, a multitude of MOEs were created as an instrument of expanding of local responsibilities in service provision in what was labeled "corporatized municipal socialism" (for details see Tsekos and Trantafyllopoulou 2016). Since the mid 1990s this "wild growth" of MOEs has however been trimmed by legislation adopted in 2002 under which hitherto only "companies of public benefit" can be established

In CEE countries, after 1990, as a key element of post-socialist transformation, the socialist state-based ownership and operation of public and social services was largely "municipalized," i.e. transferred to local authorities, which often established "hived-off" ("corporatized," in CEE countries termed "budgetary") organizations and enterprises. As in WE countries, this paved the way for private sector, not least international, companies to acquire shares and thus for further (at least partial) asset privatization.

"Outsourcing"

On the one hand, "outsourcing" service provision, that is, "contracting it out" to outside providers continued to be widely and even increasingly employed well into the late 1990s and beyond. This holds true particularly for CEE countries where the transfer of public functions to outside providers can be seen as a late and deferred move in institutional transformation and ("isomorphic") adaptation. On the other hand, in some countries and service sectors the "outsourcing" of public functions and services has been reversed and counteracted by steps to "re-insource" and "re-municipalize" them as the local authorities decide to take them back into their own hands (see below).

Asset (Material) Privatization

In WE countries local level asset privatization has been further advanced as private sector investors and companies have continued acquiring (in most cases minority) shares of MOEs or engaging themselves in (organizational or contractual) PPPs. For instance, in Germany and Austria shares in some 40 percent of all MOEs are held by private investors (see Grossi and Reichard 2016).

In South European countries the current budgetary ("sovereign debt") has increased the pressure to privatize public/municipal assets. For the case of Greece, see Tsekos and Triantafyllopoulou 2016; for Spain see Magre and Pano 2016).

In CEE countries the privatization of public/municipal assets is high on the political agenda as well, as the (post-socialist) institutional transformation and adaptation is still "unfinished" and since the current budgetary crisis has further fuelled this process.

Comeback of the Public/Municipal Sector

In some countries, moves towards the "remunicipalization" of public services have gained momentum. This is driven by sundry factors: disenchantment with the neo-liberal belief in the superiority of the private sector over the public sector; rising interest and resolve of local authorities to regain control over the provision of public utilities; politico-cultural value change in favor of public sector service provision and ensuing political pressure "from below" in local referendums; expiry of the concession contracts, and so on. This may be undertaken through "re-insourcing" the previously "outsourced" service provision or by purchasing back the previously sold assets.

In internationally comparative perspective the most conspicuous example of a "comeback" of the municipal sector in the provision of public utilities is the energy sector in Germany where the municipal companies (*Stadtwerke*) which had lost ground to market-dominating ("Big Four") energy companies have regained operational strength and ground (Wollmann et al. 2010; Hall 2012; Wollmann 2014; Kuhlmann and Wollmann 2014; Bönker et al. 2016). In other countries, too (even in France where the still largely state-owned energy giant EdF holds an all but monopolist market position) the municipalities and their MOEs have recently made (moderate) advances, particularly in the renewable energy field (see Alleman et al. 2016).

Similarly in the water sector, "remunicipalization" can be observed (Wollmann 2014; Bönker et al. 2016; Lieberherr et al. 2016 with references).

Hungary offers a conspicuous case of remunicipalization and "renationalization" as, under the (ultra-)conservative government lead by Viktor Orbán that came to power in 2010, the larger cities (particularly Budapest) and the national government started to purchase back assets and shares of companies that had been privatized in the course of the post-socialist transformation after 1990. The Orbán government has justified such (from an ultra-conservative position seemingly paradoxical) measures by asserting that the private companies abuse their dominant position by overcharging prices and tariffs (see Horvath 2016).

While in some countries and some service sectors such a "comeback" of the municipalities and their companies in the provision of public utilities can be empirically ascertained, the trend appears, pending further empirical evidence, still bounded. It should be pointed out that of the total number of the concession contracts which expire (for instance, in France and Germany), currently the lion's share continue to be extended with the previous private sector company, while only a minority of municipalities have availed themselves of the opportunity of "re-insourcing" and thus of "remunicipalizing" the services. For instance, in Germany this applies to just 2 percent of the expired concession contracts (see Grossi and Reichard 2016; Bönker et al. 2016). However, as regards future development it can be plausibly anticipated that changes in EU and national policies, for example, on "renewable energy policy turn-around," and the persisting politico-cultural preference for the public/municipal sector as service provider will foster further "remunicipalization" (for a cautious assessment, see Bönker et al. 2016; Bauer and Markmann 2016).

Provision of Personal Social Services and Care for Those in Need

Provision of Personal Social Services Between Local Government, Private, Non-Profit, and Societal Actors

On the one hand, the local authorities and their enterprises/companies still assert themselves in social service provision. Among WE countries, this holds true for Sweden where, reflecting the persistently strong role of local government, the lion's share (up to 80 percent) of personal social services are still rendered by the municipalities or their MOEs. However, service provision by local government units and MOEs has been guided by NPM principles, such as "purchaser–provider split" and performance management. Thus, since the early 1990s "market oriented reforms within elder care have transformed the role of local government from being the only provider towards being both purchasers and providers" (Montin 2016).

In most CEE countries, too, the public/municipal sector prevails as provider of personal social services. A reason for this public/municipal preponderance can plausibly be seen in the still persistent state-centered legacy of the socialist state whose "dismantling ... is still in a very early starting phase" (Nemec and Soukopoa 2016). Thus, in the Czech Republic and in Croatia, residential care homes for the elderly are almost entirely run by the municipalities and their staff (see Nemec and Sokoupova 2016; and Kopric et al. 2016 respectively). While in most CEE countries the share of non-for-profit (NGO type) providers is corresponding very small (possibly still pointing at their almost total elimination under the former communist regime), in Poland 25 percent of the homes for elderly and disabled persons are operated by NGOs, primarily by church-affiliated organizations which, in the exceptional case of Poland, "have a long tradition unbroken even in the communist period" (Mikula 2016).

In Germany, where the (path-dependent) quasi-monopoly of the non-public, non-profit (NGO-type) "welfare organizations" was conspicuously abolished in 1994 by "market liberalization" legislation, the composition of service providers has changed greatly. This shows particularly in the provision of residential elderly care where by 2011 the share of private sector commercial providers had jumped to 40 percent while that of municipal personnel proper dropped to almost zero—with traditional NGOs still retaining a share of 55 percent (see Bönker et al. 2016).

More recently in some countries the institutions and actors of personal social services have been impacted by the budgetary crisis and related fiscal austerity policies on sundry scores.

Social Enterprises

An institutional impulse came in 2011 from an EU policy initiative (and funding program) which hinges on the concept and goal of "combining a social purpose with entrepreneurial activity" in a kind of "hybrid" orientation and profile. It can be seen as a remarkable move by the EU to complement and also to rectify the fixation on "economic efficiency" which otherwise marks the EU's general market liberalization drive (see EC 2014a and its country reports on all EU countries). For instance, in Greece, such "social enterprises" have recently been founded "in a wide spectrum of services mostly in the social sector (child and elder care)" (Tsekos and Triantafyllopoulou 2016; EC 2014b).

Political "Top-Down" Initiatives to Get Social Actors (Re-)Involved

Some national policies are clearly aimed at turning the provision of personal social services and of help for the needy over and back to the individual and the family; in a broader sense, to the "societal" or "civil society" sphere which, all in all, amounts to returning to a "pre-welfare state" profile.

In the case of Italy the municipalities have traditionally played rather a residual role in direct delivery of personal social services, leaving much to family networks and non-profit (especially church-affiliated) organizations. "Recent policy moves set by the Italian governments had the direct effect to further residualize public social services and to force people to rely ever more heavily on private provision ... (including) the search for informal (and possibly cheap) solutions such as "grey" care by migrants" (Bönker et al. 2010, p. 114; Citroni et al. 2016).

Similarly in the UK where, under a "Big Society" shibboleth proclaimed in 2010 by David Cameron's coalition government (see McEldowney 2016; see also Buser 2013 with references), a policy and program are pursued which seem, in their neo-liberal—if not "arch" neo-liberal—essence, to be targeted at shifting the operational and financial burden back to the individual, the family, and social peers in what may plausibly be seen as a "pre-welfare state" stance.

"Bottom-Up" Initiatives to Get Societal Actors (Re-)Engaged

Mention should be made of the "comeback" of cooperatives and similar associations of citizens who, on a somewhat traditional track, organize to help themselves and/or others (for the *Genossenschaften* in Germany see Bönker et al. 2016; for the "renaissance" of cooperatives see Bauer and Markmann 2016).

Moreover, against the backdrop of the financial and socio-economic crisis and of fiscal austerity measures, societal and civic-society type groups and organizations have sprung up as voluntary groups, non-public non-governmental organizations (NGOs), largely non-profit and often acting outside "formal" structures. They have emerged as "grass roots" and "counter movements" (Warner and Clifton 2013 with references) that aim at establishing "social networks" to provide help for themselves and for others.

In Greece local voluntary groups have come to life, at first in big cities, such as the *Atenistas* in Athens, then spreading "all over the country" (Tsekos and Trantafyllopoulou 2016).

In Poland "the dynamic activity of NGOs is often seen as a crucial element of "social capital" (and) ... as the remarkable symbol of the shift from the socialist period (as) ... citizens began to organize many new social organizations that aim to support (or even replace) state institutions in solving social problems" (Mikula 2016).

In Turkey a momentous "bottom-up" self-help movement has evolved in the housing area where, vis-à-vis the failure of national housing policies, squatter-type (*gecekondu*, literally translated "overnight") groups have emerged in the mushrooming big cities. They "have become the main self-help mechanism of urban settlement," with 27 percent of the urban population, or 1.1 million people, living in such *gecekondu* quarters as of 2002 (Bayraktar and Tansug 2016).

Comeback of the "Social Community"?

In the recent ascent of societal and civil society types of actors and in the newly invoked complementary, if not primary, commitment of individuals and their families to coping with their socio-economic plight, some resurfacing and re-emergence of the nineteenth-century (pre-welfare-state) "social community" (Wollmann 2006) might be deciphered.

Pendulum Swinging Back?

Could the signs of the "comeback" of the municipal sector in the provision of public utilities and of a newly emerging and invoked engagement of the societal sphere in social services provision be interpreted, in historical perspective, as the movement of a "pendulum swinging back"?

The "pendulum" image goes back to Polanyi's seminal work on the "Great Transformation" (Polanyi 1944) in which long-term swings from state regulation to the markets and back again were hypothesized (Stewart 2010). Reiterated by Millward (2005), the pendulum image has received increasing attention in the international comparative debate on the institutional stages of provision of public and social services (Röber 2009; Wollmann and Marcou 2010b; Hall 2012; Wollmann 2014).

While the pendulum metaphor, besides being intellectually intriguing, provides a useful heuristic lens to identify possible developmental stages and "waves," two inherent limits and traps should be borne in mind. For one, the differences must not be ignored that do exist in the respective historical settings and contextualities, that is, between the current situation and the historical point of reference. Second, the image should not mislead one to assume a kind of determinism or "cyclism" in the movement of the pendulum "back and forth" (Bönker et al. 2016; Bauer and Markmann 2016).

REFERENCES

Alleman, R., M. Dreyfus, M. Magnusson, and J. McEldowney. 2016. Local governments and the energy sector—in France, Iceland and the United Kingdom. In *Public and Social Services in Europe. From Public and Municipal to Private Sector Provision* ed. H. Wollmann, I. Kopric, and G. Marcou. Palgrave Macmillan, forthcoming.

Bauby, P., and M. Similie. 2014. Europe. In *UCLG 2014, Basic services for all in an urbanizing world* (GOLD III 2014). London: Routledge p. 94–132.

Bauer, H., and F. Markmann. 2016. Local public service delivery between privatisation and publicisation: The renaissance of the cooperatives? In *Public and Social Services in Europe. From Public and Municipal to Private Sector Provision*, ed. H. Wollmann, I. Kopric, and G. Marcou. Palgrave Macmillan, forthcoming.

Bayraktar, U., and C. Tansug. 2016. Local service delivery in Turkey. In *Public and Social Services in Europe. From Public and Municipal to Private Sector Provision*, ed. H. Wollmann, I. Kopric, and G. Marcou. Palgrave Macmillan, forthcoming.

Bönker, F., M. Hill, and A. Marzanat. 2010. Towards marketization and centralization? The changing role of local government in long-term care in England, France, Germany and Italy. In *The provision of public services in Europe. Between state, local government and market*, ed. H. Wollmann and G. Marcou. Cheltenham/Northampton: Edward Elga.

Bönker, F., J. Libbe, and H. Wollmann. 2016. Re-municipalization revisited: Long-term trends in the provision of local public services in Germany. In *Public and Social Services in Europe. From Public and Municipal to Private Sector Provision*, ed. H. Wollmann, I. Kopric, and G. Marcou. Palgrave Macmillan, forthcoming.

Buser, M. 2013. Tracing the democratic narrative. Big society, localism and civil engagement. *Local Government Studies* 39(1): 3–21.

Citroni, G. 2010. Neither state nor market: Municipalities, corporations and municipal corporatization in water services: Germany, France and Italy Compared. In *The provision of public services in Europe. Between state, local government and market*, ed. H. Wollmann and G. Marcou. Cheltenham/Northampton: Edward Elgar.

Citroni, G., A. Lippi, and S. Profeti. 2016. Local public service in Italy: Still fragmentation. In *Public and Social Services in Europe. From Public and Municipal to Private Sector Provision*, ed. H. Wollmann, I. Kopric, and G. Marcou. Palgrave Macmillan, forthcoming.

European Commission (EC). 2011. *Communication from the Commission to the European Parliament, the Council, the European Economic and Social Committee and the Committee of the Regions. A quality framework for services of general interest in Europe.* Brussels: European Commission.

European Commission (EC). 2014a. *A map of social enterprises and their ecosystems in Europe.* http://ec.europa.eu/social/main.jsp?langId=en&catId=89&newsId=2149.

European Commission (EC). 2014b. *A map of social enterprises and their ecosystems in Europe*, Country Report Greece. Brussels: European Commission.

European Federation of Public Service Unions (EPSU) (ed.). 2010. *Public services in the European Union & in the 27 member states.* http://www.epsu.org/IMG/pdf/MappinReportDefEN.pdf

Grossi, G., and C. Reichard. 2016. Institutional variants of public service provision—Evidence from European Countries. In *Public and Social Services in Europe. From Public and Municipal to Private Sector Provision*, ed. H. Wollmann, I. Kopric, and G. Marcou. Palgrave Macmillan, forthcoming.

Hall, D. 2012. *Re-municipalising municipal services in Europe. A report commissioned by EPSU to public services.* London: PSIRU.

Horvath, T. 2016. From municipalization to centralism. Changes in the Hungarian local public service delivery. In *Public and Social Services in Europe. From Public and Municipal to Private Sector Provision*, ed. H. Wollmann, I. Kopric, and G. Marcou. Palgrave Macmillan, forthcoming.

Kopric, I., V. Dulabic, and A. Musa. 2016. Local government and local public services in Croatia. In *Public and Social Services in Europe. From Public and Municipal to Private Sector Provision*, ed. H. Wollmann, I. Kopric, and G. Marcou. Palgrave Macmillan, forthcoming.

Kühl, U. (ed.). 2001. *Munizipalsozialismus in Europa*. München: Oldenbourg.

Kuhlmann, S., and H. Wollmann. 2014. *Public administration and administrative reforms in Europe. An introduction in comparative public administration*. Cheltenham: Edward Elgar.

Lieberherr, E., C. Viard, and C. Herzberg. 2016. Water provision in France, Germany and Switzerland. In *Public and Social Services in Europe. From Public and Municipal to Private Sector Provision*, ed. H. Wollmann, I. Kopric, and G. Marcou. Palgrave Macmillan, forthcoming.

Magre Ferran, J., and E. Pano Puey. 2016. Spanish municipal services delivery: An uncertain scenario In *Public and Social Services in Europe. From Public and Municipal to Private Sector Provision*, ed. H. Wollmann, I. Kopric, and G. Marcou. Palgrave Macmillan, forthcoming.

Marcou, G. 2016a. The impact of EU law on local public service provision: Competition and public service In *Public and Social Services in Europe. From Public and Municipal to Private Sector Provision*, ed. H. Wollmann, I. Kopric, and G. Marcou. Palgrave Macmillan, forthcoming.

Marcou, G. 2016b. Local government public service provision in France. In *Public and Social Services in Europe. From Public and Municipal to Private Sector Provision*, ed. H. Wollmann, I. Kopric, and G. Marcou. Palgrave Macmillan, forthcoming.

McEldowney, J. 2016. Delivering public services in the United Kingdom in a period of austerity. In *Public and Social Services in Europe. From Public and Municipal to Private Sector Provision*, ed. H. Wollmann, I. Kopric, and G. Marcou. Palgrave Macmillan, forthcoming.

Mikula, L. 2016. The evolution of local public services provision in Poland. In *Public and Social Services in Europe. From Public and Municipal to Private Sector Provision*, ed. H. Wollmann, I. Kopric, and G. Marcou. Palgrave Macmillan, forthcoming.

Millward, R. 2005. *Public and private enterprise in Europe: Energy, telecommunication and transport 1830–1990*. Cambridge: Cambridge University Press.

Montin, S. 2016. Local government and the market. The case of public services and care for the elderly in Sweden. In *Public and Social Services in Europe. From Public and Municipal to Private Sector Provision*, ed. H. Wollmann, I. Kopric, and G. Marcou. Palgrave Macmillan, forthcoming.

Munday B. (2010) Privatization of social services in the United Kingdom. In Comparing Public Sector Reform in Britain and Germany, ed. H. Wollmann and E. Schröter. Ashgate: Aldershot, pp. 264-284.

Nemec, J., and J. Soukopova. 2016. Mixed system: Provision of local public services in the Czech and Slovak Republics. In *Public and Social Services in Europe. From Public and Municipal to Private Sector Provision* ed. H. Wollmann, I. Kopric, and G. Marcou. Basingstoke: Palgrave Macmillan, forthcoming.

Norton, A. 1994. *International handbook of local and regional government.* Aldershot: Edward Elgar.

Peters, G.B. 2011. *Institutional theory in political science. The 'new institutionalism'*, 3rd ed. London: Bloomsbury.

Polanyi, K. 1944. *The great transformation.* Boston: Beacon.

Rhodes, R.A.W. 1997. *Understanding governance.* New York: Open University Press.

Röber, M. 2009. Privatisierung ade? Rekommunalisierung öffentlicher Dienstleistungen im Lichte des Public Managements. *Verwaltung und Management* 15(5): 227–240.

Stewart, F. 2010. Power and progress. The swing of the pendulum. *Journal of Human Development and Capacities* 11: 371–395.

Tsekos, T., and A. Triantafyllopoulou. 2016. From municipal socialism to the sovereign debt crisis. Local services in Greece. In *Public and Social Services in Europe. From Public and Municipal to Private Sector Provision,* ed. H. Wollmann, I. Kopric, and G. Marcou. Palgrave Macmillan, forthcoming.

Warner, E., and J. Clifton. 2013. Marketisation, public services and the city: The potential for Polanyian counter movements. *Cambridge Journal of Regions, Economy and Society* 7(1): 2–17.

Wollmann, H. 2006. The fall and rise of the local community: A comparative and historical perspective. *Urban Studies* 43: 1414–1438.

Wollmann, H. 2008. *Reformen in Kommunalpolitik und -verwaltung England, Schweden, Frankreich und Deutschland im Vergleich.* Wiesbaden: Springer VS.

Wollmann, H. 2014. Public services in European countries. Between public/ municipal and private sector provision—and reverse? In *Fiscal austerity and innovation in local governance in Europe,* ed. C. Nunes and J. Bucek. Farnham: Ashgate.

Wollmann, H. 2016. Definitions, concepts, methodology. In *Public and Social Services in Europe. From Public and Municipal to Private Sector Provision,* ed. H. Wollmann, I. Kopric, and G. Marcou. Palgrave Macmillan, forthcoming.

Wollmann, H., and G. Marcou. 2010a. *The provision of public services in Europe. Between state, local government and market.* Cheltenham/Northampton: Edward Elgar.

Wollmann, H., and G. Marcou. 2010b. From public sector-based to privatized service provision. Is the pendulum swinging back again? comparative summary. In *The provision of public services in Europe. Between state, local government and market,* ed. H. Wollmann and G. Marcou. Cheltenham/Northampton: Edward Elgar.

Wollmann, H., H. Baldersheim, G. Citroni, G. Marcou, and J. McEldowney. 2010. From public service to commodity: The demunicipalization (or remunicipalization?) of energy provision in Germany, Italy, France, the UK and Norway. In *The provision of public services in Europe. Between state, local government and market*, ed. H. Wollmann and G. Marcou. Cheltenham/ Northampton: Edward Elgar.

Wollmann, H., I. Kopric, and G. Marcou (eds.). 2016. *Public and Social Services in Europe. From Public and Municipal to Private Sector Provision* Palgrave Macmillan, forthcoming.

CHAPTER 11

Municipal Waste Management in Norway and the Netherlands: From In-House Provision to Inter-Municipal Cooperation

Harald Torsteinsen and Marieke van Genugten

INTRODUCTION

In this chapter, we describe and compare the institutional development of municipal waste management in Norway and the Netherlands. Our focus is on the period from the 1970s to the present. We explore how local governments have reorganized internally and externally in this period of shifting and varying financial pressures. The guiding assumption of the book is that the organization of local public services has gone through three developmental stages: from originally being organized in-house, through the New Public Management epoch of disaggregation, autonomization and contractualization (Pollitt et al. 2004), maybe even

H. Torsteinsen (✉)
Institute of Sociology, Political Science and Community Planning, UiT The Arctic University of Norway, Campus Harstad, Norway,

M. van Genugten
Institute for Management Research, Radboud University, Nijmegen, The Netherlands

© The Author(s) 2016   205
S. Kuhlmann, G. Bouckaert (eds.), *Local Public Sector Reforms in Times of Crisis*, DOI 10.1057/978-1-137-52548-2_11

privatization, to the contemporary period of post-NPM and re-municipalization (Wollmann and Marcou 2010). The research question in this chapter relates to whether these developmental stages can be observed in the field of municipal waste management in Norway and the Netherlands. We compare these two countries because they are relatively similar in many respects but quite different in terms of crisis experience. While the term crisis may be true in the case of the Netherlands in the 1980s ("the Dutch disease") and the post-2008 period, Norway has so far managed to sail clear of the worst effects of the international regressions, thanks to its strong oil-lubricated economy (Löffler 2003, p. 479; Statistics Norway 2008). This difference in terms of crisis experience leads us to expect that reform pressures may have been stronger in the Netherlands, resulting in a reform trajectory or organizational solutions different from those of Norway. Furthermore, the local government systems of Norway and the Netherlands show significant similarities but at the same time exhibit important differences. Lidström (1996) for instance labels Norway as North European and the Netherlands as Napoleonic, while John (2001) describes both countries as belonging to the northern group, although he also recognizes the legacy of Napoleonic influences on Dutch local government. A basic characteristic of the Nordic welfare states is the dominating role of local government, primarily municipalities, in public service provision. The Napoleonic system is characterized by a strong centralized state, detailed control of local government by state prefects, and mayors appointed by national government. However, decentralization reforms have gradually reduced the differences between countries in this group and the Nordic countries (Lidström 1996), and this is certainly true at the local government level in the Netherlands. These similarities would lead us to expect a similar reform trajectory in both countries.

To address the research question and these expectations, we use a typology developed by Van Thiel (2012). This typology enables us to analyze whether the emergence of organizational forms in the three different stages has occurred in the same or in different ways in the field of waste management in both countries.

We find that the trajectory of reform in Norway and the Netherlands does not match the assumption of the three developmental stages as expected. Moreover, there are significant differences between the two countries in the way waste management is organized in these stages. In the Netherlands, the most significant NPM-related changes took place in the 1970s and 1980s, while in Norway they took place from the 1990s onwards. In relation to the last stage, we find no convincing signs of re-municipalization in either of the two countries in the field of waste management. We do however observe a strong tendency towards "inter-municipalization" in a variety of forms, in spite of differences in terms of crisis experience.

In the following sections, we first present a typology of agencies before addressing the policy field of waste management. Thereafter, we analyze the three stages of local institutional reform in this field. The chapter concludes with a comparative discussion where we try to explain why the two countries which have marked differences in crisis experience end up with a rather similar institutional response in the policy field of waste management.

CONCEPTUALIZATION

Describing and analyzing public service provision across national borders can often be a challenging task in terms of identifying comparable organizational forms and finding common labels. This is not only a problem of language but also of institutional and legal regulations and traditions. In this section, we present a theoretical framework related to agentification theory and based on a typology developed by Van Thiel (2012). The intention is to make comparison between the two countries easier, irrespective of differences in language and institutional legacy.

Agentification[1] may be defined as a process whereby local government (as principal) starts to disaggregate its service provision into more or less autonomous operative units or agencies (agents) and regulates the relationship between itself and these units by contracts or quasi-contracts (Pollitt et al. 2004). Although this perspective was originally applied for analyzing processes at the national level, we find it useful for processes at the local level as well. In Table 11.1 we use this perspective to identify the institutional forms at the local government level in Norway and the Netherlands.

Type 0 agencies are actually not agencies and not at arm's length from local government. This type comprises traditional in-house provision. Type 1 agencies are at arm's length from local government but do not have legal personality, while type 2 and 3 agencies do have legal personality. Type 2 agencies are public-law-based, while type 3 agencies are private-law-based. With regard to type 4 agencies, the local government that contracts out to a public or private organization does not have an ownership relation with that organization as is the case in type 2 and 3 agencies.

Table 11.1   Types of agencies at the local level in Norway and the Netherlands

Type	Definition	Forms at the local level
0	Unit or directory of the local government	Traditional in-house provision: decentralization rather than agentification
1	Semi-autonomous organization: unit or body without legal independence but with considerable managerial autonomy	In-house provision by "agentified" units or municipal companies (in N: *resultatenheter* and *kommunalt foretak* (KF); in NL: *gemeentebedrijven*) and forms of inter-municipal cooperation that are not legally independent[a]
2	Legally independent organization with managerial autonomy (in principle public law based)	Inter-municipal companies (in NL: *Gemeenschappelijke Regeling* (GR), in N: *interkommunalt selskap* (IKS))
3	Organization established by or on behalf of the local government such as a foundation, corporation, company or enterprise (private law based)	Limited companies (in N: aksjeselskap (AS); in NL: *overheidsvennootschappen*)
4	Tendering and contracting out to public (for example other municipalities) or private organizations	

Source: Based on Van Thiel (2012, p. 20)

[a]We discuss the different types in the two countries in the next sections

THE POLICY FIELD OF WASTE MANAGEMENT

In most Western European countries waste management is a municipal responsibility, although in some cases (Ireland, Italy, Spain, and the UK) the service is split between for instance the county/province and the municipality (John 2001, p. 36). In Norway, this responsibility is linked primarily to household waste where municipalities also have a monopoly. The Pollution and Waste Disposal (PWD) Act of 1981 instructs municipalities to "make arrangements for the collection of household waste" (§ 30), and no one may collect this type of waste without the consent of the municipality. The law has been amended several times, the last time in 2013. The Norwegian Environment Agency (*Miljødirektoratet*) has the supreme authority to oversee and regulate how the municipalities practice their obligations according to this law. It may also order municipalities to collect special waste and oblige owners/manufacturers of this type of waste and industrial waste to deliver it to a municipal waste treatment center. Over time, public regulations have gradually become stronger and more detailed, for example, requiring separate collection and treatment of different types of refuse. Fees for household waste are determined by the municipal councils and should not exceed the actual total cost of providing the service.

In the Netherlands, traditionally, household waste collection has been the concern of municipalities and was practiced initially on only a small scale. With the increase in the amount of waste, the Dutch central government thought it necessary to develop a more integrated approach to waste disposal. With the Waste Act of 1979 (integrated into the Environmental Management Act in 1994) public bodies at various government levels were given legally specified tasks and responsibilities regarding the formulation, operationalization and implementation of waste policy (De Jong and Wolsink 1997). The provinces were responsible for formulating plans on the disposal of household waste, while municipalities were responsible for the implementation of these plans (Vereniging van Nederlandse Gemeenten 1979). Dutch waste collection policy focuses on prevention and separation of waste and specific recycling circuits. Prevention is one of the main priorities of waste policy. Since 1994, municipalities have had the obligation to supply an infrastructure for separate collection of organic waste. In addition, they have to provide facilities for the separate collection of glass, paper, textiles, electronic products-and hazardous materials. Furthermore, local authorities are free to decide how citizens have to pay for waste collection, on the basis of a pricing system based on volume, frequency, bags, or weight.

INSTITUTIONAL SETUP OF MUNICIPAL WASTE MANAGEMENT

A major challenge in describing and analyzing the organizational development of waste management is the lack of research in the field (Smith 2014). At this stage, therefore, we have to resort to a combination of the general description of the organization of municipal service provision, case studies, and public statistics.

Public-Centred Delivery

Norway (Pre-1990s)

During the 20–25 year period from the mid 1960s to the mid–late 1980s, Norwegian municipalities went through several reforms intent on enabling them to harness the task of implementing ambitious national welfare policies: the amalgamation reform in 1964 and the reorganization reform in the 1980s, aligning four political subcommittees and administrative structure. Public services, especially within the dominating policy areas of education and health and social services, requiring formal professional training and authorization, were placed in the hands of public employees (type 0). As for technical services, including waste management, the situation seems to have varied more, for instance, depending on size and density of population and settlement patterns. Traditionally, there has been a more pragmatic openness to the use of private subcontractors in this field (types 0 and 4). Therefore, when the PWD Act of 1981 placed the responsibility for providing household waste collection and treatment in the hands of the municipalities, they were free to organize it as they saw fit.

The Netherlands (Pre-1980s)

In the Netherlands, waste management has long since been a task for the municipalities. In the nineteenth century and the first half of the twentieth century, local governments established municipal services to collect and dispose of household waste (type 0). Although municipalities bear the responsibility for the periodical collection of household waste from any property on their territories, already under the Waste Act of 1979 municipalities were explicitly allowed to decide whether to provide this service in-house, to contract it out to a private firm (type 4) or to organize household waste collection in cooperation with other municipalities (type 2). Local governments were even encouraged to cooperate in household waste management (VNG 1979). Furthermore, in 1950 a special law, the Joint Provisions Act, was enacted to stimulate and regulate cooperation between municipalities (Hulst 2005, p. 101).

NPM Reforms

Norway (1990s Onwards)

While the waves of neo-liberalism and NPM spread in the 1980s, first in the English-speaking countries and later in Europe and other parts of the world, Norwegian public opinion and the public sector seemed rather hesitant and even reluctant to embark on this voyage. Olsen (1996) used the metaphor of a tortoise to describe Norway's position. It was during the 1990s that the NPM ideas first started to influence public discourse and reforms in any significant way (Klausen and Ståhlberg 1998).

In 1992 the new Local Government Act was passed, opening up opportunities for municipalities to organize their administrations generally as they liked. The act marked a milestone in the development of Norwegian local government, gradually leading to less standardization and more variation in organizational forms. This new freedom seems to have opened up a window of opportunity for the introduction of NPM-inspired principles and practices. A general feature of the reforms now emerging was to separate politics and administration and to design arm's-length structures. Two reforms with special relevance for our topic illustrate this feature: the "agency" model and the municipal companies.

The first reform, the agency model, is an example of internal agentification—Van Thiel (2004) uses the term internal autonomization—whereby service-providing units, for instance waste services, are structurally more separated from the strategic apex of the municipal administration and given a higher degree of autonomy to make decisions concerning internal operational matters (economy, personnel, organization) than before. They remain, however, legally integrated parts of the municipality. Also, contract-like agreements were set up to formulate the performance obligations of the agency managers towards the municipal CEO (Torsteinsen 2012). In other words, they were transformed into type 1 "agents" in relation to the "principal," the CEO (*rådmann*).

The second reform, the creation and use of municipal companies (types 2 and 3) in public service provision, also gained momentum during the 1990s (Ringkjøb et al. 2008; Bjørnsen et al. 2015). Besides many pragmatic grounds, there was a strong belief that "companification" or "corporatization" would result in greater transparency, thereby making accountability and control easier. Further, many grounds for introducing company forms had a pragmatic character. For example, the traditional organizational setup in local government was perceived as less and less adapted to the growing scope and complexity of municipal service provision. This explanation, in addition to the fact that Norwegian municipalities are rather small, may have made municipal companies an attractive solution, especially within policy fields of low political controversy like, for instance, waste management. Service provision through municipal companies makes it easier to facilitate and formalize inter-municipal cooperation, thereby avoiding highly controversial amalgamation processes.

The private law limited company (AS) is the most prevalent form and accounts for more than 80 percent of all municipal companies (type 3), compared with 66 percent in 2003. Further public law company forms are the inter-municipal company (IKS), based on the Inter-Municipal Company Act of 1999 (type 2) and the municipal firm (KF), regulated according to an amendment of 1999 in the Local Government Act (type 1). The IKS is, like the AS, a separate legal entity with its own board of directors. However, it is not a limited-liability company like the AS; the participating municipalities are responsible for the IKS's total economic obligations on a pro-rata basis. The KF, however, does not hold a separate legal status.

Given our focus on waste management, the IKS and the AS are the most relevant and interesting forms of municipal companies. After a period of considerable reorganization, from in-house and private sector provision to provision through inter-municipal companies, the inter-municipal companies represent the most prevalent form in terms of the total political science and community plannin number of municipalities that they serve; now 334 municipalities out of a total of 428 municipalities (78 percent) cooperate in almost 60 IKS form companies; 63 organize their waste services through 17 inter-municipal AS companies, whereas 28 municipalities run this service in-house (see Table 11.2). In addition, some municipalities have exposed their waste service to competitive tendering, resulting in (often partially) out-of-municipality provision, either by public companies from other municipalities or by private companies. All in all, waste management appears to be one of the municipal services in Norway with the highest degree of variation in organizational forms (The Competition Authorities of the Nordic Countries 1998).

The Netherlands (1980s Onwards)

In comparison with Norway, in the Netherlands at the end of the 1970s the interest in contracting out and inter-municipal cooperation with regard to waste collection had already increased. One of the most important arguments for contracting out or cooperating with other municipalities was to improve the efficiency of policy implementation and to reduce costs as an answer to the need to achieve cutbacks and enhance the quality of public services (Van Thiel 2004). The expectation was that the market could perform some of the tasks more efficiently and effectively (Ter Bogt 1998).

Table 11.2 Institutional forms of waste management in Norway and the Netherlands 2013–14

Type	Institutional form	Norway		The Netherlands	
		No. of municipalities (M)	Percentage of M	No. of municipalities (M)	Percentage of M
0, 1	In-house, decentralized and agentified units	28	6.6	60	15
2	Inter-municipal companies	334	78.0	60	15
3	Limited companies	63	14.7	121	30
4	Contracting out to public[a] or private companies	3	0.7	145	36
Total		428	100.0	386	96[b]

Source: Norway, based on www.loop.no and own calculations; the Netherlands, based on Rijkswaterstaat Leefomgeving (2014)

[a]Municipal, inter-municipal, limited companies, and so on

[b]Only 96 percent of the Dutch municipalities are included here because 4 percent of the municipalities have an institutional form that does not fit into the typology

Furthermore, smaller municipalities in particular expected to gain economies of scale by contracting out or cooperating with other municipalities. Another argument for these reforms was to separate policy and administration so that politicians, policy makers and policy implementers could concentrate on their core business (Van Thiel 2004). The total number of tasks was growing rapidly, and, to prevent overload, it was held that tasks that were not genuinely public in character should not be provided by local governments.

Against this background, local governments rapidly changed the institutional form of waste collection. Consequently, a variety of institutional modes came into being. The two alternative modes that were chosen the most were contracting out to a private firm (type 4) and inter-municipal cooperation (type 2). In 1984, 249 municipalities out of a total of 750 municipalities (33 percent) contracted out waste collection to a private firm (Bokkes 1989). In the case of contracting out, activities are conducted by private organizations, but local governments are still engaged as commissioner (Ter Bogt 2003). In this mode of production, local governments put the performance of a service out to tender. Usually, the lowest bidder gets the award. Contracts differ in duration but are generally short term, for a fixed number of years (three to five) (Van Genugten 2008).

The number of inter-municipal cooperations also increased in the period from 1978 to 1982 by 112 municipalities (Bokkes 1989). In each inter-municipal cooperation, the municipalities establish a separate legal entity, with transfer of authority, in which they have both governance (that is voting rights or a representative on the board) and financial interests (De Kruijf 2011). These inter-municipal companies are mostly single-purpose organizations and are established on the basis of public law (more specifically, the Joint Provisions Act). They take the form of a public body or joint organ. The participating municipalities—*burgomaster*, aldermen or members of the local councils—are members of the supervisory board and the board of directors, and in that role have final responsibility. Furthermore, local governments enter into service level agreements in which the requirements of the tasks are stipulated. Municipalities can only withdraw from the inter-municipal company by paying a fine (Van Genugten 2008).

At the end of the 1990s a new institutional mode became popular in the Netherlands: the private-law-based limited company (type 3). After 2000, Dutch local governments increasingly chose this institutional form because they were experiencing high decision-making costs because of the multiple board levels in the public-law-based inter-municipal cooperations. They were hesitant to contract out to private firms because they did not think that the continuity and quality of service delivery could be guaranteed. With a limited company, they expected to stay in control of the company, while at the same time benefiting from the scale effects— most limited companies are owned by more than one municipality—and therefore a reduction of costs.

Like inter-municipal cooperations, limited companies are separate legal entities at arm's length from the local administration. Local governments are shareholders of the company and at the same time, as commissioners, they have a long-term contractual relationship with the limited company as their agent (Van Genugten 2008). Local governments have crucial powers by virtue of their shareholding. For example, they have powers to appoint and discharge the executive board and the supervisory board of the limited company and to influence the main lines of its strategic policy (Van Genugten 2008). Furthermore, local governments enter into service level agreements in which the requirements of the tasks are stipulated. Aspects of the production of the public service, for example quantity, quality and price, are specified in the contract. Local governments can only withdraw from the limited company by paying a fine (Van Genugten 2008). The rise in limited companies in this period is primarily at the expense of in-house municipal services, although there is a small decline in contracting out to private firms and inter-municipal cooperations too.

In 2014, one municipality in six collected waste themselves, while in a third of the municipalities waste collection was organized by a limited company, and in another third it was contracted out to a private firm (see Table 11.2). Contracting out to private companies is still chosen mainly by small municipalities, while municipal services can mainly be found in large municipalities (Rijkswaterstaat Leefomgeving 2014).

Effects of NPM Reforms in Both Countries

As to the effects of different forms of organizing waste collection and treatment in Norway and the Netherlands, only a few studies are available. In a Norwegian study, Sørensen (2007) argues that in some cases dispersed and indirect ownership, as in inter-municipal companies, leads to efficiency losses that are greater than the gains of economies of scale. User fees and costs are about 10 percent higher when waste services are provided by such companies compared with services provided by a single municipality. On the other hand, a couple of studies indicate that arm's-length-waste management stimulates entrepreneurship and innovation (Smith 2014; Andersen and Torsteinsen 2015).

In the Netherlands, studies have mainly investigated the economic effects of the different institutional forms. Based on data from 1996, Dijkgraaf and Gradus (2003) show that on average outside provision leads to 15 percent lower total costs than in-house provision. In two later studies, they show that this result is not stable over time. The cost advantage of private provision in the period 1998–2010 is much larger at the beginning than at the end, when costs for municipalities with private provision rise significantly (Dijkgraaf and Gradus 2008). Furthermore, short-term contracts (up to five years) with private providers are nearly always the most cost-saving option. However, overall the cost advantage of inter-municipal cooperation turns out be greater than private provision (Dijkgraaf and Gradus 2013). In addition, a study of the transaction costs of the different institutional forms shows that municipalities with a limited company have a higher level of transaction costs than in-house provision and municipalities that contract out to private firms (Van Genugten 2008).

Post-NPM: Has It Started?

There are few if any signs of a post-NPM development in Norwegian municipalities. However, the share of municipalities practicing the agency model has leveled off and recently decreased (Blåka et al. 2012). Also, most municipalities have started to merge some of their agencies into larger organizational entities (Olsen and Torsteinsen 2012). As for municipal companies, the growth in numbers also seems to have leveled off lately (Bjørnsen et al. 2015). At the same time, we find no convincing signs of municipalities dissolving municipal companies and moving tasks back in-house. To the contrary, there are increasing pressures from the EU to liberalize the waste market and open it up to private business, an idea that seems to be met with sympathy in the liberal-conservative government now in power. This being said, many municipalities seem to have kept at least rudimentary administrative functions in-house to oversee the statutory obligations linked to waste management. Neither do we find any signs of post-NPM development in local waste collection in the Netherlands. In 2015, after decades of institutional change, the waste market can be qualified as rather stable. In the future only incidental changes are to be expected, or else changes that will be the result of the reduction of the number of Dutch municipalities because of municipal amalgamations.

Comparison of Reform Trajectories

Comparing the institutional developments in Norway and the Netherlands, we observe that local waste management has undergone many reforms in both countries. First, the Netherlands seems to have entered the NPM age a decade before Norway. In the Netherlands we observe the enactment of many reforms in the 1980s and the rise of a large diversity of types, namely type 1, 2, and 4 agencies, while reforms were still limited in Norway at that time, with type 0 agencies as the main form and some type 4 agencies. Second, from 1990 to the present, we observe the development of type 3 agencies in the Netherlands, although other types remain popular. In comparison, there are more reforms in Norway in this period with the rise of type 1, 2 and 3 agencies. In the post-NPM stage, we observe a consolidation of a large variety of comparable institutional forms in both countries with an emphasis on inter-municipal cooperation. In Norway the inter-municipal company (type 2) is the dominating organizational form, while in the Netherlands the limited company (type 3) and contracting out (type 4) are the most prevalent forms.

In spite of the fact that the Netherlands was hit hard by the oil crisis in the 1970s and the financial crisis in 2008, while Norway was hardly hit at all, both countries have developed relatively similar organizational solutions for municipal waste, although they were introduced at different points in time. This could indicate similarities in institutional conditions (decentralized public service provision, strong local identities), isomorphic pressures (NPM-inspired agentification), and structural configurations (municipalities too small to harvest the economies of scale necessary for waste management).

Conclusion

The reform trajectory of waste management in Norway and the Netherlands does not match the three developmental stages discussed in the introduction. Moreover, there are significant differences in the reform trajectories of Norway and the Netherlands. In the Netherlands the most significant NPM-related changes (second stage) took place in the 1970s and 1980s, while in Norway these took place from the 1990s onwards. Nonetheless, increasing agentification seems to be a common feature. In relation to the last stage, we do not find any convincing signs of re-municipalization in the field of waste management. The main explanation for this is that the influence of NPM in these countries never led to the massive de-municipalization and privatization of local services—and more specifically waste management—that seem to have affected the larger European countries, for example, Germany (Dreyfus et al. 2010). Although agentification has left its mark on local government in Norway and the Netherlands, ownership has always been and is still mostly in the hands of local government. Instead of re-municipalization we observe a strong focus on inter-municipalization in a variety of forms.

NOTE

1. We prefer this term to 'agencification' in order to underline the link to agency theory and to make the approach more general.

REFERENCES

Andersen, O.J., and H. Torsteinsen. 2015. Selskapsreisen: En casestudie av fristilling som innovasjonskatalysator. In *Innovasjon i offentlig tjenesteyting*, ed. O.J. Andersen, T. Bondas, and L. Gårseth-Nesbakk. Bergen: Fagbokforlaget.

Bjørnsen, H.M., J.E. Klausen, and M. Winsvold. 2015. *Kommunale selskap og folkevalgt styring gjennom kommunalt eierskap*, Rapport 2015:1. Oslo: Norsk institutt for by- og regionforskning (NIBR).

Blåka, S., T. Tjerbo, and H. Zeiner. 2012. *Kommunal organisering 2012. Redegjørelse for Kommunal- og regionaldepartementets organisasjonsdatabase*, Rapport 2012: 12. Oslo: NIBR.

Bokkes, W. 1989. *Privatisering Belicht vanuit de Transactiekostenbenadering*. PhD thesis, Universiteit Twente, Enschede.

De Jong, P., and M. Wolsink. 1997. The structure of the Dutch waste sector and impediments for waste reduction. *Waste Management & Research* 15: 641–658.

De Kruijf, J.A.M. 2011. Controlling externally autonomised entities by Dutch local governments. *International Journal of Productivity and Performance Measurement* 60: 41–58.

Dijkgraaf, E., and R. Gradus. 2003. Cost savings of contracting out refuse collection. *Empirica* 30(2): 149–161.

Dijkgraaf, E., and R. Gradus. 2008. Institutional developments in the Dutch waste collection market. *Environment and Planning C: Government and Policy* 26(1): 110–126.

Dijkgraaf, E., and R. Gradus. 2013. Cost advantage cooperations larger than private waste collectors. *Applied Economics Letters* 20: 702–705.

Dreyfus, M., A.E. Töller, C. Iannello, and J. McEldowney. 2010. Comparative study of a local service: Waste management in France, Germany, Italy and the UK. In *The provision of public services in Europe: Between state, local government and market*, ed. H. Wollmann and G. Marcou. Cheltenham/Northampton: Edward Elgar.

Hulst, R. 2005. Regional governance in unitary states: Lessons from the Netherlands in comparative perspective. *Local Government Studies* 31(1): 99–120.

John, P. 2001. *Local governance in Western Europe*. London: Sage.

Klausen, K.K., and K. Ståhlberg. 1998. New public management. In *New public management i Norden*, ed. K.K. Klausen and K. Ståhlberg. Odense: Odense Universitetsforlag.

Lidström, A. 1996. *Kommunsystem i Europa*. Stockholm: Publica.

Löffler, E. 2003. The administrative state in Western democracies. In *Handbook of public administration*, ed. B.G. Peters and J. Pierre. London: Sage.

Olsen, J.P. 1996. Norway: Slow learner—or another triumph of the tortoise? In *Lessons from experience*, ed. J.P. Olsen and B.G. Peters. Oslo: Scandinavian University Press.

Olsen, T.H., and H. Torsteinsen. 2012. Enhetslederrollen. In *Resultatkommunen. Reformer og resultater*, ed. H. Torsteinsen. Oslo: Universitetsforlaget.

Pollitt, C., C. Talbot, J. Caulfield, and A. Smullen. 2004. *Agencies: How governments do things through semi-autonomous organizations*. Houndmills: Palgrave Macmillan.

Rijkswaterstaat Leefomgeving. 2014. *Afvalstoffenheffing 2014*. Utrecht: Rijkswaterstaat Leefomgeving.

Ringkjøb, H.-E., J. Aars, and S.I. Vabo. 2008. *Lokalt folkestyre AS. Eierskap og styringsroller i kommunale selskap*, Rapport 1/2008. Bergen: Rokkansenteret.

Smith, E. 2014. Entrepreneurship at the local government level. *Public Management Review* 16: 708–732.

Sørensen, R. 2007. Does dispersed public ownership impair efficiency? The case of refuse collection in Norway. *Public Administration* 85: 1045–1058.

Statistics Norway. 2008. *Samfunnsspeilet 2008/5-6*. http://www.ssb.no/nasjonalregnskap-og-konjunkturer/artikler-og-publikasjoner/det-svinger-i-norsk-okonomi. Accessed 19 Mar 2015.

Ter Bogt, H. 1998. *Neo-Institutionele Economie, Management Control en Verzelfstandiging van Overheidsorganisaties*. PhD thesis, Rijksuniversiteit Groningen, Groningen.

Ter Bogt, H. 2003. A transaction cost approach to the autonomization of government organizations: A political transaction cost framework confronted with six cases of autonomization in the Netherlands. *European Journal of Law and Economics* 16(2): 149–186.

The Competition Authorities of the Nordic Countries (De nordiske konkurransemyndigheter). 1998. *Konkurranseutsetting av kommunal virksomhet*, Rapport nr. 1/1998. http://www.konkurransetilsynet.no/iKnowBase/Content/395675/98_1_KONKURRANSEUTSETTING_KOMMUNAL_VIRKSOMHET.PDF. Accessed 25 June 2015.

Torsteinsen, H. 2012. Bakgrunn, diagnose og inspirasjon. In *Resultatkommunen. Reformer og resultater*, ed. H. Torsteinsen. Oslo: Universitetsforlaget.

Van Genugten, M.L. 2008. *The art of alignment. Transaction cost economics and public service delivery at the local level*. Enschede: University of Twente.

Van Thiel, S. 2004. Quangos in Dutch government. In *Unbundled government: A critical analysis of the global trend to agencies quasi-autonomous bodies and contractualization*, ed. C. Pollitt and C. Talbot. London: Routledge.

Van Thiel, S. 2012. Comparing agencies across countries. In *Government agencies: Practices and lessons from 30 countries*, ed. K. Verhoest, S. Van Thiel, G. Bouckaert, and P. Lægreid. Houndmills: Palgrave Macmillan.

Vereniging van Nederlandse Gemeenten. 1979. *Gemeente en Afvalstoffenwet. Het zich Ontdoen en het Inzamelen van Huishoudelijke en Andere Afvalstoffen.* Den Haag: Uitgeverij van de Vereniging van Nederlandse Gemeenten.

Wollmann, H., and G. Marcou (eds.). 2010. *The provision of public services in Europe: Between state, local government and market.* Cheltenham: Edward Elgar.

CHAPTER 12

On the Road Towards Marketization? A Comparative Analysis of Nonprofit Sector Involvement in Social Service Delivery at the Local Level

Lars Skov Henriksen, Steven Rathgeb Smith,
Malene Thøgersen, and Annette Zimmer

INTRODUCTION

Although, particularly at the local level, nonprofit organizations have played a central role in the development of modern welfare policies, with few exceptions (Wollmann, Chap. 10 in this volume) the topic of nonprofit social service provision has been on the margins of both local public administra-

L.S. Henriksen
Department of Sociology and Social Work, Aalborg University, Aalborg, Denmark

S.R. Smith
American Political Science Association, Washington, DC, USA

M. Thøgersen
The Danish Institute for Non-formal Education, Aarhus, Denmark

A. Zimmer (✉)
University of Münster, Münster, Germany

© The Author(s) 2016
S. Kuhlmann, G. Bouckaert (eds.), *Local Public Sector Reforms in Times of Crisis*, DOI 10.1057/978-1-137-52548-2_12

tion and welfare state research. We will take a fresh look at nonprofit social service provision by first focusing on the varieties of nonprofit–government relationships. The distinctive models identified by research into nonprofit organizations (Zimmer 2010) will facilitate the understanding of country differences in the role of nonprofit organizations in social service delivery. Second, with a special eye to a selection of countries, we will discuss changes in the welfare mix of local social service provision that are the outcome of processes of adaptation to a significantly changed local environment. The results of these case studies will be summarized in the concluding section which from a comparative perspective will highlight common developments at the local level in social service provision despite the divergence in welfare regimes and nonprofit–government relations.

DIFFERENT WORLDS OF NONPROFIT CAPITALISM

A common terminology for nonprofit organizations was developed by Salamon and Anheier (1992a, b, 1994), who define nonprofits as private organizations that are self-governing, voluntary, and not profit-distributing. Nonprofits operating in a certain limited context (country, region, city) constitute the nonprofit sector. With a focus on the national level, several typologies have been developed to help in understanding the relationships between the public, the private commercial, and the nonprofit sectors (Salamon and Anheier 1998; Najam 2000; Young 2000). Drawing heavily on historical institutionalism (see Wollmann, Chap. 10 in this volume), most typologies focus specifically on nonprofits in the social service domain (Janoski 1998; Freise and Zimmer 2004), exploring differences in the role of nonprofits in a liberal, a social democratic and a conservative welfare regime on several dimensions (Esping-Andersen 1990) (Table 12.1).

In the liberal stance, according to tradition and political culture, government is not responsible for individual wellbeing. This leaves ample space for nonprofit and for-profit social service providers and there is no preferential treatment of nonprofits that have to compete with commercial providers on competitive markets of social service provision. The strongholds of the liberal regime are the Anglo-Saxon countries, the British Commonwealth, and particularly the United States.

The social democratic regime stands out for generous public spending on welfare and a broad spectrum of social services provided by public institutions. In this situation, there is little room for nonprofit social service provision. Scandinavian countries, specifically Denmark, Sweden and Norway, represent the social democratic regime.

Table 12.1 Welfare regimes and nonprofit social service provision

	Liberal regime	*Social democratic regime*	*Conservative regime*
Government spending	Low	High	Medium or high
Position of NPOs within social policy	Competing with for-profit enterprises	Advocacy function vis-à-vis government	Privileged position/ protected against commercial competition
Major supplier of social services	Nonprofit sector on par with the market	Government	Nonprofit sector
Impact and side-effects on NPOs	Professionalization and marketization of NPOs	Marginalization of NPOs as social service providers	Development of nonprofit cartels within the field of social services

Source: Freise and Zimmer (2004)

Close cooperation between selected nonprofit social service providers, affiliated with either churches or parties, and government constitutes the hallmark of the conservative regime in which government serves a subsidiary function vis-à-vis a selected number of nonprofits. Social service provision is decentralized and nonprofit organizations enjoy a privileged position because they are protected by law against competition from for-profit as well as public social service providers. The conservative regime has been found in central Europe and particularly in Germany.

CASE STUDIES

The case studies focus on Germany, Denmark, and the UK. Each "case" serves as an illustrative example of one of the described models. Germany and Denmark come closest to the "ideal types" of conservative and social-democratic regimes while the UK constitutes a deviant case. Originally very close to the liberal regime, the UK developed in the socialist direction after 1945, but embraced neo-liberalism earlier and even more rigorously than the US.

From Subsidiarity to Marketization: Germany

Subsidiarity-Based Primacy of the Nonprofit Sector in Decline
In Germany, alongside the growth of the welfare state, the "dual system" (Sachße 1995), which is characterized by close cooperation between pub-

lic and nonprofit social service provision at the local level, was "uploaded" to the federal level of government. It was firmly established by the support of the developing welfare bureaucracy and the umbrella associations of the nonprofit social service and health care providers, the famous German Free Welfare Associations (Sachße 1995; Hammerschmidt 2005).[1] Still today, the Free Welfare Associations are the most important social service and health care providers in Germany (Boeßenecker and Vilain 2013).

Their extraordinary success story is closely linked to a very specific interpretation of the "principle of subsidiarity" that was incorporated into German social laws after the Second World War and redefined in favor of the Free Welfare Associations. Local governments had to abstain from establishing public social service facilities as long as a nonprofit organization, affiliated with the Free Welfare Associations, was able to provide the service. The subsidiarity-based primacy of nonprofit service delivery (see Wollmann, Chap. 10 in this volume) prohibited commercial competition in the social policy domain. As a result, nonprofit organizations worked more or less on par with public organizations in the areas of social service provision.

However, the "principle of subsidiarity" never resulted in homogeneous levels of public support for social service provision. In Germany, the federal government in close cooperation with the regional level (*Länder*) is responsible for policy-making, whereas the *Länder* and primarily local communities are in charge of policy implementation. Hence municipalities have to ensure that the social services are provided, but in terms of financing the situation is more complex (Scharpf 1976). In some areas the federal and regional level provides co-financing, while in some fields— for example, in the area of child care—the local level is the sole funder (Dahme and Wohlfahrt 2011). In any field of social service provision, however, the Free Welfare Associations, working more or less on par with public social service providers, had a very strong market position. Due to Germany's tradition of local self-government, the level of financial support for social service delivery is not fixed; instead it varies according to the policy field and also according to the economic strength of the local community. Despite this caveat, German nonprofit social service providers used nevertheless to operate in a beneficial and protected environment.

Starting in the 1990s, the German version of the conservative model of nonprofit–government relationship has been undergoing significant changes: First, the federal government put in place cost containment strategies in every area of social service provision. Second, the federal government modified the "principle of subsidiarity" by allowing commercial providers to operate in the areas of social and health care provision and hence become eligible for obtaining public grants and contracts (Backhaus-Maul and Olk 1994). Third, many municipalities, in particular in the north and east of Germany, when faced with severe fiscal deficits, introduced austerity measures which have had a serious impact on the local infrastructure.

One strategy to reduce the municipal deficit consists of selling the local public hospital to a for-profit health care provider. Another approach the municipalities have increasingly turned to since the 1990s aims at reducing the costs for social service provision by applying NPM techniques such as competitive tendering and contract management. As a consequence, the "dual system" of public and nonprofit social service provision has significantly declined in importance and relevance. Local nonprofit organizations are today faced with an increasingly competitive environment and are significantly challenged by for-profit providers.

Current Challenges
Today, German nonprofit organizations have to cope with increasingly "hostile" local environments in terms of funding, stricter regulations, and competition from commercial providers. The nonprofits trying to deal with these challenges have embarked on various strategies. First, large nonprofits in particular—such as hospitals or institutions for the care of the elderly— have become more businesslike (Strünck 2010). By now, the big service providers are almost universally incorporated as limited companies, but with tax-exempt status (Priller et al. 2012, p. 18). Some nonprofits have even opted in favor of becoming a "real business." Second, similar to for-profits, nonprofits in social services are trying to reduce personnel costs. This is clearly reflected in changes in the staff structure of the membership organizations of the Free Welfare Associations (Priller 2013, p. 165). Part-time jobs and even honorary positions are on a steady increase. "Flexibilization" and the introduction of so-called "mini-jobs" have in recent years developed into a major cost-cutting strategy of the Free Welfare Associations. Third, nonprofits in social service provision highly welcome government programs that substitute "voluntary labor." By now, there are several federal government programs in place that channel individuals interested in volunteering to nonprofits (Haß and Serrano-Velarde 2015). The "volunteers" are supported by a government stipend that also could be looked upon as an incentive for "cheap labor" in the sense that this labor force bypasses the normal

labor market with its legal regulations for employment and payment. Finally, the tradition of local self-government in Germany leads to further complexity. Public support of social service provision is compulsory by federal law, but the respective amount of support is not fixed and depends on the financial situation of the community.

In sum, the conservative model of nonprofit–government relationships has undergone significant changes during the last decades. However, how these changes have played out depends on both the respective policy field and the economic situation of the local government.

Persistent Public Dominance: Denmark

Local Government and the Role of Nonprofit Organizations in Social Service Delivery

Despite its large public sector, Denmark has always had a substantial contribution from nonprofit organizations in the social service areas. Though diminished in its service role after the Second World War, the nonprofit sector continued to play a role in certain niches—often in close collaboration with the public sector (Henriksen and Bundesen 2004; Goul Andersen 2008). The actual division of labor between public and private (nonprofit as well as for-profit) providers, however, differs substantially from field to field because of different legal regulations (Thøgersen 2013). Moreover, Denmark's political and administrative system is among the most decentralized in Europe. The high level of local autonomy results in large variations in the share of nonprofit providers across Danish municipalities (Thøgersen 2013).

Nonprofit Providers in the Fields of Child Care and Elderly Care

Nonprofit providers in the fields of elderly care and child care are typically regulated by contracts with local governments. Until 1976, when a new act on social assistance made the local and regional municipalities responsible for both the administration and the provision of most social services, child care was almost exclusively dominated by nonprofit institutions. After the reform, the number of nonprofit day care providers decreased significantly. Traditionally, nonprofit institutions for the elderly have also had a substantial share of the market. Their role declined sharply, however, as a result of a law passed in 1987 which made it possible for municipalities to close down homes and institutions and convert them into individual apartments which are rented by the elderly (Thøgersen 2013).

In line with an encompassing municipal reform in 2007 that reduced the number of municipalities from 275 to 98, social services became subject to closer central government regulation for two reasons. First, in an effort to contain total expenditures, owing to the fiscal crisis, municipalities became subject to a centrally controlled tax ceiling which means that they are not allowed to raise taxes beyond a certain level. Second, state monitoring increased by introducing citizens' rights, quality standards, control systems, and evaluation procedures. These measures have made the municipalities insist on closer coordination and scrutiny of services and many municipalities seek to contain costs by relying upon their own institutions. Much as in Germany, nonprofit service providers are no longer treated preferentially.

Instead, because of a number of recent legal changes, for-profit institutions and for-profit service delivery have become more accessible and presumably also preferable compared with the nonprofit form in the eyes of (local) government. Since 2005, it has been possible to establish private for-profit day care institutions. This reflects governmental efforts to expand the choice between public and private providers. In contrast to public and nonprofit institutions, private for-profit organizations can introduce user charges. Also in regard to homes and institutions for the elderly, legal changes have favored the private, for-profit form. In 2007, a new type of institution, the so-called "free care institution," was made possible with the double aim of giving users a free choice between public and private providers and giving for-profit providers access to the care market. In 2012, 7 percent of all users of elderly care services were placed in a free care institution (Thøgersen 2013). Though it is possible under these new regulations to take out profit, most of the institutions do not take advantage of this option but run the institution under the classic non-distribution constraint. In some cases, for-profit organizations have been established because municipal contracts with former nonprofit institutions were terminated.

Current Challenges

The expansion of for-profit institutions is indicative of a political orientation which equates private actors with the for-profit legal form and pays only marginal attention to the nonprofit form (Produktivitetskommissionen 2014). In some cases, strong local governments even seem to avoid nonprofit organizations because their taste for self-determination is not attractive in the current economic climate which demands strong cost-containment strategies.

This development is paradoxical for two reasons. First, many of the organizations that are set up under the new for-profit legal frameworks are actually run under the classic non-distribution constraint. Instead of profit, the new legal frameworks seem to be attractive because they provide the institutions with some of the administrative and professional flexibility that used to characterize traditional nonprofit organizations.

Second, the hostility towards the nonprofit form is advanced in a political climate which otherwise pays a lot of attention to the potentials of civil society for innovation in social services. However, this interest is directed elsewhere. First, effort has been focused on supporting and channeling volunteering for social purposes in voluntary associations but also in public institutions. In the same way as volunteers are attractive to the Free Welfare Associations in Germany because they supplement professional staff and reduce the costs of personnel, so they are in Danish municipalities. The difference is that Denmark does not have national volunteer programs but relies on local government initiatives and cooperation between local government and local organizations. Despite these efforts, the share of the population volunteering within the social or health fields remains constant (Fridberg and Henriksen 2014). Second, a great deal of interest has been directed towards so-called social enterprises and social entrepreneurs. The specific content of these terms is not clear and it is often hard to detect if and to what degree they actually differ from former nonprofit initiatives. They typically target the same problem groups (such as the long-term unemployed or people with disabilities), they are often founded on the same legal framework (typically as an association or a foundation), and they are often subsidized by public money. It is true that they sell goods and services on a market, but that is also the case for many classic nonprofit organizations. Social enterprises are few in Denmark and they are generally small in terms of employment and annual turnover (Thuesen et al. 2013). That said, their contribution is valuable for the groups that benefit in terms of employment and quality of life. Their problem, as for the volunteers, is the diminutive scale.

Regime Hybridity: The United Kingdom

Changing Nonprofit–Government Relations

Originally and in accordance with the liberal regime of nonprofit–government relations, local government and nonprofit organizations were largely responsible for social service delivery in the United Kingdom, with a relatively minor role for the national state (Lewis 1999). However, with the growth of the welfare state in the mid twentieth century, the central government assumed greater responsibility in social care and support. With the introduction of major national programs, the nonprofit sector was increasingly regarded as providing supplemental services to the state in social care (Lewis 1999). Particularly after the Second World War, government–nonprofit relationships shifted from the "liberal model" increasingly to the "social democratic model".

A major change began in the late 1980s and 1990s, however, as London started to delegate tasks downwards (Kuhlmann and Wollmann 2014, p. 144) and simultaneously embraced New Public Management (NPM). The result for nonprofits in social service delivery was twofold: intensified nonprofit–government cooperation and a shift from the longstanding system of grants and subsidies to greater reliance on competitive tendering and formal contracts (Gutch 1992; Lewis 1999).

In accordance with the overall policy of privatization, cooperation between local authorities and nonprofits providing social services proliferated during the 1990s and 2000s. Indeed, the Blair government was very supportive of community-based nonprofits, viewing them as a more responsive alternative to state agencies. Hence, at the local level, nonprofit–government cooperation changed significantly again. This time, with the introduction of "compacts" (Kendall 2003; Taylor 2005) that guaranteed nonprofit organizations providing social services preferential treatment compared with other providers, in particular for-profits, nonprofit-government cooperation moved in the direction of the conservative model.

The extension of contract-based cooperation with local authorities created new management challenges, however. The emphasis on competition and a direct relationship between government and nonprofit organizations contributed to a fragmentation of services; and many smaller nonprofits, especially those representing immigrant or ethnic communities, encountered difficulty competing for contracts with larger, more established nonprofits (Smith and Smyth 2010; Baring Foundation 2015).

Recent Developments
Since the Cameron government assumed power in 2010, the role of nonprofit social service providers has changed significantly. In a dramatic fashion, Prime Minister David Cameron announced his "Big

Society" initiative. Although this has been subject to a wide variety of interpretations, it was basically an effort by the Cameron government to involve nonprofit organizations as well as community members and volunteers more fully in addressing social problems. In practice, the Big Society has meant more contracting with nonprofit organizations, but unlike the 1990s it has also been accompanied by sometimes sharp budget cuts (Wiggins 2012; LVSC 2013a; UNISON 2014; NCIA 2015). Moreover, the Cameron government has not given preference to nonprofits in the contracting process. Instead, for-profit firms have been actively solicited for contracts and in some cases for-profits have won contracts that were previously the sole responsibility of nonprofits (Aiken 2010; Baring Foundation 2015). Overall, the current procurement system has tended to reward large for-profits and larger nonprofits, with many small locally-based nonprofit organizations at a distinct disadvantage. Many of these have lost significant funding (LVSC 2013b; NCIA 2015).

Spending cuts are spurring significant interest in innovation in local nonprofits especially regarding co-production, which generally refers to the joint production of public services by professional staff in government and/or nonprofits and users and community members (Bovaird 2007, 2014). Part of the motivation for this interest is an effort to shift the cost of service delivery to community members. This type of co-production is also evident in government support for the "personalization of care," which has meant shifting more control over service decisions to the users of services. Indeed, the UK government has just released a report calling for greater use of personal budgets and legal rights for the disabled (Department of Health 2015). One other key development in social services in the UK is the broad enthusiasm for social investment including hybrid nonprofit/for-profit models (Travis 2010; Social Finance 2010, 2014; Goldman Sachs 2015).

This investment approach fits with many trends evident in the UK affecting social services: the drive for greater accountability and performance assessment; the engagement of the private sector in the funding and delivery of social services; greater competition for scarce public and private funds; and support for social innovation and social enterprise. These trends are also apparent in the creation in the UK of Community Interest Companies (CICs) which are regular for-profit companies with a requirement that they need to fulfill a "community purpose."

COMMON TRENDS

Overall, the comparison of social services reveals surprising commonalities despite the wide divergence in institutional histories. The advent of a formal system of social services was rooted in a private culture of local welfare in all of the countries (Sachße 1995). Typically, these early nonprofit organizations were dependent upon individual philanthropy including wealthy donors to support their services to the poor and disadvantaged.

The growth of the welfare state in the twentieth century, though, brought significant divergence in the trajectories of the respective countries pertaining to social services. Germany integrated the system of local nonprofit service providers into an important part of the government's social safety net support. Thus, the nonprofit organizations received extensive public subsidies, greatly reducing the role of philanthropy in nonprofit revenues, while at the same time granting the nonprofits substantial autonomy under the policy of subsidiarity. Denmark followed a classic Scandinavian, social democratic trajectory: gradual assumption by the state of previously nonprofit social service providers with local government becoming the key direct provider of services. As a result, the role of nonprofit social services withered significantly even as the diversity and comprehensiveness of social services increased. The UK presents something of a hybrid trajectory: the original model of social service delivery was a liberal one with ample space for nonprofit or voluntary organizations; then direct government provision at the local level increased greatly, especially after the Second World War, and hence assigned a more supplementary role to locally active nonprofit social service providers.

In recent years, common trends and developments have again been apparent, to varying degrees, in all of these countries: increasing competition among social service providers including the growing presence of for-profit firms in service categories previously dominated by either government or the nonprofit sector; a widespread interest in social enterprise and mixed nonprofit/for-profit models of service delivery; and new models of user and citizen engagement in service delivery, including more co-production and personalization of care. Yet, social services in each country remain profoundly influenced by the institutional development of the local environment and the relationship between local government and the nonprofit sector. In Germany and Denmark, countries with a strong tradition of local self-government, "the continental fused system" of politics and policy results in a heterogeneous development that differs from municipality to municipality owing to disparities as regards the fiscal situation of the respective community, different legal regulations within different service fields, and the local tradition of nonprofit sector involvement in social service delivery. In contrast, in the UK with its vertical separationist system, the government in London enjoys comparatively much more leeway to foster, increase, or reduce cooperation with nonprofit social service providers.

Hence, doubtless there are strong tendencies of convergence as regards the provision of social services at the local level demonstrating the powerful effect of the diffusion of ideas across countries, but at the same time path dependency is still strongly in place as regards the ways local governments and authorities are changing and further developing the modes of cooperation with nonprofit social service providers.

Acknowledgements The authors would to like to recognize the excellent research and editorial assistance of Meghan McConaughey in the preparation of this chapter.

NOTE

1. There are six associations: the German Caritas Association (Caritas/Catholic), the Welfare Services of the Protestant Church in Germany (Diakonie/Diaconia/Protestant), the Worker's Welfare Service (AWO/Social Democrat), the Association of Non-Affiliated Charities (Parity), the German Red Cross (Red Cross), and the Central Welfare Agency of Jews in Germany.

REFERENCES

Aiken, M. 2010. Taking the long view: Conceptualizing the challenges facing UK third sector organizations in the social and welfare field. In *Third sector organizations facing turbulent environments*, ed. A. Evers and A. Zimmer. Nomos: Baden-Baden.

Backhaus-Maul, H., and T. Olk. 1994. Von Subsidiarität zu „outcontracting": Zum Wandel der Beziehungen zwischen Staat und Wohlfahrtsverbänden in der Sozialpolitik. In *Staat und Verbände*, ed. W. Streeck. Wiesbaden: Westdeutscher Verlag.

Baring Foundation. 2015. *The independent mission: The voluntary sector in 2015.* London: The Baring Foundation. http://www.baringfoundation.org.uk/wp-content/uploads/2015/02/IP-Mission.pdf. Accessed 20 Apr 2015.

Boeßenecker, K., and M. Vilain. 2013. *Spitzenverbände der Freien Wohlfahrtspflege*. Weinheim: Beltz-Verlag.

Bovaird, T. 2007. Beyond engagement and participation: User and community coproduction of public services. *Public Administration Review* 67(5): 846–860.

Bovaird, T. 2014. http://gov.wales/docs/caecd/research/2014/141218-community-democratic-governance-evidence-synthesis-advice-en.pdf. Accessed 20 Apr 2015.

Dahme, H.J., and J. Wohlfahrt (eds.). 2011. *Handbuch Kommunale Sozialpolitik*. Wiesbaden: VS Verlag.

Department of Health. 2015. *No voice unheard, no right ignored—a consultation for people with learning disabilities, autism and mental health conditions*. http://www.parliament.uk/business/publications/written-questions-answers-statements/written-statement/Commons/2015-03-06/HCWS355. Accessed 20 Apr 2015.

Esping-Andersen, G. 1990. *The three worlds of welfare capitalism*. Princeton: Princeton University Press.

Freise, M., and A. Zimmer. 2004. Der Dritte Sektor im wohlfahrtsstaatlichen Arrangement der post-sozialistischen Visegrád-Staaten. In *Wohlfahrtsstaatliche Politik in jungen Demokratien*, ed. A. Croissant, G. Erdmann, and F.W. Rüb. Wiesbaden: VS-Verlag.

Fridberg, T., and L.S. Henriksen. 2014. *Udviklingen i frivilligt arbejde 2004–2012*. Copenhagen: SFI, Rapport 14:09.

Goldman Sachs. 2015. *What is a social impact bond?* New York: Goldman Sachs. http://www.goldmansachs.com/our-thinking/trends-in-our-business/social-impact-bonds.html?cid=PS_02_47_07_00_00_00_01. Accessed 20 Apr 2015.

Goul Andersen, J. 2008. *Welfare state transformations in an affluent Scandinavian state: The case of Denmark*, Welfare state transformations: Comparative perspectives. Basingstoke: Palgrave Macmillan.

Gutch, R. 1992. *Contracting lessons from the US*. London: NCVO Publications.

Hammerschmidt, P. 2005. *Wohlfahrtsverbände in der Nachkriegszeit. Reorganisation und Finanzierung der Spitzenverbände der freien Wohlfahrtspflege 1945 bis 1961*. Weinheim/Munich: Juventa.

Haß, R., and K. Serrano-Velarde. 2015. When doing good becomes a state affair: Voluntary service in Germany. *VOLUNTAS: International Journal of Voluntary and Nonprofit Organizations* 26(5). doi:10.1007/s11266-015-9577-z.

Henriksen, L.S., and P. Bundesen. 2004. The moving frontier in Denmark: Voluntary–state relationships since 1850. *Journal of Social Policy* 33(4): 605–625.

Janoski, T. 1998. *Citizenship and civil society*. Cambridge: Cambridge University Press.

Kendall, J. 2003. *The voluntary sector*. London: Routledge.

Kuhlmann, S., and H. Wollmann. 2014. *Introduction to comparative public administration. Administrative systems and reforms in Europe.* Cheltenham: Edgar Elgar.

Lewis, J. 1999. Reviewing the relationship between the voluntary sector and the state in Britain in the 1990s. *VOLUNTAS: International Journal of Voluntary and Nonprofit Organizations* 10(3): 255–270.

LVSC (London Voluntary Service Council). 2013a. *The big squeeze 2013: A fragile state.* London. http://www.lvsc.org.uk/media/132319/bigsqueeze-final-smaller.pdf. Accessed 20 Apr 2015.

LVSC (London Voluntary Service Council). 2013b. *London voluntary and community sector (VCS) funding cuts (a working document).* London. http://www.lvsc.org.uk/research-policy/big-squeeze/london-vcs-cuts-reports.aspx. Accessed 20 Apr 2015.

Najam, A. 2000. The four-C's of third sector-government relations: Cooperation, confrontation, complementary, and co-optation. *Nonprofit Management and Leadership* 10(4): 375–396.

NCIA (National Coalition for Independent Action). 2015. *Fight or fright: Voluntary services in 2015: A summary and discussion of the inquiry findings.* London. http://www.independentaction.net/wp-content/uploads/2015/02/NCIA-Inquiry-summary-report-final.pdf. Accessed 20 Apr 2015.

Priller, E. 2013. Scope, structure, and development of civil society in Germany. In *Civil societies compared: Germany and the Netherlands,* ed. A. Zimmer. Nomos: Baden-Baden.

Priller, E., M. Alscher, P.J. Droß, F. Paul, C.J. Poldrack, C. Schmeißer, et al. 2012. *Dritte Sektor Organisationen heute: Eigene Ansprüche und ökonomische Herausforderungen.* Berlin: WZB-Arbeitsbericht.

Produktivitetskommissionen. 2014. *Offentlig-privat samspil.* Copenhagen: Analyserapport 6.

Sachße, C. 1995. Verein, Verband und Wohlfahrtsstaat. Entstehung und Entwicklung der dualen Wohlfahrtspflege. In *Von der Wertgemeinschaft zum Dienstleistungsunternehmen,* ed. T. Rauschenbach et al. Frankfurt: Suhrkamp Taschenbuch.

Salamon, L.M., and H.K. Anheier. 1992a. In search of the nonprofit sector. I: The question of definitions. *VOLUNTAS: International Journal of Voluntary and Nonprofit Organizations* 3(2): 125–151.

Salamon, L.M., and H.K. Anheier. 1992b. In search of the nonprofit sector. II: The question of definitions. *VOLUNTAS: International Journal of Voluntary and Nonprofit Organizations* 3(3): 267–309.

Salamon, L.M., and H.K. Anheier. 1994. *The emerging sector revisited. A summary.* Baltimore: The Johns Hopkins University Institute for Policy Studies.

Salamon, L.M., and H.K. Anheier. 1998. Social origins of civil society: Explaining the nonprofit sector cross-nationally. *VOLUNTAS: International Journal of Voluntary and Nonprofit Organizations* 9(3): 213–248.

Scharpf, F. 1976. *Politikverflechtung. Theorie und Empirie des kooperativen Föderalismus in der Bundesrepublik.* Kronberg/Ts: Scriptor Verlag.

Smith, S.R., and J. Smyth. 2010. The governance of contracting relationships: "Killing the golden goose": A third-sector perspective. In *The new public governance? Emerging perspectives on the theory and practice of public governance*, ed. S.P. Osborne. London: Routledge.

Social Finance. 2010. *A new tool for scaling social impact: How social impact bonds can mobilize private capital for the common good.* http://www.socialfinanceus. org/sites/socialfinanceus.org/files/small.SocialFinanceWPSingleFINAL_0. pdf. Accessed 20 Apr 2015.

Social Finance. 2014. *Peterborough social impact bond reduces re-offending by 8.4%; investors on course for repayment in 2016.* http://www.rockefellerfoundation. org/uploads/files/a5de37d9-f46d-40b8-859c-2dcbdbc6098f-peterborough. pdf. Accessed 20 Apr 2015.

Strünck, C. 2010. Contested solidarity? Emerging markets or social services in Germany and the changing role of nonprofit organizations. In *Third sector organizations facing turbulent environments*, ed. A. Evers and A. Zimmer. Nomos: Baden-Baden.

Taylor, M. 2005. Der Dritte Sektor und der Dritte Weg. Erfahrungen aus Großbritannien. In *Arbeiten im Dritten Sektor. Europäische Perspektiven*, ed. S. Kottlenga, B. Nägle, N. Pagels, and B. Ross. Mössingen-Thalheim: Thalheimer Verlag.

Thøgersen, M. 2013. *Selvejende institutioner i Danmark. Institutionernes udvikling, udbredelse og karakter på udvalgte samfundsområder.* Arbejdsnotat 01. Netværk for forskning i Civilsamfund og Frivillighed.

Thuesen, F., H.B. Bach, K. Albæk, S. Jensen, N.L. Hansen, and K. Weibel. 2013. *Socialøkonomiske virksomheder i Danmark. Når udsatte bliver ansatte.* Copenhagen: SFI, rapport 13:23.

Travis, A. 2010. Will social impact bonds solve society's most intractable problems? *The Guardian*, October 6. http://www.theguardian.com/society/2010/oct/06/social-impact-bonds-intractable-societal-problems. Accessed 20 Apr 2015.

UNISON. 2014. *Community and voluntary services in the age of austerity.* London: UNISON. https://www.unison.org.uk/upload/sharepoint/On%20line%20 Catalogue/21929.pdf. Accessed 20 Apr 2015.

Wiggins, K. 2012. *Spending cuts are "knocking out" sector's capacity to support big society, NCVO head says.* London: Third Sector. http://www.thirdsector.co. uk/spending-cuts-knocking-out-sectors-capacity-support-big-society-ncvo-head-says/infrastructure/article/1120432. Accessed 20 Apr 2015.

Young, D.R. 2000. Alternative models of government-nonprofit sector relations: Theoretical and international perspectives. *Nonprofit and Voluntary Sector Quarterly* 29(1): 149–172.

Zimmer, A. 2010. Third sector-government partnerships. In *Third sector research*, ed. R. Taylor. New York: Springer.

CHAPTER 13

The Governance of Childcare in Transition: A Comparative Analysis

Nikos Hlepas, Pekka Kettunen, Dagmar Kutsar,
Muiris MacCarthaigh, Carmen Navarro, Philipp Richter,
and Filipe Teles

N. Hlepas (✉)
National and Capodistrian University of Athens, Athens, Greece

P. Kettunen
Abo Akademi University, Jyväskylä, Finland

D. Kutsar
University of Tartu, Tartu, Estonia

M. MacCarthaigh
Queen's University Belfast, Belfast, UK

C. Navarro
University Autónoma of Madrid, Madrid, Spain

P. Richter
University of Potsdam, Potsdam, Germany

F. Teles
University of Aveiro, Aveiro, Portugal

© The Author(s) 2016   237
S. Kuhlmann, G. Bouckaert (eds.), *Local Public Sector Reforms in Times of Crisis*, DOI 10.1057/978-1-137-52548-2_13

INTRODUCTION

Local governments are important providers of childcare service but the features of this provision vary considerably across Europe. Furthermore, local government roles are changing owing to public budget reductions arising from the current economic crisis, while demands to increase the working population strengthen claims for daycare services. This chapter explores change in childcare governance since the beginning of this century and comparatively discusses its consequences for the different local government systems across Europe.

Increased demands arising from changes in demographics, labor markets, and social values have turned childcare services into a particularly dynamic, future-oriented field of the welfare state, the third (non-profit, social) sector, and the market. The correlation between existing intergovernmental infrastructure and welfare state development has been highlighted and systematized by Sellers and Lidström (2007, p. 610). They emphasize the close relationship between decentralization to local government and the strength of the welfare state, based on the examples of universal, egalitarian, and public systems of social provision known as social democratic welfare states.

Andreotti et al. (2012) agree that many local government systems have gained power as actors in planning, financing, and implementing social policies in the past two decades, and conclude that welfare systems should be viewed as a mix of central and local policies. However, Kokx and Van Kempen (2010) argue that, besides downscaling from central government to regional and local tiers, there has also been up-scaling to supranational agents, that is, to the EU and the International Monetary Fund. Kröger (2011) describes changes in social service provision resulting in "yo-yo effects" of vertical governance patterns between up-scaling and down-scaling of the central political power, and turns attention to the most recent up-scaling tendencies·in Finland. This phenomenon can also be observed in Spain (Navarro and Velasco 2015) and other Southern European countries owing to the fiscal crisis (Teles 2014).

Kuronen and Caillaud (2015) present a classification of 11 European countries (and respective cities) regarding childcare service policies, vertical governance structures, and legal frameworks. A first group includes countries with national legal regulations providing rights to publicly organized or subsidized childcare services, which place a large degree of responsibility on local authorities to organize them (Denmark, Finland,

France, and, with some reservations, Estonia). The second group consists of countries with national legal regulations for public childcare services and municipal responsibility in service provision, but they are more limited or divided between the state and local authorities. An important factor is the age of the child, as service provision for children over three years of age is more extensive and rights to services are legally binding (Italy, Germany, Hungary, and Spain). Third, there are some countries where both national and local public responsibility to organize childcare services is either limited or even non-existent, or where it has been left to local (and/or regional) authorities to create their own policies and provide services (Czech Republic, England, Ireland). There may still be some legal regulation and inspection of the existing services (Kuronen and Caillaud 2015). This typology is close to comparative European local government classifications which distinguish between Nordic municipalities with many tasks and municipalities in the south of Europe which have fewer tasks (Lidström 2003; Kuhlmann and Wollmann 2014).

In respect of the institutionalization of childcare, reforms in several European countries have included both vertical redistribution of competences among the jurisdictions and levels (up-scaling, down-scaling) as well as horizontal re-allocation of responsibilities among different actors (public, private, non-profit sector, inter-municipal cooperation) (trans-scaling). Across Europe, there is a common increased demand for formalized childcare services, as well as the explicit, goal-oriented ("Barcelona targets") European policy for the development of childcare (European Commission 2013; Eurofund 2014). A central question arising is whether the field of childcare has, as seen in other aspects of welfare state provision, also been a field of converging tendencies promoted through European policies, many of which are threatened by the financial crisis and retrenchment measures.

In this chapter, the seven selected country cases (Estonia, Finland, Germany, Greece, Ireland, Portugal, and Spain) represent distinctive local government and state models (Loughlin et al. 2011, p. 11) as well as welfare state traditions (Esping-Andersen 1990; Ferrera 1996) and family policy types (Eurofund 2014). The choice is primarily based on the fact that in relation to childcare governance structures, most of them have been assigned to different groups (Kuronen and Caillaud 2015). These countries offer, therefore, a wide range of possibilities for comparison. Second, they represent geographically different parts (north, south, east, and west) of Europe and different local government systems with strong "welfare municipalities" in the north and weak, and mostly "residual" municipalities in the south.

Based on secondary literature and existing research in this field, we will analyze and compare changes in childcare governance within a common framework, explaining how local governments" responsibility for this social service has evolved, the extent to which this evolution has affected the role of local government in the countries under consideration, and the extent to which we find converging and diverging trends.

Conceptual Framework

According to institutionalist theory, institutional change can mainly be defined by influential actors ("actor-centered" institutionalism), dominant discourses shaping the "mind frames" (discursive institutionalism), or strong legacies (historical institutionalism). The latter seems to offer a useful framework not only for understanding change but also for understanding inertia and setbacks. Historical institutionalism offers a set of concepts such as "path dependence," "critical junctures," and "increasing returns" that illuminate the temporal dimension of change and inertia. Remaining on the same path is usually a low-risk and low-cost option ("increasing returns"). On the contrary, changing paths normally brings higher risks and costs, and that is why path dependence occurs (Pierson 2004). Administrative reforms and policy changes are more likely at "critical junctures" or when "windows of opportunity" emerge.

Looking back at the development of childcare during the last two decades, it seems that in several European countries the economic growth of the nineties in correlation with ongoing decentralization policies and societal change (for example, labor relations, social values, and demography) offered such "windows of opportunity." In Southern Europe particularly, decentralization reforms were combined with an emerging new welfare role for municipalities, sometimes activating effectively nonexistent policy fields, such as public childcare. The effects of such functional reforms can be classified as "political decentralization" (devolution, when tasks and decision powers are assigned), "administrative decentralization" (when tasks are transferred to local governments) and "administrative de-concentration" (when tasks are delegated to state or semi-state entities) (Kuhlmann and Wollmann 2014). On occasion, recentralizing tendencies can also be observed.

Sellers and Lidström's (2007) correlation of decentralization with welfare patterns leads to the assumption that territorial allocation of childcare tasks and responsibilities can, on the one hand, affect the nature of local government ("welfare municipality"), while on the other hand it is closely related to prevailing perceptions of childcare policy. An emerging question is why and how far childcare service policies, corresponding governance structures, and legal frameworks have changed in the seven different countries under investigation during the past two decades, and how they have been affected by the crisis. Hall's (1993) sociological institutionalist approach is useful here, because it distinguishes between simple changes, which are incremental in nature, and radical transformation (or paradigm shift), which involves changes of the framework of ideas and standards that "specifies not only the goals of policy and the kind of instruments that can be used to attain them, but also the very nature of the problems they are meant to be addressing" (Hall 1993, p. 279). The concept of a paradigm shift is a good starting point in our discussion of re- and trans-scaling of organized childcare. According to the historical institutionalist approach, the authority over a specific policy is of particular importance. During a paradigm shift, changes occur "in the locus of authority over policy," which means that the ownership of the policy and eventually the corresponding role of local government will change (Hall 1993, p. 280).

LOCAL GOVERNANCE AND CHILD DAYCARE IN COMPARISON

The following country cases highlight the institutional evolution of local governance of child daycare in the seven countries in focus. Our emphasis is placed on the interplay between national, regional, and local levels of government, and the dynamics of change characterizing this evolution. The case descriptions focus on two major questions: first, to what extent child daycare has been a public service and, second, how the role of local government has evolved.

Estonia

Much as in the Eastern bloc (for example, Eastern Germany), extensive but low-quality centrally governed public childcare infrastructures had been developed in Estonia during the Soviet occupation in order to facilitate workforce recruitment. After Estonia regained independent statehood in 1991 there was strong political pressure against institutional legacies (Kutsar et al. 1998). As the whole society required reconstruction, childcare policies were left in a political vacuum until the institutional shift towards down-scaling of central power took place with the Local Government Administration Act introduced in 1993. The Act obliged local governments to organize childcare within their respective territories. The services did not materialize, however. In 2014 the organization of childcare services in Estonia gained priority in national political discussions affected by the launch of a new Operational Program for Cohesion Policy Funds 2014–20, according to which it is planned to improve the availability and variety of childcare services. The Pre-School Child Care Institutions Act was amended in 2014.

Finland

In Finland local governments have been responsible for child daycare since 1972. Local governments have had a relatively free hand in arranging the service, though there are regulations defining such issues as the competence of employees, and in the late 1990s child daycare became a subjective right of families. The coverage of organized public childcare is, however, not particularly high, as many parents take the opportunity to stay home with their child and this option is supported by public means. The economic viability of the municipalities varies and hence cuts in local government services are common. The economic crisis, reflected in the budgetary cuts at the national level and through diminishing tax incomes also at the local level, will put further pressure on child daycare, which represents a universal service to all citizens. Rights once granted are difficult to pull back, however, and hence local governments are likely to use their innovativeness in finding other ways to cut the costs.

Germany

The tradition of conservative welfare regime in combination with a highly decentralized political system resulted in a situation in Germany whereby "the federal government has had no part to play and the role of the Länder has been confined historically to the setting of basic regulatory frameworks." (Evers 2005, p. 198). Owing to the reframing of the childcare policy in a demographic and economic context and the fact that the childcare rate for the under-threes was very low in Germany and far away from achieving the Barcelona objectives, the federal government, the *Länder* governments, and representatives of the local level agreed in 2007 to establish 750,000 new childcare places for the under-threes until 2013. The new commitment of the federal level for improving provisions for the under-threes marked "a move away from Germany's firmly decentralized approach towards more multi-level responsibility" (Evers 2005, p. 199). This is mainly expressed by the fact that the federal level provides financial funds to establish new childcare places. In contrast with 2004, a legal right to childcare places for the under-threes was also introduced and came into effect in 2013. The federal level provides an additional €4 billion to the *Länder*, which are obliged to transfer the funds to the local authorities as well as to non-profit organizations providing childcare places. What becomes obvious is that the increasing demand for childcare places in Germany has resulted in a partial centralization of the financing structure for daycare places, but not of the normative or delivery structures, which are still the responsibility of the local and *Länder* level.

Greece

In Greece a mix of public and private entities offers organized childcare. Up to the late nineties a sparse network of state units was unable to meet the rapidly growing demand, leaving space for profit-oriented businesses. In 1997, European funding offered a window of opportunity and the Ministry of Welfare opted to transfer childcare units to the municipalities, thus decentralizing responsibility for a socially sensitive task. Local authorities proved their responsiveness and managed to increase the range of childcare services significantly (60 percent increase in units, more than 100 percent increase in children served) from 1997 to 2013, causing considerable decommodification and defamilization of this service. In fact, municipal childcare threatened to collapse in 2012 because of the unprecedented drop in state grants (down 60 percent in five years) that was a result of rigid austerity policies following the crisis, and the respective bail-out agreements. Municipal childcare was temporarily sustained in 2013 and 2014 through additional EU funds mobilized by the central government. It is obvious, however, that this is not a sustainable solution. At the same time, centrally imposed fiscal constraints leave no discretion even to municipalities that could find their own way of cross-financing their childcare services. A successful case of decentralization is therefore existentially threatened by "locally blind" top-down policies of austerity and fiscal centralization.

Ireland

Traditionally, childcare services in Ireland have been mainly provided by the private sector, with little by way of state subsidies for this service. What regulation exists has been decided at central rather than local levels. After 2000, however, a combination of EU targets (the "Barcelona goals") combined with demands to support female labor force participation saw the creation of approximately 65,000 partially state-funded childcare places. These new childcare services were coordinated (though with no requirement to ensure access) and supported (but not funded) at the local level in Ireland through a network of city and county "childcare committees," each operating within a local authority territory and with local authority members on their governing boards. Thus the immediate effect of the push to provide more childcare facilities was one of partial down-scaling of childcare service coordination to the subnational level. A recent development in the provision of childcare services was the creation of a new Child and Family Agency ('Tusla"), which further centralized the inspection system. Local childcare committees retain mainly informational and advisory roles only, as well as child protection and training which are accredited centrally by the new national agency. Thus there has not been any significant scaling or further down-scaling of responsibility to subnational level since the initial creation of the local childcare committees in 2001.

Portugal

In Portugal, the childcare system is comprised of public and private (as well as cooperative and nonprofit) institutions that form a national network to provide a universal pre-school education, overseen by the national government. The centralized structure of the welfare regime and restricted public budgets are, however, impeding factors. Owing to economic growth and European funding, notable progress in early childhood education has been achieved. In 1996, the coverage rate for children of up to three years was 12.65 percent (Vasconcelos et al. 2002). By 2015 the coverage rate had surpassed 38 percent (between three years and the mandatory school age it is slightly above 78 percent). The main source of finance for education in Portugal is central government, which also ensures institutional coordination. The recognition of the critical importance of education policies at the local level has urged the government to initiate conversations with local authorities in order to extend and prepare a significant transfer of competencies to municipalities in this field. This is still under discussion given the negative feedback, both from the Portuguese National Association of Municipalities and from parents' and teachers' organizations. Although using different arguments against this process, financial constraints or simply mistrust towards changes, these reactions disclose Portuguese political culture and the perceived function of local governments. Though this drive towards decentralization appears to be on the move, the next step in this process is also threatened by austerity and post-bailout centralized control measures.

Spain

Our final case, Spain, is a latecomer in developing public childcare services, though dramatic changes in both outcomes and re-scaling of these services have taken place over the last two decades. Soon after their establishment in the early 1980s, the regional governments confronted overcrowded agendas that included the expansion of the welfare state. They neglected "infant education" (as childcare is called in Spain, where it is integrated in the education system), although it was part of their policy responsibility, and focused on more urgent needs such as compulsory education and pre-school years (3–6 years). Taking advantage of a flexible general competence clause, local governments took a distinctive approach and started building the childcare network, compelled by new demands arising from the increase of women in the labor force in a context of transition from a traditional "male breadwinner" model to a dual earner type of family organization. Local authorities were able to respond to citizens' demands owing to their favorable financial situation. Later on, the Autonomous Communities, being aware of the strong social demand for wider public coverage, took two complementary paths. First, they created their own "infant schools" networks; and second, they stimulated the creation of new nurseries in municipalities by transferring subsidies to town halls (Navarro and Velasco 2015). The outbreak of the financial crisis in Spain led to a retrenchment of municipal work. In 2013, the national parliament passed the Rationalization and Sustainability of Local Administration Act, which determined that municipalities would not continue developing activities beyond a list of basic services that increases with population size, including childcare services, unless they fulfill some exigent criteria. Spain thus represents a case of successful decentralization to local authorities in a first stage, overlapping of responsibilities between local and regional entities later on, and a limitation of local action imposed by the central government triggered by the financial crisis.

Change Evaluation and Dynamics: A Discussion

The above country cases reveal that the local governance of child daycare has been in flux. First, EU incentives as well as domestic changes, followed by the economic crisis, have all put the childcare governance system in motion. This becomes obvious when comparing the corresponding two columns in the following table 13.1, presenting the situation in 2000 and 2015. What we see is that there are major differences in how this particular public good, child daycare, is governed across Europe. For the first, the question is to what extent it is a public good, and second, what kind of governance structure there is. Our particular emphasis here was on the role of the local governments.

Local governments are important providers of organized child daycare across Europe and the growth of this service (percentage of coverage) is particularly spectacular in Ireland and Southern Europe. This does not seem to lead, however, to the emergence of "welfare municipalities" (replacing the traditional "residual municipalities") in the South of our continent. Traditional typologies are still valid and suggest that Southern European local governments are strongly dependent on decisions made and resources provided by upper levels of governance. In Germany and Ireland, the services are more heterogeneous, reflecting the way public services are provided in these two countries (Wollmann 2014). In Estonia and Finland, private services exist reflecting the purchasing power of well-to-do families, but the principal actor is local government.

Second, the provision for care of children under three years has obviously increased, even though the Barcelona targets (90 percent coverage for children over three years and 33 percent for younger children) have not been met everywhere (see Table 13.1).

We find growth in daycare services in all of the countries, except Finland and Estonia, which already entitled all families to obtain a daycare place in the late 1990s. In Germany, for example, due to a paradigm shift, there was an impressive increase in public childcare services, with the number of

Table 13.1   Coverage of child daycare in 2000 and 2014 and responsible public authority in 2014

	Coverage of under 3 2000–15		Coverage of over 3 2000–15		Provision	Regulation	Financing
Estonia	no data	34	79	88	Local	Central/local	Mixed
Finland	31	35	55	63	Local	Central	Mixed
Germany	8,5	20	90	92	Local	Regional	Mixed
Greece	2	8	15	69	Local	Central	State/EU
Ireland	15	24	no data	90	Local	Central	State
Portugal	31	38	72	79	Local/ regional	Central	Mixed
Spain	8,9	39	95	95	Local/ regional	Central/regional	Mixed

Sources: Eurofund, National Statistical data, elaborated by the authors

Notes: Germany 2002, Ireland 2003

children under three years in organized daycare doubling between 2006 and 2012. We witness rapid increase in the coverage in Portugal, Spain, and Greece. In other states, namely Estonia and Ireland, it is more a question of recent commitment to growth, the results of which remain to be seen. The growth of childcare promotes the role of local and regional authorities for welfare policies and care services, even though in most cases it does not mean devolution but simply administrative decentralization (Kuhlmann and Wollmann 2014).

Thirdly, the dynamics of the growth differ significantly. Activation has been facilitated by domestic resources in times of economic growth (Spain), and larger and stronger municipalities (Greece), while in Portugal local governments have not been involved in a similar manner. EU resources and policies (Barcelona targets) have played a crucial role too, promoting changes in policy ownership. Local government activity in organized childcare promoted decommodification of this service while it also influenced stratification in affected societies (Fenger 2007). However, these dynamics proved to be vulnerable to restraints imposed by the financial crisis and austerity policies from above triggering recentralization and/or trans-scaling tendencies. Thus, they reflect the Napoleonic model of local government, which is weak.

In Germany, the situation has varied between east and west. The main change agent has been the federal state, which does not usually engage in welfare policy. This reflects the high political profile of child daycare services and also changes in policy ownership. Ireland bears witness to an emerging commitment to break the traditionally low coverage of child daycare and adopt new policy goals (paradigm shift). Estonia is broadening the opportunities for parents to choose between different types of childcare facilities; the number of children in formal childcare is increasing unequally across local areas, however. A "yo-yo effect" of down- and up-scaling central powers and trans-scaling of service provision influenced both by institutional shifts and EU policies is shaping this process. Finally, in Finland, the change is more a rhetorical than concrete one, but if finally completed and realized · it will radically break the universal commitment of welfare services.

Child daycare does not belong to the core competency areas of the European Union, but it has affected the change in this policy in any case. The Barcelona objectives represent a soft way of influence (Kettunen and Wolff 2010), but alongside visible tendencies towards more convergence in life attitudes and aspirations across Europe (Eurofund 2014; European Commission 2013) they do trigger institutional dynamics of decentralization.

In institutional terms child daycare represents a radical change in several countries, connecting partly to transnational pressures and incentives to integrate and reach European standards, while in other countries most of the change is home-made. Not surprisingly, in order to facilitate a paradigm shift, new kinds of actions are required, such as redefining the role of the federal state in Germany, or empowerment of local governments in Estonia, or making principal decisions concerning the rights of children in Ireland. European funds (or federal funds in the case of Germany) can be seen as a window of opportunity, as a leap from, say, 20 percent of the parents having a child daycare place to 50 percent or 80 percent requires extraordinary dynamics.

CONCLUSIONS

We asked at the beginning of this chapter how the local governance of a specific policy field, child daycare, has evolved over time and specifically during the recent crisis. Europeanization, and especially the 2002 Barcelona protocol for the development of childcare services, in combination with the economic growth of the nineties and converging life aspirations across Europe (especially the shift from the male breadwinner to the dual earner type of family organization) have triggered the development of public childcare structures in several countries. It has also led to paradigm shifts where public childcare barely existed in previous years (mostly in Southern Europe). In several European countries, there was a trans-scaling from family networks and a decommodification from private businesses to the third sector and public childcare and a down-scaling of funds and responsibilities to local government, which was considered to be more responsive towards local needs and contexts (Wollmann 2014). However, the growth of childcare did not signify the end of traditional local government systems and dichotomies in the European continent, since the role of local government continued to vary and "residual" municipalities in the South did not transform into welfare municipalities of the Northern type.

From 2008 onwards, the division of labor between the public, private, and third sectors has been seriously affected by the crisis and prevailing austerity policies. There were significant cut-backs in the so-called "social budgets," replicating a vicious circle that increased needs for social welfare. Multi-level social governance has also been affected by the crisis, since in many cases national governments have tended to devolve social responsibilities to the regional and to the local levels. Devolution of competence to lower tiers is often combined with a contrary trend, that of the "up-scaling" of control and supervisory powers to upper levels of governance. National governments in particular have tended to exert direct control over local government financial autonomy, resource management, and decision-making on social policies.

Child daycare belongs to the core of social service provision in EU member countries while it marks a social service that is nearly everywhere provided by municipalities. The recent changes in this policy area, arising from the economic crisis, policy-specific motivations, and more generic reforms concerning municipal tasks and obligations, have led to redefinitions of who is entitled to the service, withdrawal of services, and service reorganization in terms of scaling and re-scaling. A converse policy shift seems to have emerged in some countries, following a decade of generous regional and local investment in daycare centers. The public debt crisis in 2010 put an end to this growth and recent local government reforms have limited the autonomy of municipalities in the sector (for example, in Spain). With the retrenchment of local government, public coverage of childcare is threatened, while tendencies of up- and trans-scaling could be enhanced.

This study could not do more than compare broad institutional and policy developments, however, often taking advantage of secondary data.

Details of systemic differences, of service organization, delivery, and quality that would be crucial for in-depth comparison would require case studies which lie beyond the scope and intention of this chapter and are left open for future research in this particularly dynamic and understudied challenging topic.

References

Andreotti, A., E. Mingione, and E. Polizzi. 2012. Local welfare systems: A challenge for social cohesion. *Urban Studies* 49(9): 1925–1940.

Esping-Andersen, G. 1990. *The three worlds of welfare capitalism*. Princeton: Princeton University Press.

Eurofund. 2014. *Third European quality of life survey—Quality of life in Europe: Families in the economic crisis*. Luxembourg: Publications Office of the European Union.

European Commission. 2013. *Barcelona objectives*. Luxembourg: Publications Office of the European Union.

Evers, A. 2005. Developing child-care provision in England and Germany: Problems of governance. *Journal of European Social Policy* 15(3): 195–209.

Fenger, H.J.M. 2007. Welfare regimes in central and Eastern Europe: Incorporating postcommunist countries in a welfare regime typology. *Contemporary Issues and Ideas in Social Sciences* 3(2):1–30.

Ferrera, Maurizio (1996) "The 'Southern Model' of Welfare in Social Europe" Journal of European Social Policy (6) 1: 17–37.

Hall, P.A. 1993. Policy paradigms, social learning, and the state: The case of economic policymaking in Britain. *Comparative Politics* 25: 275–296.

Kettunen, P., and C. Wolff. 2010. Europeanisation through the back door: EU social policy and the member states. *Politicka Misao (Croatian Political Science Review)* 47: 144–158.

Kokx, A., and R. van Kempen. 2010. Dutch urban governance: Multi-level or multi-scalar? *European Urban and Regional Studies* 17(4): 355–369.

Kröger, T. 2011. Retuning the Nordic Welfare Municipality. Central regulation of social care under change in Finland. *International Journal of Sociology and Social Policy* 31(3/4): 148–159.

Kuhlmann, S., and H. Wollmann. 2014. *Introduction to comparative public administration. Administrative systems and reforms in Europe*. Cheltenham: Edward Elgar.

Kuronen, M., and P. Caillaud. 2015. Vertical governance, national regulation and autonomy of local policy making. In *Local welfare policy making in European cities*, ed. D. Kutsar and M. Kuronen, 71–85. Cham: Springer International Publishing.

Kutsar, D., A. Trumm, and U. Oja. 1998. New democracy: Boundaries and resources for development. In *Social development and societies in transition*, ed. S. MacPherson and Hoi-Kwok Wong. Aldershot: Ashgate.

Lidström, A. 2003. *Kommunsystem i Europa. Demokrati i förändring.* Malmö: Liber.

Loughlin, J., F. Hendriks, and A. Lidstrom (eds.). 2011. *The Oxford handbook of local and regional democracy in Europe.* Oxford: Oxford University Press.

Navarro, C., and F. Velasco. 2015. "In wealth and in poverty?" The changing role of Spanish municipalities in implementing childcare policies. *International Review of Administrative Sciences* 81. doi:10.1177/0020852315576707.

Pierson, P. 2004. *Politics in time: History, institutions, and social analysis.* Princeton: Princeton University Press.

Sellers, J., and A. Lidström. 2007. Decentralization, local government, and the welfare state. *Governance* 20: 609–632.

Teles, F. 2014. Local government and the bailout: Reform singularities in Portugal. *European Urban and Regional Studies.* doi:10.1177/0969776413517249 (published online 27 January 2014).

Vasconcelos, T., et al. 2002. *Educacao de infancia em Portugal.* Lisbon: Conselho Nacional de Educacao.

Wollmann, H. 2014. *Public and social services provision in European countries. From public/municipal sector to market liberalisation—and then what?* Discussion Paper, Berlin.

CHAPTER 14

Rescaling of Planning Power: Comparing Functional Planning Reforms in Six European Countries

Panagiotis Getimis

Introduction

There are differences between the spatial planning systems in EU countries. Planning power is exercised at different levels (national, regional, local), but local government is a crucial key player in planning procedures. Planning refers to a wide spectrum of spatial regulations, restrictions, and artifacts which extend from the permit system and land use plans to strategic spatial planning. In this chapter, we will focus on the rescaling of planning power in six EU countries foreseen in several institutional planning reforms, mainly in the preordained conventional hierarchical framework (local, regional, and national). However, we will examine additionally new planning instruments which signify the shift from government to governance and refer to new "soft spaces" overcoming institutional boundaries. Rescaling of planning power refers·both to vertical

P. Getimis (✉)
Universities of Dortmund and Darmstadt, Dortmund/Darmstadt, Germany

© The Author(s) 2016
S. Kuhlmann, G. Bouckaert (eds.), *Local Public Sector Reforms in Times of Crisis*, DOI 10.1057/978-1-137-52548-2_14

redistribution of planning competences among the jurisdictions and levels (up-scaling, down-scaling) and to horizontal reallocation of competences and roles (trans-scaling) among different actors (public, private, nonprofit sector, and inter-municipal cooperation).

The section focuses on the conceptual framework upon which we draw our main hypothesis. The section "Institutional Changes of Functional Planning Reforms and New Planning Instruments" analyses the institutional changes of functional planning reforms (rescaling of power, down-, up-, and trans-scaling) and the new planning instruments (strategic planning, tools of territorial governance) in the six countries over the last few decades. Furthermore, the different responses of the national planning systems to the common driving forces of Europeanization, marketization, and economic crisis are comparatively analyzed and explained. In the conclusion (section "Conclusions") the main findings are summarized, as we reflect on the hypothesis of the chapter.

CONCEPTUAL FRAMEWORK AND SELECTION OF THE SIX COUNTRIES

The theoretical framework of concepts used in this study stems, on one side, from *actor-centered institutionalism* (Mayntz and Scharpf 1995; Ostrom 2007), and, on the other side, from the approach of *multi-level governance* (Hooghe and Marks 2003; Heinelt 2010) and the *politics of scale* (Smith 2004; Swyngedouw et al. 2002).

Our conceptualization of the causes and effects of planning reforms relies on the interdependence between institutions and actors, which means that the institutional contexts influence, but do not totally determine, the action arena (action situations, actors) (Ostrom 2007). Institutions constitute the initial conditions, the framework for the actors to interact. Political and administrative actors have some room to develop their own options, choices, and agendas in trying to influence the decisions for their own benefit (Scharpf 2000). Actors have the ability to mobilize resources for action, to develop discourses and practices, in ways that can change institutional conditions (Scharpf 1997)—always, however, within restricted corridors (Benz 2004).

From another theoretical debate on "multi-level governance" (Heinelt 2010 ; Hooghe and Marks 2003) and on the "politics of scale" (Smith 1984; Swyngedouw 1998, 2004), we draw the conceptualization of the "rescaling of planning power" within a "flexible political geometry" and the opportunities of "jumping of scales." In the framework of the restructuring of statehood and the doubts raised about the capacity of the political system to govern modern societies (Heinelt 2010)-the existing system of formal hierarchical political-territorial structures is questioned. There is a need for it to be complemented with horizontal networks (Benz 2004), reflecting the shift from "government" to "governance." Moreover, new "soft spaces" of action emerge, referring to "fuzzy" boundaries, which overcome existing institutional boundaries (Allmendinger and Haughton 2012). Actors reorganize their strategies, while institutions change "scalar configurations," shifting competences and power upwards, downwards, and horizontally. Scales are restructured, redefined and contested, depending on the socio-spatial transformation and the actor constellation that prevails in each country (Swyngedouw et al. 2002).

Drawing from the above theoretical approach, we attempt to explain the different directions of rescaling of planning power among the six countries. The chapter focuses on the overarching questions of the book (reform implementation, driving forces/causes) and particularly on the following:

(a) Are there different directions and intensities of planning reform (rescaling: up-, down-, trans-scaling of competencies and power) between different countries or groups of countries?
(b) How can we explain similarities and differences? What are the main driving forces (causes) of planning rescaling?
(c) How important are the initial institutional conditions, as factors explaining the heterogeneity of rescaling of planning processes?

The main hypothesis of the study is:

Countries with different starting conditions (local government type, degree of centralization, capacities, supervision, and planning type), because of external and internal driving forces (Europeanization, privatization, economic crisis and austerity policies, and territorial and functional domestic reforms) follow different paths of rescaling of planning power.

The countries to be investigated in the comparison of the planning reforms and the rescaling of planning power are selected under the following criteria:

1. Belonging in different types of local government typologies (Heinelt and Hlepas 2006; Hesse and Sharpe 1991; Sellers and Lidström 2007).

2. Belonging in different groupings of countries, concerning local capacities and supra-local supervision (low, medium, and high) (Sellers and Lidström 2007).
3. Belonging in different types of planning systems (CEC 1997; EU Compendium, four "planning families").

The following six countries were selected, which cover to a great extent all the types of local government systems and belong to the four planning families (see Annex, Table 14.A.1):

(a) *Denmark* and *Germany* belong to the "comprehensive/integrated" planning family. Denmark belongs to the Northern local government type, with a high level of local capacities and a low degree of supra-local supervision, while Germany belongs to the Middle local government system, with moderate/high degree of local capacities and higher degree of supra-local supervision.
(b) *France*, belongs to the "regional economic" planning type and to the Napoleonic/Franco local government type, with low local capacities and strong supra-local supervision
(c) *Italy* and *Greece*, within the tradition of "urbanism" planning type, belong to the Napoleonic/Franco local government type, with even lower capacities and strong supervision.
(d) *United Kingdom*, within the "land use management" planning type, belongs to the Anglo-Saxon local government system, with low capacities and medium/high supra-local supervision.

INSTITUTIONAL CHANGES OF FUNCTIONAL PLANNING REFORMS AND NEW PLANNING INSTRUMENTS

Planning "Power" and "Functions"

The term "planning power" is used here in distinction with the legal term "planning function" (competence), since we refer not only to the duties of local government in the subject of "planning," but also to the relations of local government to the central state and the regional authorities, which determine the relative degree of freedom of the local level and its strength of planning power. In that sense we focus on planning power as a relation between the main institutional tiers and on the trends of rescaling of planning power caused by the dynamic of planning reforms, changing the relations among scales. In the same way, Marcou distinguishes municipal "powers" and "functions" in his important study on comparing the situation of local government in 2007 across several European countries (Marcou 2007). However, this is a synchronic study, comparing the different country situations in the same period, without analyzing diachronic trends of the rescaling of local government power, due to functional or territorial reforms.

Institutional changes concerning vertical and horizontal power relations in the subject field of planning emerge owing to planning reforms (incremental or comprehensive), which differ among the EU countries. They can refer to all the substantive contents of planning competences of the mainstream planning system at different scales (for example, land use planning, urban and town planning, building permits, planning of specific areas like housing, coastal zones, tourism, green, environmental, and vulnerable areas). Additionally, they can also refer to "new" functions and planning tools, for example, for geographically coherent spaces, cross-border areas, functional urban areas, and strategic planning spaces.

Relevant research has shown that Europeanization (ESDP, European Territorial Agenda, ESPON) has resulted in both convergence and divergence trends among the national planning systems (Farinos Dasi 2006; Nadin and Stead 2008). However, while the trends of convergence and divergence have been deeply analyzed (for example, referring to strategic planning), there is a lack of comparative research on the multi-faceted institutional rescaling of planning, concerning both te vertical and horizontal power relations (Getimis 2012; Reimer et al. 2014).

Institutional Changes of Planning Reform: Vertical Rescaling of Planning Power

A general trend that has taken place during recent decades in all six of the countries examined is the devolution and/or decentralization of planning power from the central level to lower administrative tiers (downscaling). This trend concerns both mainstream planning functions (for example, land use planning, town planning, the permit system, and so on) and new planning instruments (for example, strategic planning and territorial governance tools). Municipalities gain more planning functions and power, while the processes of down-scaling are accompanied by participatory processes. This trend is either part of a nationally driven broader territorial and administrative reform, as in Denmark (2007) and

Greece (1994, 1998, 2010), or it is a long process of incrementally driven planning reforms, taking place at different periods, without being part of a broader territorial or functional reform (for example, France, Italy, UK, Germany) (Wollmann and Marcou 2010). For example, in *France* the devolution policy started in the 1980s, followed by a decentralization planning policy from the 1990s until today (with constitutional reform in 2003 and planning reforms in 2004 and 2010) (Marcou 2007). In *Italy* the planning reform in the 1990s further enhanced the strong regions ("neo-regionalism"), the provinces (Act 142, the territorial provincial planning reform) and the municipalities (Lingua and Servillo 2014). In the *UK* the devolution of planning functions and power to the local level with the Localism Act 2010 ended a period of experimental attempts to establish regional authorities (Nadin and Stead 2014; Olesen 2010).

However, parallel to this functional down-scaling to the local level, there is evidence of an opposite trend: a functional up-scaling of planning power to the central state, transferring certain competences or veto functions to the central ministries in crucial issues of strategic planning decisions, such as natural environment, water resources, metropolitan management, retail planning, coastal zone management, housing, privatization of publicly owned land, and others. This evidence is drawn from all the countries examined, with the exception of France,[1] with its strong hierarchical "Jacobin" state tradition, where a continuing devolution and decentralization process still prevails.

In *Denmark* ("comprehensive-integrated" planning type), parallel to the devolution of planning power to the merged 98 municipalities (2007), there emerged a contrasting shift towards the enhancement of planning power at the central state level through the exercise of veto rights in crucial issues (strategic decisions for environment, water resources, retail sector, central ministries taking over the strategic planning responsibilities of the Greater Copenhagen Region).

In *Germany* ("comprehensive/integrated planning type") scale-shifting processes can be observed in two directions: on the one hand there is a continuing trend of decentralization of competencies. On the other hand there are signs of functional "up-scaling" of planning tasks, exceeding the "traditional" administrative boundaries of single municipalities (for example, shifting competences and informal governance arrangements to upper levels with regard to retail development and allocation decisions at a regional scale) (Blotevogel et al. 2014; Zimmermann 2011, pp. 52–6).

In *Greece* ("urbanism" planning type), while during the decentralization reforms (1994, 1998) planning competencies had been transferred to the 13 regions and to merged municipalities, owing to legal objections from the Council of State (spatial planning is considered as a "state" function) planning power has again been concentrated in the central state (Ministry of Environment and Planning, up-scaling trend) (Getimis and Giannakourou 2014).

In *Italy*, despite the continuing down-scaling of planning power to the regions and to the municipalities, which became more politically powerful after the reforms regarding the direct election of mayors (Lippi 2011), a contrary shift towards the recentralization of planning power to the state has also emerged, concerning especially the coordination of sector policies and the management of "crisis" situations (for example, in case of earthquakes). Furthermore, the recent abolition of the provinces transferred competences to both the local and regional levels (Lingua and Servillo 2014).

Finally, in the *United Kingdom* ("land use management" planning type) although the recent reform in 2011 claims to emphasize localism ("Localism 2011"), and "down-scaling" of planning power to the municipalities (district councils, Local Development Schemes) (Gallent et al. 2013), central government intervention in the planning reform towards "simplification and streamlining" was very crucial. It reinforces central planning procedures, especially when delivering major transport and energy infrastructures (Baker and Wong 2012; Nadin and Stead 2014).

Summing up, concerning the vertical rescaling of planning power, devolution and decentralization is combined with the—often neglected in the literature—up-scaling trends appearing in all planning types. Central state intervention in core planning fields is suggested to be a necessary response to the fragmented and differentiated landscape, which emerges owing to devolution (Reimer et al. 2014). Pressures towards a "centralized decentralization" (Allmendinger and Haughton 2012; Baker and Wong 2012) are due to the emergence of new spatial problems which cannot be resolved at the local level.

Planning reforms in each country foresee different roles and planning powers for the intermediary levels (regions, provinces, and municipalities). While in some countries (for example, Greece and Italy) the regions are gaining planning power, in other countries they have lost planning power or have been abandoned (for example, UK in 2011, Denmark in 2007) in favor of the local level (Mouritzen 2011). These differences reflect both the historic role of the intermediary tiers and the different scope and priorities of the administrative and planning reforms prevailing in each country. For example, other reasons have led the Greek government to establish 13 regional authorities with development and planning competences (with the assistance of EU structural funds for Objective 1 regions) and other priorities have been chosen by the Danish and British governments to abolish or downgrade the regional level (economies of scale, decentralization, localism).

It is worth mentioning that diverse trends exist among the countries in terms of the binding or non-binding/optional nature of the planning regulations for the lower tiers, and the latitude and flexibility of the competences of planning institutions at the local level. Here again we detect a bipolarity among countries concerning the variables of centralization, of local capacities, and of the degree of supervision of local government. In countries with strong local government capacities and a relatively low degree of supervision, like Denmark and Germany, regional plans are indicative and non-binding for the municipalities, enabling more options for local planning authorities. On the other hand, in countries, like Greece and Italy, with hierarchical planning regulations, regional plans are strictly binding on the lower tiers and reduce the flexibility and latitude of planning practices at the local level. In the UK particularly, the recent "downscaling," giving emphasis to localization for land use planning, promoted greater consensus around a more open local system of planning, in which "decisions are localized and taken closer to affected communities" (Gallent et al. 2013, p. 564).

Horizontal Trans-Scaling of Planning Power and New Planning Instruments (Strategic Planning, Instruments of Territorial Governance, "Market-Led" Planning)

Planning reforms affect not only the vertical relations of planning institutions, but also the horizontal relations among multiple institutions and actors involved in the new planning processes. The European Spatial Planning Agenda (including territorial cohesion, strategic planning, ESPON) had an influential role on the national planning systems. However, while different paths of the vertical rescaling of planning power have emerged in the countries examined, all countries have introduced similar new planning instruments (strategic planning, territorial governance tools), which enhance "trans-scaling" of planning power to multi-actor cooperation schemes (inter-municipal cooperation, and public and private partnerships).

Furthermore, deregulation (privatization and marketization) and the recent economic crisis have strengthened the market orientation of planning, with a variety of manifestations. In the last two decades in all the countries examined there has been a common shift towards a more *development-oriented* spatial planning approach, aiming at better coordination of economic planning, regional development, and sector policies (especially infrastructure networks). This shift represents the need to facilitate investments (*"market-led"* planning) and to involve private stakeholders in the framework of territorial governance.

A characteristic example of enhancement of the horizontal trans-scaling of planning power is the case of *France*. The spatial planning reform of 1999–2000 focused on "territorial coherence and coordination" (*Plan local d'urbanism* (PLU), *Schéma de cohérence territoriale* (SCoT) 2003), placing emphasis on coordination between cities and regions in spatial planning practices. It was based on a non-binding national strategic development perspective (SNADT). The need for horizontal cooperation and complementarity is based on new institutional settings (*Établissement public de coopération intercommunale* (EPCI), development councils) developing planning strategies for "geographical coherent spaces" beyond and across jurisdictions ("soft" planning and "fuzzy boundaries"). Furthermore, the French planning system is shifting from the "regional economic" planning type to the "comprehensive/integrated" type, incorporating elements of horizontal integration and participatory procedures (for example, development councils) (Geppert 2014, pp. 118–20). However, horizontal networking in planning arrangements refers mainly to the "inter-municipal" coordination and secondary to the contractual involvement of private stakeholders (PPPs). Thus the shift towards "market-led" planning in France is moderate and partial, following the general trend of the French model of "functional privatization" through delegated contracts of specific functions to private stakeholders (Citroni 2010; Kuhlmann and Wollmann 2011, p. 153).

Similar new planning instruments enhancing horizontal trans-scaling of planning power and multiple actors' participation are found in the countries belonging to the "comprehensive/integrated" planning type (for example, Denmark and Germany). In *Denmark*, the decentralization reform (2007) enhanced further multi-actor participation and strategic planning in relation to economic planning and sustainability at the regional level and at the local level (traditional land use plans, broad spatial development plans, and land use planning as a strategic management tool). In *Germany*, incremental reforms have aimed at the enhancement of multi-actor participation, promoting new informal strategic planning instruments and concepts at all spatial levels (especially the regional level), complementing the existing mainstream formal instruments. The role of private stakeholders in spatial planning processes is limited in consultation procedures, initiated and organized by the planning authorities (Blotevogel et al. 2014). Therefore, in both countries, the impact of "privatization/ marketization" on the trans-scaling of planning power is moderate, since the role of private stakeholders in strategic planning and territorial governance arrangement is reduced to within certain limits which are set by the public actors (municipalities, regions, and metropolitan governance arrangements) (Kuhlmann and Wollmann 2011; Waterhout et al. 2012).

In the countries belonging to the "urbanism" planning family (Greece and Italy), there is evidence of similar trends, which introduced new planning instruments of horizontal trans-scaling. Thus, in *Greece*, there is evidence of a complementary approach to the mainstream "physical planning" (statutory, ex post land use regulations); a strategic, development-oriented planning, supported through horizontal networks of actors (Getimis and Giannakourou 2014, pp. 161–2). It is worth mentioning that the recent economic crisis, which has hit Greece dramatically, has strengthened the market orientation of planning since 2010. The new, "fast-track" planning licencing for strategic investments (Law3894/2010) and the simplified planning regime for privatization of public land (Law 3986/2011) is evidence of a strong shift to "market-led" planning which is a response to the fiscal and economic crisis (facilitating the prerequisites for new investments, and the "outsourcing" of planning competences) (Getimis and Giannakourou 2014, p. 164).

In *Italy* since the "Single Act" reform of 1999, strategic planning regulations have introduced territorial governance and increased municipal power (Constitutional Reform 2001). A series of instruments have been introduced for the enhancement of territorial governance (Lingua and Servillo 2014, p. 141). Among them the "Territorial Pact" and the "Program Agreement" have been used in specific domains, mobilizing multi-actor networking and PPPs. The recent economic crisis has strengthened in Italy the shift from the "conformative" model towards a "performance-oriented" planning approach and "market-led" planning. However, despite the strong political will for extended "privatization" and "marketization," in both Mediterranean countries of the "urbanism" planning type (Italy and Greece), the pace and the degree of privatization is moderate, owing to the lack of interest on the part of private investors and the persistence of bureaucratic obstruction by the public sector (Cotella and Rivolin 2011).

In the *United Kingdom* ("land use management" planning type) strategic planning approaches, first initiated in the 2000s, are strongly "market-led," mainly oriented to developmental aims and private investment, enhancing "place-based strategies" and horizontal trans-scaling of planning power. This effort coincided with the devolution of power to local governments, resulting in enhanced PPPs, voluntary agreements between local authorities, and "local strategic partnerships" with the cooperation of business and civil society. The UK is characterized as a forerunner of a market-led planning transformation and "investor-friendly" planning culture (Kuhlmann and Wollmann 2011, pp. 140–1; Waterhout et al. 2012).

Summing up the trends of horizontal trans-scaling of planning power, despite the common orientation towards developmental goals, the pace and the intensity of privatization/marketization differs among the different groupings of countries.

Conclusions

The comparative analysis of the planning reforms in six European countries with different starting conditions (local government type, capacities, supervision, and planning type) has shown both different and common features concerning the trends of rescaling of planning power.

First, concerning the *vertical power relations*, there is a common trend towards a devolution and/or decentralization of planning power ("*down-scaling*") from the central level to lower administrative tiers (regions, local). This trend is independent of the different starting conditions (local government types, capacities, supervision, and planning family). It refers both to regulatory planning functions (for example, land use planning, town planning, permit system, and so on) and to new planning instruments (for example, strategic planning and territorial governance tools).

However, devolution and decentralization (down-scaling) is combined with an opposite, "*up-scaling*" trend, in all countries (except France, already a highly centralist state, within the Jacobin tradition). This "up-scaling" trend is neglected in the literature, despite the fact that it is most important and affects the vertical power relations among planning institutions. Recentralizing competence and power in core planning fields is explained as a necessary response to the fragmented and differentiated landscape which emerges because of devolution.

Diverse trends in the planning reforms exist among the countries in terms of the binding or non-binding effect of the planning arrangements for the lower tiers. This is connected with the latitude and flexibility of planning competences of the local level. Here the different starting conditions do matter. A bipolarity exists among the countries. In those with strong local government capacities and relatively low degree of supervision, like Denmark and Germany ("comprehensive/integrated" planning type), regional plans and directives are indicative and non-binding for the municipalities, enabling planning institutions at the local level to exercise a broad range of planning functions, and enjoy strong planning power. In other countries, like Greece, France, and Italy (Franco type, weak capacities, strong supervision, and "urbanism" planning type) with hierarchical planning regulations, regional plans are strictly binding on the lower tiers, while they reduce the flexibility and latitude of planning practices at the local level.

In the UK particularly ("land use management" type, medium capacities, and supervision), the recent abolition of the regions (2011) has been accompanied by the strengthening of both the local level ("Localism Act" 2010) and the central level. Moreover, there is evidence that in countries with strong hierarchical state traditions (that is, France and Greece), the preordained conventional hierarchical planning system has been not abolished but rather complemented with new, more open, participatory processes of vertical and horizontal integration.

Concerning the *horizontal power relations*, in all the countries examined new planning instruments have been introduced (strategic planning, and territorial governance tools), which enhanced "*trans-scaling*" of planning power to multi-actor cooperation schemes (inter-municipal cooperation, "soft" spaces with "fuzzy" boundaries, and the overcoming of official jurisdictions).

Europeanization, marketization, and crisis have a multi-faceted influence on the rescaling of planning power among European countries. The European Spatial Planning Agenda had an influential role on the national planning systems (trans-scaling, development oriented planning). The recent economic crisis has deepened the market orientation of planning, with a variety of manifestations. The pace and intensity of neo-liberal influence on spatial planning differs among the examined countries. While in the UK (the forerunner of neo-liberal policy, common law tradition, and public-interest culture) and in Greece (after 2010) the shift towards market planning is more radical, in Germany, in Denmark, and in France (continental legal administrative tradition) it is more balanced. Furthermore, the different responses of the EU member states have emerge as a result of the public debt crisis of the southern EU countries (since 2010). Thus, countries being hit by the global economic crisis (especially Greece and Italy) were forced to move faster towards "market-led" planning, in order to facilitate private investment. Furthermore, in order to overcome planning burdens, the outsourcing of specific planning services has additionally been employed (for example, in Greece).

ANNEX

Table 14.A.1 Local government and planning system typologies

	LG typology Lidström (2003)	LG typology Hesse and Sharpe (1991)	LG typology Heinelt and Hlepas (2006)	LG capacities: fiscal/political/administration Sellers and Lidström (2007)	Supervision of LG: fiscal/political/administration Sellers and Lidström (2007)	Planning system typology CEC (1997)
Denmark	Northern European	North-Middle European	North-Middle	1.96	0.98	EU Compendium Comprehensive integrated
Germany	Middle European	North-Middle European	North-Middle Executive mayor	1.0	1.26	Comprehensive integrated
France	Napoleonic	Napoleonic	Franco Political mayor	0.60	1.29	Regional economic planning
Italy	Napoleonic	Napoleonic	Franco Political mayor	0.34	0.93	Urbanism
Greece	Napoleonic	Napoleonic	Franco Political mayor	0.53	1.42	Urbanism
UK	British	Anglo-Saxon	Anglo	0.75	1.23	Land use management

Source: Own elaboration, based on Lidström (2003), Hesse and Sharpe (1991), Heinelt and Hlepas (2006), Sellers and Lidström (2007), and CEC (1997)

Note

1. In France also there are some attempts on the part of the central state to recover control of the ongoing processes of devolution and decentralization. However, as Geppert recognizes, these attempts (for example, Late DTA, exceptional power given to the state representatives during the various reforms), are not a revival of the authoritative and paternalistic planning style (Geppert 2014, p. 124).

References

Allmendinger, P., and G. Haughton. 2012. The evolution and trajectories of English spatial governance: "Neoliberal" episodes in planning. *Planning Practice and Research* 28(1): 6–26.

Baker, M., and C. Wong. 2012. The delusion of strategic planning: What's left after the labour government's English regional experiment? *Planning Practice and Research* 28(1): 83–103.

Benz, A. (ed.). 2004. *Governance. Regieren in komplexen Regelungssystemen.* Wiesbaden: Westdeutscher Verlag.

Blotevogel, H.H., R. Danielzyk, and A. Munter. 2014. Spatial planning in Germany: Institutional inertia and new challenges. In *Spatial planning systems and practices in Europe: A comparative perspective on continuity and changes*, ed. M. Reimer, P. Getimis, and H. Blotevogel. New York: Routledge.

CEC (Commission of the European Communities). 1997. *The EU compendium of spatial planning systems and policies.* Luxembourg: Office for Official Publications of the European Communities.

Cotella, G., and U.J. Rivoli. 2011. Europeanisation of spatial planning through discourse and practice in Italy. *disP* 186(3): 46–53.

Farinos Dasi, J. 2006. *ESPON Project 2.3.2. Governance of territorial and urban policies from EU to local level. Final Report.* Esh-sur-Alzette: ESPON Coordination Unit.

Gallent, N., I. Hamiduddin, and M. Madeddu. 2013. Localism, down-scaling and the strategic dilemmas confronting planning in England. *Town Planning Review* 84(5): 563–582.

Geppert, A. 2014. France, drifting away from the "regional economic" approach. In *Spatial planning systems and practices in Europe: A comparative perspective on continuity and changes*, ed. M. Reimer, P. Getimis, and H. Blotevogel. New York: Routledge.

Getimis, P. 2012. Comparing spatial planning systems and planning cultures in Europe. The need for a multi-scalar approach. *Planning Practice and Research* 27(1): 25–40.

Getimis, P., and G. Gianakourou. 2014. The evolution of spatial planning in Greece after the 1990s: Drivers, directions and agents of change. In *Spatial planning systems and practices in Europe: A comparative perspective on continuity and changes*, ed. M. Reimer, P. Getimis, and H. Blotevogel. New York: Routledge.

Heinelt, H. 2010. *Governing modern societies: Towards participatory governance*. Oxford: Oxford University Press.

Heinelt, H., and N.K. Hlepas. 2006. Typologies of local government systems. In *The European mayor: Political leaders in the changing context of local democracy*, ed. H. Back, H. Heinelt, and A. Magnier. Wiesbaden: VS Verlag für Sozialwissenschaften.

Hesse, J.J., and J. Sharpe. 1991. Local government in international perspective: Some comparative observations. In *Local government and local affairs in international perspective analyses of twenty western industrialised countries*, ed. J.J. Hess and J. Sharpe. Nomos: Baden-Baden.

Hooghe, L., and G. Marks. 2003. Unraveling the central state, but how? Types of multi-level governance. *The American Political Science Review* 97(2): 233–243.

Kuhlmann, S., and H. Wollmann. 2011. *Verwaltung in Europa: Verwaltungssysteme und—reformen im Vergleich*. Wiesbaden: Springer VS.

Lidström, A. 2003. *Kommunsystem I Europa* [Local Government Systems in Europe]. Malmö: Liber foerlag.

Lingua, V., and L. Servillo. 2014. The modernization of the Italian planning system. In *Spatial planning systems and practices in Europe: A comparative perspective on continuity and changes*, ed. M. Reimer, P. Getimis, and H. Blotevogel. New York: Routledge.

Lippi, A. 2011. Evaluating the "Quasi federalist" programme of decentralisation in Italy since the 1990s: A side-effect approach. *Local Government Studies* 37: 495–516.

Marcou, G. 2007. *Local authority competences in Europe, study of the European committee on local and regional democracy*. Straßbourg: Council of Europe.

Mayntz, R., and R.F. Scharpf. 1995. *Gesellschaftliche Selbstregelung und Politische Steuerung*. Frankfurt/New York: Campus Verlag.

Mouritzen, P.E. 2011. The Danish revolution in local government: How and why? In *Territorial choice. The politics of boundaries and borders*, ed. H. Baldersheim and L. Rose. London: Palgrave Macmillan.

Nadin, V., and D. Stead. 2008. European spatial planning systems social models and learning. *disP* 44(1): 35–47.

Nadin, V., and D. Stead. 2014. Spatial planning in the United Kingdom, 1990–2013. In *Spatial planning systems and practices in Europe: A comparative perspective on continuity and changes*, ed. M. Reimer, P. Getimis, and H. Blotevogel. New York: Routledge.

Olesen, K. 2010. *Danish "strategic spatial planning" in transition.* Paper presented at 24th AESOP annual conference 2010, Helsinki. http://vbn.aau.dk/files/43876932/Danish_strategic_spatial_planning_in_transition_Kristian_Olesen.pdf.

Ostrom, E. 2007. Institutional rational choice: An assessment of the institutional analysis and development framework. In *Theories of policy process*, ed. P. Sabatier. Boulder: Westview Press.

Reimer, M., P. Getimis, and H. Blotevogel (eds.). 2014. *Spatial planning systems and practices in Europe: A comparative perspective on continuity and changes.* New York: Routledge.

Scharpf, F.W. 1997. *Games real actors play. Actor-centered institutionalism in policy research.* Boulder: Westview Press.

Scharpf, F.W. 2000. *Interaktionsformen. Akteurzentrierter Institutionalismus in der Politikforschung.* Opladen: Leske + Budrich.

Sellers, J.M., and A. Lidström. 2007. Decentralization, local government and the welfare state. *Governance* 20(4): 609–632.

Smith, N. 1984. *Uneven development. Nature, capital and the production of space.* Oxford: Basil Blackwell.

Smith, N. 2004. Scale bending and the fate of the national. In *Scale and geographic inquiry*, ed. E. Shepperd and R.B. McMaster. Oxford: Blackwell.

Swyngedouw, E. 1998. Homing in and spacing out: Re-configurating scale. In *Europa in Globalisierungsprozess von Wirtschaft und Gesellschaft*, ed. H. Gebhardt, G. Heinritz, and R. Weissner. Stuttgart: Franz Steiner Verlag.

Swyngedouw, E. 2004. "Globalisation or glocalisation"? Networks, territories and rescaling. *Cambridge Review of International Affairs* 17(1): 25–48.

Swyngedouw, E., B. Page, and M. Kaika. 2002. Sustainability and policy innovation in a multi-level context: Crosscutting issues in the water sector. In *Participatory governance in multi-level context*, ed. H. Heinelt, P. Getimis, G. Kafkalas, R. Smith, and E. Swyngedouw. Opladen: Leske + Budrich.

Waterhout, B., F. Othengrafen, and O. Sykes. 2012. Neo-liberalization processes and spatial planning in France, Germany and the Netherlands: An exploration. *Planning Practice and Research* 28(1): 1–19.

Wollmann, H., and G. Marcou (eds.). 2010. *The provision of public services in Europe: Between state, local government and market.* Cheltenham/Northampton: Edward Elgar.

Zimmermann, K. 2011. Spatial planning in Germany. In *Metropolitan governance, different paths in contrasting contexts: Germany and Israel*, ed. H. Heinelt, E. Razin, and K. Zimmermann. Frankfurt/New York: Campus Verlag.

PART IV

Local Participatory Reforms, Political Leaders, and Citizens

Giving Citizens More Say in Local Government: Comparative Analyses of Change Across Europe in Times of Crisis

Angelika Vetter, Daniel Klimovský, Bas Denters, and Norbert Kersting

INTRODUCTION

At the same time as Western democracies are facing the consequences of the financial crisis, these countries are also confronted with a "crisis of democracy." In part this democratic crisis is the result of an ongoing process of trans-nationalization and an increasing scale and complexity of governance. These processes tend to reduce the chances of individual citizens effectively influencing political decisions and lead to a sense of

A. Vetter (✉)
Department of Social Sciences, University of Stuttgart, Stuttgart, Germany

D. Klimovský
Comenius University, Bratislava, Slovakia

B. Denters
University of Twente, Enschede, The Netherlands

N. Kersting
University of Münster, Münster, Germany

© The Author(s) 2016
S. Kuhlmann, G. Bouckaert (eds.), *Local Public Sector Reforms in Times of Crisis*, DOI 10.1057/978-1-137-52548-2_15

political powerlessness. This is especially problematic since at the same time, as a consequence of increasing education and value changes, citizens expect and demand more direct and effective participatory opportunities. As Robert A. Dahl (1994) argued, widening the range of opportunities for citizens to influence local, small-scale decision-making might compensate for the growing gap between actual and expected opportunities for citizen participation. In Dahl's view:

> The larger scale of decisions need not lead inevitability to a widening sense of powerlessness, provided citizens can exercise significant control over decisions on the smaller scale of matters important in their daily lives. (Dahl 1994, 33)

In recent decades, significant reforms in local governance and local democracy have been implemented (see Chaps. 16, 17, 18, and 19 of this volume, but also Baldersheim et al. 2003; Coulson and Campbell 2008; Denters and Rose 2005; Jüptner et al. 2014; Hendriks et al. 2011; Kersting and Vetter 2003; Kersting et al. 2009; Reynaert 2005; Schaap and Daemen 2012; Schiller 2011; Soós et al. 2002). As a result of these reforms, the range of participatory opportunities at the local level has been increased.

Our knowledge of the scope and patterns of these reforms is rather patchy, however. Most of the studies on local democratic reforms, for example, concentrate on a particular selection of countries, focus on a specific aspect of reform, and pertain to a particular moment in time. In this chapter we aim at providing a comprehensive overview of local democratic reforms for a wide range of European countries, over an extended period of time. Our main research question is: Did local government reforms in European countries in the years between 1990 and 2014 lead to an increase in the scope for active citizen participation in local decision-making, consistent with Dahl's vision? On the basis of this descriptive analysis we will also ask why the established patterns of reform may have emerged.

SCOPE AND METHODS OF THE ANALYSIS

Our focus is on three types of reform that indicate increasing levels of citizen control in local government:

1. The right of free access to information is essential for citizen control. First, information can be understood as a fundamental requirement for citizens' engagement. Second, information by itself is a main

criterion for the quality of local democracy supporting an enlightened understanding of the political process (Dahl 1998, p. 37).

2. In a parliamentary political system citizens vote only for their representatives in the local councils which then decide their council leader(s) or the leadership board (see also Chap. 19 of this volume). Giving citizens the opportunity to vote separately for their mayors "expands the electoral marketplace" (Dalton and Gray 2003) by giving citizens more opportunities to control more directly the fate of the local community.

3. Similarly, local referenda expand citizens' opportunities to control local decision-making directly by expressing their voices apart from in local council elections.

On the basis of an expert survey we collected data for the reforms in these three domains in the period between 1990 and 2014 in all member states of the EU with a population of more than one million, plus Switzerland, Norway, and Iceland.

FINDINGS

Before we analyze reform patterns over time and across the three dimensions, we will first discuss the reforms separately.

The Right of Free Access to Information

Since the 1990s, Central and Eastern European countries have approved various acts on free access to information related to public authorities' activities, especially within the context of their accession to the European Union. A more heterogeneous picture is presented by the so-called Western European democracies. Until the end of the 1990s, such acts had been approved in Austria, Belgium, Denmark, France, Greece, Iceland, Ireland, Liechtenstein, the Netherlands, Norway and Portugal. The most recent acts were approved in Germany (at the federal level), Spain, Switzerland, and the United Kingdom. The German case is interesting: the federal parliament of Germany passed the act on free access to information in 2005 but in some of the German states their parliaments passed such acts even earlier, including Brandenburg (1998) and North-Rhine-Westphalia (2002). In most European countries freedom of information acts do not exclusively pertain to the local government level. The provisions of these acts are likely to influence significantly the transparency and openness of local government, however, and to increase the opportunities for effective citizen control.

Of course the actual impact of these provisions also depends on the conditions under which they are implemented. First, the availability of information and telecommunication technologies (ICT) is important in facilitating free and easy access to government information. Second, despite the fact that many local authorities in the European countries have made significant progress in providing information online, the analysis of the situation and the developments in the UK proved that additional funding and staff development, combined with more fundamental changes to internal business processes and interorganizational working are usually needed if local authorities are to harness the full potential of new ICT to transform their transactions with the citizens and other service users (Beynon-Davies and Martin 2004). Third, the right of free access to information may be supplemented by the personal provision of information. Recent changes to local government law in Iceland (2011) include a duty on local councilors to inform citizens on important subjects regarding their local authority. In Slovakia such an obligation on local councilors was included already in the original text of the local government act (1990) but the fulfillment of this obligation has been questionable owing to a general lack of political accountability.

Direct Election of Mayors

While for local councils the direct election of members has been common practice in most European countries, the direct election of mayors seems in many countries to be a more recent development (Denters and Rose 2005; Hendriks et al. 2011; Koprić 2009). Since 1990, direct election of mayors has been introduced or expanded in Austria, Croatia, England, Germany, Hungary, Italy, Norway, Poland, and Lithuania. The issue of direct election of mayors was considered a serious political issue even in the countries where it has not been introduced (Czech Republic and the Netherlands; Šaradín 2010).

The context regarding the implementation of the direct election of mayors has varied a lot in Europe. For example, in Slovakia the direct election of mayors was introduced immediately after the collapse of the communist regime. A two-step implementation was used in the Hungarian case: while in 1990 direct mayoral elections were held in municipalities with population up to 10,000 inhabitants, since 1994 the mayors have been directly elected in all Hungarian municipalities regardless of size (Temesi 2000). Germany experienced a gradual spread of direct mayoral elections. While in Baden-Württemberg and Bavaria the direct elections of mayors had been practiced since the 1950s, during the 1990s all other German states adopted the direct election of mayors (for example, Kuhlmann 2009; Vetter 2006, 2009). In England citizens obtained the right to call for a local referendum whether to elect a mayor directly or not in 2000 (John and Copus 2011). The first directly elected English mayor was elected in Greater London. Since then, direct election of mayors has been introduced in several local units. In Norway experiments with direct election of mayors were carried out for three successive election periods (1999–2011) but were discontinued at the 2011 election. The Dutch national government introduced the option of having a consultative mayoral referendum in which the electorate could express their preference for the candidates to be nominated to the national government for appointment in 2001. Although it was not a direct mayoral election *sensu stricto*, the results of such referenda were accepted by the national government. However, only eight municipalities used this option and voters' interest was rather low, which led to the abandonment of this measure in 2008. Currently the influence of the local council on the appointment of Dutch mayors is so large that the system comes close to that of an indirectly elected mayor. In the Czech Republic, the direct election of mayors has not yet been introduced all over the country, but there was an intense ministerial discussion on such an option and on the basis of a recent central government resolution in 2014 the introduction of directly elected mayors was implemented in the smallest municipalities. Although there seems to be a common trend in Europe with regard to the direct election of mayors, we also find significant differences regarding the terms of election methods, the term of office and so on (for example, Klimovský 2009; Wollmann 2009).

Binding Local Referenda

The importance as well as utilization of local referenda is a popular topic both in the political and the academic discourse (see Chap. 19 in this volume as well as Qvotrup (2014), Scarrow (2001), and Schiller (2011)). Two distinctions should be kept in mind in this regard: first, whether referenda are mandatory, whether they are held only at the discretion of the local authorities, or whether they may be initiated by the inhabitants of municipalities, and second, whether they are only advisory (consultative) in nature or the result is binding for the local authority (COE 1993).

Council of Europe data from the early 1990s (1993) show that at that time 14 European countries had already experienced (usually consultative) local referenda that were called by the local councils, namely Austria, Belgium, Denmark, Finland, France, Germany, Ireland, Italy, Luxembourg, the Netherlands, Norway, Portugal, Spain, and Sweden. Referenda initiated by citizens with the approval of the local councils had at that time been introduced in Finland and Spain, and referenda initiated by citizens that had to be held in the case of certain quorums were used in Austria, Germany, Luxembourg, Norway, and Spain. Ten years later, Scarrow (2001) compared 15 countries with regard to local referenda, including 12 European countries. She stressed that almost all of them experienced the utilization of local referenda in the beginning of the twentieth century. But without doubt Switzerland remains the world champion regarding the utilization of local referenda (Ladner 2002).

Regarding the context of introduction for local referenda, it is helpful to mention a few interesting examples from Sweden, the Netherlands, and Poland. In 1994 a citizen initiative to hold local referenda was introduced in Sweden. The final decision was left to the local council which has the right to decide whether the referendum would be held. Therefore it is no surprise that by 2010, only 15 out of 150 initiatives had led to a local referendum (Eriksson and Kaufmann 2010). The Dutch constitution rules out any decisive referenda, but, recently, several municipalities in the Netherlands initiated experiments with local consultative corrective referenda. The procedures for local referenda differ markedly from one municipality to another. In the years from 1990 to 2013, more than 110 referenda were held in Dutch municipalities, about half of them linked to amalgamation proposals. In the Polish case, 10 percent of the municipal inhabitants are allowed to initiate a local referendum. The referendum is binding if turnout exceeds the legally set level of 30 percent of eligible voters in general.

Patterns of Democratic Renewal

In addition to the qualitative information per type of reform we were also able to make a systematic comparison of reform patterns, across different countries over the last 25 years (from 1990 to 2014). We asked local government experts from 28 European countries to indicate whether these three types of reforms were implemented in 1990 and in 2014. We coded their answers as either 0 = not implemented or 1 = fully implemented. In addition a score of 0.5 (not fully implemented) was given where reform was, for example, implemented in only part of the country.

We are well aware that such a rough coding scheme does not do full justice to all within-country variations and cross-national variations in institutional arrangements and practices. For example, the right of free access to information does not imply that such access is either techni- cally or culturally supported by administrative or political elites. Similarly, measuring the direct election of mayors with a binary code (0–1) does not say anything about the power of the mayors vis-à-vis the local councils, although such a detail may strongly affect citizen control. Nevertheless, simplification allows for a comparative view in order to detect and explain patterns of similarity or difference that may not otherwise become visible.

Table 15.1 summarizes the results of our expert survey. First, changes in European local democracy are obviously following Robert Dahl's vision of giving citizens more possibilities to participate in local politics. There is an overall trend towards giving citizens more information and more say in local policy-making. However, change is no universal phenomenon and the degree of change is different. In 9 out of the 28 cases no change occurred. In the majority of our cases (19 out of 28), however, change is visible, although to different degrees. There are clear politico-geographical patterns observable. In constructing the table and figure we grouped our countries into eight groups.

Changes are most distinctive in many post-communist countries even if one takes into account that the first steps of reform had already been taken early in the 1990s—before our comparison starts. There are only two "Western" local government systems where change is quite obvious: Germany and the UK. Change is least in the local government systems of the Northern and the Southern European groups with only some excep- tions in Belgium, Greece, France, and Iceland (Fig. 15.1).

It is also apparent that most changes were in the domain of free access to information. With regard to the more far-reaching reforms, like the introduction of directly elected mayors and even more so the implementa- tion of binding referenda (see Table 15.1), there is more reluctance. In these domains, at least in some countries, these democratic reforms would have led to major changes in the division of local powers and such changes would also require constitutional change in many cases. Free access to

Table 15.1 Presence of three institutional arrangements available for citizen involvement in local government in 28 European countries, 1990s and 2014

	Free access to information			Direct election of mayors			Local referenda			Total number of change
	1990s	2014	**Change**	1990s	2014	**Change**	1990s	2014	**Change**	1990s to 2014
N	1	1	0	0	0	0	1	1	0	0
SE	1	1	0	0	0	0	0	0	0	0
DK	1	1	0	0	0	0	0.5	0.5	0	0
SF	1	1	0	0	0	0	0.5	0.5	0	0
IS	0.5	1	0.5	0	0	0	0.5	0.5	0	0.5
NL	1	1	0	0	0	0	0.5	0.5	0	0
UK	0.5	1	0.5	0	0.5	0.5	0	0	0	1.0
IE	0.5	1	0.5	0	0	0	0.5	0.5	0	0.5
ES	0.5	0.5	0	0	0	0	0.5	0.5	0	0
PT	0.5	0.5	0	0	0	0	0.5	0.5	0	0
FR	0.5	0.5	0	0	0	0	0	0.5	0.5	0.5
BE	1	1	0	0	0	0	0	0.5	0.5	0.5
GR	0.5	1	0.5	1	1	0	0.5	0.5	0	0.5
IT	1	1	0	1	1	0	1	1	0	0
DE	0	0.5	0.5	0.5	1	0.5	0.5	1	0.5	1.5
CH	0.5	0.5	0	1	1	0	1	1	0	0
AT	0.5	0.5	0	0	0.5	0.5	1	1	0	0.5
LV	0	1	1	0	0	0	0	0	0	1
EE	0.5	1	0.5	0	0	0	0.5	0.5	0	0.5
CZ	0.5	1	0.5	0	0	0	1	1	0	0.5
LT	0.5	1	0.5	0	1	1	0	0	0	1.5
PL	0.5	1	0.5	0	1	1	1	1	0	1.5
HU	1	1	0	0	1	1	1	1	0	1
SK	0.5	1	0.5	1	1	0	1	1	0	0.5
SI	0.5	1	0.5	1	1	0	1	1	0	0.5
HR	0.5	0.5	0	0	1	1	0.5	0.5	0	1
BG	0.5	1	0.5	1	1	0	0	0.5	0.5	1
RO	0	1	1	1	1	0	0.5	0.5	0	1
Total	16.0	24.0	8.0	7.5	13	5.5	15	17	2	15.5
Mean	0.6	0.9	0.3	0.3	0.5	0.2	0.5	0.6	0.1	0.6
Stddev	0.3	0.2	0.3	0.4	0.5	0.4	0.4	0.3	0.2	0.5

Source: Own data collected in 2014 based on expert survey in these countries

Groups of countries are based on a combination of typologies by Hesse and Sharpe (1991) and Swianiewicz (2014). The first group comprises Northern Europe (*N* Norway, *SE* Sweden, *DK* Denmark, *SF* Finland, *IS* Iceland, *NL* Netherlands), where the degree of decentralization is traditionally high. The "Anglo" group are the UK and Ireland (IE). The "Franco" group comprises *ES* Spain, *PT* Portugal, *FR* France, *BE* Belgium, *GR* Greece, *IT* Italy, where local governments are of political rather than of functional importance. The fourth group are countries similar to the Northern European group but with federal rather than unitary systems (*DE* Germany, *CH* Switzerland, *AT* Austria). Following Swianiewicz (2014) we subdivide the post-communist countries into a number of more homogeneous clusters (comprising (a) *LV* Latvia, *EE* Estonia, *CZ* Czech Republic (b) *LT* Lithuania (c) *PL* Poland, *HU* Hungary, *SK* Slovakia (d) *SI* Slovenia, *HR* Croatia, *BU* Bulgaria, *RO* Romania information is probably less cumbersome and poses less of a threat to the status quo.

Although we find change towards more citizen control since the beginning of the 1990s, there are persistent country differences in the formal institutional opportunities offered citizens for involvement in local policy-making (Fig. 15.1). For many decades, citizens' involvement in local decision-making has been a main feature of Swiss local democracy, followed by that of Italy after the massive reforms in the beginning of the 1990s. By 2014, however, formal possibilities for citizen involvement

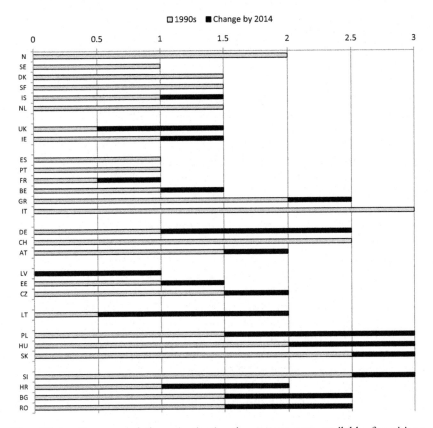

Fig. 15.1 Presence of three institutional arrangements available for citizen involvement in local government in 28 European countries. Total number in 1990s and 2014 (*Source*: Own data collected in 2014 based on expert survey)

in local policy-making seem to be even higher in many of the Central and Eastern European local government systems like Hungary, Poland, Slovakia, and Slovenia, although the data does not mirror the quality and quantity of citizen involvement in the these countries.

WHY DO WE FIND CHANGE IN SOME COUNTRIES BUT NOT IN OTHERS?

The theory of policy diffusions developed by Braun and Gilardi (2006) offers a useful starting point for explaining democratic reforms in various countries. This theory is based on the presumption that reforms can result from independent decisions of actors dependent upon internal determinants specific to particular countries. But the theory also recognizes that the introduction of new policies (reforms and innovations) may be the result of diffusion, defined as "a process where choices are interdependent, that is, where the choice of a government influences the choices made by others and, conversely, the choice of a government is influenced by the choices made by others" (Braun and Gilardi 2006, p. 299). Different mechanisms may account for such diffusion, like "learning," "competitive and cooperative interdependence," "coercion," "common norms," "taken-for-grantedness," and "symbolic imitation" (Braun and Gilardi 2006; see also Simmons and Elkins 2004).

Regarding the observed patterns of reform, "coercion" may have been a mechanism at work in the post-communist countries. "Coercion is the imposition of policies on national governments by powerful international organizations or powerful countries" (Braun and Gilardi 2006, p. 309). In post-communist countries, at least the right of free access to information was implemented, especially within the context of the EU accession period when these countries experienced pressure from international stakeholders and transparency became an important principle in order to implement good governance. Additionally, in most of the Central and Eastern European countries, the "taken-for-grantedness" mechanism (where certain policies "become accepted as the normal or even the obvious thing to do"; Braun and Gilardi 2006, p. 311) may also have been at work. After decades of centralism and communism with the democratic transitions a new generation of political leaders rose to power who accepted modern standards of transparency and citizen control inspired by Western European standards (Finnemore and Sikkink 1998). The same mechanism might also explain reforms in Italy or Greece, where strong internal pressure might have shaped an environment for breaking with the prevailing institutional setting.

"Coercion" and "taken-for-grantedness," however, do not explain change in a country like Germany. Here the change mechanisms are in all likelihood primarily domestic rather than inspired by imposition of or inspiration by external standards. In Germany, a discourse on declining political legitimacy (indicated, for example, by low and declining voter turnout) was prevalent. Moreover, inspiration was provided by progressive local government constitutions in the "new" German states after reunification. This strengthened beliefs in the value of increasing citizen participation. In this climate of opinion, and under the political pressure of opposition parties and strong civil groups, state governments—responsible for local democratic reforms—adopted democratic reforms (Vetter 2009). In other European countries domestic factors may have been less favorable to nationwide democratic reforms. In the Netherlands, for example, the adoption of reform laws that strengthen local citizens' control is made virtually impossible by the super-majorities required for the necessary constitutional changes (Andeweg and Irwin 1989). Such constitutional barriers may also explain the continuities that we observe in Fig. 15.1.

Of course these are post-hoc interpretations rather than a full-fledged explanation, but our observations suggest that, as one might expect, democratic reforms are the result of domestic political factors (electoral, competition, opinion climate, and constitutional arrangements). As diffusion theory suggests, these reforms are also externally determined by factors like coercion, learning, and imitation.

Acknowledgements We would like to thank our colleagues from the COST project as well as other research colleagues who supported us by completing our questionnaire: Harald Baldersheim (Norway), Anders Lidström (Sweden); Ulrik Kjær (Denmark); Eva Marín Hlynsdóttir (Iceland); Siv Sandberg (Finland); Colin Copus (UK); Andreas Ladner (Switzerland); Anna Gamper (Austria); Joan Font and Angel Iglesias (Spain); Paolo Fedele (Italy); Vincent Hoffmann-Martinot (France); Kristof Steyvers (Belgium); Nikos Hlepas (Greece); Carlos Nunes Silva (Portugal); Inga Vilka (Latvia); Egidius Barcevicius and Oksana Mejere (Lithuania); Ringa Raudla (Estonia); Paweł Swianiewicz and Adam Gendzwill (Poland); Michal Illner (Czech Republic); Miro Hacek (Slovenia); Gabor Soos (Hungary); Dubravka J. Alibegovic (Croatia); Desislava Stoilova (Bulgaria); Calin Hintea (Romania); Gerard Turley and John McEldowney (Ireland). Because of their small size we excluded Luxembourg, Malta and Cyprus from this study.

REFERENCES

Andeweg, R.B., and G.A. Irwin. 1989. Institutional conservatism in the Netherlands: Proposals and resistance to change. In *Politics in the Netherlands: How much change?* ed. H. Daalder. London: Frank Cass.

Baldersheim, H., M. Illner, and H. Wollmann (eds.). 2003. *Local democracy in post-communist Europe.* Wiesbaden: VS Verlag für Sozialwissenschaften.

Beynon-Davies, P., and S. Martin. 2004. Electronic local government and the modernisation agenda: Progress and prospects for public service improvement. *Local Government Studies* 30(2): 214–229.

Braun, D., and F. Gilardi. 2006. Taking "Galton's problem" seriously. Towards a theory of policy diffusion. *Journal of Theoretical Politics* 18(3): 298–322.

COE. 1993. *Local referendums.* Strasbourg: The Council of Europe Press.

Coulson, A., and A. Campbell (eds.). 2008. *Local government in Central and Eastern Europe: The rebirth of local democracy.* New York: Routledge.

Dahl, R.A. 1994. A democratic dilemma. System effectiveness versus citizen participation. *Political Science Quarterly* 1: 23–34.

Dahl, R.A. 1998. *On democracy.* New Haven/London: Yale University Press.

Dalton, R.J., and M. Gray. 2003. Expanding the electoral marketplace. In *Democracy transformed? Expanding political opportunities in advanced industrial democracies,* ed. B.E. Cain, R.J. Dalton, and S.E. Scarrow. Oxford: Oxford University Press.

Denters, B., and L.E. Rose. 2005. *Comparing local governance. Trends and developments.* Houndmills: Palgrave Macmillan.

Eriksson, P., and B. Kaufmann. 2010. *Folkinitiativ: Handbok i direktdemokrati.* Stockholm: Premiss förlag.

Finnemore, M., and K. Sikkink. 1998. International norm dynamics and political change. *International Organization* 52(4): 887–917.

Hendriks, F., A. Lidström, and J. Loughlin (eds.). 2011. *The oxford handbook of local and regional democracy in Europe.* Oxford: Oxford University Press.

Hesse, J.J., and L.J. Sharpe. 1991. Local government in international perspective: Some comparative observations. In *Local government and urban affairs in international perspective,* ed. J.J. Hesse. Baden-Baden: Nomos.

John, P., and C. Copus. 2011. The United Kingdom: Is there really an Anglo model? In *The Oxford handbook of local and regional democracy in Europe,* ed. F. Hendriks, A. Lidström, and J. Loughlin. Oxford: Oxford University Press.

Jüptner, P., M. Batorova, V. Bubeníček, S. Drezgić, D. Klimovský, and I. Kruntoradova. 2014. *Local governance between democracy and efficiency.* Novo mesto: Faculty of Organization Studies in Novo mesto and Charles University in Prague.

Kersting, N., and A. Vetter. 2003. *Reforming local government in Europe: Closing the gap between democracy and efficiency.* Opladen: Leske + Budrich.

Kersting, N., J. Caulfield, A. Nickson, D. Olowu, and H. Wollmann. 2009. *Local governance reform in global perspective.* Wiesbaden: VS Springer.

Klimovský, D. 2009. Klasifikácia spôsobov kreovania základných orgánov obecnej samosprávy v európskej perspective. *Acta Politologica* 1(3): 241–267.

Koprić, I. 2009. Roles and styles of local political leaders on the territory of the former Yugoslavia: Between authoritarian local political top bosses and citizen-oriented local managers. *Hrvatska javna uprava* 9(1): 79–105.

Kuhlmann, S. 2009. Reforming local government in Germany: Institutional changes and performance impacts. *German Politics* 18(2): 226–245.

Ladner, A. 2002. Size and direct democracy at the local level: The case of Switzerland. *Environment and Planning C: Government and Policy* 20(6): 813–828.

Meyer, J.W., and B. Rowan. 1977. Institutionalized organizations: Formal structure as myth and ceremony. *American Journal of Sociology* 83(2): 340–363.

Qvotrup, N. (ed.). 2014. *Referendums around the world.* London: Palgrave.

Reynaert, H. 2005. *Revolution or renovation? Reforming local politics in Europe.* Bruges: Vanden Broele.

Šaradín, P. 2010. Direct elections of mayors in the Czech Republic? Data from research and political support. *Contemporary European Studies* 2: 77–85.

Scarrow, S.E. 2001. Direct democracy and institutional change: A comparative investigation. *Comparative Political Studies* 34(6): 651–665.

Schaap, L., and H. Daemen (eds.). 2012. *Renewal in European local democracies: Puzzles, dilemmas and options.* Wiesbaden: VS Verlag für Sozialwissenschaften.

Schiller, T. 2011. Local direct democracy in Europe—a comparative overview. In *Local direct democracy in Europe*, ed. T. Schiller. Wiesbaden: VS Verlag für Sozialwissenschaften.

Simmons, B., and Z. Elkins. 2004. The globalization of liberalization: Policy diffusion in the international political economy. *American Political Science Review* 98(1): 171–189.

Soós, G., G. Tóka, and G. Wright (eds.). 2002. *The state of local democracy in Central Europe.* Budapest: OSI/LGI.

Swianiewicz, P. 2014. An empirical typology of local government systems in Eastern Europe. *Local Government Studies* 40: 292–311.

Temesi, I. 2000. Local government in Hungary. In *Decentralization: Experiences and reforms*, ed. T. Horváth. Budapest: OSI/LGI.

Vetter, A. 2006. Modernizing German local government: Bringing the people back in? In *State and local government reforms in France and Germany. Divergence and convergence*, ed. H. Wollmann and V. Hoffmann-Martinot. Wiesbaden: VS Verlag für Sozialwissenschaften.

Vetter, A. 2009. Citizens versus parties. Explaining institutional change in German local government 1989–2008. *Local Government Studies* 35: 125–142.

Wollmann, H. 2009. The ascent of the directly elected mayor in European local government in West and East. In *Local political leadership in Europe: Town chief, city boss or loco president?* ed. H. Reynaert, K. Steyvers, P. Delwit, and J.B. Pilet. Bruges/Baden-Baden: Vanden Broele, Nomos.

CHAPTER 16

Reforming Local Councils and the Role of Councillors: A Comparative Analysis of Fifteen European Countries

Anders Lidström, Harald Baldersheim, Colin Copus, Eva Marín Hlynsdóttir, Pekka Kettunen, and Daniel Klimovský

A. Lidström (✉)
Department of Political Science, Umeå University, Umeå, Sweden

H. Baldersheim
Department of Political Science, University of Oslo, Oslo, Norway

C. Copus
Department of Politics and Public Policy, De Montfort University, Leicester, UK

E.M. Hlynsdóttir
Faculty of Political Science, University of Iceland, Reykjavík, Iceland

P. Kettunen
Faculty of Social Sciences, Business and Economics, Turku, Finland

D. Klimovský
Institute of Public Policy, Faculty of Social and Economic Sciences, Comenius University, Bratislava, Slovakia

© The Author(s) 2016   287
S. Kuhlmann, G. Bouckaert (eds.), *Local Public Sector Reforms in Times of Crisis*, DOI 10.1057/978-1-137-52548-2_16

Introduction

European local authorities are essentially units of representative democracy (Loughlin et al. 2011; Schaap and Daemen 2012; Egner et al. 2013). Although some municipalities are ruled by municipal assemblies and, despite local referendums having become more frequent in recent decades, all European countries have local government systems that are either entirely based on representative democracy or, as is the case in Switzerland, possess significant components of it. That the most important municipal decisions are taken by elected councils and that citizens can hold the members accountable for their decisions is a cornerstone of European local democracy. However, in recent decades these institutions have been seriously challenged. The primary reason is that citizens have become increasingly well educated, critical and demanding, and the financial crisis of 2008 added to the challenge. This is expressed through decreasing turnout in local elections, weakening of political parties, reduction of citizens' trust in local councillors and questioning of whether elected representatives possess sufficient competence for their tasks (Kersting and Vetter 2003; Schaap and Daemen 2012). In some cases, local government has suffered losses of function, either through privatization or through transfer of traditional local government functions to other types of institutions or other levels of government. The quality of democracy at regional, national, and European levels has also been criticized (Crouch 2004; Norris 2011; Papadopolous 2013), but the challenges at local level show particular characteristics as the municipalities are the units of democracy closest to the citizens.

This criticism of council-based representative democracy has inspired political reforms aimed at improving local democracy (Reynaert et al. 2005; Denters and Rose 2005). Some of these, such as the introduction of binding referendums or directly elected mayors, have attempted to identify alternatives to council-based representative democracy. Other reforms have instead aimed at restoring or improving existing institutions of representative democracy, for example, by facilitating citizen participation in local elections, providing administrative support for the councillors, strengthening the role of the council vis-à-vis the executive, providing financial support for political parties, or making the council meetings more accessible and interesting to the general public (Denters and Rose 2005). Although alternatives to representative democracy may make a difference, the importance of the councillors and the council remains largely undisputed. Most key decisions on local government and the responsibility for carrying out local policies remain in their hands.

This chapter highlights and analyzes attempts to restore and improve existing institutions of representative democracy—the councils and the councillors—in 15 European countries from a comparative perspective. The chapter develops a typology of reforms and seeks to analyze drivers of, and approaches to, reform. Most of the initiatives are national, covering an entire country, but some may be specific to parts of countries or certain localities. The focus is on the extent to which there are differences and similarities between countries with regard to the occurrence of reforms, and how these may be understood.

The various *types of reform* may be related to three core functions of local councils and councillors in a representative democracy: mediation, decision making, and scrutiny. As *mediators,* local councillors represent and reflect the various, and often competing, interests found in a community. The classical debate in this respect is concerned with the councillor as delegate versus trustee; in recent decades concerns with descriptive and substantive representation have come more to the fore. The latter is reflected in worries over the socio-demographic composition of councils, especially the possible underrepresentation of women or marginal groups, and the extent to which the council actually reflects the range of opinions in the community (Mansbridge 2003; Williams 2000). As *decision makers* the councillors set the priorities regarding the tasks to be performed by the municipality, ideally in a manner that reflects the preferences of the voters as expressed in electoral outcomes. In this regard, reformers have been preoccupied with introducing more of a strategic orientation into council decision making, often inspired by New Public Management, moving away from a hands-on or clientelistic style of politics, leaving details to managers (Mouritzen and Svara 2002). The function of *scrutiny* concerns holding the executive of the municipality accountable to the council and ultimately to the voters. Accountability is pursued in several ways, especially through enhancing openness and transparency and by clarifying the lines of responsibility and division of work between the executive and the council.

The overarching ambition of the reforms of councils and the councillors is to enhance the status and legitimacy of local representative democracy. Consequently, we expect the extent to which a country's local government system generally enjoys a high level of legitimacy to have consequences for reform patterns. One general assumption in this study is that, in countries where local government enjoys a relatively high degree of legitimacy, a decline of legitimacy may still be regarded as reparable, whereas in countries where local government is generally held in low esteem, it may be more logical to look for ways of organizing local democracy other than through (improvements of) the current workings of local councils. Hence, we will assume that reforms aimed at improving the position of the council and the councillors will be more common in countries where local government is highly esteemed.

The concept of legitimacy has been referred to as "the willingness to comply with a system of rule" (Weber 1947), independent of who the current rulers are. Citizen trust in local government is a basic source of legitimacy (Roos and Lidström 2014). However, in modern political theory, a distinction is often made between input and output legitimacy (Scharpf 1999). The former denotes legitimacy derived from adherence to proper procedures for the selection of decision makers, normally electoral procedures. The latter points to legitimacy derived from citizens' satisfaction with the results of decisions, or the outputs of the political process. In this chapter, citizen support is represented by a measure of citizen trust in local and regional government based on surveys and by turnout for local elections. Thus, the concept as applied here combines aspects of input and output legitimacy.

Furthermore, when studying the legitimacy of local government, it must be remembered that local authorities are simultaneously creatures of the state and expressions of the self-government of the citizens in a locality (Lidström 1998). The range of responsibilities and extent of financial and other competencies entrusted to local government may be taken as an expression of the state's confidence in local government. For practical purposes, we take local government expenditure as a proportion of total public spending as the measure of the state's confidence in local government. The larger the proportion, the more important local government is in the overall political system of a country, and the more important the effectiveness of local decision making and service provision is to central government.

By combining the two sources of legitimacy we establish four ideal types of local government legitimacy. Local government may primarily receive its legitimacy from below or from above, from both of these sources, or from neither. Based on the measurements presented above, and using the median value of each distribution as cut-off points, all the countries can

Table 16.1 Types of local government legitimacy in selected European countries

		National government confidence in local government Local govt expenditure as % of total public expenditure; >25% = high	
		High	**Low**
Citizen trust in local government > 50% = high	High	**Strong level of legitimacy** *Norway, Sweden, Finland, Iceland, the Netherlands,* Denmark, Estonia	Bottom-up legitimacy *Germany, Switzerland, France,* Austria, Belgium, Luxembourg
	Low	**Top-down legitimacy** *Poland, United Kingdom, Italy*	**Weak legitimacy** *Slovakia, Ireland, Spain, Greece,* Czech Republic, Slovenia, Hungary, Portugal

Sources: OECD Fiscal Decentralisation Database: Consolidated government expenditure as percentage of total general government expenditure (consolidated) [Table 5: 1969–2012] http://www.oecd.org/ctp/federalism/oecdfiscaldecentralisationdatabase.htm (COR 2001; Eurobarometer 2008, 2012; Lidström 2003; Iancu 2013; Jüptner et al. 2014; Vetter 2014; Vilka and Brekis 2013). Countries in *italics* have been selected for analysis in this chapter. Sufficient data are not available to include other European countries in the table

be given a position in relationship to these ideal types. Results are summarized in Table 16.1.

Local government that has *a strong level of legitimacy*, and is supported by both the state and the citizens, is found in countries with the Nordic type of welfare state, which combines a role for local governments as implementers of national welfare policy with a significant amount of self-government. The Netherlands and Estonia are also positioned here. National and local government are closely interwoven and form a *partnership* type of local governance. Local government with *bottom-up legitimacy* is mainly found in the mid European federations. Significant functions are carried out at the *Länder/canton* level which makes local government less relevant from a national point of view, although they remain very much trusted by the citizens. Here we may identify a *communitarian* type of local governance. Although we lack data for citizens' trust in local government in Switzerland, previous studies have indicated that it is higher than for several other countries in this group (Denters et al. 2014). Here France and Luxembourg, with fairly small municipalities, can also be found.

Poland, the UK, and Italy are cases of *top-down legitimacy*. Central government has entrusted local government with significant functions; however, its legitimacy in the eyes of the citizens is low, although the UK is a borderline case. In these cases, local government is primarily regarded as *state servant*. Finally, *weak legitimacy*, where neither citizens nor the state have trust in local government, can be found in many Eastern and Southern European countries but also in Ireland. Here, local government is a *marginal* phenomenon in the overall system of governance.

Perhaps not surprisingly, how the countries end up in these different categories to some extent coincides with contemporary classifications of local government systems, although these may be based on criteria other than the legitimacy of local democracy (Heinelt and Hlepas 2006; Sellers and Lidström 2003; Loughlin et al. 2011; Swianiewicz 2014).

In the next section we will examine whether type of local government legitimacy matters for the *kind of* reforms of councils and councillor roles that have been carried out. Our assumption is that concern with these core institutions of representative democracy will be stronger the more legitimate local government is. The countries with strong legitimacy are expected not only to initiate a broad range and different types of reforms aimed at improving the position of the councils and the councillors; they are also more likely to abstain from reforms that could undermine traditional forms of representative democracy. In consequence, countries with bottom-up legitimate local government are likely to initiate reforms that strengthen its relationship with citizens by enhancing participation and responsiveness, while those with top-down legitimacy will aim at maintaining central government trust by improving local service delivery. However, in all the countries apart from those with strong local government legitimacy, we expect more willingness to introduce alternative means of democracy, such as direct election of mayors or binding referendums.

Restoring Local Representative Democracy: Reform Patterns

As the basis for comparative analysis, fifteen countries have been selected representing the different types of local government legitimacy identified in Table 19.1. Below, the main traits of reforms aimed at improving the position of council and the councillor are summarized.

Local Government with Strong Level of Legitimacy
Local authorities in these countries combine strong support from both the citizens and national government. This category consists of the

Nordic countries (Denmark, Finland, Iceland, Norway and Sweden), the Netherlands and Estonia. It is well established in the literature that Nordic local government occupies an exceptional position. Previous analyses have also suggested that local government in the Netherlands resembles the Nordic countries in terms of its welfare functions and capacity (Loughlin et al. 2011; Sellers and Lidström 2007). Estonian local government is a borderline case in terms of central government trust, but clearly enjoys strong support from its citizens.

These countries appear to be highly active in terms of initiating and implementing reforms aimed at improving the position of the councils and the councillors. At the same time, they are reluctant to open up for alternative local electoral positions, such as directly elected mayors, or to introduce stronger means of local direct democracy. Indeed, in Norway direct election of executive committee chairs was permitted on an experimental basis, but has now been discontinued.

Reform activities in these countries appear to follow mainly four paths. First, one set of reforms aims at giving the local council a more strategic role, often combined with a clarification of the position of the executive. The clearest example of such reforms is the 2002 Dutch dualization reform. All executive responsibilities were transferred to the Court of the Mayor and Aldermen (CMA) leaving the council with responsibility for governing, scrutiny, and representation. If council members are appointed to the CMA they must give up their seat on the council. The council has the power to remove aldermen with a majority vote. The primary consequence of these reforms was to strengthen the mayoral office (Hendriks and Schaap 2011; Schaap 2009). Similar reforms have been carried out in other countries in this category, sometimes linked to a New Public Management agenda aimed at improving efficiency.

The second path of reform is strengthening the council by clarifying roles and responsibilities and facilitating accountability by clarifying the roles of the political majority and the opposition. The most conspicuous initiative in this regard is the emergence of what is termed the parliamentary model in Norway, which was regarded as a revolutionary departure from the traditional consensual principles of Norwegian local politics (Baldersheim 2005). This model originated in Oslo in the 1980s and has now spread to four of the larger cities and four county councils. It means that the coalition of parties that can form a majority prevails, but if a vote of no confidence is passed the power shifts to the opposition according to principles that are familiar from national parliaments in many countries.

Third, the weakening of political parties is compensated for by municipal financial or administrative support to local parties. The argument is that this is necessary as the parties are a crucial element in a well-functioning local democracy. In Sweden, municipal financial support to political parties in the council became legal in the 1970s and is now provided by all municipalities, generally in proportion to the strength of the party in the council. With declining party membership, such support has become increasingly important as a source of finance, and has made parties less dependent on private donations and membership fees. The parties have been able to maintain their role, but at the expense of the increasing dominance of party elites (Copus and Erlingsson 2012).

Fourth, with the purpose of trying to reverse declining turnout in local elections, attempts have been made to facilitate voting. In the 2011 Norwegian local elections, ten municipalities were selected for experiments in electronic voting. Voters could cast their votes from any computer with internet connection. The initiative was well received, especially by voters with physical disabilities, but the overall level of voter turnout did not increase. Corresponding experiments were carried out in two Finnish municipalities, again without any positive results. From 1997, Sweden opened up for electors to indicate their support for a particular candidate. However, such support has seldom strengthened councillors' position in the council.

Local Government with Bottom-Up Legitimacy

Countries where local government is legitimate in the eyes of the citizens, but where they have been awarded only a limited role in the public sector as a whole, include the four mid-European federal states of Austria, Belgium, Germany, and Switzerland as well as France and Luxembourg. This is perhaps not surprising as the presence of a *Länder/canton* level and/or the small size of municipalities mean the latter are less relevant as service providers, although they remain important as units of local identification among their citizens. The reform impulse that seeks to strengthen the role of the council and the councillor seems to be weaker among these countries than in the countries where local government has strong legitimacy. Consequently, many have chosen to follow paths of democratic reform other than the restoration of the councils.

All the German states have introduced both additional elected representatives (the directly elected mayors) and local binding referendums. These reforms have exerted an impact on the position and procedures of local councils (Bogumil 2006). Governance systems with directly elected mayors seem to work better in *Länder* with more personalized electoral systems and a tradition of consensus politics (*Konkordanzpolitik*) (Banner 2006). An analysis of relationships between local councils and management demonstrated that managers tend to have the upper hand where the consensus tradition dominates while competitive, party-dominated politics provides more space for councillor control (Holtkamp 2006).

Switzerland is an extremely diverse, decentralized country with considerable differences between cantons in terms of language and religion. This is also reflected in the institutional preconditions for local government which vary between them. Swiss local democracy differs from the mainstream European tradition with its strong emphasis on means of direct democracy, carried out at municipal assemblies and through referendums. Hence, it is not surprising that Swiss local government derives its legitimacy primarily from its citizens. However, approximately 20 percent of municipalities, mainly the bigger cities and municipalities in the French-speaking parts, have a representative system using elected local councils (Ladner 2011). Among recent council reforms, a recall referendum of the council was introduced in the Uri canton in 2011.

Bottom-up legitimacy is also a feature of French municipal government, which is based on small units with a strong sense of identification. There are currently about 36,000 municipalities with an average of 1700 inhabitants. Each municipality is governed by an elected council which appoints the mayor. The mayor has traditionally held a strong position vis-à-vis the council, which is reinforced by the tradition of combining this position with membership of decision-making units at higher levels of government. The position of mayor seems to have been strengthened in recent years at the expense of the council. One reason is the transfer of municipal functions to units of inter-municipal cooperation. It has even been suggested that there are tendencies towards "urban presidentialism" in France (Hoffmann-Martinot and Wollmann 2006). Many of the council reforms in France have aimed at improving the responsiveness of the electoral system. For example, from 2014 majority voting was replaced by a proportional system in municipalities with a population of between 1000 and 3500 inhabitants. The same year, direct elections to intercommunal bodies were introduced.

Local Government with Top-Down Legitimacy
The local authorities in this category have been entrusted with extensive public tasks, however they suffer weak support from their citizens. Many of these countries have chosen alternative means of democracy rather than

reforming councils. In Poland, the position of the council was weakened by the introduction of directly elected mayors in 2002, although the council retains significant functions. For example, both the budget and the selection of the local treasurer must be approved by the council, and the mayor cannot chair the municipal council. Political parties are less important than in other European countries (Aars et al. 2012). Almost 74 percent of all seats in municipal councils were won by independent (non-party) candidates in the 2010 elections, and this is particularly common in the rural areas.

In the UK, council reforms have primarily aimed at improving the efficiency of local decision making by strengthening the executive functions of local government. In 2000, executive managers and cabinets, as well as an option to elect mayors directly, were introduced (ODPM 2004). All municipalities with a population of more than 85,000 were required to adopt an executive system which would include a cabinet of not more than ten councillors. They would also need to set up an overview and scrutiny committee with the task of holding the executive to account and reviewing its policies. The smaller municipalities would have a non-executive, slimmed-down committee system with an overview and scrutiny function. Reforms in 2013 relaxed these requirements, which resulted in 14 councils returning to the previous committee system. Research has found, however, that the aims of these reforms have not yet been fully realized (Copus 2008).

Italian local government was significantly reformed in 1993 in order to clarify lines of responsibility. Directly elected mayors were introduced and they also guaranteed a majority in the council. Localist and personalized political parties replaced national and ideological parties at local level. However, no further reforms of significance have been introduced (Piattoni and Brunazzo 2011).

Local Government with Weak Legitimacy

In the final group of countries, local governments have a weak position in relation to both national government and their own citizens. This group includes many countries in eastern, central and southern Europe and also Ireland. Some of them are among the poorest in the EU and experience serious problems of corruption. These countries have also been severely affected by the financial crisis that began in 2008. Probably as a consequence, citizens' trust in local and regional government fell dramatically between 2008 and 2012 in Ireland, Greece, Portugal, and Spain. There have been only limited attempts to strengthen the position of the councils and councillors in these countries. The focus has been on managing the financial crisis, rather than on reforming the councils.

The local councils in this category are often weak, in particular in countries where there are directly elected mayors. In Slovakia, the mayors' position has repeatedly been strengthened. Since 2010, they have been entitled to appoint their own deputies who were previously elected by the council. In Spain the mayor used to be constrained in his/her executive capacities by having to pass most decisions through the council, however, the situation changed in 1999 with a reform that increased the mayoral powers (Guérin and Kerrouch 2008). In recent years the position of the councils has improved as they have been allocated supervisory powers.

Irish local government also finds itself distrusted by both the citizens and central government. It has a history of being stripped of many key functions, such as education, police, and social welfare, which are local government functions in most other European countries. There has also been a trend to transfer powers from local councillors to the city manager, who is subordinate to central government. A major territorial reform in 2014, largely initiated as a response to the financial crisis, resulted in a new two-tier system, and almost halved of the number of councillors (Callanan et al. 2014).

Reforms in Greece have also primarily been carried out in response to the financial crisis. Two amalgamation reforms drastically reduced the number of councillors, thereby increasing the citizen:councillor ratio. Larger municipalities have also changed their style of policy making from traditional patronage to machine politics (Hlepas and Getimis 2011) although the legitimacy crisis of the political parties has appeared to enhance, once again, personal ties and the role of personalities in local politics. The financial squeeze has significantly reduced resources and scope for action by the municipalities.

CONCLUSIONS

In most European countries, the workings of representative local democracy have come under scrutiny in recent decades. Critics have questioned whether local councils and councillors will be able to continue to function as key institutions of local democracy, or whether they need to be replaced by, or complemented with, other instruments for citizen involvement. This has triggered reform activities, aimed at strengthening or restoring the position of these institutions. This chapter has examined the occurrence of such reforms and tried to explain contrasts between countries.

It is clear from this overview that countries vary with regard to both the intensity of their reform activities and their content. This variation appears, to a great extent, to reflect the type of legitimacy that each local government enjoys. Where local government has a strong level of legitimacy, that is, where it is supported by both central government and the citizens, many different types of reforms aimed at improving the position of the councils have been initiated continuously over several decades. Where local government has support from central government but not from citizens, reforms tend to focus on strengthening the executive and increasing decision-making efficiency. Reform activity seems generally to be lower in countries where local government enjoys only bottom-up legitimacy, that is, where it is supported by the citizens but not the state. Where local government lacks support from both the state and the citizens, reform activity level is even lower and has primarily been a response to the financial crisis and is not concerned with local representative democracy as such.

REFERENCES

Aars, J., A. Offerdal, and D. Ryšavý. 2012. The careers of European local councillors: A cross-national comparison. *Lex Localis—Journal of Local Self-Government* 10: 63–84.

Baldersheim, H. 2005. From aldermen to ministers. The Oslo model revisited. In *Transforming political leadership in local government*, ed. R. Berg and N. Rao. London: Palgrave.

Banner, G. 2006. Führung und Leistung der Kommunen. *Deutsche Zeitschrift für Kommunalwissenschaften* 45: 57–69.

Bogumil, J. 2006. Verwaltungsmodernisierung und die Logik der Poltik. Auswirkung des Neuen Steuerungsmodells auf das Verhältnis von Kommunalpolitik und Kommunalverwaltung. *Deutsche Zeitschrift für Kommunalwissenschaften* 45: 13–24.

Callanan, M., R. Murphy, and A. Quinlivan. 2014. The risks of intuition: Size, costs and economies of scale in local government. *The Economic and Social Review* 45: 371–403.

Copus, C. 2008. English councillors and mayoral governance: Developing a new dynamic for political accountability. *Political Quarterly* 79: 590–604.

Copus, C., and G. Erlingsson. 2012. Parties in local government: A review. *Representation* 48: 235–47.

COR. 2001. *Voter turnout at regional and local elections in the European union 1990–2001*. Brussels: EU Committee of the Regions.

Crouch, C. 2004. *Post-democracy.* Cambridge: Polity Press.

Denters, B., and L.E. Rose (eds.). 2005. *Comparing local governance. Trends and developments.* Houndmills: Palgrave Macmillan.

Denters, B., M. Goldsmith, A. Ladner, P.E. Mouritzen, and L.E. Rose. 2014. *Size and local democracy.* Cheltenham: Edward Elgar.

Egner, B., D. Sweeting, and P.-J. Klok (eds.). 2013. *Local councillors in Europe.* Wiesbaden: Springer VS Verlag für Sozialwissenschaften.

Eurobarometer. 2008. Special Eurobarometer no. 307, Autumn 2008.

Eurobarometer. 2012. No. 77, Spring 2012.

Guérin, É., and É. Kerrouch. 2008. From amateurs to professionals: The changing face of local elected representatives in Europe. *Local Government Studies* 34: 179–201.

Heinelt, H., and N.-K. Hlepas. 2006. Typologies of local government systems. In *The European mayor. Political leaders in the changing context of local democracy,* ed. H. Bäck, H. Heinelt, and A. Magnier. Wiesbaden: VS Verlag für Sozialwissenschaften.

Hendriks, F., and L. Schaap. 2011. The Netherlands: Subnational democracy and the reinvention of tradition. In *The Oxford handbook of local and regional democracy in Europe,* ed. J. Loughlin, F. Hendriks, and A. Lidström. Oxford: Oxford University Press.

Hlepas, N.-K., and P. Getimis. 2011. Impacts of local government reform in Greece: An interim assessment. *Local Government Studies* 37: 517–32.

Hoffmann-Martinot, V., and H. Wollmann (eds.). 2006. *State and local government reforms in France and Germany: Divergence and convergence.* Wiesbaden: VS Verlag für Sozialwissenschaften.

Holtkamp, L. 2006. 'Kommunalpolitik zwischen Konkordanz- und Konkurrenzdemokratie—Ausmass. *Ursachen und Probleme des Parteieneinflusses',* *Deutsche Zeitschrift für Kommunalwissenschaften* 45: 70–83.

Iancu, D.-C. (ed.). 2013. *Local reforms in transition democracies.* Iaşi: Institutul European.

Jüptner, P., M. Batorova, V. Bubeníček, S. Drezgić, D. Klimovský, and I. Kruntoradova. 2014. *Local governance between democracy and efficiency.* Novo mesto: Faculty of Organization Studies in Novo mesto & Charles University in Prague.

Kersting, N., and A. Vetter (eds.). 2003. *Reforming local government in Europe.* Opladen: Leske + Budrich.

Ladner, A. 2011. Switzerland: Subsidiarity, power-sharing and direct democracy. In *The Oxford handbook of local and regional democracy in Europe,* ed. J. Loughlin, F. Hendriks, and A. Lidström. Oxford: Oxford University Press.

Lidström, A. 1998. The comparative study of local government systems - a research agenda. *Journal of Comparative Policy Analysis: Research and Practice* 1: 97–115.

Lidström, A. 2003. *Kommunsystem i Europa*. Malmö: Liber.

Loughlin, J., F. Hendriks, and A. Lidström (eds.). 2011. *The Oxford handbook of local and regional democracy in Europe*. Oxford: Oxford University Press.

Mansbridge, J. 2003. Rethinking representation. *American Political Science Review* 97(4): 515–28.

Mouritzen, P.E., and J.H. Svara. 2002. *Leadership at the Apex. Politicians and administrators in Western local government*. Pittsburg: University of Pittsburg Press.

Norris, P. 2011. *Democratic deficit. Critical citizens revisited*. Cambridge: Cambridge University Press.

ODPM. 2004. *The future of local government: Developing a ten year vision*. London: Office of the Deputy Prime Minister.

Papadopolous, Y. 2013. *Democracy in crisis? Politics, governance and policy*. Houndmills: Palgrave Macmillan.

Piattoni, S., and M. Brunazzo. 2011. Italy: The subnational dimension to strengthening democracy since the 1990s. In *The Oxford handbook of local and regional democracy in Europe*, ed. J. Loughlin, F. Hendriks, and A. Lidström. Oxford: Oxford University Press.

Reynaert, H., K. Steyvers, P. Delwit, and J.-B. Pilet (eds.). 2005. *Revolution or renovation. Reforming local politics in Europe*. Bruges: Vanden Broele.

Roos, K., and A. Lidström. 2014. Local policies and local government legitimacy. The Swedish case. *Urban Research and Practice* 7: 137–52.

Schaap, L. 2009. De Burgmeester'. Netherlands' mayoral leadership in consensual democracy and collegial policymaking? In *Local political leadership in Europe*, ed. H. Reynaert, K. Steyvers, P. Delwit, and J.-B. Pilet. Bruges: Vanden Broele.

Schaap, L., and H. Daemen (eds.). 2012. *Renewal in European local democracies*. Wiesbaden: Springer VS Verlag für Sozialwissenschaften.

Scharpf, F.W. 1999. *Governing in Europe: Effective and democratic?* Oxford: Oxford University Press.

Sellers, J., and A. Lidström. 2007. Decentralization, local government, and the welfare state. *Governance* 20: 609–32.

Swianiewicz, P. 2014. An empirical typology of local government systems in Eastern Europe. *Local Government Studies* 40: 292–311.

Vetter, A. 2014. Just a matter of timing? Local electoral turnout in Germany in the context of national and European parliamentary elections. *German Politics*. doi:10.1080/09644008.2014.984693.

Vilka, I., and E. Brekis. 2013. Comparing local government elections in Latvia and other European countries. *Socialiniai tyrimai/Social Research* 32: 5–16.

Weber, M. 1947. *The theory of social and economic organization*. New York: Free Press.

Williams, M. 2000. The uneasy alliance of group representation and deliberative democracy. In *Citizenship in diverse societies*, ed. W. Kymlicka and W. Norman, 124–53. Oxford: Oxford University Press. Ch. 5.

CHAPTER 17

Have Mayors Will Travel: Trends and Developments in the Direct Election of the Mayor: A Five-Nation Study

Colin Copus, Angel Iglesias, Miro Hacek, Michal Illner, and Anders Lidström

INTRODUCTION

The debate about whether citizens or councilors should choose the political head of the council has spread across Europe (Berg and Rao 2005; Denters and Rose 2005). At the heart of discussion about the route to local leadership are questions about the legitimacy to act, the visibility and

C. Copus (✉)
De Montfort University, Leicester, England

A. Iglesias
University Rey Juan Carlos, Madrid, Spain

M. Hacek
University of Ljubljana, Ljubljana, Slovenia

M. Illner
Institute of Sociology - Academy of Sciences, Prague, Czech Republic

A. Lidström
Umeå University, Umeå, Sweden

© The Author(s) 2016
S. Kuhlmann, G. Bouckaert (eds.), *Local Public Sector Reforms in Times of Crisis*, DOI 10.1057/978-1-137-52548-2_17

301

profile of local leaders, the transparency of political decision-making processes, the most effective mechanism for political accountability, and the role of citizens in local democracy (Kersting and Vetter 2003; Magre and Betrana 2007; Elcock 2008; Wollmann 2008).

It would be a simplistic truism to point out that the debates around these facets of local political leadership reflect national political culture and existing structures and processes of politics within any country, or that leadership's need to respond to political crisis or concerns about political legitimacy. Such a point does, however, need to be made before moving on to examine the nature of the international debate around the direct election of the mayor, as it has taken place in various particular settings. The point needs to be made because it enables us to understand the national similarities and differences over the issues involving local political leadership that are of concern for reformers, and which can then be considered against broader international factors.

The literature suggests that policy transfer is facilitated by similarity in contexts such as policy conditions, geography, and ideology (Rose 1993; Peters 1997; Evans 2009). Continental reform trends, such as New Public Management, multi-level governance, and decentralization and devolution have been easily transferred across Europe (Denters and Rose 2005; Kuhlmann and Wollmann 2014), and we will examine whether the same applies to the direct election of the mayor. Our concern in this chapter is to examine the extent to which the debate about the direct election of the mayor has influenced change in local government and how, if at all, this model of local leadership has been adopted in our chosen countries. We use our selected countries to examine the source of the reform initiative, the intentions of reform, and the debates around the desirability of the election of the mayor in country-specific settings. We examine the principles and arguments used by supporters and opponents of the direct election of the mayor in our chosen countries.

In assessing the arguments about the direct election of the mayor we focus on countries where direct election has, so far, been rejected (Sweden and Spain), where it has been fully implemented (Slovenia), where there is a mixed system of direct and indirect election (England), and where mayors are indirectly elected, but the debate is still alive (Czech Republic and to some extent England, Sweden, and Spain). Moreover, we have selected countries from established democracies (England and Sweden), from a now established but newer democracy (Spain) and from more recent entrants to the democratic club (Slovenia and the Czech Republic). The last two countries represent transition states moving from a communist past to democracy but provide two counterpoints in how transition states have reacted to questions about local government legitimacy, accountability, and democracy.

We explore the debate about the direct election of the mayors through the lens of local political legitimacy and accountability so as to examine reform intentions within different conceptualizations of political leadership—presidential (individualized systems) where power rests with the mayor, or collectivist (where decision making is diffused across committees). In so doing we examine how accountability and visibility have been reflected in the reform of local political leadership (Steyvers et al. 2008; Loughlin et al. 2011; Rhodes and t'Hart 2014). We focus on accountability and legitimacy to assess whether the direct election of the mayor arrives as a result of concerns about local democracy reflecting common national or international themes and which therefore transfer across national boundaries (Dolowitz and Marsh 1996, 2000; Evans 2009). In addition, the size of local government in our selected countries varies considerably and that variation enables us to consider whether the introduction of elected mayors also varies with local government size.

The concentration of political decision-making power in the mayor alone, while enabling him or her to act quickly, can sit uncomfortably in countries where a more fragmented, collectivist approach to political power and decision making is usual. Elected mayors exist across Europe, however, often as part of a series of reform packages designed to enhance the legitimacy and accountability of local government in, for example, Germany, Greece, Italy, and Poland; meanwhile many European nations remain wedded to indirect appointment of the mayor.

In the next section a brief outline is given of the local government systems in our chosen countries as a contextual setting for the chapter. The third section explores the common themes and debates about the reform of local political leadership across our countries, concentrating on local political legitimacy, accountability, and visibility as central concepts within a wider debate on reform. The final section draws out the main lessons for the reform of local political leadership.

The Local Government Landscape

In this section a brief overview of local government is given for each of our countries where we explore the debates about the direct election of the mayor so as to be able to elicit whether there are systemic distinctions within countries that make elected mayors more or less likely.

Czech Republic

The 1993 Constitution of the Czech Republic decreed municipalities as the basic territorial self-governing units, entrusting them with the execution of local self-administration and some state administrative "transferred responsibilities." Since 1990 municipal elections have taken place every four years, with a 74 percent turnout in that year, which gradually declined to 49 percent in 2010. Elections use a proportional system and voters are faced with choosing from the following: registered political parties and movements; coalitions of political parties and movements; independent candidates; associations of independent candidates; associations of political parties or movements; independent candidates. The local proportional electoral system means that in most cases municipal councils are multi-party and typically the winning party has the strongest position in the municipal board and holds the mayoralty which is chosen by councilors.

England

England, some 84 percent of the United Kingdom, is the only country excluded from the Celto-centric devolution introduced by the Labour government of 1997, which created national chambers for Scotland, Wales, and Northern Ireland—there is no English Parliament. There are however, 352 councils with a mix of two-tier county and single-tier unitary authorities and all councilors serve for four years. The electoral system is simple majority, first-past-the-post.

There are 16 directly elected mayors in England (excluding the mayor of London); 14 of these result from a "Yes" vote in a local referendum, two from a resolution of the council. The electoral system used is the supplementary vote where voters mark a cross "X" by their first and second preference candidates and if no one candidate has over 50 percent of the vote all but the top two are eliminated and the second preferences redistributed to provide a winner. As a result of the 2015 local elections in England just over 90 percent of all councilors are members of the Conservative or Labour parties or Liberal Democrats. In the first mayoral elections in 2002 independent candidates were successful in five of 11 contests; in 2015, 14 elected mayors are from the three main parties and three are independents.

Slovenia

The current Slovenian single-tier local government system was introduced in 1994. The municipal council (legislative) and the mayor (executive) are directly elected using either majority voting (the mayor, in smaller municipal councils) or proportional voting (in larger municipal councils). Mayors are directly elected by local citizens and along with councilors have four-year terms and can be re-elected an unlimited number of times. Local electoral participation was high in the elections just after 1994 but recently turnout rates have fallen to under 50 percent. Nonetheless there is still a very lively local democracy with many non-partisan candidates and local lists presenting themselves for election; since 2006 political parties have been losing support while independent candidates and lists have been gaining in mayoral and council elections. At the local elections in 2014 there were 115 independent mayors elected and independent lists and candidates received 29.2 percent of the votes.

Spain

Despite Spanish municipalities' proportional representation ensuring a multi-party system at the local level, the electoral threshold of 3 percent favors the large parties and makes the electoral results more a bipolar system. The voting lists are closed and blocked and the councilors, whose number depends upon the size of the locality, serve a four-year term and are subject to strong party discipline which means they are more dependent on the party machine than on their electorate. In this context the election of independent councilors is rare. There are no elected mayors in Spain, rather the mayor is normally the candidate who heads the victorious party list and is therefore a choice of the party rather than the voters directly.

Sweden

Local government in Sweden consists of two tiers: municipalities and counties. Councilors are elected for four-year terms and the elections to the municipalities and county councils are held on the same day as the national elections. A system of proportional representation is used and a party label is compulsory on the candidate list; there is no room for non-party candidates. There is however, no limit to forming local parties, but as would be expected from the system there is a dominance of the national parties in local politics and about 95 percent of councilors represent one of the eight main parties in parliament. There are no directly elected mayors in Sweden, where a grip is maintained on collectivist decision-making through the existence of an executive committee, drawn from the council, and a range of other committees through which the collective involvement of councilors in decision making takes place.

LOCAL POLITICAL LEADERSHIP: POLITICAL POWER, LEGITIMACY, AND ACCOUNTABILITY

If mayors are the solution to local government, it is fair to ask: What is the question (Orr, 2014)? In this section we consider the policy debates about the legitimacy and accountability of local political leaders. It is in this context that we need to consider the different political interpretations and conceptions at play and how those lead policy makers and local politicians to varying conclusions about the structures and processes needed to achieve the effective use of local political power and to ensure its legitimacy and accountability.

Local Political Leadership and Accountability

Collectivist and individualized decision-making both find opponents and supporters in all political parties and internationally. In England, where prior to the Local Government Act 2000 a committee system was the norm, no individual councilor had any legal executive powers; since 2000, elected council leaders and cabinets have had executive responsibilities. In Sweden, with similar collectivist traditions, the chairperson of the executive committee, who represents the majority administration and in practice often has a strong informal position but has no formal individual powers, rather depends on the council or committee for the ability to take action. Nor does the chairperson function as head of the administration.

In Spain mayors are not directly elected, although such an idea was supported by the Spanish Socialist Party in 1998 and the conservative Popular Party in 2014 and both parties were motivated by the need to strengthen their own political control of municipalities and not local executive power. The arguments put forward at the time recognized the need for a strong democratic link between political leaders and citizens and a system more representative of the democratic process than one controlled by councilors alone. Part of the Spanish argument also reflected questions of legitimacy caused by councilors crossing the floor and changing the political control of a council without an election, a pertinent problem where the electoral system delivers a large number of parties into the council chamber. Elected mayors thus equal stability, and this particular systemic factor also enhances accountability and legitimacy by stressing the importance of the visibility of the decision makers. While the main Spanish parties have seen advantages in elected mayors, the debate is stalled because of the lack of public support, the entrenched nature of local political elites more used to having influence over a mayor who heads a party list, and a broader reform focus on mechanisms of citizen participation generally.

When we look at the two most recent members of the democratic club—Slovenia and the Czech Republic—we see concerns with the same questions of power, legitimacy, and accountability, but two different responses in these post-communist countries. In the Czech Republic local political leadership is based on the indirect election of the mayor by the council, with the mayor's responsibility to the council rather than to local citizens. The assumption is that local political power is best constrained by elected councilors whose role it is to focus more acutely than would citizens on the actions and use of power by the mayor. Thus, accountability and legitimacy are products of a political process internal to parties and political institutions and of a collectivist turn.

Slovenia took a different approach to accountability and legitimacy, with mayors held directly to account by the public. Indeed, the stress lay on the idea that politicians, locally, are acutely aware of the fact that periodic elections enable voters to evaluate their accomplishments when deciding on their vote. Election and local electoral behavior was the way of providing an opportunity for citizens to entrust either an incumbent or some other candidate with the functions of local political leadership, rather than the internal working of political groupings. The emphasis here is on the direct link of accountability between mayor and citizens, rather than such accountability resting with a council.

We also see in four of our countries that a final settlement has yet to emerge as to whether accountability and legitimacy is best served by direct or indirect election. Elected mayors are still being debated in the Czech Republic, a debate inspired by direct mayoral elections across Europe (Šaradín and Outlý 2004; Jüptner 2004, 2009; Balík 2009), and in Sweden independent analysts and academics have discussed such a reform along with the Swedish Association of Local Authorities and Regions. A recent survey of Swedish councilors showed that 33 percent favor direct election of chairs of municipal executive committees (Gilljam et al. 2010), suggesting interest in the mayoral approach but one yet to overcome the collectivist local political tradition. England and Spain continue to grapple with the strengthening of accountability and legitimacy locally through the office of elected mayor, with the government of the UK insisting that new powers and responsibilities devolved to combinations of English authorities will only come with an elected mayor. It is only Slovenia that made an early and steadfast commitment to elected mayors and tellingly there we see independent candidates have improved their performance in mayoral elections since the inception of the office (Kukovič and Haček 2013).

The concern with independent candidates for mayoral office and their performance, relative to national political parties, is also related to questions of accountability and legitimacy. If mayoral offices are held by members of national political parties and those same parties are also well represented on the council, then unless councilors fully adopt a separation of powers in their work, party politics will interfere with accountability (Copus 2008, 2011). Mayors from outside national parties provide an additional democratic element in the local political landscape and are a way of undermining national party control of local government (Elcock 2008; Aars 2009). Indeed, without a party machine to support them the enhanced visibility of action that comes with direct election could serve independent candidates well, while visibility in leadership action also provides a bonus for accountability.

Local Political Leadership: Visibility and Profile

In the countries studied here, the debate about the merits of elected mayors has been accompanied by consideration of how local politics can become more visible and therefore more meaningful to citizens. Visibility of the local political leadership was a central feature of the Blair government's support for elected mayors in England: where committees hid responsibility, direct election made it clear and identifiable and would strengthen the link with the voters that leaders chosen by the council lacked (DETR 1998, paras 5.4:29, 5.14:31). The argument that direct election enhances visibility reflects a general attitude across our case study countries, but in these countries visibility can also be secured by municipalities of a smaller size than those in England. Where municipalities are small, visibility of the local political leader is easier to achieve and yet that was no barrier to the introduction of elected mayors in Slovenia and the ongoing debate in the Czech Republic where the large number of small municipalities make visibility of the local political leader far less of an issue. Yet increases in the size of local government units and the need to ensure visible local leadership do not automatically lead to the arrival of elected mayors. Despite local electoral turnout and trust in local government in Sweden being among the highest in Europe (Loughlin et al. 2011) there has been serious concern for the state of local democracy since the 1974 amalgamations, which generated a large flow of reform proposals, none of which included elected mayors.

Slovenian local government rests on the notion of a visible mayor as the public face of the municipality and council; indeed, the mayor is the external representative of the municipality. In the Slovenian case mayors are very much the "masters" of the municipality (Kukovič 2014, pp. 23–25). It is not only the legitimacy of the power to act that matters; it is also that citizens are aware of who is taking action. We see a contrast in Spain, however, where the institutionalization of local political parties and the power of the party group in municipalities (Sweeting 2009; Iglesias and Mendieta 2010) and the path-dependent response to reform have acted as a barrier to direct election. But again, in the Spanish context, with many small municipalities visibility is less of an issue.

Although elected mayors are a widespread phenomenon across Europe (Borraz and John 2004; Back et al. 2006; Magre and Bertrana 2007), our five countries have come to different stages in the debate about their adoption. Despite resistance to elected mayors in four of the countries, reformers remain concerned with the legitimacy, accountability, and visibility of local government. Given that we have selected only one country where elected mayors are the norm and one where there is a partial, minor adoption, we are concerned now to explore what our selection tells us about the nature of political ideas travelling across borders (Peters 1997; Dolowitz and Marsh 2000; Evans 2009).

WILL MAYORS TRAVEL?

When we look at the issues of legitimacy and accountability it is surprising that directly elected mayoral leadership has not been adopted more widely in our selected countries. It is surprising because each has explored, in its own terms, how to make political power locally more effective and more democratic—that is, legitimate, accountable, and with a direct link to the voters. It is also surprising because in each of our countries the preconditions for policy transfer are favorable as each shares a number of cultural, economic, and political characteristics with other European countries and because our two former communist countries have looked westwards in devising new systems of local government.

Direct election appears an obvious reform when representative democracy faces challenges such as citizen disengagement and problems associated with party decline (Blondel 2002; Drummond 2006; Blyth and Katz 2005, p. 40; Seyd and Whiteley 2004, p. 358). Even though politically in England and Sweden individualism has a strong cultural hold this has not transferred into support for individualistic political decision-making which in these two countries has remained stubbornly collectivist (Pettersson and Geyer 1992; Inglehart and Welzel 2005). Each of our countries has shown little reluctance in reforming its system of local government, generally. England and Sweden comprehensively reformed their structures of local government with mergers in the mid 1970s and England has since seen a gradual reduction in the number of councils. Slovenia and the Czech Republic reinstated democratic local government when faced with the need to develop a system of representative local democracy rapidly after the fall of communism. The Spanish constitution guarantees the right to self-government of the nationalities, regions, and autonomous communities of Spain, which suggests that a partial and gradual development of mayoral local government is more likely than wholesale reform. What are the reasons for the reluctance to introduce mayors in England, Sweden, and Spain, and why the delay in the Czech Republic? We can explain this by taking a historical institutional perspective and examining the power and resilience of the norms and practices of local politics that contribute to systemic resistance to reform of political decision-making within our chosen countries. There are a number of components to such resistance which themselves reflect political, constitutional, institutional, and cultural factors which make elected mayors more or less likely to be introduced.

One component is the traditional strength of political parties in local politics (Saiz and Geser 1999; Buch Jensen 2000; Copus 2004; Ringkjøb 2004; Clark 2007; Copus and Erlingsson 2012). We have seen that 94 percent and 90 percent respectively of councilors in Sweden and England come from the main national political parties; in Spain currently the two major political parties account for 71 percent of councilors and if nationalistic parties are taken into account the figure rises to nearly 80 percent. In Slovenia, however, the rate of councilors from parties in parliament stands at just 51 percent. Where the nationalization of local politics has taken place, with national party control of local government, elected mayors introduce an element of uncertainty among local elites that independent candidates may win mayoral office.

A tradition of collectivist, committee-based councilor decision-making—even in a single-party cabinet—displays a reluctance to cede power to directly elected mayors (Goldsmith and Larsen 2004; Aars 2009). Not only is this a cultural consideration but it is also about raw, practical politics—why would councilors willingly hand power first to the electorate to decide who the mayor should be and second to the mayor? Elected mayors not only break the tradition of collective, party-based decision-making, they also challenge the dominant role of political parties in local government (Copus 2011; Wollmann 2012).

Where the shift from local government to local governance is most pronounced there is more of an institutionalized challenge to the status and role of local government, and such a shift has been marked in England. In cases where networks between local government and other local interests have been less important, such as in Sweden, there has not been the need for a powerful, directly elected local political leader to establish the position of the council within networks (Aars 2009). Thus, traditional collectivist democracy can cope with the shift to governance which does not necessarily stimulate the arrival of elected mayors (Montin and Hedlund 2009).

It would appear that longstanding patterns of political organization can resist change. But if we look at countries such as Germany and Italy, when a particular point of historical or political crisis occurs it can stimulate the arrival of elected mayors; in transition countries the direct election of the mayor is a widespread phenomenon as a result of the political crisis of the fall of communism (Swianiewicz 2014); there is even a debate taking place in Ireland as to whether Dublin, as the capital city, should have an elected mayor. In these few examples we see that historical institutionalism can help explain the arrival or not of mayoral governance, a suggestion that future research could confirm especially in more established Western European democracies.

CONCLUSION

Directly elected mayors have been introduced into an increasing number of European countries as a response to the crisis of legitimacy, visibility, and accountability facing local representative democracy (Kersting and Vetter 2003; Berg and Rao 2005; Loughlin et al. 2011). Elected mayors were intended to provide a swifter and legitimate response to the pressures local government experienced from urbanization, globalization, Europeanization, increasing demands on services, and growing participatory pressure. There has, however, been an uneven spread of elected mayors and in our countries, at least, we have seen that existing traditions of local political decision-making are hard to shift.

What we have presented in this chapter is a first analysis of the debates as they have occurred within and across the five countries studied. It will be necessary for future comparative research and analysis to consider the appropriate analytical framework within which such exploration should take place. Moreover, future analysis will need to explore the link between path-dependent policy development, historical institutionalism, and the transfer and diffusion of policy across local, regional, and national boundaries. The limit of space has meant that it is only possible to highlight rather than to explore those issues at this stage, but we can conclude that, despite debates about the accountability, legitimacy, and visibility of local political leadership, the direct election of the mayor is not completely acknowledged as the appropriate way of enhancing those features of local democracy. Indeed, we see that collectivist decision-making results in a conceptualization of accountability and legitimacy of local leadership as directed toward councilors, not citizens, and which downgrades leadership visibility to an unimportant characteristic. Direct election of the mayor fundamentally challenges existing patterns of behavior among political parties and councilors by transferring power to the public. The processes of reforming local political leadership by the adoption or rejection of the direct election of the mayor will come up against the power of local political elites. In our chosen countries elected mayors have not traveled well, indicating that for reforms to travel across borders, policy makers and practicing politicians must agree with them!

REFERENCES

Aars, J. 2009. Immune to reform? The Nordic mayor. In *Local political leadership in Europe. Town chef, city boss or loco president?* ed. H. Reynaert, K. Steyvers, P. Delwit, and J.-B. Pilet. Bruges: Vanden Broele.

Back, H., H. Heinelt, and A. Magnier (eds.). 2006. *The European mayor: Political leaders in the changing context of local democracy.* Urban and Regional Research International. Wiesbaden: VS Verlag for Sozialwissenschaften.

Balík, S. 2009. *Komunální politika. Obce, aktéři a cíle místní politiky* (Communal politics. Municipalities, actors and aims of local politics). Prague: Grada.

Berg, R., and N. Rao (eds.). 2005. *Transforming local political leadership.* Basingstoke: Palgrave.

Blondel, J. 2002. Party government, patronage, and party decline in Western Europe. In *Political parties: Old concepts and new challenges,* ed. R. Gunther, J.R. Montero, and J.J. Lintz. Oxford: Oxford University Press.

Blyth, M., and R. Katz. 2005. From catch-all politics to cartelization: The political economy of the cartel party. *West European Politics* 28: 33–60.

Borraz, O., and P. John. 2004. The transformation of urban political leadership in Western Europe. *International Journal of Urban and Regional Research* 28(1): 107–120.

Buch Jensen, R. 2000. *Lokale partiorganisationer.* Odense: Odense universitetsforlag.

Clark, A. 2007. Local party organisation, activism and campaigning in post-devolution Scotland. In *Paper presented at the 'European Consortium for Political Research' conference in Helsinki,* https://ecpr.eu/Events/PaperDetails.aspx?PaperID=12544&EventID=52.

Copus, C. 2004. *Party politics and local government.* Manchester: Manchester University Press.

Copus, C. 2008. English councillors and mayoral governance: Developing a new dynamic for political accountability. *Political Quarterly* 79(4): 590–604.

Copus, C. 2011. Elected mayors in English local government: Mayoral leadership and creating a new political dynamic. *Lex Localis: The Journal of Local Self-Government* 9: 335–351.

Copus, C., and G.Ó. Erlingsson. 2012. Parties in local government: A review. *Representation* 48(2): 235–247.

Denters, B., and L. Rose. 2005. *Comparing local governance: Trends and developments.* Basingstoke: Palgrave Macmillan.

DETR. 1998. *Modern local government: In touch with the people.* London: cmnd 4041.

Dolowitz, P.D., and D. Marsh. 1996. Who learns what from whom: A review of the policy transfer literature. *Political Studies* 46(2): 343–357.

Dolowitz, P.D., and D. Marsh. 2000. Learning from abroad: The role of policy transfer in contemporary policy-making. *International Journal of Policy and Administration* 13: 5–24.

Drummond, A. 2006. Electoral volatility and party decline in Western democracies: 1970–1995. *Political Studies* 54(2): 628–647.

Elcock, H. 2008. Elected mayors: Lesson drawing from four countries. *Public Administration* 86(3): 795–811.

Evans, M. 2009. Policy transfer in critical perspective. *Policy Studies* 30(3): 243–268.

Gilljam, M., D. Karlsson, and A. Sundell. 2010. *Politik på hemmaplan: tiotusen fullmäktigeledamöter tycker om politik och demokrati.* Stockholm: SKL Kommentus.

Goldsmith, M., and H. Larsen. 2004. Local political leadership: Nordic style. *International Journal of Urban and Regional Research* 28(1): 121–133.

Iglesias, A., and M. Mendieta. 2010. Local political leadership in urban governance and public administration modernisation: the role of the mayor and councillors in a Spanish municipality (1979–2007). *Lex Localis* 8(2): 185–201.

Inglehart, R., and C. Welzel. 2005. *Modernization, cultural change, and democratization.* New York: Cambridge University Press.

Jüptner, P. 2004. *Česká komunální politika a její problémy* (Czech communal politics and its problems). Prague: Charles University, Faculty of Social Sciences, The Institute of Political Sciences.

Jüptner, P. 2009. 'Ministerská diskuse k případnému zavedení přímé volby starostů: velmi nízká priorita' (Ministerial discussion on the potential adoption of the direct election of mayors: 'a very low priority'). *Acta Politologica* 1(3): 305–331.

Kersting, N., and A. Vetter (eds.). 2003. *Reforming local government in Europe: Closing the gap between democracy and efficiency.* Opladen: Springer VS.

Kukovič, S. 2014. *Local self-government in Slovenia: Organisational aspects.* Ljubljana: Faculty of Social Sciences.

Kukovič, S., and M. Haček. 2013. The re-election of mayors in the Slovenian local self-government. *Lex Localis* 11(2): 87–99.

Kuhlmann, S., and H. Wollmann. 2014. *Introduction to Comparative Public Administration: Administrative Systems and Reforms in Europe.* Cheltenham, UK and Northampton, MA: Edward Elgar.

Loughlin, J., F. Hendricks, and A. Lidström. 2011. *The Oxford handbook of regional democracy in Europe.* Oxford: Oxford University Press.

Magre, J., and X. Bertrana. 2007. Exploring the limits of institutional change: The direct election of mayors in Western Europe. *Local Government Studies* 33(2): 181–194.

Montin, S. and G. Hedlund (eds.). 2009. *Governance på svenska.* Stockholm: Santérus förlag.

Peters, G. 1997. Policy transfers between governments: The case of administrative reforms. *West European Politics* 20(4): 71–88.

Pettersson, T., and K. Geyer. 1992. *Värderingsförändringar i Sverige. Den svenska modellen, individualismen och rättvisan.* Stockholm: Utbildningsförlaget Brevskolan.

Rhodes, R., and P. t'Hart. 2014. *The Oxford handbook of political leadership.* Oxford: Oxford University Press.

Ringkjob, H. 2004. *Partia i lokalpolitikken.* Bergen: Institutt for administrasjon og organisasjonsvitenskab, universitetet i Bergen.

Rose, R. 1993. *Lesson-drawing in public policy.* New York: Chatham House.

Saiz, M., and H. Geser (eds.). 1999. *Local parties in political and organisational perspective.* Boulder, CO: Westview Press.

Šaradín, P., and J. Outlý. 2004. *Studie o volbách do zastupitelstev v obcích* (A study on the elections of local assemblies). Olomouc: Palacký's University.

Seyd, P., and P. Whiteley. 2004. British party members: An overview. *Party Politics* 10(4): 355–366.

Stevyers, K., T. Bergstrom, and H. Back. 2008. From princeps to president? Comparing local political leadership transformation. *Local Government Studies* 34(2): 131–146.

Sweeting, D. 2009. The institutions of 'strong' local political leadership in Spain. *Environment and Planning C: Government and Policy* 27(4): 698–712.

Swianiewicz, P. 2014. An empirical typology of local government systems in Eastern Europe. *Local Government Studies* 40(2): 292–311.

Wollmann, H. 2008. Reforming local leadership and local democracy: The cases of England, Sweden, Germany and France in comparative perspective. *Local Government Studies* 34(2): 279–298.

Wollmann, H. 2012. Local government reforms in (seven) European countries: Between convergent and divergent, conflicting and complementary developments. *Local Government Studies* 38(1): 41–70.

CHAPTER 18

Local Democratic Renewal by Deliberative Participatory Instruments: Participatory Budgeting in Comparative Study

Norbert Kersting, Jana Gasparikova, Angel Iglesias, and Jelizaveta Krenjova

INTRODUCTION

The crisis of local representative democracy can be seen, on the one hand, in growing political apathy, cynicism, and a decline of voter turnout as well as political party membership (invited space) in a number of cities; and, on the other hand, in growing political protest and violent and non-violent demonstrations (invented space) (see Kersting et al. 2009, 2013a). Both

N. Kersting (✉)
Department of Political Science, University of Muenster, Münster, Germany

J. Gasparikova
School of Economic Management and Public Administration, Bratislava, Slovakia

A. Iglesias
University Rey Juan Carlos, Madrid, Spain

J. Krenjova
Ragnar Nurkse School of Innovation and Governance, Tallinn University of Technology, Tallinn, Estonia

© The Author(s) 2016   317
S. Kuhlmann, G. Bouckaert (eds.), *Local Public Sector Reforms in Times of Crisis*, DOI 10.1057/978-1-137-52548-2_18

phenomena are influenced by the financial restrictions and an omnipresent financial crisis at the local, regional, and national levels (see Denters et al., Chap. 19 in this volume). Democratic innovation focusing on local representative democracy and direct-democratic democracy seem to have little effect (see Vetter et al., Chap. 15 in this volume). New forms of talk-centric deliberative democracies are implemented in some cities (Kersting 2008; see "deliberative turn"). Most of these new participatory instruments are implemented at the local level by local administration and in the 2010s Participatory Budgeting (PB) processes became one of the most important instruments (see Sintomer et al. 2008; Diaz 2014).

We focus on three questions, which include an analysis of implementations, actors, and goals as well as results. Who are the driving and promoting actors supporting these instruments? It is hypothesized that local administration and directly elected mayors are key actors, while the councils are more hesitant in implementing these instruments (see Kersting 2008). What kinds of instruments are implemented and for what purposes (goals)? We argue that despite a broad variety in different countries, PB in Europe focuses more on public brainstorming and less on planning, conflict resolution, social capital generation, and pro-poor welfare policies. What is the influence of new information and communication technologies (ICT) on the development of new instruments and local governance strategies (the online component)? We argue that in most PB processes the online component becomes more important, which may reduce the quality of discourse and the possibilities of increasing social capital (see Kersting 1995, 2013a).

Owing to its informal, non-constitutionalized character, local deliberative democracy is facing a lack of comparative research and data. Consequently, other questions such as the level of integration (who is included and who is excluded?), and the impacts on local groups (what are the reactions by citizens, politicians, and administration?) cannot be covered here, and need further comparative research (see also Gabriel and Kersting 2014). Here typical case studies from Spain and Germany as well as Estonia and Slovakia will be analyzed. These countries differ in the local political and administrative culture (Eastern, Central, and Southern European), socialist past (Slovakia, Estonia), size, level of decentralization, and federalism. Some countries were early adopters of the new participatory instruments (Spain) and others are latecomers such as Germany, Slovakia, and Estonia (see Kersting and Vetter 2003; Kersting et al. 2009).

DELIBERATIVE DEMOCRACY IN THE CONCEPTUAL FRAMEWORK FOR POLITICAL PARTICIPATION

According to Kersting (2013a), political participation can be divided into four different political spheres: participation in representative democracy (elections, voting for representatives), participation in direct democracy (referenda, voting on issues), deliberative participation (talk on issues) and demonstrative participation (demonstrations, symbolic expressive participation). These spheres can have online and offline components. Kersting (2013a) argues that, due to the specific character of online participation, these instruments focus more on demonstrative participation as well on direct democratic participation (votes and likes, for "clicktivism" and "slacktivism"; see Christensen 2011). This direct democratic participation includes crowd sourcing instruments which allow citizens to make suggestions and which allow everybody a vote on these recommendations (such as by e-petitions).

In 1992, after the Rio de Janeiro Conference on Sustainability and Development most countries introduced the Local Agenda 21 process. In the European countries some Local Agenda 21 activities started early and some were latecomers (Germany). In the global South, democratic innovations such as PB processes were already implemented in the late 1980s at the local level, supported by donor agencies such as the World Bank, especially in Latin America (see Sintomer et al. 2008).

There are different definitions of PB which do to a certain extent overstretch the instrument. For the purposes of this study, PB is defined as a process that encompasses participatory methodologies and participatory instruments for information, communication, and decision making in the local, regional, and national budgetary process. According to Sintomer et al. (2008, 2010), PB processes encompass an information phase, a consultation phase, a prioritization/evaluation phase, and an accountability phase. In its original type, local representatives (from the neighborhood or from organized interest groups) and open forums are informed (the information phase), make recommendations (the consultation phase), and discuss and deliberate on new projects. In some cases at the neighborhood level a certain budget is given to the neighborhood to develop these projects. Then these groups prioritize (often using criteria such as poverty) (the prioritization/ evaluation phase). These lists of projects are included in the local budget discussion in the city council. Local government has to inform the neighborhood about the status of implementation (the accountability phase).

There is a broad range of talk-centric and vote-centric participatory methods and instruments (open forums, mini-publics, and stakeholder conferences). Certain goals can be identified. The primary goal of PB is to influence directly or indirectly the decision-making processes. Secondary goals can focus on political civic education, community building, conflict resolution, pro-poor policies, and so on. In Latin America in the 1990s these forms of political participation development were sometimes strongly related to pro-poor self-help strategies (see Kersting et al. 2009). In Europe only some countries and cities have followed the Brazilian example in implementing and focusing on open forums. Some had stakeholder conferences that included only organized interests. In Italy most instruments were predominantly organized as mini-publics with a smaller group of randomly selected representatives. Around the world in 2013— depending on the definition and the status—there were around 2000–2700 participatory budget processes (Sintomer et al. 2013). In 2010, Europe had around 200 cases. The leading countries were Spain, Italy, and Portugal. Owing to the financial crisis some of them stopped in the 2010s. These were cases where mostly informal instruments were transferred into formal institutionalized processes; for example, in the province of Tuscany (Italy) or in Poland participatory budgets are prescribed by law as well.

Deliberative Turn in European Cities: Comparative Studies

In the following, deliberative democracy instruments will be analyzed in different European countries using the criteria for evaluation (goals, main promoting actors, and online component). Other evaluative criteria such as openness, control, transparency, and impact (see Kersting et al. 2008, pp. 45f.; Geißel and Newton 2012) will not be analyzed. The case studies are regarded as typical PB processes in their countries.

Spain

Since the second half of the 1990s there has been a sustained engagement with democratic innovations in Spain (Iglesias and Barbeito, 2014). In Spain there exists a wide array of participatory practices concerning the whole of Spanish territory. Although systematic studies are still lacking, these include information gathered from citizens' juries and forums, consensus conferences, and City Strategic Planning agendas, as well as consultations and satisfaction surveys.

The most recent innovative practices and instruments favored by local democratic Spanish governments have been online participation and participatory budgets. PB processes have been in operation in Spain since 2001 and represents a great variation to the participatory instruments that local governments have already implemented. There is no national policy, per se, on PB; all of the experiences are the isolated initiatives of local governments. However, the Spanish National Federation of Municipalities (FEMP) promoted and contributed to the awareness of these experiences by providing a framework within which PB could be developed on a larger scale. Most of the experiences have been in large and medium-sized local governments, with no evidence of what has occurred in small and rural localities.

It could be argued that PB practices in Spanish local governments are, in general, applied within a more broad-based participatory model, and that therefore PB has been coordinated with other participatory practices. In terms of numbers, since 2001, approximately 80 cases can be identified, originally inspired by Brazilian experiences, concerning large and medium urban localities. Regarding territorial diversity, some Autonomous Communities have been more active than others; for example, more experiences of PB practices are concentrated in the regions of Andalucía, the Basque Country, Valencia, and Catalonia. The first experiences with PB, and likewise the largest number of cases, have been designed and implemented by local governments led by left-leaning political parties (IU and PSOE). In addition, the number of experiences and experiments with PB boomed following the 2007 local elections; however, after the 2011 local elections there was a sharp decline in such practices.

Case Study of Seville

Seville is a large Spanish city with a population of approximately 720,000. The governance structure of the city includes a "strong mayor" form (Mouritzen and Svara 2002) where the mayor is elected within a proportional representation electoral system whereby all council members are elected in closed party lists. Under the mayor, a heavily top-down administrative structure operates which includes district governments. Community activism operates mainly through neighborhood civic associations and within a legal framework provided by a local participatory ordinance. The size, capacity, and resources of these civic associations vary across the city.

Inspired by the Porto Alegre experience, PB was introduced in Seville in 2004. The initiative to introduce PB originated from one of the minority members of the coalition government (IU) and was consistent with previous participatory policy, as well as being framed within a broader pragmatic strategy of public–private collaboration. Initially there was weak political support for PB since most executive councilors were not involved, arguing a potential lack of ability on the part of the populace to understand complex bureaucratic issues and processes. They were, therefore, skeptical of the efficiency of deliberative democracy. The opposition councilors were, quite simply, against a process that involved only a small portion of the total operating budget; namely 0.7 percent of the total financial resources (2005). This was the environment within which the process of PB was initiated and implemented.

The main objective was to empower local citizens (mostly at an individual level, although some neighborhood associations were also invited) and citizen participation through deliberative experimentation. Although most of the participants had previous participatory experience, particularly in terms of representation, the method of participant selection was biased towards those civic associations linked to the political group that initiated the process. The immediate implication was that some key civic associations and social movements were excluded, although there was a Participatory Unit that supported the development process and assisted civic associations in organizing meetings, the attendance at which was uneven in that most of the participants were citizens who had previous been involved in the city's local politics. Furthermore, the steering committee for the PB was composed mainly of members of the local administration. What is more, while citizens were involved in designing the process, their deliberations were often mediated by experts. Nevertheless, within this context, citizens identified some priority proposals, and after deliberation those projects were voted on at a district level.

During the first three years the total number of participants amounted to 12,000 with more than 200 suggestions, but they were concentrated in a few neighborhoods. In addition, most of these suggestions were modified in order to be included within the broader and technocratically designed urban projects, which makes it impossible to evaluate to what extent the proper citizens' proposals were implemented.

Furthermore, the huge cuts in public sector spending (required by the EU) have particularly affected local Spanish governments. Within this restrictive environment of the 2011 local elections there was a change of political leaders in most local governments that had PB in operation, which has essentially resulted in a shutting down of these experiments. Finally, the 2013 Local Government Act was passed by the Spanish central government, promoting a recentralization process and the privatization of local public services which have, with democratic issues being absent, had a negative impact on participatory policies including, but not limited to, PB.

Slovakia

After the Velvet Revolution in Czechoslovakia in 1989 and the founding of the independent Slovak Republic in 1992, one of the most important manifestations of participatory democracy has been PB, in operation since 2012.

It is necessary to understand that PB is a new instrument included within previous political instruments that have influenced the political culture of Slovak public officials regarding decision-making processes concerning municipal budgets and also their level of acceptance of active citizen participation in these decision-making processes.

Interest among citizens in full participation in the public arena was increased after the accelerated development of municipal policy, especially in various locations over the last several years in both small villages and also in larger towns, where active citizens started organizing themselves into various community and non-profit organizations. This interest in involvement in public issues has been manifested in several cities such as Banská Bystrica (population 78,000), Bratislava and Ružomberok (population 27,000).

A common thread in these three cases that has influenced the concept of PB has been the special interest of many citizens in the restoration of community life, which had been partly destroyed during the long socialist era of industrialization. The interest in PB represents desire for the restoration of their community in general, for better planning so as to support adequate municipal projects, as well as dedication to local needs in their communities. The local actors in these three cities have mostly been various civic associations that are interested in participation in budgeting and the implementation of local projects. One of the most important national civic associations has been pushing for the implementation of the PB process in Bratislava and has backed various participatory projects in the Slovak Republic. The other type of actors are those who normally gather together in participatory activities based on local interests groups, professional groups, students and neighborhoods and their activity is often more targeted and brings better results.

Case Study of Bratislava

In Bratislava (population 450,000) PB was defined as civil budgeting because acceptance of PB has been supported by citizens and activists in accord with their interest in upgrading Bratislava's public, community space. Citizens' different ideas about the implementation of various public projects culminated in the development of an online instrument labeled the "public stock exchange." This was internet-based and its web address was advertised on Bratislava's city council webpage. All citizens over 18 years old could contribute their ideas and projects and post information on the website.

Finances allocated for PB were not distributed via various public grants but were and have remained part of the municipal budget. Locally elected officials decided how much financial support should be allocated for different projects based on what they considered the primary public interest. The sum of money allocated for public projects was between 0.2 and 1 percent of the municipal budget. In Bratislava, the PB in 2014 for six public agendas was €46,000 (of the total €370 million city budget). Bratislava's PB has several agendas such as for traffic and roadways, environment, culture, sport, social aid, and social assistance.

The primary public interest in PB is concentrated on a selection of appropriate projects from within the abovementioned agenda. All projects that are selected by the public must be executed according to the regulations for public procurement and a municipality's internal budgetary regulations. This process has to be controlled by the public, particularly by participatory civic forums that are expected to be very active in the process.

The primary interest of these forums is solidarity and cooperation based on rational support of real spontaneous activities, support of various participatory networks, and participatory communities. Bratislava's PB was subject to severe criticism in 2014 by the general public, especially concerning the legality of the decision-making processes developing from cooperation between public forums and public officials, resulting in ignorance on the part of public officials from the municipality of Bratislava. This ignorance damaged the true functionality of PB in Bratislava, because active participation of citizens on a local level was not supported by positive and transparent interest on the part of municipal officials. Paradoxically the possibility of strengthening public participatory measures owing to the political culture of municipal officials was reduced in Bratislava.

In Slovakia, the online component and the strong role of the civil society become obvious. The true functionality of PB depends not only on the active participation of citizens at the local level but also on real supportive interest on the part of the municipal officials. Support for PB at the local political level (invited space) is, perhaps somewhat paradoxically, one of the prerequisites for strengthening public participatory space (invented space) in Slovakia.

Estonia

Estonia, like other Central and Eastern Europe (CEE) countries, experienced the change from an undemocratic to a democratic regime (Mishler and Rose 2001; and Titma Rämmer 2006). This has had a definite impact on the formation of the political culture as well as on the perception of the state in general. The same can be argued about the local government level, as the prevailing culture of the public's mistrust of politicians is contributing to the perception of the citizen's role in a "legal" manner, that is, as a legal status and the opportunity to guarantee oneself civil and political rights, rather than presuming social obligation to participate in the governing of one's own state/municipality (Kalev et al. 2009). Hence, the experience of local administrations in Estonia in the field of citizens' participation is rather limited. In view of the rapid growth of ICT, e-participation has received much attention in Estonia. At the local level, however, it has not developed as much as at the national level, not least perhaps because cities mainly use ICT for information dissemination rather than for the genuine inclusion of their citizens (Hänni 2009).

Hence, Tartu was the first city in Estonia to try PB during the pilot project in autumn 2013. By autumn 2014 four cities in Estonia had already implemented PB initiatives. Tartu, with a population of 95,600, is by far the largest of these; the other municipalities are rather small, Viljandi counting 17,600 residents, Kuressaare 14,000, and Elva 5800. All four PB cases have minor differences but the same overall structure, involving initially the gathering citizens' input followed by the selection of proposals by the experts; the process is finalized by citizens voting. All cities have the obligation to bring to fulfillment the idea that has gathered most votes.

Case Study of Tartu

The topic of PB was first introduced to Estonian local decision-makers during autumn 2011 in the framework of the project "Participatory Budgeting in Local Governments" implemented by an Estonian non-governmental organization, the e-Governance Academy Foundation (eGA). The idea of PB fell upon fertile ground in Tartu, as there was strong political will among the members of the city government and city council to pilot this initiative. In particular, the mayor of the city was very enthusiastic about integrating new participatory practices into the everyday governance of the city.

One of the main objectives of PB was the improvement of understanding of the city budget as well as the decision making within the city government (see City of Tartu, 2014). Other important objectives have been cooperation between communities, increased civic participation, and the learning factor. Planning and executing projects have to teach those involved to carefully consider problematic areas as well as to try to find possible solutions.

As a result of numerous discussions, arguments, and the exchange of ideas during the preparatory stage of PB (Krenjova and Reinsalu 2013), it was agreed that the PB in Tartu was to consist of the following stages (City of Tartu, 2014). First, from late August to early September, the presentation of ideas was to take place (via both offline and online tools). Everyone was eligible to present ideas for an investment of up to €140,000 (which constituted approximately 1 percent of the municipal investment budget). In total 158 ideas were submitted, one of them on paper while all the others were submitted electronically. After this the experts analyzed and consolidated similar ideas, assessed them, and commented on their estimated cost until October 2013. As a result of this stage, 74 ideas were selected for the public vote. The presentation of the ideas took place in mid November 2013. The event was broadcast online and the ideas were accessible on the city's webpage. Every Tartu resident of 16 years or over was eligible to vote. In total, 2645 votes were cast, 2370 of them electronically and 275 on paper, which constitutes approximately 3.3 percent of all eligible voters in the city of Tartu. The most active cohort was voters aged 30–36 (36 percent of all voters). The idea that won the largest number of votes (773) was named "Investment in Presentation Technology for Culture Block." Tartu city council confirmed its adoption by accepting the budget on 19 December 2013.

After the pilot project, the city of Tartu decided to continue with the implementation of PB, but with its structure amended. The idea was to provide the citizens with more opportunities to present and discuss their proposals among themselves as well as with the experts in the field. The PB structure now includes thematic workshops where both the owners of the ideas as well as experts in the field are participating and discussing the proposals. The objective was to select five ideas during every thematic session that would be put up for public vote. Also, the voting system was changed by giving everyone three votes, so that "small ideas" would have better chances. The amount of money allocated for PB remained the same—€140.000; however, the new rule of two winning ideas was established. The submitted proposals had to be either an investment object or a public event; the maximum cost of each could not exceed €70,000 (Krenjova and Reinsalu 2013).

In Estonia, the online component and the strong role of the mayor and the executive became obvious. Estonia is one of the leading countries in e-administration. There exists little research about the potential of PB to transform administration (see Baiochhi and Gamuza 2014). One of the decisive factors in combating political confrontations is to give the leading role in designing the process to neutral and independent institutions and experts. Furthermore, the political will to initiate and to implement the process can aid in paving the way to go beyond the limits of financial autonomy (Krenjova and Reinsalu 2013).

Germany

In Germany, participatory instruments were implemented in the 1970s, but the country was a latecomer in the Local Agenda 21 process. From 1998 a broad variety of local participatory instruments were implemented. In 2006 PB processes were imported, by 2012 PB was booming in Germany and in 2013 it was implemented in more than 100 large cities. A further 100 other cities had already experienced or are planning to implement this instrument. Some 90 percent of the cities use PB as a kind of electronic suggestion box (see Kersting 2013b). Most cities have predominantly only online participation and some cities have additional "face-to-face regional workshops" mostly characterized by low turnout. These included cities such as Cologne, Bonn, Oldenburg, and Frankfurt. An exception is the most prominent German PB process in the Berlin district of Lichtenberg. It focused more on offline instruments and neighborhood networks.

Nevertheless, in these forums just a small number among the population takes part. Only in Lichtenberg did the face-to-face forum have high rates of participation.

Case Study of Münster

In 2010 the city of Münster (population 300,000) decided to implement a PB process. The initiative came from civil society, the administration, and the directly elected mayor himself. Due to the local financial crisis the council decided that from 2012 onwards PB process would only be implemented bi-annually. Furthermore, in 2012 suggestions were accepted only if they reduced local government spending.

In March 2011 an online instrument was implemented whereby citizens could make recommendations. This was controlled for hate speech, supervised (and "censored"). There was also the chance to send suggestions by ordinary mail. Additionally in five city districts, open forums were implemented, but these had a very low turnout. There was a much higher rate of participation online and more citizens participated (27,000 comments from 1400 voters), in accord with empirical findings in other cities. Online proposals were controlled and supervised in that period, to avoid inappropriate suggestions. In the following period of six weeks, citizens voted for certain proposals via the internet. It could be shown that some societal groups utilized the instrument for their purposes. Thus in 2011 the renovation of one school building was suggested and was ranked high. It can be argued in this case particular interest groups (parents and pupils at this school) were successfully mobilized. In 2011 in total around 440 proposals were made. There were 2700 comments and 1400 citizens voted. The comments were proofed beforehand, were in general very short and there was no adequate dialogical deliberation. The votes allowed Yes, No, or a neutral vote. In 2012 and 2014 the administration used a representative survey to poll opinion on the top suggestions. This was to give them greater legitimacy and to avoid the overrepresentation of particular interest groups. The results were included in the ranking and additionally presented to the council members. In the third phase the most popular recommendations were transferred to the administration, which had to approve them regarding the legality and feasibility. Although this was regarded as additional work, most administrative staff were quite open towards the suggestions. After the approval, the best recommendations were transferred to the city council and included in the budget talks of the council, or rather the local political party factions within the council.

In 2011, 63 suggestions were transferred to the council and 36 were immediately approved by the council and implemented shortly afterwards. In 2012, 102 suggestions made it onto the list and 51 were accepted.

Although some of the recommendations were cost-intensive big projects, it is interesting that those chosen as top recommendations were not the major topics in Münsteranian politics. Suggestions focused on traffic issues, followed by infrastructure and local finance.

German PB is not related to a certain budget, but to the budget as a whole. Here it has only a consultative character. In Germany, as stated, it is more an electronic suggestion box as an aid to prioritization, an instrument imported to assist public management to be implemented by the directly elected mayor. Councillors, who are excluded, often criticize it for being too small.

LOCAL DELIBERATIVE TURN? CONCLUSIONS

In the last decade, a democratic renewal has become obvious (see Dryzek 2002; Fung and Wright 2003; Kersting et al. 2009; Smith 2009; Kersting 2015). The Rio Summit and Local Agenda 21 gave the impulse for some participatory pilot instruments. A broad range of deliberative democratic instruments were implemented sporadically and new advisory boards were installed. In the late 2000s a trend towards PB became obvious. This instrument was developed in the global South and in the young democracies such as Brazil, and exported to the old democracies in Europe and Northern America. But in the implementation different trends could be observed.

Political and other environmental variables influence not only the goals of the PB model but also the design, mechanisms, and outcomes. In Europe the older Spanish cases (Seville and Cordoba) were closest to the traditional deliberative Brazilian pilot projects. Slovakian cases also include a stronger deliberative offline component. Deliberative democracy focuses on communication and community-building processes. It allowed the development of social capital within the group. Nevertheless our country study showed that in most other countries the instruments do not focus preliminary on deliberation and community development. In Germany and Estonia PB processes led to new forms of online participation. PB became more of an electronic suggestion box. In this regard, new PBs follow the first examples of PBs in New Zealand where these budgets were implemented during the New Public Management reform processes and where PB focused on customer orientation and less on community development.

Second, in a climate of strong political competition, the institutionalization of a participatory practice is not possible when political opponents do not support it in their initial platform, or freely eliminate it when they do reach power. New participatory instruments are frequently implemented by the mayors and the administration, but highly criticized and sometimes even obstructed by councilors. This tendency seems to be stronger in the young democracies in Eastern Europe. Nevertheless, the new deliberative instruments are consultative and cannot lead—with exceptions at the sub-local level and in certain policy fields—to binding decisions. Power still lies in the hands of elected representatives such as councilors who, however, are feeling sidelined by the new participatory instruments.

Finally the obvious trend is that in most European cities the instruments are no longer pro-poor oriented, and in some of them no funds are allocated. So the different advisory functions in some cases concentrate only on suggestions on how to save money and not how to spend it. With the financial crisis which hit the Southern European countries extremely hard, only a few of these participatory instruments have been applied.

References

Baiochhi, G., and E. Gamuza. 2014. Participatory budgeting as if emancipation mattered. *Politics & Society* 42: 29–50.

Christensen, H.D. 2011. Political activities in the Internet, slacktivism or political participation by other means? *First Monday* 18(2).

Diaz, N. 2014. *Hoped-for democracy. 25 years of participatory budgeting worldwide.* São Brás de Alportel: In Loco.

Dryzek, J. 2002. *Deliberative democracy and beyond: Liberals, critics, contestations.* Oxford: Oxford University Press.

Fung, A., and E.O. Wright (eds.). 2003. *Deepening democracy.* London: Verso.

Gabriel, O., and N. Kersting. 2014. Politische Beteiligung und lokale Demokratie: Strukturen politischer Partizipation und ihre Wirkungen auf die politischen Einstellungen von Bürgerschaft, Verwaltung und Politik. In *Wandel politischer Beteiligung*, ed. Bertelsmann Stiftung. Gütersloh: Bertelsmann Stiftung.

Geissel, B., and K. Newton. 2012. *Evaluating Democratic Innovations: Curing the Democratic Malaise.* London: Routledge.

Hänni, L. 2009. Kohalike omavalitsuste veebilehed e-kaasamise vahendina. In *2002: E-participation in local government*, ed. I. Kearns, J. Bend, and B. Stern. London: Premier Print Group.

Iglesias, A., and Barbeito, R.,2014. ¿Es posible más y mejor democracia?. Democracia como empoderamiento político del ciudadano. Barataria, Revista Castellano-Manchega de Ciencias sociales, 18, pp. 215-242.

Kalev, L., L. Ott, and S. Tõnis. 2009. Eesti poliitiline kultuur: poliitikastiilid ja poliitikaprotsess. Riigikogu toimetised 19. Accessible at: http://www.riigikogu.ee/rito/ index.php? id=13766 &op=archive2 25.04.2012.

Kersting, N. (ed.). 2008. *Politische Beteiligung. Einführung in dialogorientierte Instrumente politischer und gesellschaftlicher Partizipation.* Wiesbaden: VS Springer.

Kersting, N. 2013a. Online participation: From "invited" to "invented" spaces. *International Journal of Electronic Governance* 4: 270–280.

Kersting, N. 2013b. Bürgerhaushalte in Deutschland. *Haushaltszeitung* 1: 15–16.

Kersting, N. 2015. Local political participation in Europe. Elections and referendums. *Croatian and Comparative Public Administration* 2: 319–334.

Kersting, N., and A. Vetter. 2003. *Reforming local government in Europe. Closing the gap between democracy and efficiency.* Opladen: Leske und Budrich.

Kersting, N., P. Schmitter, and A. Trechsel. 2008. Die Zukunft der Demokratie. In *Politische Beteiligung. Einführung in dialogorientierte Instrumente politischer und gesellschaftlicher Partizipation,* ed. N. Kersting. Wiesbaden: VS Springer.

Kersting, N., J. Caulfield, A. Nickson, D. Olowu, and H. Wollmann. 2009. *Local governance reform in global perspective. Urban and regional research international.* Wiesbaden: VS Springer.

Krenjova, J., and K. Reinsalu. 2013. Good governance starts from procedural changes: Case study of preparing participatory budgeting in the city of Tartu. *Socialiniai Tyrimai* 3: 32, 28–40. Accessible at: http://connection.ebscohost. com/c/case-studies/91943793/good-governance-starts-from-procedural-changes-case-study-preparing-participatory-budgeting-city-tartu20.11.14.

Mishler, W., and R. Rose. 2001. What are the origins of political trust? Testing institutional and cultural theories in post-Communist societies. *Comparative Political Studies* 34: 30–62.

Mouritzen, P.E., and J.H. Svara. 2002. *Leadership at the apex: Politicians and administrators in Western local governments.* Pittsburgh: University of Pittsburgh Press.

Sintomer, Y., C. Herzberg, and N. Röcke. 2008. *Der Bürgerhaushalte in Europa.* Wiesbaden: VS.

Sintomer, Y., C. Herzberg, and A. Röcke 2010. Der Bürgerhaushalt. In *Europa— eine realistische Utopie? Zwischen partizipativer Demokratie, Verwaltungsmodernisierung und sozialer Gerechtigkeit.* Wiesbaden: VS Verlag für Sozialwissenschaften, GWV Fachverlage GmbH.

Smith, G. 2009. *Democratic innovation.* Cambridge: Cambridge University Press.

Titma, M., and A. Rämmer. 2006. Estonia: Changing value patterns in a divided society. In *Democracy and political culture in Eastern Europe,* ed. H. Klingemann, D. Fuchs, and J. Zielonka. London: Routledge.

CHAPTER 19

Reforming Local Governments in Times of Crisis: Values and Expectations of Good Local Governance in Comparative Perspective

Bas Denters, Andreas Ladner, Poul Erik Mouritzen, and Lawrence E. Rose

INTRODUCTION

Among both practitioners and scholars in politics and public administration, a consensus is emerging that good (democratic) governance should be based on active involvement of citizens, not only as voters and clients but also as "problem-solvers, co-creators, and governors actively engaged in producing what is valued by the public and good for the public" (Bryson

B. Denters
University of Twente, Enschede, The Netherlands

A. Ladner (✉)
University of Lausanne, Lausanne, France

P.E. Mouritzen
University of Southern Denmark, Odense, Denmark

L.E. Rose
University of Oslo, Oslo, Norway

© The Author(s) 2016
S. Kuhlmann, G. Bouckaert (eds.), *Local Public Sector Reforms in Times of Crisis*, DOI 10.1057/978-1-137-52548-2_19

333

et al. 2014, p. 446). In light of this emerging consensus, recent local government reforms—implemented in reaction to recent political, economic and financial crises—typically have dual aims. They attempt to "keep the voter/client satisfied" by meeting their service needs and policy demands and/or they aim at broadening the scope for active citizen involvement and seek to improve the quality of local democracy. But how do these reforms relate to citizens' perceptions of the performance of municipalities (what they *actually* do) and citizens' ideas about what these governments *should* do?

Because little is known about such questions, in this chapter we first ask: (1) *How satisfied are citizens with the way local democracy works in a general sense, but also with respect to local services, facilities, and policies as well as the perceived responsiveness of elected officials.* We also try to understand some of the value orientations underlying these evaluations of local government performance. Hence, we ask: (2) *What do citizens expect from their local governments? How much do they value good services, facilities, and policies (functional criteria), and how important do they consider various aspects of a well-functioning democracy (procedural criteria)?*

This chapter therefore provides an evaluation of local government from a citizens' perspective using data from four countries: Switzerland, Norway, Denmark, and the Netherlands.[1] We begin by describing patterns of citizens' satisfaction in these countries. After this we explore underlying (functional and procedural) value orientations of citizens by asking how important citizens judge functional considerations regarding the performance of their governments (for example, in solving local problems, in facing societal challenges and in providing facilities and services) to be, and the same with respect to procedural norms pertaining to, for example, a well-functioning system of political representation and opportunities for citizen participation. Knowledge about these questions is highly relevant, not only because as yet we do not know much about such issues, but also because such knowledge represents an important component in the local government reform debate. Would citizens appreciate, for example, a Singapore-inspired reform scenario (Subramaniam 2001) in which excellent functional performance (in terms of policies, facilities and services) at the expense of the democratic quality of governance? Or would they rather prefer local government reforms of a more balanced character?

The four countries used in our analyses are all relatively wealthy. Where, if not here, according to arguments of post-materialism (compare Inglehart 1977), do democratic values have a chance to compete and match up with system effectiveness? The four countries are also relatively similar in terms of the general quality of local democracy (Denters et al. 2014; Chapter 3). Yet there are differences regarding the organization and role of local government and the democratic rights accorded to citizens. Switzerland is a federalist country characterized by small, autonomous municipalities in which citizens have far-reaching rights of direct democracy, while Norway, Denmark, and the Netherlands are unitary countries based in large measure on indirect representative democracy. Compared with Switzerland and Norway, municipalities in Denmark and the Netherlands are also quite large. Finally, municipalities in the Netherlands, and even more so in Norway and Denmark, are important pillars in the welfare state model.[2]

In the next section, data from these four countries are used to describe patterns of citizens' satisfaction with the local government (Question 1), and subsequently used to present information on the value orientations underlying these evaluations (Question 2). On this basis, we then draw some tentative conclusions.

Satisfaction with Local Government

A common point of departure in considering citizens' satisfaction with local governments is to ask how citizens evaluate municipal performance in general terms. For this purpose, we use a general measure for citizens' satisfaction with the way in which "local democracy in their municipality works," But as has been indicated in the literature (Dalton 2004, p. 39; Denters 2014), responses to this question are likely to be influenced by a variety of factors, including both outputs (for example, services) and the quality of democratic procedures. Hence, in addition to this general municipal performance measure, we also use four specific measures. Three measures are about satisfaction with outputs (respectively, satisfaction with policies, services, and facilities). A fourth specific measure relates to a composite measure for the extent to which citizens think that their local political system satisfies a key value in representative democracy—namely responsiveness to citizens' demands and needs.[3]

When it comes to citizens' evaluations of the performance of their local governments, the results are unambiguous. Switzerland scores highest on all five indicators (see Fig. 19.1). By comparison, Denmark ranks second on all but one indicator, whereas Norway and the Netherlands rank third or fourth on all but one of the indicators.

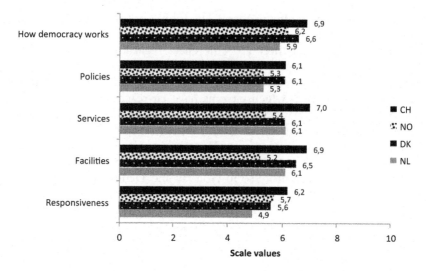

Fig. 19.1 Mean satisfaction with different aspects of municipal government performance by country (0 = very dissatisfied, 10 = very satisfied. Minimum *N*: CH = 1637, NO = 1570, DK = 1776, NL = 921.)

This pattern of findings makes us curious as to how these variations in satisfaction are related to citizens' normative expectations with respect to what constitutes good local governance. Before turning to this issue, however, we have to determine what these normative expectations actually are.

Normative Expectations for Good Local Government

How important are functional and procedural value orientations for citizens' ideas about good local governance? Following democratic theorists (for example, Sabine 1952; Pennock 1979; Thomassen 1995), we can distinguish two fundamentally different normative theories that are relevant for conceptualizing good democratic governance—collectivism and individualism. These theories differ in a number of respects. Two issues are particularly important. One issue, which reflects a *governance* perspective, concerns the proper role of government. What should governments do *"for the people"*? In the collectivist view, governments are responsible for "directing societal development and taking care of people's welfare" (Thomassen 1995, p. 389), whereas in the individualist view, "government intervention should be limited to a minimum" (Thomassen 1995, p. 389). A second issue, which reflects a *democratic* perspective, is what procedures are appropriate to realize government "*by the people*," Here, collectivists hold that "true" democracy requires widespread and effective opportunities for direct citizen participation, which in the individualistic interpretation of democracy is in essence a more limited form of representative democracy.

The national surveys conducted in each of the four countries contained twelve items in two batteries that allow us to assess how important citizens consider each of these values for them personally. The items are as follows:

1. *The municipality is effective in solving local problems.*
2. *The municipality provides services and facilities that are well suited to the needs of residents.*
3. *The municipality seeks to provide services and facilities as cheaply as possible.*
4. *The municipality provides only the most critical services and leaves the provision of additional services to others.*
5. *The municipality recognizes that for many problems private initiatives provide better solutions than government.*
6. *All residents have ample opportunity to make their views known before important local decisions are taken.*
7. *Residents participate actively in making important local decisions.*
8. *The municipality seeks to involve residents, voluntary organizations, and private business in finding solutions to local problems.*
9. *Local elected officials pay attention to the views of residents.*
10. *Local (elected) officials can be held accountable to residents for their actions and decisions.*
11. *The outcome of local elections is decisive for determining municipal policies.*
12. *Municipal decisions reflect a majority opinion among residents.*

The first five items all pertain to functional considerations about the proper role of the state. Among these five items, the first three relate to a collectivist orientation in which government should play a major role in solving major community problems and providing for public services and facilities. The two other functional items (4 and 5) refer to an individualist orientation in which the desirability of limited or minimal government intervention is emphasized. The remaining seven items pertain to proper democratic procedures. Again, some of these items reflect a collectivist view (items 6–8) while others relate to an individualist orientation (items 9–12).

Factor analysis of these twelve items indicated that they indeed tapped four underlying value dimensions. Four scales were therefore constructed in order to establish how important citizens considered each of the four facets of good local governance for them personally.[4]

Figure 19.2 presents the aggregate mean scores per country for each of the value orientations. In the functional domain, a collectivist orientation (Collective Provision) clearly dominates an individualist interpretation (Private Provision) of the state's role in all four countries. In the two most pronounced welfare states, Norway and Denmark, differences for the mean values of these orientations are larger than in the Netherlands and Switzerland. In the procedural domain, on the other hand, both participatory and representative democratic norms are generally considered equally important. Differences between mean values for each country are

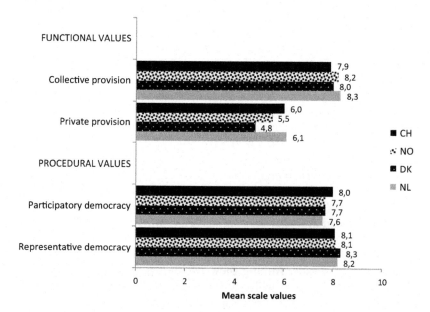

Fig. 19.2 Mean scores for four value orientations by country (0 = of little importance, 10 = very important. Minimum *N*: CH = 1648, NO = 1564, DK = 1736, NL = 959.)

quite small, but in three of the four countries, representative democratic values are slightly more important than participatory democratic values. Only in Switzerland, where direct democracy plays an important role, is there no statistically significant difference between these two democratic orientations.[5]

If we consider the average country scores displayed in Fig. 19.2, we can also see that the scores for collective provision (as the overall highest scoring factor in the functional domain) and representative democracy (highest scoring in the procedural domain) do not differ much. It is only when we force people to make a choice, between functional and procedural concerns that a clear priority emerges. When asked what they personally consider to be most important for good local governance, either (a) "meeting their ideas of what is essential for local democracy," or (b) "dealing adequately with local problems and providing relevant services and facilities," three-fourths or more of the citizens in each country indicated that functional considerations were most important. The majority is higher in Denmark (84 percent) and Norway (82 percent) than it is in Switzerland (79 percent) and the Netherlands (74 percent), but the dominant tendency is similar in all four countries.

Summarizing the main findings, we can conclude that a minimalist conception of local government is of minor importance for a majority of the citizens in these four countries. Citizens expect local government to play an important role when it comes to solving major community problems and providing for public services and facilities. While these functional considerations are of primary importance, democracy and participation are not unimportant. Here, representative democracy prevails, but there are also important sympathies for participatory democracy. Local governments in all four countries, in short, have to be "jacks of all trades": they have to meet citizens' demands for effective policies and cheap, high-quality services and facilities, but at the same time have to provide for a well-functioning, responsive representative democratic system with adequate opportunities for direct citizen involvement.

NORMATIVE EXPECTATIONS AND EVALUATION OF LOCAL GOVERNMENT

The final step in our exploratory analysis is to link citizens' evaluations of municipal governance with individual value orientations. We begin by looking at the aggregate level (Fig. 19.3). This provides an idea as to what

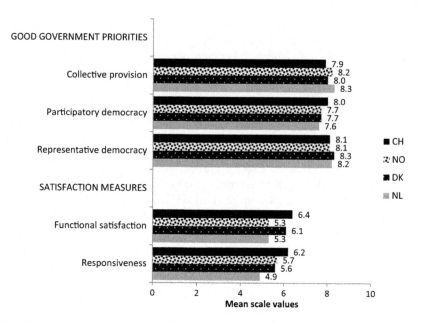

Fig. 19.3 Mean scores for good local governance value orientations and satisfaction measures by country (Values for the good governance priorities are taken from Fig. 19.2. Functional satisfaction scores are based on the added average scores of each country as presented in Fig. 19.1 with respect to satisfaction with policies, services, and facilities (see Note 6 for an explanation). Responsiveness scores are based on the relevant item presented in the same figure.)

extent the performance evaluations of local governments in the respective countries meet the relevant expectations of their citizens.

Swiss municipalities appear to come closest to meeting these varied demands. Not only do Swiss municipalities receive the highest overall functional satisfaction scores and political representatives are rated as being relatively responsive, but the Swiss political system—with its small municipalities and its direct-democratic institutions—also appears to offer ample opportunities for direct citizen participation in local matters.

For the Danish case, local governments at the time of our fieldwork did a pretty good job in meeting citizen expectations for good policies, services and facilities.[6] If there was a gap between expectations and results achieved it was most evident in the domain of democratic responsiveness.

Danes put a relatively high value on a well-functioning representative democratic system but were not entirely satisfied with the responsiveness of their elected officials.

For the Dutch and the Norwegian cases, the picture is a little less rosy. In both countries, citizens have relatively high expectations regarding the functional performance of their local governments but are relatively less satisfied with actual performance. In the Dutch case, this problem is exacerbated by lower satisfaction with the responsiveness of elected officials.

If we turn our attention to the individual level, we have analyzed correlations between value orientations and different aspects of citizens' satisfaction.[7] Such correlations provide us with an indication of the degree to which various values may shape citizens' satisfaction. On the basis of this analysis, we draw the following conclusions. First, in all four countries we find that the more a respondent is in favor of a more limited government role and private provision, the more negative this person is likely to be in his/her evaluations of the responsiveness of local representatives. Second, in three of the four countries we also find that the more important one considers representative democratic principles to be, the more likely one is to have a relatively negative view on the responsiveness of local politicians. Third, adherence to participatory democratic values is not related to evaluations of municipal governance in three of the four countries. Results for the final value orientation (collective provision), on the other hand, are ambiguous.

CONCLUSIONS AND DISCUSSION

In light of the emerging consensus on what constitutes good local governance and the prominent role accorded citizens therein, we have in this chapter adopted a citizens' perspective of the quality of local governance. Results from surveys conducted at the beginning of the millennium offer not only the possibility of analyzing citizens' evaluations of local government along several dimensions, both functional and procedural, but also of interpreting these evaluations in the light of underlying value orientations. This provides a frame of reference for considering local public sector reforms in times of crisis.

All four countries considered here are relatively well-off with a well-functioning state sector and a high quality of democracy. It is therefore not especially surprising that in the eyes of their citizens, local governments in these countries achieve satisfactory (but by no means supreme) marks in many respects. But there are nonetheless some noteworthy differences.

First, there are differences across the four countries. In Switzerland, satisfaction, both with policies, services, and performance and with meeting democratic norms, is generally higher than in Norway and the Netherlands, while Denmark takes a position in between. This satisfaction with policies, services, and facilities is especially remarkable in so far as Switzerland has small municipalities, where the capacity for effective and efficient governance is often considered to be problematic (for example, Dahl and Tufte 1973). This might suggest that the system capacity of small-scale local government is oftentimes underestimated. But we should also take into account not only the functional responsibilities of local government but also the expectations of citizens. In Switzerland, municipalities provide only a limited range of services, whereas municipalities in Denmark are larger and constitute an important pillar of the welfare state model. It is plausible that these variations in formal responsibilities shape citizens' expectations; hence, it might be expected that local governments undertaking a wide range of responsibilities would find it more difficult to satisfy the high expectations of their citizens, especially because in larger municipalities these expectations may be not only high but also more diverse and conflicting (Dahl and Tufte 1973). To address this prospect in a satisfactory manner requires a more comprehensive analysis in which data on both actual municipal performance and the democratic quality of local politics are included.

Second, there are differences across evaluative dimensions. On the whole, satisfaction with municipal output performance (in terms of policies, services, and facilities) is higher than people's satisfaction with the responsiveness of local elected officials. Despite different mean scores, the latter is a challenge for all four countries. But this challenge is larger to the extent that citizens consider democratic norms (like responsiveness) more important. However, if citizens endorse a Singaporean conception of good governance based on effectiveness rather than democracy (Subramaniam 2001), this may pose less of a problem. Therefore, it is useful to consider citizens' value orientations. In all four countries, the endorsement of collective provision, implying the desirability of extensive state responsibilities, clearly dominates over a more individualist value orientation (asking for a small state sector). Likewise, representative democratic values are considered more important than participatory concerns but in a less pronounced manner. Finally, we also found that citizens equally value the most important concern in the functional domain (collective provision) and representative democracy (the highest scoring factor in the procedural domain). It is only when we force people to make a choice between functional and procedural concerns that a clear priority for functional concerns emerges. This finding indicates that at least in these countries, a Singaporean conception of good governance, that is dominated by effectiveness and efficiency in policy-making, service delivery, and providing facilities, is not widely endorsed. Effectiveness and efficiency are important, but not all-important! Future research will have to demonstrate whether this dominant value orientation—that combines functional and democratic values—is also prevalent in other less-well-off European countries.

When it comes to reforming the local public sector or to interventions in times of crisis, there are three lessons to be drawn from our findings. First, even in the four relatively well-off countries that we have examined, there is ample room for improving the performance of local governments. Both in the functional domain—in making policies and providing services and facilities—and in securing good democratic governance, citizens are only moderately satisfied.

Second, even though these countries are rather similar in many respects, there are some clear differences in the value orientations across these countries. It would therefore appear unreasonable to suggest that there is any single "best way" to improve local governance. In some cases more collectivistic approaches may be more appropriate than individualistic ones, and for others participation may be more important than representative democracy.

Third, even though there are some clear national variations—at least in these four countries—it is important to recognize the need for adopting a balanced reform package combining administrative and democratic reforms. Of course, on balance, functional considerations are very high on the priority lists of citizens, but this by no means implies that procedural values can be completely ignored. Citizens also value a well-functioning representative democracy, and ample opportunities for citizen participation.

NOTES

1. The data were gathered by means of citizen surveys conducted as part of a larger comparative research project (see Denters et al. 2014).
2. For additional information on local government in these four countries, see Chapter 3 in Denters et al. (2014).

344 B. DENTERS ET AL.

3. Unlike the other satisfaction measures, this measure is not based on a 10-point performance rating, but is, rather, a scale constructed on the basis of four survey items. For details on scale construction, see Denters et al. (2014, pp. 178–179). Unfortunately, we have no adequate measure for citizen satisfaction with participatory opportunities offered by their municipalities.

4. The approach taken is similar to that in Denters et al. (2011). Results of the analysis are available upon request. Scales were computed as the mean value of the respective items (allowing for one missing value per case, with the exception of the two-item scale, where no missing values were allowed). For reasons of comparability with other measures used, we have transformed the original 1–5 scale values to a 0–10 scale. In the light of the limited number of items per index, the internal consistency of these indices is satisfactory. Cronbach alphas for the four dimensions are: 0.55 (Collective Provision, 3 items); 0.69 (Private Initiative, 2 items) 0.64 (Participatory Democracy, 3 items) and 0.72 (Representative Democracy, 4 items).

5. Paired sample t-tests were used to establish significance, using an α of 5 percent.

6. The past tense is used here because the data for this project were collected prior to the Danish amalgamation reforms of 2007.

7. Comments here are based on inspection of results that are not presented in detail.

REFERENCES

Bryson, John M., Barbara C. Crosby, and Laura Bloomberg. 2014. Public value governance: Moving beyond traditional public administration and the new public management. *Public Administration Review* 74(4): 445–456.

Dahl, R.A., and E.R. Tufte. 1973. *Size and democracy.* Stanford: Stanford University Press.

Dalton, Russell J. 2004. *Democratic challenges, democratic choices: The erosion of political support in advanced industrial democracies.* Oxford: Oxford University Press.

Denters, Bas. 2014. Beyond 'What do I get?' functional and procedural sources of Dutch citizens' satisfaction with local democracy. *Urban Research & Practice* 1–16. doi:10.1080/17535069.2014.910921

Denters, Bas, Oscar Gabriel, and Lawrence E. Rose. 2011. Citizens' views about good local governance. In *How democracy works: Political representation and policy congruence in modern societies*, ed. M. Rosema, B. Denters, and K. Aarts. Amsterdam: Pallas Publications.

Denters, Bas, Goldsmith Mike, Andreas Ladner, Poul Erik Mouritzen, and Lawrence E. Rose. 2014. *Size and local democracy*. Cheltenham: Edward Elgar.

Inglehart, Ronald. 1977. *The silent revolution: Changing values and political styles among Western publics*. Princeton: Princeton University Press.

Pennock, J. Roland. 1979. *Democratic political theory*. Princeton: Princeton University Press.

Sabine, G.H. 1952. The two democratic traditions. *The Philosophical Review* 61: 451–474.

Subramaniam, Surain. 2001. The dual narrative of "Good Governance": Lessons for understanding political and cultural change in Malaysia and Singapore. *Contemporary Southeast Asia* 23(1): 65–80. doi:10.2307/25798528.

Thomassen, J. 1995. Support for democratic values. In *Citizens and the state*, ed. H.D. Klingemann and D. Fuchs, 383–416. Oxford: Oxford University Press.

Conclusion: Tensions, Challenges, and Future "Flags" of Local Public Sector Reforms and Comparative Research

Geert Bouckaert and Sabine Kuhlmann

The country comparisons presented in this book have revealed four areas of research addressing major cross-cutting issues of local public sector reforms in Europe: (1) Rescaling, restructuring, and multilevel governance. (2) Output legitimacy, citizen satisfaction, and service delivery. (3) Input legitimacy, trust, and participation. (4) Local autonomy, austerity, and the fiscal crisis.

1. The need to cope with increasingly complex policy issues in uncertain situations and under uncertain conditions (so-called "wicked" problems) has challenged local institutional structures, organizational arrangements, and modes of multilevel coordination. Different

G. Bouckaert (✉)
Public Management Institute, Kath Universiteit Leuven, Leuven, Belgium

S. Kuhlmann
Chair for Political Science, Public Administration and Organisation, House 7, Zi. 2.22, University of Potsdam, Campus Griebnitzsee, Potsdam, Germany

© The Author(s) 2016   347
S. Kuhlmann, G. Bouckaert (eds.), *Local Public Sector Reforms in Times of Crisis*, DOI 10.1057/978-1-137-52548-2_20

trajectories, actors, and outcomes of reforms in European local government systems notwithstanding, up- and down-scaling and the reallocation of powers, resources, and functions across levels and jurisdictions, combined with new forms of interinstitutional collaboration and coordination, have been revealed as salient features of local public sector reforms in Europe. Strikingly, after a phase of decentralization characteristic of many European countries, the recent fiscal crisis has prompted many reverse developments directed at functional recentralization. Territorial upscaling and consolidation are also common institutional reactions to fiscal constraints, yet differences between various administrative traditions tend to persist, and being affected by (financial) crisis does not appear to be a reliable predictor for municipal mergers.

2. Local government being the level closest to the citizens, deals with concerns about effective service delivery, citizen satisfaction, and output legitimacy tend to be more salient and visible than at superior levels of government. Therefore, rearrangements in organizational structures, procedures of service provision, and techniques of local management have turned out to be another core issue of local public sector reforms across the European continent. However, the attempts at redefining the boundaries between the public, private, and societal spheres as well as the degree of contestation regarding the classical Weberian bureaucracy as contrasted with NPM are highly diverse in various local government systems. Not surprisingly, the answers of the contributions to this volume to the questions of whether, when, and to what extent the "pendulum is swinging back" (from private to public; from NPM to "re-Weberianization") are not uniform, but rather differentiated. Nevertheless, the picture of a "swinging pendulum" and subsequent phases seems to be appropriate for characterizing the overall institutional change at the local level in the long run, different directions and temporal structures across countries and policy sectors notwithstanding.

3. Concerning input legitimacy, the findings presented in this book show that we have, on the one hand, a common trend across Europe towards reforming local democracy. On the other hand, there seems to be only limited convergence between the countries regarding the preferred tools of modernization and even fewer similarities regarding the outcomes of the reforms. We have learnt from the contributions that these differences must be explained, inter alia, in light of the already existing level and type of legitimacy local governments enjoy

in a given country. A general conclusion to be drawn from the chapters is that innovations in local participation are not regarded as a value as such, but must be judged by their outcomes and improvements in the views of the citizens. If the results of citizen participation are not implemented in the end, for example, for fiscal or political reasons, the participation procedure tends to be discredited in general, and input legitimacy is even likely to decrease. This mechanism has not been taken into account sufficiently by the initiators of these reforms.

4. The fiscal crisis and austerity policies that hit local governments in Southern Europe and in the UK most seriously, but also to a significant degree in Continental and Eastern Europe, have fuelled many attempts at reform, which have been partly locally driven, but often also centrally imposed. It is cause for concern that we observe a growing tendency towards recentralizing powers, reducing local autonomy, cutting back local resources, and intensifying upper-level control and supervision measures over local authorities. These trends must be assessed as threatening local authorities and local democracy, and contradicting the idea of a politically accountable and functionally viable local self-government in Europe. Against this background, from the point of view of this COST-Action, there is an urgent need for reinvesting in local governments and restrengthening local autonomy in order to guarantee political and institutional stability not only at the local level of government but also at the national and European ones.

These four clusters of analysis result in four concluding reflections.

Public Sector Reforms in a Multilevel System

Obviously, in this COST-Action and in this volume, we have proceeded from the assumption that upper-level/central government reform patterns are different from local government reforms for a range of reasons: there is a top-down versus bottom-up choice or none; tangible service delivery is located less at central and more at the local level; there are different legal and fiscal degrees of freedom; citizen–politician interactions are different; and so on. Against this background, the question as to whether reforms should be more coherent across levels of government, and are likely to be consolidated in the intergovernmental setting, must be answered with scepticism. However, the centrality of central government and its international platforms, such as OECD, have made local government reform part of central government reforms, specifically in unitary countries. In federal countries, the state level (*Länder, cantons*) is responsible for fundamental parts of locally relevant policy-making and sub-central reforms. A crucial discussion then should be:

- How do local government reforms match with upper-level reforms?
- How different are patterns of upper-level reform from those of local government reform?
- Are efforts made towards the consolidation of upper- and lower-level reforms, and do they make sense?

Central government is on the one hand increasingly subject to European governance, and on the other hand dependent on the dynamics of local government. There is also a tendency to expand functional recentralisation and to tighten central controls on decentralized financial and fiscal frames. In this sense, central government becomes "more local" in the contexts of some countries. Also, in the cases of a number of countries, local government is increasingly facing higher levels of governance through amalgamation, mergers, cooperation, and of central de-concentration. In this sense, local government becomes more central. Yet, even if central government seems to be "less central," and local government seems to be "less local," it remains useful to distinguish between the levels and their reforms, in order to reveal, by analysis, the multilevel interactions, interweaving, and changes in the institutional weight of certain levels. Starting from such a multilevel analysis, the question as to whether and where there is a need and a possibility of consolidating local government reform with central government and/or upper-level reform policies can be answered.

The Nature of Trajectories: Shifting Models versus Pendulums

Several metaphors are used to describe the shifts and patterns of change and reform. Depending on the level of analysis, one can see both more and less of the same phenomena. Local governments become bigger and smaller (population versus number of representatives). They are more and less autonomous (choices of service delivery versus more central control). They are more and less democratic (regarding referendums and the direct election of mayors versus representation). They are more territorial and less territorial (mergers versus more functional decentralisation, more cross-boarder governance). They are more horizontal and less horizontal (with the private sector and NGOs versus more vertical integration with intermediate and central government). Depending on the starting positions, a mechanism of pendular movement seems to emerge, even if the speed of the shift varies and the starting positions are different.

LEARNING BY COMPARING LOCAL GOVERNMENT REFORM POLICIES

European countries have been clustered for the convenience of reducing complexities to better understand existing realities, and for increasing comparability to facilitate learning between these comparable units. Obviously, each cluster of countries depends on how distinct the criteria are, and therefore remains uncertain. Even with an awareness of different starting positions, and of sometimes less clear-cut clusters, there are commonalities within and between clusters. These commonalities allow learning by comparing local government reform policies, even if the outcomes seem to be quite different. Between clusters, organized pressure seems to be brought by central/state government on local government through hiving off more competencies than resources, while simultaneously centralizing financial controls and fiscal frames, and imposing functional recentralization. This pressure on local government organizations produces a pattern of reactions in the shape of internal managerial reforms (performance-oriented measures), external reforms (mergers, cooperation, and so on), and/or marketized measures. Even if imitation is not actually the model of transfer, a contingent mix of hierarchy, market, and network-type measures are inspiring reforms and triggering learning what to do, or what not to do.

DEFINING WHAT IS NEXT

Three related major tensions seem to determine what will come next for local governments.

There is a logic of consequences, which defines the allocation of resources, and the internal and external organization to guarantee economic, efficient, and effective delivery of services. There is also a logic of appropriateness, with democratic values such as participation, involvement, co-decision, and so on. The tension between these two logics will increase to the extent that increasing scales to enhance service delivery will cause a trade-off with transparent democratic control.

There should be a proportionality between the span of control of local government and its span of performance. The span of control includes legal and fiscal degrees of freedom and choice to contract (out or in), to set up Public-private Partnerships (PPPs), to develop market-type mechanisms, network-type mechanisms, and hierarchy-type mechanisms. The span of performance is higher to the extent that a level is internally economic and efficient, or externally effective, or even trustworthy and satisfactory. A bigger span of performance requires a bigger span of control. When the expectations of citizens for an extended span of performance is high, this conflicts with a stricter financial and legal span of control of that local government.

The third tension is between responsibility and accountability. Local governments may be confronted with situations where they are considered to be (politically) accountable but not (legally) responsible. The types of responsibility and accountability should correlate and should be proportional. To the extent that more competencies are decentralized to local government than resources, a common and hidden central government saving strategy, or to the extent that central "wicked" problems are politically defined at the local level—to that extent will local responsibility and local accountability be in tension.

These concluding discussions could lead to the following future research "flags" for local government which at the same time address major tensions and challenges of European local governments and governance:

(I) Autonomy vs. austerity: reinvesting in local governments and fostering local discretion under the fiscal crises?

(II) Structures of local government in a context of multiple levels, coordination, and collaboration: fit for resolving wicked problems?

(III) Participation, involvement, and input-legitimacy: how to ensure citizen satisfaction and trust in local governments?

(IV) Challenges of local service delivery, management, and performance: striving for (more) quality, efficiency, and output-legitimacy?

Finally, while researching local public sector reforms from a comparative perspective and with regard to these four cross-cutting key issues, the academic community of this COST-Action and beyond is requested to further develop its own analytical and methodological tool kit. On the one hand, comparative researchers should jointly invest in the elaboration of more comprehensive comparative databases, indicators, indices, and statistics—thus into their quantitative tools for research. On the other hand, there is still an urgent need for more contextual country-case-specific information to understand reforms, their triggers and effects, differences and similarities, and convergences and divergences on a European and international scale—and, hence, an improved qualitative data basis and context-knowledge for sound comparisons.

INDEX

A

accountability, 103, 130, 289, 303, 306–8, 352

actor-centered institutionalism, 155, 189, 240

administrative culture and tradition, 8–9

administrative reforms
external, 4–5
internal, 5–6

amalgamation reforms
bottom-up to top-down strategies, 26–7
characteristics, 24
comprehensive to incremental approaches, 26–8, 30, 31
municipal structure development, 28–31
objectives, 25–6, 32–3
outcome, 24, 28, 35–7
patterns of conflicts and implementation, 27–8, 33–5
phases of reform process, 36–9
reform strategy, 24, 26–7

in 2004–13; consensual political systems, 63, 69; countries experiences in, 74; decentralization, 62, 68–9; dependent variable, 71; fiscal stress pressures, 60–1, 68; functional status, 70–1; historical absence, 64–5, 69; intermunicipal cooperation, 70; large local governments, 64; model specification, 70; municipal size, 70; protection, of local self-government, 63–4, 69; reform histories, 62; territory, 70; theoretical model, 60; urbanization, 61

Ämter, 89

Anglo-Saxon type administration, 13

asset (material) privatization, 195

autonomy, 47
of local governments, 9
vs. austerity, 352

© The Author(s) 2016
S. Kuhlmann, G. Bouckaert (eds.), *Local Public Sector Reforms in Times of Crisis*, DOI 10.1057/978-1-137-52548-2

B

Belgium, municipal amalgamations in, 47–8
Big Society initiative, 229–30
Bilbao (Spain)
budgetary constraints, 161
change management, 166–8
change process difficulties, 165
change process measures, 163
communication and cooperation, 165–6
holistic reform process, 161
HRM/personnel unit role, 163
leadership, 164–5
municipal council and the staff council, 163
organizations' focus, 169–70
performance and economic incentive, 166
staff motivation, 169
bonuses, performance related
in France, 144
in Germany, 142
in Italy, 148
bottom-up legitimacy, 291, 294–5
Brandenburg, 86
forms of IMC, 89; micro-region, 90–1; for particular tasks, 90; regional planning association, 90; special-purpose associations, 90; voluntary, 90–2
legal provisions, 86
municipal territorial structures, 86
Bratislava (Slovakia), Participatory Budgeting in, 324–5
burgomaster, 212

C

Central Eastern European (CEE) countries
administration, CEE type, 13

institutional development; asset (material) privatization, 195; bottom-up initiatives, 199; outsourcing, 195; personal social services and care, 197–8; political top-down initiatives, 198; public/municipal sector comeback, 195–7; public utilities, 193–5; social community, 199; social enterprises, 198
provision of public services, 191
childcare service
decentralization, 241
development of, 240
Estonia, 241–2
Finland, 242
Germany, 242–3
Greece, 243–4
institutional changes, 240
institutionalization, 239
Ireland, 244
local government roles, 238
national legal regulations, 238–9
Portugal, 244–5
Spain, 245–6
coercion, democratic reforms, 282, 283
co-governance, 47
Collective Agreement for the Public Service, 141
committee systems, 10
Community Interest Companies (CICs), 230
companification/corporatization, 211–12
consensual political systems, 63, 69
context conditions, of reforms
administrative culture and tradition, 8–9
autonomy, of local governments, 9
features of, 11–12

functional responsibilities, 9
local democracy, 10
state structure and government
    type, 8
territorial structures, 9–10
Continental European Federal type
    administration, 11
Continental European Napoleonic
    type administration, 10–11
cooperation, inter-municipal. *See*
    inter-municipal cooperation
    (IMC)
cooperative democracy, 6
corporatization, of service provision,
    194
corporatized municipal socialism, 194
COST Action LocRef, 2–3
country clusters
    Anglo-Saxon type, 13
    Central Eastern European (CEE)
        type, 13
    Continental European Federal type,
        11
    Continental European Napoleonic
        type, 10–11
    Nordic type, 12–13
    South European type, 13
Court of Mayor and Aldermen
    (CMA), 293
Czech Republic
    direct election of mayor, 304
    direct election of mayors, 277
    local political leadership, 307, 309
    municipal development, 31

D

decentralization, 48, 62, 68–9
decision makers, 289
deliberative participatory
    instruments. *See* Participatory
    Budgeting (PB)

democratic reforms, 6
    coercion, 282, 283
    democratic renewal, 278–82
    direct election of mayors,
        276–7
    free access to information, right of,
        275–6
    local referenda, 277–8
    scope and methods, 274–5
    taken-for-grantedness, 282, 283
    theory of policy diffusions, 282
Denmark
    amalgamation reforms in, 66
    comprehensive-integrated planning
        type, 259
    marketization, persistent public
        dominance, 226–8
    planning power, 256
    reforms in, 34
Dienstvereinbarung, 142
different style of accountingization,
    102
direct democracy, 6
direct election of mayor. *See* mayor,
    direct election of
discursive institutionalism, 189, 240

E

economic rationality, 194
energy sector, in Western European
    countries, 190
England
    direct election of mayor, 304–5
    mayors election in, 277
Environmental Management Act
    (1994), 208
Estonia, 241–2
    Participatory Budgeting, 325–7
European Spatial Planning Agenda,
    260
external administrative reforms, 4–5

F

Finland, 242
  aging population, 159
  amalgamation reforms in, 66
  budgetary constraints, 159
  political motives and legal gaps, 160
  public employment across levels,
    158
fiscal crisis and austerity policies, 349
fiscal stress pressures, 60–1, 68
Flanders, municipal amalgamations in
  austerity governments and policy, 47
  bottom-up process, 52
  central government, 50
  decentralization of tasks, 48
  incremental change *vs.* large waves,
    46
  intermunicipal cooperation, 53
  local political system, 49
  political pressure, 51
France
  bottom-up legitimacy, 295
  civil service in, 141
  decentralization process, 125
  imminent departure from
    performance administration,
    129–31
  local PMM reforms, 125
  paradigmatic case selection strategy,
    122
  performance incorporation, 130
  performance measurement, 130
  performance-related pay systems, .
    144–6; design, 144–5;
    implementation and criticalities,
    145–6; origin, 144
  performance use, 131
  planning power, 256, 261
free access to information right,
    275–6
functional bonus, in France, 144, 145
functional planning reforms

G

Germany, 242–3
  amalgamation reforms in, 66
  civil service in, 141
  comprehensive/integrated planning
    type, 259, 262
  human resource management;
    budgetary constraints, 159;
    case selection, 155–6; public
    employment across levels, 158;
    reform driver, 159
  municipal development, 31
  Participatory Budgeting, 327–9
  performance budgeting; accounting
    system, 108; budget and
    performance management, 108;
    budget formulation and
    execution, 107, 112; budget
    statement, 107, 111; external
    pressure role, 110; financial
    autonomy, 106; financial data,
    106, 112; fiscal crisis role, 110;
    focus on results, 107; level of
    detail, 107; main structural
    units, 107; new budget status,
    109; NPM role, 110;
    promoters/drivers, 110; reform
    waves, 109, 113–15; role and
    quality, 109; strategic
    documents, 108; time-period,
    106, 113–14; traditional
    budgeting, 106
  performance-related pay systems;
    design, 142; implementation
    and criticalities, 143–4; origin,
    141
  personal social services, 190
  planning power, 256, 262
  subsidiarity to marketization, 223–6
Greece, 243–4
  amalgamation reforms in, 66
  bottom-up initiatives, 199

planning power, 256
reforms in, 34
urbanism planning type, 259

H
historical institutionalism, 240
holistic reform process, 161
horizontal power relations, 260–4
human resource management (HRM)
  administrative reform process, 155
  change process description, 162–4
  institutional changes, 157, 173
  institutional reform changes; change
    process assessment, 166–8,
    174; communication and
    cooperation, 165–6;
    instruments assessment,
    168–70, 174–6; leadership,
    164–5, 178–80; organizational
    level, 171–2; performance and
    economic incentives, 166, 181;
    personnel level motivation, 171
  institutional setting, 160–2
  most-similar case design concept,
    156
  multi-perspective approach, 156–7
  public management reforms, 154
  reform profiles, 158–60

I
Iceland
  amalgamation reforms in, 66
  municipal development, 30
incentive bonus payments, Italy, 148
information and telecommunication
  technologies (ICT), 276
input legitimacy, 348–9
institutional development, in WE and
  CEE countries
  asset (material) privatization, 195

bottom-up initiatives, 199
outsourcing, 195
personal social services and care,
  197–8
political top-down initiatives, 198
public/municipal sector comeback,
  195–7
public utilities, 193–5
social community, 199
social enterprises, 198
institutionalization, 239
institutional policies
  administrative reforms, 4–6
  context conditions of reforms, 8–10
  country clusters, 10–14
  democratic reforms, 6
  institutional analysis, 3–4
institutional reform changes, HRM
  change process assessment, 166–8,
    174
  communication and cooperation,
    165–6
  instruments assessment, 168–70,
    174–6
  leadership, 164–5, 178–80
  organizational level, 171–2
  performance and economic
    incentives, 166, 181
  personnel level motivation, 171
inter-municipal company, 212
inter-municipal cooperation (IMC),
  53, 70
  advandages and disadvandages, 84–5
  forms of, 89–92
  impacts, 92–5
  legal frameworks, 87–9
  local governments and size, 82–4
  municipal territorial structures, 86–7
  reasons for development, 87
  waste management in Netherlands,
    214, 215
internal administrative reforms, 5–6

Ireland, 244
Italy
  civil service in, 141
  performance budgeting of local
    governments; accounting
    system, 108; budget and
    performance management, 108;
    budget formulation and
    execution, 107, 112; budget
    statement, 107, 111; external
    pressure role, 110; financial
    autonomy, 106; financial data,
    106, 112; fiscal crisis role, 110;
    focus on results, 107; level of
    detail, 107; main structural
    units, 107; new budget status,
    109; NPM role, 110;
    promoters/drivers, 110; reform
    waves, 109, 113–15; role and
    quality, 109; strategic
    documents, 108; time-period,
    106, 113–14; traditional
    budgeting, 106
  performance-related pay systems;
    design, 147–8; implementation
    and criticalities, 148–9; origin,
    146–7
  planning power, 256, 259, 262–3
  reward structure in, 147
  top-down legitimacy, 296

K
key reform actors, 155
Kommunale Arbeitsgemeinschaften, 92

L
large local governments, 64
legitimacy, 289–92
  bottom-up legitimacy, 291, 294–5
  strong level of legitimacy, 291–4

    top-down legitimacy, 292, 295–6
    weak legitimacy, 292, 296–7
Lijphart's executive-parties index, 63
Lithuania, performance budgeting
    accounting system, 108
    budget and performance
      management, 108
    budget formulation and execution,
      107, 112
    budget statement, 107, 111
    external pressure role, 110
    financial autonomy, 106
    financial data, 106, 112
    fiscal crisis role, 110
    focus on results, 107
    level of detail, 107
    main structural units, 107
    new budget status, 109
    NPM role, 110
    promoters/drivers, 110
    reform waves, 109, 113–15
    role and quality, 109
    strategic documents, 108
    time-period, 106, 113–14
    traditional budgeting, 106
local councils and councillors
    bottom-up legitimacy, 291, 294–5
    decision making, 289
    legitimacy, 289–92
    mediation, 289
    scrutiny, 289
    strong level of legitimacy, 291–4
    top-down legitimacy, 292, 295–6
    weak legitimacy, 292, 296–7
local democracy, 10
Local Government Act, Norway, 212
Local Government Act, Slovenian, 88
Local Government Administration
      Act, Estonia (1993), 242
local government reform
    autonomy vs. austerity, 352
    fiscal crisis and austerity policies, 349

input legitimacy, 348–9
local service delivery, 352
logic of consequences, 351–2
output legitimacy, 348
participation and involvement, 352
policies, 351
rescaling and restructuring, 349–50
responsibility and accountability, 352
structures of local government, 352
local political leadership
  and accountability, 306–8
  visibility and profile, 308–9
local political system, 49
local public sector reforms. *See also*
    institutional policies
  democratic reforms, 6
  external administrative reforms, 4–5
  institutional analysis, 3–4
  internal administrative reforms, 5–6
  types of, 7
local self-government, protection of,
    63–4, 69
local service delivery, 352
  re-organizing, 5

M
managerial reforms, 5–6
Mannheim (Germany)
  budgetary constraints, 161
  change management, 166–8
  change process difficulties, 165
  change process measures, 163
  communication and cooperation,
    165–6
  holistic reform process, 161
  HRM/personnel unit role, 163
  leadership, 164–5
  municipal council and the staff
    council, 163
  municipal strategies and visions, 162
  organizations' focus, 169–70

performance and economic
    incentive, 166
  staff motivation, 169
marketization
  common trends, 231–2
  nonprofit capitalism, 222–3
  persistent public dominance, 226–8
  principle of subsidiarity, 225
  regime hybridity, 228–30
  subsidiarity to, 223–6
mayors, direct election of, 276–7
  Czech Republic, 304
  England, 304–5
  local political leadership; and
    accountability, 306–8; reform
    of, 310–12; visibility and
    profile, 308–9
  Slovenia, 305
  Spain, 305
  Sweden, 306
mediators, 289
miestne akčné skupiny, 91
mikroregióny, 90
mini-jobs, 225
most-similar case design (MSCD),
    155–6
municipal amalgamations
  administrative system; bottom-up
    process, 52; intermunicipal
    cooperation, 53
  analytical framework and research
    design, 44–5
  change events, 51–2
  elite decision making, 50–1
  incremental change *vs.* large waves,
    45–6
  political system; consensus *vs.*
    consensus in making, 47–8;
    decentralization of tasks, 48;
    local politics and identity, 49
  socio-economic forces, 46–7
municipal empires, 190

municipal firm, 212
municipal size, 70
municipal socialism, 189
municipal structure development,
    28–31
municipal territorial structures, 86–7
Münster (Germany), Participatory
    Budgeting in, 328–9

N
Napoleonic local governments. *See also*
    France; Portugal; Turkey
    financial performance
        administration, 131–3
    imminent departure from
        performance administration,
        129–31
    model stability and performance
        management issues, 123–4
    performance administration, 133–4
    research methodology, 127–8
    variations of, 124–7
neo-institutionalist approach, 155
neo-liberal market-liberalization, 191–2
Netherlands
    municipal amalgamations in, 66;
        austerity governments and
        policy, 46–7; bottom-up
        process, 52; central
        government, 50;
        decentralization paradox, 48;
        incremental change *vs.* large
        waves, 45; intermunicipal
        cooperation, 53; local political
        system, 49; national and local
        government, 47; political
        pressure, 51
    waste management; economic
        effects, 215; household waste
        collection, 209; institutional
        forms, 213; inter-municipal

cooperations, 214, 215; policy
    implementation and cost
    reduction, 212; private firm,
    213; private-law-based limited
    company, 214; public-centred
    delivery, 210
New Public Management (NPM), 1,
    2, 102
New Steering Model (NSM), 159
nonprofit capitalism, 222–3
    Denmark, 226–8
    Germany, 223–6
    United Kingdom, 228–30
Nordic type administration, 12–13
Northern European municipality
    systems, 124
Norway
    Norwegian Environment Agency,
        208
    performance budgeting of local
        governments; accounting
        system, 108; budget and
        performance management, 108;
        budget formulation and
        execution, 107, 112; budget
        statement, 107, 111; external
        pressure role, 110; financial
        autonomy, 106; financial data,
        106, 112; fiscal crisis role, 110;
        focus on results, 107; level of
        detail, 107; main structural
        units, 107; new budget status,
        109; NPM role, 110;
        promoters/drivers, 110; reform
        waves, 109, 113–15; role and
        quality, 109; strategic
        documents, 108; time-period,
        106, 113–14; traditional
        budgeting, 106
    waste management;
        companification/
        corporatization, 211–12;

economic effects, 215; household waste collection, 208–9; institutional forms, 213; internal autonomization, 211; Local Government Act (1992), 211; municipal companies, 212; public-centred delivery, 210

Nuclei di Valutazione, 147

O

optimal territorial size, 194

output legitimacy, 348

outsourcing strategies, 195

P

Participatory Budgeting (PB)
  advisory functions, 330
  environmental variables, 329
  Estonia, 325–7
  Germany, 327–9
  new participatory instruments, 330
  non-constitutionalized character, 318
  political participation, 319–20
  Slovakia, 323–5
  Spain, 320–3
participatory reforms, 6
performance appraisal, in Germany, 142, 143
performance bonus
  in France, 144
  in Germany, 142
performance budgeting of local governments
  analytical framework, 105–6
  design and implementation; accounting system, 108; budget and performance management, 108; budget formulation and

execution, 107, 112; budget statement, 107, 111; external pressure role, 110; financial autonomy, 106; financial data, 106, 112; fiscal crisis role, 110; focus on results, 107; level of detail, 107; main structural units, 107; new budget status, 109; NPM role, 110; promoters/drivers, 110; reform waves, 109, 113–15; role and quality, 109; strategic documents, 108; time-period, 106, 113–14; traditional budgeting, 106
  institutional arrangements, 104
  public management reforms, 104
  transformative approach, 103–4
  variants of, 103
performance management and measurement systems (PMMS)
  characterization, 128–9
  financial performance administration, 131–3
  incorporation of performance, 128
  paradigmatic case selection strategy, 122
  performance administration, 133–4
  performance information uses, 128
  performance measurement, 127–8
performance management reforms (PMR), 122. *See also* Napoleonic local governments
performance-related bonus, in France, 144, 145
Performance-related pay (PRP) systems
  in France, 144–6
  in Germany, 141–4
  in Italy, 146–9

planning power
  actor-centered institutionalism, 254
  market-led planning, 261–2
  multi-level governance, 254–5
  and planning function, 256–7
  planning system typologies, 266
  rescaling of, 255–6
  strategic planning, 260–1
  territorial governance, instruments
    of, 261
  vertical rescaling, 257–60
Poland, bottom-up initiatives, 199
polder model, 47
policy diffusions, theory of, 282
political rationality, 194
politico-administrative supervision, 64
Pollution and Waste Disposal (PWD)
    Act (1981), 208
Portugal, 244–5
  local PMM reforms, 126
  paradigmatic case selection strategy,
    122–3
  performance incorporation, 132
  performance measurement, 131–2
  performance use, 132
prime de résultats (PR), 145
private law limited company, 212
privatization, asset (material), 195
projektová medziobecná spolupráca, 91
provision of public services,
    institutional development analysis
  analytical and explanatory
    framework, 188–9
  asset (material) privatization, 195
  bottom-up initiatives, 199
  Central Eastern European (CEE)
    countries, 191
  country selection, 188
  developmental analysis, 189
  guiding question, 189
  neo-liberal market-liberalization,
    191–2

nineteenth-century development, 189
  outsourcing, 195
  personal social services and care,
    197–8
  political top-down initiatives, 198
  politico-administrative model, 192
  public/municipal sector comeback,
    195–7
  public utilities, 193–5
  social community, 199
  social enterprises, 198
  West European (WE) countries,
    190–1
Public-Private Partnerships (PPPs), 352
public sector reforms, in multilevel
    system, 349–50
public service motivation (PSM), 143
purchaser–provider split, 197

R
reforming local governments, in times
    of crisis
  citizens' satisfaction, 335–6, 342
  expectations and evaluation, 339–42
  value orientations, 336–9, 343
Regionale Planungsgemeinschaft, 90
remunicipalization, of public services,
    195–6
renationalization, 196
re-organizing local service delivery, 5
rescaling and restructuring, 349–50
responsibility, 352
Rio de Janeiro Conference on
    Sustainability and Development
    (1992), 319

S
scrutiny, 289
Seville (Spain), Participatory
    Budgeting in, 321–3

shifting models, *versus* change and reform, 350–1
skupna obèinska uprava, 91
Slovakia, 86
 forms of IMC, 89
 legal provisions, 86
 local governments, 92
 municipal territorial structures, 86
 Participatory Budgeting, 323–5
Slovenia, 86
 direct election of mayor, 305
 forms of IMC, 89
 legal provisions, 88
 local governments, 92
 municipal council, 305
 municipal territorial structures, 86
 Slovenian Local Government Act, 88
Southern municipality systems, 123–4
South European type administration, 13
Spain, 245–6
 budgetary constraints, 159
 direct election of mayor, 305
 local political leadership, 307
 Participatory Budgeting, 320–3
 political motives and legal gaps, 160
 public employment across levels, 158
Spanish National Federation of Municipalities (FEMP), 321
spoloèné obecné podniky, 91
spoloèné obecné úrady, 90
staff motivation, 169
strategic development perspective (SNADT), 261
strong level of legitimacy, 291–4
strong mayor-systems, 10
Sweden
 direct election of mayor, 306
 municipal development, 31
 public services, 193
Swiss cantons, municipal development in, 30, 31

Switzerland
 amalgamation reforms in, 66, 67
 bottom-up legitimacy, 295

T
taken-for-grantedness, 282, 283
Tampere (Finland)
 budgetary constraints, 161
 change management, 166–8
 change process difficulties, 165
 change process measures, 163
 communication and cooperation, 165–6
 customer-oriented approach, 161
 HRM/personnel unit role, 163
 leadership, 164–5
 municipal council and the staff council, 163
 municipal strategies and visions, 162
 organizations' focus, 169–70
 performance and economic incentive, 166
 staff motivation, 169
Tartu (Estonia), Participatory Budgeting in, 326–7
territorial fragmentation, 31
territorial re-scaling, 4–5. *See also* amalgamation reforms; inter-local cooperation
territorial structures, 9–10
territory, 70
Tiebout's model, 83
top-down legitimacy, 292, 295–6
Turkey
 bottom-up initiatives, 199
 local PMM reforms, 125–6
 paradigmatic case selection strategy, 122
 performance incorporation, 134
 performance measurement, 133–4
 performance use, 134

U

United Kingdom. *See also* England
  land use management planning type,
    259
  marketization, by regime hybridity,
    228–30
  planning power, 256, 263
  top-down legitimacy, 296
urbanization, 61

V

vertical power relations, 257–60
voluntary labor, 225

W

Waste Act (1979), 208
waste management
  conceptualization, 207–8
  NPM reforms, 210–16
  policy field, 208–9
  post-NPM development, 216

public-centred delivery, 210
  reform trajectories, 216–17
water sector, in Western European
  countries, 190
weak legitimacy, 292, 296–7
West European (WE) countries
  institutional development; asset
    (material) privatization, 195;
    bottom-up initiatives, 199;
    outsourcing, 195; personal
    social services and care, 197–8;
    political top-down initiatives,
    198; public/municipal sector
    comeback, 195–7; public
    utilities, 193–5; social
    community, 199; social
    enterprises, 198
  provision of public services, 190–1
  waste management, 208

Z

Zweckverbände, 90

.

Printed by Printforce, the Netherlands